D0148553

Political Reform
in Francophone Africa

Political Reform in Francophone Africa

edited by

John F. Clark
Florida International University

David E. Gardinier
Marquette University

WestviewPress

A Division of HarperCollins*Publishers*

Copyright © 1997 by Westview Press, A Division of HarperCollins Publishers, Inc.

Published in 1997 in the United States of America by Westview Press, 5500 Central Avenue, Boulder, Colorado 80301-2877, and in the United Kingdom by Westview Press, 12 Hid's Copse Road, Cumnor Hill, Oxford OX2 9JJ

Library of Congress Cataloging-in-Publication Data
Political reform in francophone Africa / edited by John F. Clark,
    David E. Gardinier.
        p.   cm.
    Includes bibliographical references and index.
    ISBN 0-8133-2785-7. — ISBN 0-8133-2786-5 (pbk.)
    1. Africa, French-speaking—Politics and government.   2. Africa,
West—Politics and government—1960–   I. Clark, John Frank.
II. Gardinier, David E.
DT532.6.P65   1996
320.966′0917541—dc20
                                                                                96-38176
                                                                                CIP

The paper used in this publication meets the requirements of the American National Standard for Permanence of Paper for Printed Library Materials Z39.48-1984.

10   9   8   7   6   5   4   3   2   1

For Janie and Josefina

Contents

Tables

Acknowledgments

We wish to express our appreciation to those who assisted us in the preparation of this volume. First and foremost are the contributors, who exhibited both diligence and patience during the long process of editing and revising their chapters. We also would like to express our thanks to Barbara Ellington, senior acquisitions editor, and Libby Barstow, senior production editor, at Westview Press and to copy editor John J. Guardiano for their efforts in bringing out this volume. Any errors of fact or interpretation, of course, are our responsibility. John Clark would like to thank two former research assistants for their work on this manuscript: Laura Boudon, particularly for her translation work, encouragement, and perpetual enthusiasm, and John Woolridge, especially for his technical wizardry in computer formatting. Professor Clark also thanks his senior colleague, Susan Waltz, for her cooperation and encouragement. David Gardinier expresses his thanks to his own computer wizard, his daughter Annemarie, for all her help in preparing the manuscript for publication. Finally, we wish to dedicate this volume to the women whose support sustains us in all our work: Janie Valdes for John Clark, and Josefina Sevilla-Gardinier for David Gardinier.

John F. Clark
David E. Gardinier

Acronyms

AAC	All Anglophone Conference [Cameroon]
ADF	Alliance pour la Démocratie et la Fédération [Burkina Faso]
ADP	Alliance pour la Démocratie et le Progrès [Central African Republic]
AEC	All-Ewe Conference [Togo]
AEF	Afrique Équatoriale Française
AFC	Alliance des Forces du Changement [Niger]
AFC	Allied Front for Change [Cameroon]
AJ/PADS	And Jef/Parti Africain pour la Démocratie et le Socialisme [Senegal]
AND	Alliance Nationale pour la Démocratie [Congo]
ANDP	Alliance Nigérienne pour la Démocratie et le Progrès
AOF	Afrique Occidentale Française
APRT	Association Professionnelle des Revendeurs des Tissus [Togo]
BDS	Bloc Démocratique Sénégalais
BET	Borkou-Ennedi-Tibesti (Prefecture) [Chad]
BNA	Bloc Nigérien d'Action
BPN	Bureau Politique National [Chad]
CAM	Cameroon Action Movement
CAR	Central African Republic
CAR	Comité d'Action pour le Renouveau [Togo]
CCCCN	Comité Coordonnateur pour la Convocation d'une Conférence Nationale [Central African Republic]
CCLD	Comité de Coordination des Luttes Démocratiques [Niger]
CDP/G-G	Convention des Démocrates and Patriotes/Garabi-gi [Senegal]
CDR	Coalition pour la Défense de la République [Rwanda]
CDR	Comités pour la Défense de la Révolution [Burkina Faso]
CDS	Convention Démocratique et Sociale [Niger]
CFA	Communauté Financière Africaine
CFD	Caisse Française de Développement
CFD	Concertation des Forces Démocratiques [Central African Republic]

CFP	Convention des Forces du Progrès [Burkina Faso]
CGSL	Confédération Gabonaise des Syndicats Libres
CMS	Conseil Militaire Suprême [Niger]
CNCA	Caisse Nationale de Crédit Agricole [Togo]
CND	Conseil National de Développement [Niger, Rwanda]
CNDH	Commission Nationale des Droits de l'Homme [Togo]
CNPP/PDS	Convention Nationale des Patriotes Progressifs/Parti Démocrate Social [Burkina Faso]
CNR	Conseil National de la Révolution [Burkina]
CNS	Conseil National du Salut [Chad]
CNTT	Confédération Nationale des Travailleurs du Togo
COD	Collectif pour l'Opposition Démocratique [Togo]
CPDM	Cameroon People's Democratic Movement
CPPO	Conseil Permanent des Partis de l'Opposition [Central African Republic]
CR	Comités Révolutionnaires [Burkina]
CR	Commune Rurale [Senegal]
CRA	Coordination de la Résistance Armée [Niger]
CSC	Confédération Syndicale Congolaise
CSM	Conseil Supérieur Militaire [Chad]
CSNPD	Comité de Sursaut National pour la Paix et la Démocratie [Chad]
CSON	Conseil Supérieur d'Orientation Nationale [Niger]
CSR	Conseil Supérieur de la République [Various states]
CST	Conseil Supérieur de la Transition [Chad]
CSTC	Confédération Syndicale des Travailleurs Congolais
DGSE	Direction Générale de la Sécurité Extérieure [France]
DSP	Division Spéciale Présidentielle [Zaire]
EEC	European Economic Community
FAN	Forces Armées Nigériennes
FAR	Front des Associations pour le Renouveau [Togo]
FARF	Forces Armées pour la République Fédérale [Chad]
FC	Forum Civique [Central African Republic]
FDU	Forces Démocratiques Unies [Congo]
FLNC	Front pour la Libération Nationale du Congo [Zaire]
FLPC	Front de Libération du Peuple Centrafricain
FOD	Front pour l'Opposition Démocratique [Togo]
FP	Front Populaire [Burkina Faso]
FPI	Front Populaire Ivoirien
FPP	Front Patriotique pour le Progrès [Central African Republic]
FR	Front Républicain [Côte d'Ivoire]
FROLINAT	Front de Libération Nationale du Tchad
GECAMINES	Générale des Carrières et des Mines [Zaire]

GRAD	Groupe de Réflexion et d'Action des Jeunes pour la Démocratie [Togo]
HCR	High Council of the Republic; Haut Conseil de la République [various states]
HCR/PT	Haut Conseil de la République/Parlement de la Transition [Zaire]
IFIs	international financial institutions
IMF	International Monetary Fund
JMNR	Jeunesse du Mouvement National de la Révolution [Congo]
LD/MPT	Ligue Démocratique/Mouvement pour le Parti du Travail [Senegal]
LDP	Liberal Democratic Party [Cameroon]
LIPAD	Ligue Patriotique pour le Développement [Burkina Faso]
LTDH	Ligue Togolaise des Droits de l'Homme
MCDDI	Mouvement Congolais pour le Développement et la Démocratie Intégrale [Congo]
MDD	Mouvement pour la Démocratie et le Développement [Chad]
MDDR	Mouvement Démocratique pour la Défense de la République [Cameroon]
MDP	Mouvement des Démocrates Progressistes [Burkina Faso]
MDP	Mouvement pour la Démocratie et le Progrès [Cameroon]
MDP	Mouvement pour le Développement et le Panafricanisme [Niger]
MDR	Mouvement Démocratique Républicain [Rwanda]
MEDAC	Mouvement d'Évolution Démocratique de l'Afrique Centrale [Central African Republic]
MELD	Mouvement Étudiant pour la Lutte Démocratique [Togo]
MESAN	Mouvement pour l'Évolution Sociale de l'Afrique Noire [Central African Republic]
MFDC	Mouvement des Forces Démocratiques de la Casamance [Senegal]
MIBA	Société Minière de Bakwanga [Zaire]
MLPC	Mouvement pour la Libération du Peuple Centrafricain
MNC-L	Mouvement National Congolais-Lumumbiste [Zaire]
MNR	Mouvement National de la Révolution [Congo]
MNSD	Mouvement National pour une Société de Développement [Niger]
MONESTO	Mouvement National des Étudiants et Stagiaires du Togo
MORENA	Mouvement de Redressement National [Gabon]
MP	Mouvance Présidentielle [Congo]
MP	Mouvement des Progressistes [Cameroon]
MPR	Mouvement Populaire de la Révolution [Zaire]
MPS	Mouvement Patriotique du Salut [Chad]

MRND	Mouvement Révolutionnaire National pour le Développement [Rwanda]
MRP	Mouvement Républicain Populaire [France]
MRS	Mouvement Républicain Sénégalais
MSA	Mouvement Socialiste Africain (Sawaba) [Niger]
NDI	National Democratic Institute for International Affairs (Washington, D.C.)
NRA	National Resistance Army [Uganda]
OAU	Organization for African Unity
OCAM	Organisation Commune Africaine et Malgache
ODP/MT	Organisation pour la Démocratie Populaire/ Mouvement du Travail [Burkina Faso]
OPT	Office des Postes et Télécommunications
OULD	Organisation Universitaire de Lutte pour la Démocratie [Togo]
PAI	Parti Africain de l'Indépendance [Senegal]
PALU	Parti Lumumbiste Unifié [Zaire]
PARMEHUTU	Parti du Mouvement pour l'Émancipation Hutu [Rwanda]
PCD	Parti Communiste du Dahomey [Benin]
PCF	Parti Communiste Français
PCT	Parti Congolais du Travail
PDCI	Parti Démocratique de la Côte d'Ivoire
PDG	Parti Démocratique Gabonais
PDS	Parti Démocratique Sénégalais
PDS/R	Parti Démocratique Sénégalais/Rénovation
PDSC	Parti Démocrate et Social Chrétien [Zaire]
PEP	Parti Écologique pour le Progrès [Burkina Faso]
PG	Presidential Guard [Benin, Chad, and Gabon]
PGP	Parti Gabonais du Progrès
PIT	Parti de l'Indépendance et du Travail [Senegal]
PIT	Parti Ivoirien des Travailleurs
PLD	Parti Libéral Démocratique [Central African Republic]
PMT	Parti des Masses pour le Travail [Niger]
PNDS	Parti Nigérien pour la Démocratie et le Socialisme
PPD	Programme Populaire du Développement [Burkina Faso]
PPN	Parti Progressiste Nigérien
PPR	Parti Populaire de la Révolution [Benin]
PPT	Parti Progressiste Tchadien
PRD	Parti du Renouveau Démocratique [Benin]
PS	Parti Socialiste [Senegal]
PSD	Parti Social-Démocrate [Rwanda]
PSDN	Parti Social Démocrate Nigérien
PSI	Parti Socialiste Ivoirien
PSR	Parti Socialiste Révolutionnaire [Niger]

PUND	Parti Nigérien pour l'Unité et la Démocratie
RDA	Rassemblement Démocratique Africain
RDC	Rassemblement Démocratique Centrafricain
RDPC	Rassemblement Démocratique du Peuple Camerounais
RDPS	Rassemblement pour la Démocratie et le Progrès Social [Congo]
RDR	Rassemblement des Républicains [Côte d'Ivoire]
RFP	Rassemblement des Forces Patriotiques [Cameroon]
RNB	Rassemblement National des Bûcherons [Gabon]
RND	Rassemblement National Démocratique [Senegal]
RPF	Rwandan Patriotic Front
RPT	Rassemblement du Peuple Togolais
RSDG	Rassemblement Social et Démocrate Gabonais
SAA	Syndicat Agricole Africain [Côte d'Ivoire]
SAP	structural adjustment program
SDF	Social Democratic Front [Cameroon]
SFIO	Section Française de l'Internationale Ouvrière
SNC	sovereign national conference
TPC	Tribunaux Populaires de la Conciliation [Burkina Faso]
UDC	Union Démocratique du Cameroun
UDDIA	Union Démocratique pour la Défense des Intérêts Africains [Congo]
UDFP-Sawaba	Union Démocratique des Forces Progressistes–Sawaba [Niger]
UDI	Union des Démocrates Indépendants [Zaire]
UDN	Union Démocratique Nigérienne
UDPS	Union pour la Démocratie et le Progrès Social [Niger and Zaire]
UDSR	Union Démocrate et Sociale de la Résistance [France]
UFERI	Union des Fédéralistes et des Républicains Indépendants [Zaire]
UMAD	Union des Masses pour une Action Démocratique [Niger]
UMHK	Union Minière du Haut Katanga [Zaire]
UN	United Nations
UNC	Union Nationale Camerounaise
UNDP	Union Nationale pour la Démocratie et le Progrès [Cameroon]
UNDP	United Nations Development Programme
UNIR	Union Nationale pour l'Indépendance et la Révolution [Chad]
UPADS	Union Panafricaine pour la Démocratie Sociale [Congo]
UPC	Union des Populations du Cameroun
UPDP	Union des Patriotes Démocrates et Progressistes [Niger]
UPS	Union Progressiste Sénégalaise
UR	Union pour la République [Congo]
URD	Union pour la République et la Démocratie [Zaire]

URD	Union pour le Renouveau Démocratique [Congo]
USD	Union des Sociaux-Démocrates [Côte d'Ivoire]
USN	Union des Scolaires Nigériens
USOR	Union Sacrée de l'Opposition Radicale [Zaire]
USTN	Union des Syndicats des Travailleurs du Niger
UTRD	Union pour la Triomphe du Renouveau Démocratique [Benin]

Chapter One

Introduction

JOHN F. CLARK

This book has several sources of inspiration, not the least of which was the star-tling outburst of political reform that began in sub-Saharan Africa in the waning months of 1989. From the mid-1960s to the end of the 1980s, both Africans and Western observers had come increasingly to take the presence of the one-party state in Africa for granted. The few cases of quasi democracy (Gambia, Botswana, and Senegal) seemed tentative, isolated, and anomalous; as a result, and as one would expect, few scholarly studies of democracy in Africa were undertaken, and these dealt much more with democratic potential than actual democratic experi-ence.[1] Beginning with the revolution in Benin in 1989, however, democracy seemed to gain renewed credibility in sub-Saharan Africa. Fascination with dem-ocratic political reforms soon swept the subcontinent, leading to the eventual overthrow of many longtime dictators, some of whom had ruled their countries since independence. Even if one believes that "development"—broadly under-stood as the alleviation of the severe material deprivation that plagues the lives of so many Africans—is the continent's most pressing need, one cannot help but to be impressed with the possibilities for change represented by such reform efforts.

The roots of this dramatic turn of political events are destined to be long de-bated by scholars. Some point to the rather obvious coincidence of political revo-lutions in Africa with the end of the Cold War and the end of Eastern Europe's one-party states. Scholars of a more materialist bent point to the long-brewing economic crises of sub-Saharan Africa occasioned by stagnation, debt, and ini-tially unsuccessful structural adjustment programs imposed by the multilateral lending institutions (the International Monetary Fund and the World Bank). Per-haps the best metaphor to describe the sources of revolt and reform is one of an intellectual spark (the broad notion of freedom stemming from the collapse of communist states) landing in a socioeconomic powder keg (the social frustration created by declining economic prospects and unrelenting authoritarianism).

By 1996 the strength of the opposition movements seems largely to have dissipated. It may be that those countries that had not experienced significant transformation by 1993 simply were not destined to do so in this "wave" of democratization.[2] Meanwhile, in the cases in which political transitions took place, it became clearer that political change did not necessarily spell an end to corruption or undemocratic politics and that it can lead to increased social (especially ethnic) strife.

This book was also inspired by the distinctiveness of the political reform processes that have taken place in francophone Africa. Most notably, sovereign national conferences became the critical aspect of political reform movements throughout francophone Africa.[3] One reason for this development is the distinct political culture that France and Belgium bequeathed to their former colonies.[4] A second source of francophone Africa's distinctiveness is the continuing influence of France itself in the reform processes. Since the independence of the various francophone African states, France has consistently sought to develop and maintain close relations with them, showing little regard for democracy in the process. Indeed, former French Prime Minister (now president) Jacques Chirac insisted that multipartyism might not be right for Africa even as the national conference in Benin was unfolding.[5] At the June 1990 Franco-African summit at La Baule, France, however, President François Mitterrand suddenly announced that France would thereafter link its aid to African states to the pace of democratic political reforms.[6] This volte-face had a catalyzing effect on reform movements throughout francophone Africa. No less important, however, has been the direct engagement of France since then with the political forces, both status quo and reformist, of its former colonies as well as those of Belgium.

Finally, this book was also inspired by the fact that francophone Africa has been slighted—not to say ignored—in Anglo-American settings.[7] This tendency is both understandable and regrettable. The political experiences of certain anglophone countries, notably South Africa, Kenya, Nigeria, and Ghana, have had a disproportionate influence on American thinking about Africa, perhaps because they have been more accessible to researchers. (A principal exception has been Zaire, because of that country's notoriously close relationship with the United States since the early 1960s.) As a result, those who were so amazed by Zambia's 1991 elections might have been less so if they had been following events in Benin and Congo eighteen months before.

The uniqueness of the francophone African experience has been brought into relief during the recent years of political reform. It is the singularity of the francophone African political experience that binds this book together. Each of the chapters that examine a particular country addresses national conferences (or campaigns for them), the role of France, and the legacy of French and Belgian colonial rule (including, for example, the influence of the Catholic Church,[8] where applicable). Chapter 2, by David Gardinier, details the sources of such francophone African unity as exists on the subcontinent. France and Belgium introduced political forms into their former colonies that blended with indigenous political patterns to create new and lasting political cultures. Since independence, France has maintained its influence over its former colonies through military cooperation agreements and the financial discipline—some would say hegemony—of the so-called "franc zone." Moreover, France has extended its influence strongly into the former Belgian colonies as well, as evidenced by its military activities in Zaire during the 1960s and 1970s and in Rwanda very recently, and by its inclusion of these countries in the annual summits of francophone African states with France. In addition to the annual Franco-African Summit Conferences of Heads of State, France has held several conferences just for heads of francophone states. It was during the fourth such conference in November 1991 at the Chaillot Palace in Paris that Mitterrand retreated from the strong support that he had given to democratization at La Baule in June 1990.

Chapter 3 addresses some of the theoretical issues of political reform and democratization. Specifically, it identifies some of the more important variables in the process of political reform and assesses the potential of reform to lead to the institutionalization of democracy. Although such a chapter could scarcely be comprehensive, it pinpoints underdevelopment, weak or inappropriately constituted civil society, and "defective" political culture as impediments to democratization. It also points to the important role of external actors in transitions from authoritarianism and in democratization.

The remaining chapters, which take up the course of political reform in a number of francophone African countries, are grouped by the apparent degree of political reform achieved. Obviously, the assignment of the various states to different categories is open to dispute, especially since reform processes are ongoing, but a reasonable typology has been attempted. Since not all francophone African countries could be included because of limitations of space, representative examples for each category have been included. Zaire and Rwanda are included despite their having been Belgian, not French, colonies, and despite their not being members of the franc zone, because of the vitally important role that France has played in their politics since independence and during the recent period of political reform.

Part Two contains the cases of "peaceful regime change," including Benin, Congo, Niger, and the Central African Republic. "Peaceful regime change" should by no means be taken to be synonymous with "successful democratization"; all of the countries in question have a long way to go before democracy can be considered to have been consolidated. Congo very nearly had civil war, and the new political system was only maintained there by the president's dissolution of the Parliament and the staging of new elections, which was of dubious constitutionality. In Benin, the new regime has committed human rights abuses and taken some steps that bring its democratic credentials into question. Moreover, despite the political successes in this group of countries, the authors of these chapters all emphasize that democratic transitions have had only limited impact thus far on the lives of ordinary citizens. Thomas O'Toole, author of the chapter on the Central African Republic, is particularly skeptical about the promise of Western-style democracy in Africa. Most discouraging of all for democrats, Niger's experiment with democracy ended by a coup d'état in late January 1996 (after the chapter on Niger in this volume was completed).

Part Three contains five cases of "moderate reform," including Burkina Faso, Gabon, Cameroon, Côte d'Ivoire, and Senegal. In each of these countries there have been elections of some credibility, but in each case there have also been serious charges of fraud. In all of these cases except that of Côte d'Ivoire, where the redoubtable Félix Houphouët-Boigny died in December 1993, the old presidents were returned to office. In the cases of Cameroon and Burkina Faso, divisions among the opposition groups, as much as authoritarianism, were responsible for the lack of transition. In Côte d'Ivoire, the Speaker of the National Assembly (and Houphouët-Boigny's designated successor), Konan Bédié, has become president. Nevertheless, in each case, the dominant party and/or president has less leeway for acting arbitrarily because of an opposition presence in parliament, legal reforms, and new constitutions. Senegal, of course, entered the 1990s boasting the strongest liberal institutions of any of the francophone countries. Relatively speaking, however, it represents a case of only moderate reform, since it has not maintained its status as the most clearly democratic francophone African state.

The third category, in Part Four, is labeled "Opposition Without Reform" and includes the cases of Togo and Zaire. In these two countries there were national conferences that seemed to deal death blows to long-standing dictatorships, but in both cases the dictators proved to be more durable than expected. Though opposition continues in both countries, the short-term prospects for political reform seem dim at present. In the case of Zaire, France has been a key player in the ongoing negotiations over a power transition.

Two francophone African countries, Chad and Rwanda, have experienced severe and sustained civil conflict as well as transitions over recent years but without significant political reform. Interestingly, both have seen regime transformations in the midst of war. These two cases are grouped in Part Five under the label "Transition Without Reform." Despite the conduct of elections in Chad, any real political reform there must await restoration of basic civil order.

In these studies, the authors reflect on the meaning of political reform in the countries that they analyze, assessing the extent to which the polity has moved towards becoming more democratic and speculating on the possibilities for further movement towards democracy. In their conclusions to the individual country studies, most of the authors also reflect on the costs and gains of political reform. We leave it to our readers to digest the evidence from this selection of francophone African countries and to determine for themselves what future democracy has in the distinct political environment of francophone Africa.

Notes

1. Two exceptions were Larry Diamond, Juan J. Linz, and Seymour Martin Lipset, eds., *Democracy in Developing Countries*, vol. 2, *Africa* (Boulder: Lynne Rienner, 1988), and Walter Oyugi et al., eds., *Democratic Theory and Practice in Africa* (London: James Currey, 1988).

2. This image comes from Samuel Huntington's *The Third Wave: Democratization in the Late Twentieth Century* (Norman: University of Oklahoma Press, 1991).

3. See John F. Clark, "The National Conference as an Instrument of Democratization in Francophone Africa," *Journal of Third World Studies* 11, no. 1 (Spring 1994):304–335; Pearl T. Robinson, "The National Conference Phenomenon in Francophone Africa," *Comparative Studies in Society and History* 36, no. 3 (July 1994):575–610; and F. Eboussi Boulaga, *Les conférences nationales en Afrique noire: Une affaire à suivre* (Paris: Karthala, 1993). As Marina Ottaway has pointed out, Ethiopia, Somalia, South Africa, and Namibia—all "anglophone" states—also had national conferences to address political reformulation in the early 1990s. It should be noted, however, that the national conferences in these countries generally did not have the same importance for the political reform processes as those in the francophone countries. See Marina Ottaway, "Democratization in Collapsed States," in I. William Zartman, ed., *Collapsed States: The Disintegration and Restoration of Legitimate Authority* (Boulder: Lynne Rienner, 1995), p. 246.

4. See David E. Gardinier, "Historical Origins of Francophone Africa," in this volume.

5. Robinson, "The National Conference Phenomenon," p. 585.

6. "Le seizième sommet franco-africain de La Baule," *Le Monde*, June 20, 1990, p. 5. Cited in Robinson, "The National Conference Phenomenon," p. 589.

7. The recent volume edited by Anthony Kirk-Greene and Daniel Bach, *State and Society in Francophone Africa Since Independence* (New York: St. Martin's Press, 1995), makes a contribution to informing anglophone audiences about the distinctiveness of francophone Africa. Since that volume has a much broader scope and is based on essays originally written in 1988, however, it scarcely touches on the issues of concern in the present study. Other recent works of interest are cited in Chapter 2.

8. See Metena Nteba, "Les conférences nationales et la figure de l'évêque-président," *Zaïre-Afrique*, no. 276 (1993):361–372; and the chapters on Congo, Cameroon, and Rwanda in Paul Gifford, ed., *The Christian Churches and the Democratisation of Africa* (Leiden, Netherlands: Brill, 1995), pp. 148–204.

Part One

Historical and Theoretical Perspectives

Chapter Two

The Historical Origins
of Francophone Africa

DAVID E. GARDINIER

The term "francophone Africa" ordinarily refers to fourteen West and Central African states formerly under French rule and three Central African states formerly under Belgian rule that have retained French as an official or national language. In nearly all of them, French is the principal language of public life and international communication. Important portions of the adult population in many of these countries speak French fluently, while smaller numbers read and write it.[1] The term further serves to differentiate these countries from the anglophone and lusophone states, which were, respectively, British or Portuguese colonies. That the former Belgian territories are now grouped together with the former French territories reflects not merely their continuing use of the French language but also their inclusion since the 1960s among the sub-Saharan African states with which France maintains a special relationship.[2]

It is to this special relationship that we turn in this chapter in order better to understand why the recent movements for political reform in the francophone states have so many similarities.[3] The special relationship, the features of which continued to evolve through the periods of colonial rule and decolonization into the era of national independence, has helped to maintain and to develop further a common francophone African political culture. Just as the collaboration of the African elites with France made the special relationship possible, their maintenance of French-derived political and educational systems and their policy of spreading knowledge of the French language and culture to much larger portions of their peoples facilitated the further growth of this common political culture. This culture has contributed to a certain distinctiveness in the set of responses the francophone African states have had in the face of some of the same problems being experienced by some nonfrancophone African countries.

The special relationship has been shaped and strengthened in important ways by a remarkable continuity in French policy concerning Black Africa since at least the 1870s. France's involvement in the sub-Saharan regions of the continent has resulted, above all, from a desire to maintain and increase its power and prestige in Europe and in the world. Economic aims such as securing raw materials, markets, and places for investment have ordinarily been seen in relation to this basically political goal—and so has the goal of spreading the French language and culture. It is this persistent vision of Africa as an arena for advancing French power that has contributed to the maintenance of such a strong French presence on the continent throughout the postcolonial era.[4]

Prior to the 1870s French possessions in West and Central Africa were limited to several offshore islands and coastal fringes of commercial or strategic value. Then, as a result of the colonial expansion of the late nineteenth century, and in competition with other European powers, France acquired control of vast regions inland. At the start of the twentieth century, it organized them into two federations in order to promote more effective administration and development. The first, French West Africa (Afrique Occidentale Française, AOF), contained the territories that were to become today's states of Mauritania, Senegal, Guinea, Mali, Côte d'Ivoire, Burkina Faso, Niger, and Benin; the second federation, French Equatorial Africa (Afrique Équatoriale Française, AEF), included present-day Gabon, Congo, Central African Republic, and Chad. As a result of the outcome of World War I, France obtained the largest portions of two German colonies, Togo and Cameroon, which were administered separately, first as League of Nations mandates and after 1946 as UN trust territories.

Despite the diversity of peoples or ethnic groups and geographic regions placed within the often artificial boundaries of these territories, France developed broad common policies for their administration. Thus French rule everywhere involved centralization, hierarchy, and uniformity. The fourteen territories were administered by a single bureau within the Ministry of Colonies in Paris. The ministry was headed by a member of the cabinet or government, which was responsible to the Parliament for its policies and practices. The minister appointed the governors-general of the two federations and the governors of the territories who were responsible to them. The governors appointed the Frenchmen who headed the local administrative districts. In carrying out their duties, French administrators employed legal codes that were basically uniform for all of Black Africa.

France was able to rule these vast areas with small numbers of French officials by securing the collaboration of Africans after its military conquest. Under a system of mainly direct rule, Africans, often traditional rulers, became agents for the transmission of French commands to their African subjects and in time became Western-educated subordinates.

French rule also led to the development of cash crops that remain the economic mainstay of these countries today and to the exploitation of woods, metals, and minerals needed in Europe. France undertook the construction and maintenance of the infrastructure necessary to export these products to Europe and to import European manufactures into Africa. In general, France followed protectionist policies that largely eliminated the possibility of any significant amount of trade between its colonies and other industrial states.[5]

In the cultural realm, France organized schools to train auxiliaries for its administration, European commerce, and the educational system. Through the schools it also sought to spread the French language and culture among as many Africans as was financially possible, beginning with the families of the traditional rulers and government employees. Even during the period between the two world wars, when France largely abandoned its efforts to assimilate the bulk of the population, it still sought to create an elite of gallicized auxiliaries who could serve as intermediaries between the French administrators and the masses who remained oriented to more traditional ways.

In order to maximize the resources available for education, the French gave small subsidies to the primary schools of the Catholic and Protestant missions from France (but not to those of Protestants from other European countries or the United States). These schools were required to teach the official programs, which were entirely in French, but they were allowed to give religious instruction in the vernacular. After the separation of church and state in France in 1905, the colonial administration opened more public schools, which were frequently headed by Frenchmen who were hostile to religion. But regardless of whether young Africans acquired a secularist or a Christian orientation, all of them gained a knowledge of the French language and culture that attached them to France. As for the Muslims, who were numerous in many of these countries (particularly Mauritania, Senegal, Guinea, Mali, Niger, Chad, and northern Cameroon), most preferred to seek a traditional Quranic education. Ordinarily the only Muslims who enrolled in the public schools prior to World War II were the sons of chiefs and government employees.

During the interwar period the seminaries and bible schools of the missions not only prepared clergy and other church workers but also provided an education beyond the primary level to other church members. At the same time, specialized public post–primary schools at Dakar, Yaoundé, and Brazzaville trained government employees for teaching, general administration, health care, and technical services. Bringing together African students from many different regions of a single territory or from several territories helped to create a French African consciousness among this educated elite. It was mainly from this group that would come the members of representative bodies during the period of decolonization after World War II.[6]

World War II unleashed decolonizing trends that undermined the political and ideological foundations of Western colonial rule in Africa and Asia. Given the French view that retention of its control in Africa was essential for the maintenance of its power and prestige in Europe and in the world, France opposed independence for its territories. Instead it sought, beginning with the Brazzaville Conference of early 1944 and continuing through the constitution-making of the Fourth Republic in late 1946, to reform colonial rule in order to make its presence acceptable for the foreseeable future. France thus aimed to promote the advancement of the Africans within a framework that for the time being would be dominated by Frenchmen but within which Africans would undergo preparation to play progressively larger parts. This policy would lead to the integration of the African territories into the Republic and the gradual emancipation of their inhabitants as individuals rather than to the severing of ties with France. As a result of this essentially assimilationist policy, Africans acquired French citizenship and representation in territorial assemblies, federation councils, and such metropolitan bodies as the National Assembly in Paris.

In order to promote the more rapid advancement of its African territories, France undertook a much larger role in their economic development through planning and public investment. It also hoped that the territories' advancement would aid French recovery from the war. Through the construction and improvement of infrastructure (ports, roads, railroads, airfields, telecommunications), France sought to increase the output of such tropical products as cocoa, coffee, palm oil and nuts, bananas, cotton, woods, metals, and minerals. In the process it linked the African economies more closely with those of France and the Western world. From 1956 on, as the creation of the European Economic Community (EEC) approached, France for the first time invited capital investment from other Western nations (e.g., Germany, the United States) in order to accelerate the development of its territories' metals and minerals, particularly aluminum, manganese, and petroleum. It should be noted that the development of the territories' economies was centered upon increased production of raw materials for French and international markets. France continued to provide Africa with industrial goods under near monopolistic conditions and to restrict local manufactures to foodstuffs, beverages, and household items.[7]

At the Brazzaville Conference France established the goal of providing a primary education in French for all children of both sexes in Africa. It aimed as well to give further education to the most gifted students at the secondary, technical, and higher levels in order to enable Africans to play larger roles in the management of their own affairs. As a result of African pressures to secure equal opportunities with Frenchmen, the school programs became nearly identical to those in the metropole. Material on African history, geography, science, and daily life was added instead of substituted for French subjects. The result of this policy was the creation of a much larger and better educated elite even more closely linked to France by language and culture; its members, educated in France itself at the higher levels, were able to communicate with one another across territorial boundaries.[8]

The reforms undertaken during and after World War II, on the whole, served to strengthen the ties between France and its African territories far more than to loosen them. Nevertheless, these countries achieved self-government in 1957 and

1958 and independence from the Republic in 1960 (with the exception of Guinea, which opted for independence in September 1958). The integration of the African territories into the French state and the assimilation of their inhabitants into citizenship on a par with Europeans had failed to win the acceptance of either the French or the Africans. The French ultimately were unwilling to accept the many consequences for their state and society of full integration of an African population nearly equal in size to their own. At the same time, the Africans came to desire control of their own affairs at the territorial level. The example of the Gold Coast (later Ghana) achieving independence in 1957 and the neighboring trust territory of Togo (under French administration) moving towards self-rule under UN pressures spurred the francophone African leaders to seek similar measures of political advancement for their countries. Decolonizing forces elsewhere in the French Union (particularly Indochina and North Africa), which ultimately contributed to the collapse of the Fourth Republic and the return to power of General Charles de Gaulle as the head of a new Fifth Republic, made possible the negotiation of a peaceful transition.

The circumstances of decolonization led to a transfer of power not to the federations of AOF and AEF but to the dozen territories that collectively composed them. Some of the richer territories, particularly Côte d'Ivoire in AOF and Gabon in AEF, had long objected to the use of their resources for the benefit of their poorer neighbors; they argued for the dismantling of the federations. The leaders of the Fourth Republic did so in 1958, choosing to support the view of these richer territories rather than those of Senegal, Guinea, and the Central African Republic, which advocated the transformation of the federations into two large, economically viable, self-governing states. France may have dismantled the federations in order more easily to perpetuate its control,[9] but its action also prolonged dependency indefinitely by creating twelve small (populations from a half million to a few millions), weak states that lacked the resources to maintain, much less to develop, their administrations, economies, and social services.[10]

In this situation France devised the policy of *coopération* in order to provide its former territories with the necessary financial aid, technical expertise, and personnel for administration and development. Through this policy, it also sought to maintain a privileged relationship with them despite their attainment of international sovereignty. Thus France signed with the African states at independence or shortly thereafter agreements in such key areas as foreign policy, defense and strategic materials, education and culture, monetary policy and currency, economic, financial, and technical assistance, and such matters as fishing, civil aviation, and merchant marine.[11]

In a very real sense, French aid and assistance to education and culture underpin all other efforts to maintain and perpetuate the French presence and influence in these countries. Through the provision of financial aid and French teachers, France has enabled the African states to maintain and expand the French-derived educational system inherited from the decolonization era. Although mother-tongue instruction has been introduced in some countries in the early primary grades, and the quality of instruction in French has diminished as a result of over-crowded classes and poorly prepared instructors, students who reach the sec-ondary, technical, and higher levels continue to receive good instruction in French. At those levels teachers from France and better-trained African nationals instruct an elite whose modes of thought, professional orientation, and tastes are very French. While France has aided in the establishment of universities in most of the African states, more than 100,000 African students continued throughout the 1980s to attend universities in France. There they are further acculturated into French life.[12] In a recent work, Anton Andereggen has noted that French success in making the African elite French oriented contributes much to the special rela-tionship that France enjoys today with its former African dependencies.[13]

France promotes its culture not only through education but also through radio, television, and the press. In most countries French personnel prepare programs for broadcast over African-owned facilities that have been constructed and main-tained with French aid and assistance. In addition, Radio France Internationale broadcasts several hours daily throughout francophone Africa, and since 1989 Canal France International has been sending television programs six hours daily via satellite. French books and newspapers have a wide audience among the African elite as do French films.[14]

Further strengthening the special relationship are the measures taken to protect the African states' security under the terms of defense and military assistance agreements. Senegal, Côte d'Ivoire, Togo, Cameroon, Gabon, and the Central African Republic (as well as Djibouti and the Comoros) have defense agreements that enable their governments to seek French military intervention whenever their security is threatened. Under the terms of these agreements France main-tains bases in Senegal, Côte d'Ivoire, Gabon, the Central Africa Republic, Dji-bouti, and Réunion (an overseas department of the French Republic), at which several thousand marines are stationed to defend Africa. Far more numerous are the Forces of Rapid Action stationed at bases in southern France, from where they can be transported quickly into Africa as needed. (These forces are also available to defend Western Europe.) French strategy involves close collaboration between French and African national forces, toward which end joint maneuvers are held annually in several countries.

France maintains military assistance agreements with nearly all of its former African possessions as well as with the former Belgian territories. Under the terms of these agreements France provides aid and assistance in training the African states' armed forces and in supplying equipment, most of it at no cost. French of-ficers train troops and provide technical advice to African officers in the states themselves. African officers are sent to France for advanced instruction and in-service training. French troops frequently construct roads and bridges, and they staff medical units that serve African military personnel and their families.

While in theory French military intervention should have taken place only in those states having defense agreements, this has not been the case in practice. France has come to the rescue of some states menaced from the exterior with which it had only assistance agreements. The most notable examples are Chad in the early 1980s when it was invaded by Libya, Zaire in 1977 and 1978 when it was attacked by troops coming from Angola seeking to overthrow the Mobutu regime, and Rwanda in 1993 and 1994 when a regime perceived as favorable to French interests was threatened with overthrow.

A positive response from France to an appeal from an African government threatened from the exterior or the interior has never been automatic; France has been selective, especially in the case of internal threats. But regimes in the more prosperous coastal states with governments that have collaborated closely with French official and business interests have had strong assurances of French assistance when threatened. The presence of French bases in several of them, moreover, has diminished the possibility of external attacks as well as of internal upheavals.[15] As John Chipman has noted: "The network of defense and [military assistance] cooperation agreements maintained between France and the francophone African states is itself an important factor contributing to security within the states and in the region as a whole."[16] Thus, without the French military presence, there might well have been less stability in these states and in their relations with their neighbors. At the same time, however, this presence has served to prop up corrupt and abusive single-party regimes that ruled without much regard for the welfare or the wishes of their peoples.[17]

A second key aspect of France's special relationship with the African states has been economics. During the post-independence era, as in the colonial period, France viewed the benefits to be gained by perpetuating its control over African economies more in terms of power than of enrichment, though economic motives were hardly absent. To gain African leaders' acceptance of arrangements that bound their economies closely to that of France, the French had to offer them benefits that they could not have obtained otherwise. These arrangements proved to be mutually beneficial, in a great many respects, for a quarter of a century, until changing international conditions after 1985 increasingly called them into question.[18]

The arrangements for the franc zone were central to providing a stability that could facilitate growth and development of the African economies. At independence the African states agreed to maintain the CFA franc (Communauté Financière Africaine), which had been established following World War II, as their currency. Its value was pegged to that of the French franc, into which it was freely convertible. The CFA franc was issued in two forms, one by a monetary union of the West African states (including Togo) and another by a monetary union of the Equatorial African states (including Cameroon). Both unions maintained operations accounts into which their member states paid and from which they drew.[19]

The guarantee extended by the French government to the member states of both monetary unions through the functioning of the operations accounts was the main foundation of the Franc Zone. This system stabilized the currencies throughout the Franc Zone and greatly facilitated exports and imports with France and other member states. Thanks to this system the Franc Zone countries were able to avoid currency black marketing, parallel economies, and overvalued currencies that have damaged the economies in many African countries outside the Franc Zone.[20]

The franc zone made its member states less vulnerable to economic crises in cash crop production. It also provided security for foreign investments and helped to attract multinational corporations (most often their French-based divisions) to Côte d'Ivoire, Cameroon, Gabon, and Congo. Between the early 1960s and the early 1980s the arrangements contributed to progressive economic growth, a comparatively low rate of inflation, and economies more open to the outside than was the case for nonfrancophone states.[21] On these matters, John Chipman has commented that "the existence of the franc zone and the tradition of bilateral aid provided by France have created order where otherwise there would be near total unpredictability. They have also created some dependence on France."[22]

As for the bilateral arrangements, "reciprocal advantage within a preferential system was the central theme of these accords, including quotas, freedom from customs duties, guaranteed commodity prices, and unrestricted movement of goods between France and its trading partners."[23] Thus France continued to be the main trading partner of the African states and their major source of investment capital and development aid. Even though the associate status of the African states in the EEC granted its European members greater access to African markets and increased opportunities for investment in exchange for aid from the European Development Fund, France retained its predominance in the franc zone. France also retained influence in some of the states through its subsidies to their operating budgets, including the salaries of civil servants, and its provision of technical and administrative expertise.

The cooperation of the leaders of several coastal states (in particular, Senegal, Côte d'Ivoire, Cameroon, and Gabon) enabled France to hold and to consolidate its position in sub-Saharan Africa. The greatest share of French commercial interest is centered in these countries, which are sufficiently developed to offer attractive markets and investment opportunities, or which contain valuable energy and mineral reserves. These states have thus received the largest shares of imports and exports, in part because their leaders have pursued trade and investment policies that cater to French business and government interests. As a result, the African leaders have been able to increase the income of their governments—as well as to enrich themselves personally in ways that maintain their hold and that of their associates on political power.[24]

Chipman has noted that

the Francophone African states which are the objects of French economic assistance and development aid are generally weak. The political structures of these states, with some exceptions, are not strong enough to sustain long and well paced development policies, with specific projects carefully integrated into an ordered macro-economic design. There is equally an inherent sociological problem of inculcating new entrepreneurial attitudes both in the urban population and, further afield, in those working in the traditional agricultural sector.[25]

Because cereal production had fallen 20 percent during the 1970s, thereafter the African states were importing an increasingly large proportion of their foodstuffs. At the same time, few of them had developed an industrial capacity capable of producing goods suitable for export. The dramatic fall in global market prices for the major exports of these countries (e.g., cotton, petroleum) in 1985 and after contributed to a prolonged recession that continued, with only minor upturns, into the first half of the 1990s.[26]

These circumstances led to constantly rising costs of economic assistance, currency stability, and convertibility that France could bear only with great difficulty. The African states had to obtain assistance from such international agencies as the International Monetary Fund and the World Bank under terms that proved to be very hard to implement in view of their social costs. France has sought to coordinate its aid with that of these international bodies, for it can no longer afford to absorb the balance of trade deficits of the African states. Moreover, France itself has been troubled by budgetary constraints that are linked to repeated devaluations of the franc.[27] In January 1994, in an effort to deal with these various problems and to stimulate the international trade of the African states, it took the unprecedented step of devaluing the CFA franc by 50 percent in relation to the French franc.[28] The increased integration of France into the European Union under the terms of the Maastricht Accords (1992) will require further adjustments in its economic relations with the African states.[29]

Much of France's success in maintaining the military and economic dimensions of its special relationship with the African states has resulted from the special diplomacy that accompanies them. France's close and often affectionate relations with African leaders and peoples have involved the skillful use of both personal ties and formal structures. The representation of the African countries in the institutions of the French Republic and Union between 1945 and 1958 had already established foundations at the personal level. For example, both Félix Houphouët-Boigny of Côte d'Ivoire and Léopold Senghor of Senegal had served as deputies in the National Assembly, from which they were selected for ministerial posts in the mid-1950s.

Under the distribution of powers in the Fifth Republic, foreign affairs lay more within the domain of the president than of the government headed by the prime minister and responsible to the majority in the National Assembly. Under President de Gaulle (1958–1969), a secretariat for African and Malagasy affairs was organized at the Elysée Palace under Jacques Foccart to manage interstate relations at a personal level. Within the secretariat operated the secret service responsible for creating security services within several African states as a part of the defense agreements. Most of the secretariat's activities were hidden from the public eye and beyond parliamentary scrutiny. At the same time, the Ministry of Foreign Affairs and the Ministry of Cooperation, which was created to handle France's aid and assistance, had formal and bureaucratic responsibilities.

In 1973, in the wake of a revision of the cooperation agreements that somewhat lessened France's involvement in certain aspects of the African states' affairs, and at the request of the president of Niger, France under President Georges Pompidou agreed to hold the first Franco-African summit for heads of state to discuss matters of mutual concern. By 1975, under President Valéry Giscard d'Estaing, the summit had become an annual event as a result of its usefulness, and the former Belgian states were beginning to attend. The summit became an opportunity for settling problems through personal contacts as well as a forum for discussing issues in Franco-African relations.[30]

Chipman has noted that changing international conditions were making it increasingly difficult by the 1980s for France to utilize the bilateral relationships that it had maintained with the African states for the purposes of extending its global influence, as had been its original design. In fact, the entire special relationship had become a subject of discussion in France as a result of changing conditions.[31]

During the course of the post-independence decades, domestic politics in the African states had developed along their own paths, but within the context of the special relationship with France. Keeping in mind the features of that relationship, we may turn now to certain general developments in the African states since 1960 that form the broad context for the movements for political reform during the late 1980s and early 1990s.

During the early 1960s the multiparty, liberal democratic political systems that France had introduced into its African territories foundered nearly everywhere and were replaced by single-party regimes of an authoritarian character, several of them under military direction. Most of these regimes had a client or neopatrimonial character, which led to personal enrichment of office-holders and their families and associates as well as to corruption and mismanagement. The state came to play a much larger role in the economy, which gave further opportunities for abuses. In the face of attempts at regime change, the governments of the French Fifth Republic responded in ways that best protected France's interests, which in some cases meant military intervention to restore those ousted by coups and in others to prevent the overthrow of incumbents.

Although single-party regimes did not have to risk their tenure in office to elections, they did have to take account of ethnic and regional interests. At independence the strongest loyalties of most Africans remained those to their extended family, ethnic group, and region rather than to the nation-state that was still coming into being. Therefore, in order to promote stability, clientalist and neopatrimonial regimes had to try to incorporate individuals representing these various loyalties and the resulting interests. Financial rewards and benefits had to be distributed as evenhandedly as possible. Because of the state's control of such a large portion of the national wealth, participation in government and administration by individuals from the various ethnic groups and regions was necessary for the well-being of their kin and associates.[32]

The period from the early 1960s through the mid-1980s saw roughly a doubling in the population of the francophone states and an even higher rate of urbanization. African governments had to find the means to develop their economies further so that they could provide basic social services to burgeoning populations increasingly concentrated in large towns and cities. Given the relatively high rate of population growth in many countries, half of the population came to be under twenty years of age, thereby placing an inordinately large burden upon governments to supply education.[33]

In these circumstances education costs came to require 25 to 30 percent of national budgets without even meeting the basic requisite of giving each child at least a primary education. Secondary, technical, and higher education proved to be extremely costly because of the need to employ so many expatriates and because of the maintenance of the French tradition of free instruction. In addition, at higher levels subsidies for room and board were generally provided as well as scholarships for study in France and elsewhere overseas for advanced programs not available at home.[34]

Health care costs, too, went up. In all of francophone Africa (with the exception of Zaire), practically all health care is provided by the government, with the greatest share of the facilities and the personnel concentrated in urban areas. Given the age distribution of the population, a large part of the services is devoted to young mothers and children.

In order to ensure an adequate food supply for the populations of the urban areas, governments had a tendency to regulate the prices of locally produced foodstuffs to such an extent that many rural producers could not realize a profit. At the same time, foodstuffs had to be imported to meet the needs. To prevent urban unrest, governments frequently subsidized part of the costs of basic items. Food subsidies, along with the provision of education and health care, placed growing burdens on national budgets, especially in cases not accompanied by comparable levels of economic growth.[35] Demands by international lenders that governments reduce such social expenditures in order to meet the requirements of structural adjustment programs have led to serious popular unrest.

The immediate context of the growth of most movements for political reform was shaped by several years of comparative economic downturn linked to deteriorating international market conditions for Africa's exports, which diminished the abilities of governments to provide basic services, including maintenance of infrastructure, health care, and education during a period in which real incomes were declining. The immediate context also included the impact of the rapid demise of long-established communist regimes in Eastern Europe—regimes that had failed to bring either liberty or prosperity to their citizens. Francophone African states, whose populations had experienced a lack of freedom, mismanagement of resources, corruption, and oppression at the hands of one-party regimes, began to think that beneficial changes might be possible in their countries as well. About the same time, the celebration of the 200th anniversary of the French Revolution, transmitted by radio and television, drew attention to a successful revolution against oppression and privilege. In France, the return to power of the Left in the presidential and parliamentary elections in May and June 1988, which put an end to two years of Center-Right control of the government (albeit with a president of the Left), offered new encouragement to those who advocated reform.[36] But then in March 1993 the overwhelming electoral victory of the Center-Right parties restored the French allies of authoritarian regimes to influential positions in the Parliament and government. The election of Jacques Chirac as president of France in May 1995 and the reelection thereafter of the Center-Right coalition controlling Parliament raised further questions about France's commitment to political reform in Africa.[37]

Notes

1. UN statistics from 1991 indicate the percentage of persons aged fifteen years and over who are literate as follows: Benin, 23.4 percent; Burkina Faso, 18.2 percent; Cameroon, 54.1 percent; Central African Republic, 37.7 percent; Chad, 29.8 percent; Congo, 56.6 percent; Gabon, 60.7 percent; Guinea, 24.0 percent; Côte d'Ivoire, 53.8 percent; Mali, 32.0 percent; Mauritania, 34.0 percent; Niger, 10.8 percent; Senegal, 28.6 percent; Togo, 39.1 percent. Cited in Anton Andereggen, *France's Relationship with Subsaharan Africa* (Westport, Conn.: Praeger, 1994), p. 111.

2. The best brief introduction to the francophone states, past and present, is Patrick Manning, *Francophone Sub-Saharan Africa* (Cambridge, England: Cambridge University Press, 1988). Also see Anthony Kirk-Greene and Daniel Bach, *State and Society in Francophone Africa Since Independence* (New York: St. Martin's Press, 1995). Francis Terry McNamara's *France in Black Africa* (Washington, D.C.: National Defense University, 1989) provides the best introduction to French involvement in Africa.

3. The most recent useful works for understanding the special relationship between France and the francophone African countries are John Chipman, *French Power in Africa* (Oxford: Basil Blackwell, 1989); Andereggen, *France's Relationship with Subsaharan Africa*; and Guy Martin, "Francophone Africa in the Context of Franco-African Relations in Africa," in John W. Harbeson and Donald Rothchild, eds., *Africa in World Politics: Post–Cold War Challenges,* 2d edition (Boulder: Westview Press, 1995), pp. 163–188. See also McNamara, *France in Black Africa,* pp. xiii–xvii, 217–238.

4. For an understanding of the continuity in French policy, see Chipman, *French Power in Africa,* pp. 1–13, and Andereggen, *France's Relationship with Subsaharan Africa,* pp. 1–32.

5. Manning, *Francophone Sub-Saharan Africa,* pp. 24–86; Denise Bouche, *Histoire de la colonisation française,* vol. 2, *Flux et reflux (1815–1962)* (Paris: Fayard, 1991), pp. 128–148, 161–206; McNamara, *France in Black Africa,* pp. 3–40.

6. David E. Gardinier, "The Impact of French Education in Africa, 1817–1960," in G. Wesley Johnson, ed., *Double Impact: France and Africa in the Age of Imperialism* (Westport, Conn.: Greenwood, 1985), pp. 333–344.

7. Manning, *Francophone Sub-Saharan Africa*, pp. 112–163; Andereggen, *France's Relationship with Subsaharan Africa*, pp. 21–32; Bouche, *Flux et reflux*, pp. 377–386, 452–462.

8. David E. Gardinier, "Education in French Equatorial Africa, 1945–1960," *Cultures et développement* 16, no. 2 (1984):303–334.

9. See Joseph-Roger de Benoist, *La balkanisation de l'Afrique occidentale française* (Dakar: Nouvelles Éditions Africaines, 1979).

10. Andereggen, *France's Relationship with Subsaharan Africa*, pp. 31–66; Manning, *Francophone Sub-Saharan Africa*, pp. 135–163; Bouche, *Flux et reflux*, pp. 463–475; Chipman, *French Power in Africa*, pp. 85–109.

11. Chipman, *French Power in Africa*, pp. 109–113; Andereggen, *France's Relationship with Subsaharan Africa*, pp. 63–66; McNamara, *France in Black Africa*, pp. 95–115; Guy Martin, "The Historical, Economic, and Political Bases of France's African Policy," *Journal of Modern African Studies* 23, no. 9 (June 1985):189–208.

12. William Bosworth, "The Rigid Embrace of Dependency: France and Black Africa since 1960," *Contemporary French Civilization* 5 (Spring 1981):327–345; David E. Gardinier, "Schooling in the States of Equatorial Africa," *Canadian Journal of African Studies* 8, no. 3 (1974):517–538; Suzie Guth, "Africanisation, enseignement, et coopération bilatérale française," *Genève-Afrique* 29, no. 2 (1991):77–85.

13. Andereggen, *France's Relationship with Subsaharan Africa*, pp. 94–99.

14. Ibid., pp. 100–102; David E. Gardinier, *Historical Dictionary of Gabon*, 2d edition (Metuchen, N.J.: Scarecrow Press, 1994), pp. 220–221.

15. Chipman, *French Power in Africa*, pp. 114–167; Pascal Chaigneau, *La politique militaire de la France en Afrique* (Paris: Centre des Hautes Études Africaines et Musulmanes, 1984); Robin Luckman "French Militarism in Africa," *Review of African Political Economy* 2, no. 5 (May 1982):55–84.

16. Chipman, *French Power in Africa*, p. 183.

17. Ibid., pp. 168–185.

18. Nicolas van de Walle, "The Decline of the Franc Zone: Monetary Politics in Francophone Africa," *African Affairs* (London) 90, no. 4 (1991):383–405; Guy Martin, "The Franc Zone: Underdevelopment and Dependency in Francophone Africa," *Third World Quarterly* 8 (January 1986):205–235; Martin, "Francophone Africa in the Context of Franco-African Relations," pp. 171–178.

19. Chipman, *French Power in Africa*, pp. 186–226; Andereggen, *France's Relationship with Subsaharan Africa*, pp. 105–126; McNamara, *France in Black Africa*, pp. 115–127.

20. Andereggen, *France's Relationship with Subsaharan Africa*, p. 115.

21. Ibid., pp. 105–111.

22. Chipman, *French Power in Africa*, p. 190.

23. Andereggen, *France's Relationship with Subsaharan Africa*, pp. 136–138.

24. Ibid., pp. 105–111.

25. Chipman, *French Power in Africa*, p. 190.

26. Andereggen, *France's Relationship with Subsaharan Africa*, pp. 105–126, 135–139; Chipman, *French Power in Africa*, pp. 189–192; Jacques Alibert, ed., "Trente années d'Afrique," *Afrique contemporaine* 31, no. 164 (October-December 1992):59–87, 99–144, 224–244.

27. van de Walle, "The Decline of the Franc Zone," pp. 383–405; Tony Chafer, "French African Policy Towards Change," *African Affairs* 91, no. 1 (1992):37–51.

28. "Franc Zone News," *Economist* Intelligence Unit, *Country Report: Gabon, Equatorial Guinea*, no. 1 (1994), pp. 25–28.

29. See Serge Michailof, ed., *La France et l'Afrique: Vade-mecum pour un nouveau voyage* (Paris: Karthala, 1993), particularly the chapters by Michailof, "Faut-il brûler la coopéra-tion française?," pp. 63–99, and by Patrick Guillaumont and Sylviane Guillaumont, "La zone franc à un tournant vers l'intégration régionale," pp. 411–422; François Gaulme, "France-Afrique: Une crise de coopération," *Études*, January 1994, pp. 41–52.

30. Andereggen, *France's Relationship with Subsaharan Africa*, pp. 75–91; Chipman, *French Power in Africa*, pp. 227–255.

31. Chipman, *French Power in Africa*, pp. 253–255.

32. There is a vast literature on these subjects. For a good introduction to them in Eng-lish, see Richard Sandbrook, *The Politics of Africa's Economic Stagnation* (Cambridge, Eng-land: Cambridge University Press, 1985). In French, see the various chapters in Gérard Conac, *L'Afrique en transition: Vers le pluralisme politique* (Paris: Économica, 1993), and Jean-François Bayart, *L'état en Afrique: La politique du ventre* (Paris: Éditions Fayard, 1989). Bayart's volume is also available in English translation, *The State in Africa: The Poli-tics of the Belly* (London: Longman, 1993).

33. Roland Pourtier, "L'expansion urbaine," *Afrique contemporaine* 31, no. 164 (October-December 1992), pp. 153–167.

34. Gardinier, *Historical Dictionary of Gabon*, pp. 123–129.

35. Louis Sanmarco, "Le monde rural sacrifié: De l'injustice au risque écologique," *Afrique contemporaine* 31, no. 164 (October-December 1992), pp. 168–177; and Pourtier, "L'expansion urbaine," pp. 153–167.

36. Gardinier, *Historical Dictionary of Gabon*, pp. 20–26.

37. Larry Diamond has noted that in 1990, at the time of Benin's national conference, Chirac declared that "multipartyism was 'a political error' and a 'luxury' for developing countries." Larry Diamond, "Promoting Democracy in Africa," in Harbeson and Rothchild, *Africa in World Politics*, p. 275.

Chapter Three

The Challenges of Political Reform in Sub-Saharan Africa: A Theoretical Overview

JOHN F. CLARK

This chapter provides a basic theoretical overview of the challenge of political reform in sub-Saharan Africa. It begins with a brief exploration of some of the
terms employed to discuss political change, justifying our use of the term "political reform" in the current context. Following that is a discussion of some of the
philosophical problems that underlie any discussion of political reform and democratization in the developing world. The chapter concludes with an outline of
some of the constraints that may impede the course of political reform in sub-Saharan Africa.

Reform, Liberalization, or Democratization?

At this point in Africa's history, it is difficult to know how best to characterize the
political events that have unfolded on the subcontinent since 1989. To be sure, the
majority of African states have undergone profound political transformations, at
least at the constitutional level. One could simply refer to these events, most
vaguely and defensively, as a period of "political change," implying no particular
directionality in them, while acknowledging the obvious rupture with existing

I have previously published an article containing many of the same ideas but directed toward a different point under the title "The Constraints on Democracy in Sub-Saharan Africa: The Case for Limited
Democracy," *SAIS Review* 14, no. 2 (Summer-Fall 1994):91–108.

political practice. More subjectively, one could refer to the recent period as one of political "reform," "liberalization," or, perhaps, "democratization."

This series of appellations represents, of course, a progressively more optimistic valuation (from a liberal perspective) of events in Africa since 1989. Further, they seem to betray a teleological tendency in the thinking of those who might choose to apply them, a tendency that envisions the eventual evolution of African states, as envisioned in 1950s developmentalism, to a point of mass production and liberal political participation through democratic institutions. An honest analysis of reform in Africa must avoid this temptation to assume that African states will achieve such a happy outcome, especially in the short term.

Accordingly, scholars should hesitate before attempting to give a name to the recent period in Africa's history. Clearly, the wave of political turmoil that swept through sub-Saharan Africa after 1989 should not be minimized, as much as Marxist thinkers might want to emphasize the continuities of class domination spanning the pre- and post-1989 periods,[1] or democratic skeptics the daunting odds against the consolidation of democratic regimes.[2] It is true, as some radicals protest, that the recent changes in the political life of African states have had only a superficial impact on the quality of life for ordinary Africans. Peasants, for instance, who form a majority in most African states, may well have experienced only marginal changes in their daily lives, and their material welfare may even have suffered.

Yet, to ignore or dismiss the recent events in Africa is to allow a particular historical vision of Africa's political development to obfuscate the irrepressible element of human will that has been influencing the course of affairs on the continent. The democratic skeptics, Marxist and "realist," often overestimate the power of deterministic social forces to prevent change.

Conversely, it would certainly be to judge recent events in Africa too hopefully to refer to them as "democratization," since it is far from certain that the transitions that have thus far occurred will end up with the consolidation of any democratic regimes. Short of democratization, one could speak of "liberalization,"[3] which would seem to characterize the changes both in formal institutions and in the civil society in Africa, but the depth and durability of these changes are still unclear.

Hence we have adopted the term "reform" in this volume as the best label available, though it remains an unsatisfactory one. As the term suggests, most of the political change that has occurred since 1989 has been "progressive" insofar as many longtime dictators have had to give way to popular opposition coalitions— though the term does not suggest that such change is permanent or irreversible.[4] "Reform" is also broad enough to encompass both the "revolutionary" changes in Benin and Congo and the more gradual—and grudging—concessions made to the opposition movements in Gabon, Côte d'Ivoire, and Burkina Faso. The question posed by this book is whether recent political events in Africa represent a historical turning point leading towards a more democratic future or merely a soon-to-be-forgotten episode in a centuries-long evolution along some unforeseeable path. In short, can liberalization be expected in the medium term, and democratization in the long term?

The Prospects for Democracy:
Some Philosophical Questions

To begin our analysis of political change in francophone Africa, we start with a brief account of some of the general problems of democratization in the developing world. Nearly all sociopolitical struggles may be understood as a series of contests between the deterministic social forces of history, culture, and material welfare, on the one hand, and the voluntaristic force of individual and collective human will on the other. As Przeworski has argued, "objective factors constitute at most constraints to that which is possible under a concrete historical situation but do not determine the outcome of such situations."[5] The same understanding applies to the current struggles for freedom and material well-being in sub-Saharan Africa. Unless one is completely cynical about the motivations of the opposition militants who have been recently engaged in campaigns to unseat African dictatorships, one has to acknowledge that at least some individuals are interested in establishing democratic regimes in their countries. Many others, of course, have struggled only to unseat those whom they oppose, often with the goal of seizing power for themselves. For them, the rhetoric of democratization is only a tool to garner internal and external support. For the democrats, though, their struggle is one of will in the face of resistant social forces, given expression in the countervailing will of their opponents. The chapters in this volume examine the course of these struggles in the specific settings in which they are occurring.

The most likely outcome in the African states now traveling the path of political reform is that some will achieve at least modestly more satisfactory political patterns and others will not. Though this seems a truism, it is an important observation if one believes that those relatively more successful outcomes reflect a significant change in the social satisfaction of the citizens who inhabit those states. If some African states do consolidate institutions that collectively merit the name "democracy" while others do not, this is certainly a victory for Jean-François Bayart's view of the "historicity" of African societies[6] as well as for the influence of human will. Conversely, it would be a defeat for those grand theorists who eschew the role of local circumstance and dynamics in their analyses.

All of the authors in this volume take seriously the idea that some African political leaders and ordinary citizens have actually been struggling for democracy, rather than merely against certain authoritarian regimes and dictatorial leaders. Certainly the recent political campaigns in Africa are more than a spurious manifestation of some other social process such as economic adjustment with the external market or underlying class struggle. Perhaps the struggle is a quixotic one, doomed to failure, or one that should be placed squarely in second place behind the imperative of providing economic sustenance, but we owe it to Africa's democrats at least to take their projects seriously. Seen through their eyes, the problem of reform in Africa can best be understood as a series of impediments to, or constraints on, the institution and consolidation of democratic regimes.[7] Some of these constraints, which are overlapping and interrelated, are examined later.

One of the most useful distinctions that can be made among the constraints on democracy in the developing world is that between transition problems and consolidation problems. That is, where authoritarianism prevails, the first problem, no small task in itself, is to overthrow existing regimes. The far more daunting, long-term task, however, is to consolidate democratic institutions. Francophone Africa has seen a great number of transitions, but it is far from certain that democratic institutions have yet been consolidated anywhere.

Transitions typically follow a regime crisis, such as those that spread across Africa in the early 1990s. As Alfred Stepan has noted, however, such transitions need not lead to protodemocracies. Rather, "[t]he most likely outcome of sharp crises of authoritarian regimes stemming from diffuse pressures and forces in society" (which aptly describes the crises manifested in national conferences in francophone Africa), "is either a newly constituted successor authoritarian government, or a caretaker military junta promising elections in the future."[8] Hence it is rather impressive that so many of the new regimes brought into being by "diffuse pressures and forces in society" in Africa have been democratic or quasi-democratic and that some have now survived for several years.

An important qualification to this "transition-consolidation" model stems from the notion that a country might achieve a democratic system very *gradually*, that is, without a transition phase. Some Western countries, including Britain, and arguably the United States as well, had their democratic systems evolve over time. Similarly, perhaps Mexico, Côte d'Ivoire, and Senegal are gradually becoming more democratic. If such a path to a more meaningfully participatory system is possible, then our choice of the word "reform" is further justified.

Nonetheless, the first step in a transition from authoritarianism is typically the dissolution of an existing authoritarian regime. Such a dissolution can of course be accomplished through capitulation in the face of popular pressures (Benin, Congo) or through coup d'état (Mali). Organizing either coups d'état or popular campaigns to unseat existing authoritarian regimes, which enjoy the advantages of being able to bring state power—ideological, economic, and military—to bear against opposition forces, is no small feat. Whether one sees the state in Africa as an instrument created by a modern ruling class to serve its interests[9] or as an organic product of indigenous political belief, the colonial legacy, and the postcolonial elites' extraction of social wealth,[10] it has served as a formidable instrument of authoritarian control, if not as an engine of development. In francophone Africa, the regimes of Mobutu Sese Seko (Zaire), Gnassingbé Éyadéma (Togo),

Lansana Conté (Guinea), and others have been able to avert any transition by undertaking certain liberalizing reforms while threatening or using force against opposition figures at critical moments. Hence, the most immediate issue for would-be democratizers in authoritarian states is to assemble opposition coalitions, at the grass roots and/or among elites, with enough solidity, stamina, courage, and resistance to corruption to face down often brutal and savvy dictators.

Researchers who focus on the transitional part of democratization are frequently preoccupied with the political compromises and formal constitutions that follow the termination of authoritarian regimes when there is strong sentiment for the institution of democratic forms.[11] Theorists who have drawn extensively from case studies in Iberia, Greece, and Latin America often emphasize the necessity of a "class compromise" (or compromise among other major social groups) in the transition to democratic institutions.[12] In relatively more economically advanced societies this approach is justified by the observable organization of social groups along class and ideological lines. As Di Palma argues, those on both ends of the political spectrum need reassurance at the moment of transition from authoritarian regimes. The downtrodden and those on the left need assurance that their social agenda will not be ignored by a minimalist democratic regime, while the middle class and those on the right demand guarantees that property rights will not be substantially undermined.[13] In Africa, where political activity, if not social oppression, along class lines has been more muted, this concern is less relevant to constitution-making and compromise. Far more important are political arrangements that reconcile the leaders of ethnic and personal constituencies to democratic processes.[14] Scholars who focus on the compromises and processes of democratic transitions, as do Di Palma and Richard Joseph, are generally more optimistic about the possibility of democratic consolidation.[15]

If constitutional "crafting" is the main preoccupation of the transitional period, other constraints on democratization apply to both the periods of transition and of consolidation. Those who focus on these "structural" problems are generally far more pessimistic than Di Palma and Joseph.[16] Although these constraints can, with sufficient Procrustean effort, be artificially separated and given discrete labels for the purposes of discussion,[17] they actually form part of an interrelated complex of concepts that can be useful in describing political behavior in any society. Consider here, for instance, the concepts of state, civil society, political culture, level of development, and economic growth. With the use of these most fundamental of tools, authoritarian states, weak civil societies, nondemocratic political cultures, and underdevelopment may all be described as important constraints on democratization. To specify the causal order of these social phenomena, one may theorize that weak civil society and nondemocratic culture are to a large degree the *product* of underdevelopment. That is, defective political culture or weak civil society serve as "important intervening variables" in the relationship between underdevelopment and authoritarianism.[18] Likewise, an authoritarian state, itself the immediate and tangible constraint on the institution of democracy, could be seen as the product of weak civil society and defective political culture. Thus, one may focus on root, intermediate, or proximate causes, emphasizing any link in a long causal chain.[19]

The Constraints on Democratization in Africa

The most basic constraint on the consolidation of democratic regimes in Africa, however, is underdevelopment itself. The positive association between development and democracy is apparent to the most casual observer, and scholars have attempted to verify the linkage between the two variables since the 1950s.[20] Most scholars have focused on the "intervening variables" just mentioned that follow from underdevelopment and impede democratization, including illiteracy, ethnic strife, fragmented civil societies, and defective political cultures. For instance, one recent study suggests that "population pressures," defined chiefly as population growth, "are related to the use of repression by policymakers."[21] Rapid population growth, of course, is a principal characteristic of developing societies.

In Africa, underdevelopment is the main contributor to the dominant political forms of the continent—neopatrimonialism, prebendal politics, and personal rule. Patrimonialism, as first described by Max Weber, is a political system in which a leader imbued with charismatic or traditional authority maintains power by rewarding the loyalty of critical elites with increased social status.[22] Neopatrimonialism is a political form in which leaders reward their clients with official bureaucratic or administrative positions that characterize modern states.[23] The clients in turn use these positions to extract wealth from the society. In the independence era, during which African states have nationalized foreign-owned businesses or created state-owned businesses outright, these enterprises have often served as rewards for loyal clients. Mobutu Sese Seko of Zaire, for instance (among many other African leaders), has used the distribution of his country's nationalized enterprises in precisely this way.[24]

As Richard Sandbrook has argued, personal rule is a form of patrimonialism that has arisen in Africa where rulers have no "constitutional, charismatic-revolutionary or traditional legitimacy." As he describes personal rule, "[a] chief or strongman emerges and rules on the basis of material incentives and personal control of his administration and armed force. Fear and personal loyalties are the mainstays of a personalistic government untrammeled by traditional or modern constitutional limitations."[25] Successful personal rule is a frequent product of underdevelopment because elites recognize that their only access to the economic rewards of state office lies in their loyalty to the ruler. Meanwhile, individual rulers often find themselves embattled by critics if they attempt to reform access to state office according to a rational, merit-based system. Bratton and van de Walle have argued that the neopatrimonial (and personalistic) quality of African regimes makes changes of regime type nearly impossible, though the particular rulers may change often.[26]

The dual tasks of democratic transition and consolidation are rendered nearly impossible when they must take place simultaneously with systemic and inevitably painful economic reforms. This has certainly been the case for the relatively more developed economies of southern and eastern Europe and of Latin America, but it has been all the more conspicuous in the utterly collapsed economies of sub-Saharan Africa.[27] Of course, virtually every country in the subcontinent is now enduring structural adjustment programs mandated by the International Monetary Fund (IMF) as a condition for relief from its debt burdens, and the social consequences of these programs, at least in the short term, are devastating.[28] Currency devaluation, the revocation of government subsidies, and privatization, whatever their long-term economic merits, lead to job losses, declining standards of living, and, frequently, economic despair in the short term. And ironically, though these social costs can be the source of strong opposition to autocratic regimes, they make the consolidation of the "democratic" regimes that follow them difficult indeed.[29] Often material expectations run high when declining economic fortunes are responsible for the dissolution of autocratic regimes, and these expectations are usually disappointed when follow-on regimes have no more creative ways of financing reform than their predecessors. Besides creating outright antipathy for new governments, economic contraction quite often creates class and ethnic conflicts at the societal level, which in turn undermine the consolidation of democracy.[30]

The nature of African civil societies presents other impediments to democratization.[31] In the classic "pluralist" model of Western democracy, civil associations, including professional groups, labor unions, voluntary associations, and other "interest groups," all make claims on the state for particular needs, and the state then mediates these claims in a roughly fair way that benefits the common good. Moreover, such societal institutions serve as a bulwark against excessive expansions of state power into the social realm. In addition, a free press plays the role of watchdog over extraconstitutional suspensions of civil liberties and other abuses. In many African countries, however, states have co-opted these institutions, rendering them subject to control by ruling authorities.[32] Only a few countries, such as Nigeria and the quasi democracies, have maintained a free press, while labor unions and youth and women's groups were frequently created as, or converted to, official organs of the state. The domination of these groups by the state thus represents a severe constraint on the transition from authoritarianism.[33] Conversely, however, if the same groups are too strong in relation to the state, they can undermine newly formed regimes that are constitutionally democratic. Some theorists of rational choice have tried to demonstrate that overly powerful social groups can impinge on the adoption of rational, growth-producing economic policies.[34] One can equally demonstrate that social organizations serving narrow constituencies, such as unions that represent urban civil service workers, sometimes push newly democratic regimes into violent confrontations that end with a return to authoritarianism.

The relationship of democratization to class and ethnicity, which represent broader social categories, is similarly complex. Generally, it must be said, African societies are marked by profound class oppression, though the "organizational bourgeoisie" rather than a traditional Marxian bourgeoisie is the dominating class.[35] The distribution of income across the economic spectrum has been far more skewed in African countries that in Western states,[36] and the absence of a large middle class is almost universally regarded as an obstacle to democratic rule. At the same time, class consciousness and classwide political activity are far less evident in Africa than they have been in Europe or the United States. In this regard, the growth of class consciousness in Africa, to the extent that it leads to a redistribution of income, could create the conditions for democratic stability over the long term. But class consciousness can also lead to civil strife or challenges to elites that provoke more rigorously repressive measures by the state-controlling class, which of course defeats democratization in the near term.

On the whole, ethnic and ethnoregional consciousness in Africa have been stronger than class consciousness; indeed, the main civil wars of the continent—in Nigeria, Sudan, Zaire, Angola, Ethiopia, and so on—have been fought mainly along ethnoregional lines. Whether one views ethnic strife primarily as a product of manipulation by political entrepreneurs (the "instrumentalist" view)[37] or as the inevitable result of competition among primordial groups whose members share common cultural symbols,[38] ethnic politics has been a constant in Africa since Europeans created the continent's artificial states a century ago. Even if the Western media take Conradian delight in reporting the outrages of ethnic violence in Africa, there is still no use in denying the frequency of ethnic conflict or in viewing it strictly as a result of deeper class or other divisions. While Marxist analysts typically—and sensibly—argue that economic contraction exacerbates ethnic tensions, the better ones concede that ethnicity is an autonomous variable in African politics.[39] In fact, the weakening or removal of a number of authoritarian regimes that had previously repressed ethnoregional protests has led to outbreaks of ethnic and ethnoregional strife in Africa. Recent events in Rwanda and Burundi are only the more visible manifestations of a wave of ethnic violence that has also affected Congo, Zaire, and many other African states, often after years of relative ethnoregional peace.

As for political culture, a well-developed literature makes a strong case for the thesis that the institution and maintenance of democracy depend largely on favorable attitudes towards democracy by elites and ordinary citizens.[40] In one sense "democracy" is a state of mind: If people *believe* profoundly that democracy *will* work, and if they are committed to a democratic form of governance, then, no matter what their material or social circumstances, democracy *can* work. Among elites serving the state, however, nondemocratic values, inspired either by conviction or simple love of power, are often insurmountable impediments to the removal of authoritarian regimes. The uncertain charms of democratic politics have rarely been more attractive to governing elites than the status and rent-generated wealth associated with holding high office. And while Western observers often delude themselves in thinking that all those who struggle against oppression are committed to liberty, it happens all too often that opposition elites who come to power are no more democratic in political values than those they replace. As the cases of Zambia and Benin demonstrate, the detention of political opponents is virtually a reflex to opposition for many African leaders, even if they come to power by election.

Among the masses, nondemocratic values—as well as outright ignorance of the realities of democratic practice—are also an impediment to democracy. The impact of mass political culture, however, is more operative over the long term, affecting the consolidation and maintenance of democratic regimes more than their creation. Many authoritarian regimes in Africa have been brought down by popular pressures, inducing the new leaders to promise elections and democratic constitutions. Yet, in nearly as many instances, the general population has acquiesced in, if not favored, the end of democratic regimes, particularly ones that were perceived to be hopelessly corrupt. In Nigeria, for instance, the population responded weakly to the seizure of power by high military officers in the mid-1980s, partly as a result of the corruption of civilian regimes. Perhaps the recurring cycle of change from military to civilian rule in Sudan[41] reflects a similar ambivalence towards democracy in that country. In general, mass opinion often despises ruling authoritarians without having any real commitment to democracy in the abstract. Finally, of course, the attitudes towards democracy of the masses and of the elites are mutually reflective and mutually reinforcing; authoritarian leaders would not survive without some measure of popular support from a non-democratically thinking public, but these same leaders promote the idea that democratic politics is undesirable, unworkable, or un-African.

According to one recent analysis, the roots of Africa's political cultures can be identified in three periods, the precolonial, the colonial, and the anticolonial (1945–1960).[42] There is no reason not to add the period of independence, especially since recent practice weighs heavily on the minds of citizens and political elites alike. In delimiting a political space of the scope of "Africa," one has to be on guard against either of two false notions about political culture, namely, (1) that there is nothing distinguishably different about African political patterns from those in other regions, or (2) that political patterns in all African countries are essentially similar. All of Africa, including Ethiopia and Liberia to some extent, carries the political legacy of the century-long direct confrontation with European colonialism. Moreover, there is some validity in viewing certain features of African culture as continent-wide (or, at least, subcontinent-wide)[43] and clearly distinguishable from those of, say, India, Indonesia, or Brazil. Even if one takes the view that "pre-colonial Africa consisted of many little traditions that did not . . .

generate a great tradition,"[44] it remains true that the "great traditions" of other large world regions rendered them distinct from Africa as a whole. At the same time, the differences among the various indigenous political forms, patterns of colonial rule, and post-independence experiences are certainly great enough to have created different political cultures for African states and other socially distinguishable ethnic and religious groups.

One can trace both protodemocratic and authoritarian, even tyrannical, strains in the political forms of precolonial Africa. Many contemporary African elites, especially those who hope to promote democracy on the continent, prefer to dwell on the popular or protodemocratic strains of precolonial political life,[45] and there is no gainsaying that there was debate, consultation, well-developed legal systems, and checks on the abuse of power in some precolonial African societies.[46] Popular inclusion, the high value placed on public goods, and decentralization were other protodemocratic values prominent in many precolonial African societies.[47]

Popular Western accounts of precolonial Africa, by contrast, often seem to relish relating the gory details of some of precolonial Africa's most tyrannical regimes, such as those of Shaka Zulu or Mutesa, king of Buganda.[48] Yet some Africans themselves are also anxious to debunk the "democratic myth" of African traditional societies.[49] Even in some of the cases in which traditional leaders consulted with the people, as through the *kgotla* (assembly) in the Tswana culture, the public was not allowed to set the agenda, and those opposing the chief had to fear reprisals.[50] Nor did Islam bring much of a democratic tradition to those parts of Saharan, West, and East Africa where it has penetrated. Traditional Islam, like medieval Christianity, usually carried with it the largely antidemocratic values of paternalism, deference to authority (religious and secular), and reservation of political rights to believers. In the majority of Black African states, though, relatively unfettered kingship was the major source of political authority. Of course this heritage should not be an embarrassment to anyone, since full democracy, including a universal franchise and reasonable protection of civil rights, was unknown *anywhere* in the world until the twentieth century.[51] Thus, the truth in the debate about precolonial cultures certainly lies between either of the extreme positions.

Formal European colonialism in Africa, typically lasting some seventy years and being largely responsible for contemporary African political borders, did not obliterate existing political cultures, but it altered them profoundly. Inasmuch as political cultures pertain only to identifiable political communities, the advent of colonial states created new loci for the evolution of syncretic political cultures. These new cultures resulted from a mixture of both existing political attitudes and behaviors of diverse peoples incorporated into colonial states, and those absorbed from the practice of colonial rule. Of course, the main contribution of colonial rule was to reinforce the arbitrary and authoritarian aspects of political behavior. After all, the root goal of colonial rule, whatever ideological or moral justifications were offered for it, was to enable a more systematic and exhaustive exploitation of Africa's economic potential. This could hardly be accomplished without an authoritarian political structure supported by a bureaucracy organized according to the principles of commercial efficiency. Naturally, the denial of Africans' self-determination, like that of other races and peoples, could only be accomplished by the constant threat and the occasional exercise of coercive means of rule. Doubtless the political behaviors of colonial authorities did not go unobserved by the new elites who were being trained for a role in administration themselves. And the class stratification engendered by the creation of a "bureaucratic bourgeoisie" dependent on the state as a source of income paralleled the less-entrenched class cleavages between traditional elites and their followers.[52]

These rather conventional observations about the effects of colonial rule on political culture, necessary though they are, should not obscure the complexity of the overall effect of the penetration of European social, moral, and political thinking in Africa in the twentieth century. For every H. M. Stanley, liberally applying force as he slashed his way across the continent in order to organize Africans according to his rationalized conception of their role in the world, there was a David Livingstone or a Savorgnan de Brazza, sometimes preceding him, seeking to promote European values in a subtler way. One legacy of this variety of European contact is that several generations of Africans in French and Belgian territories were educated in the Christian (usually Catholic) schools promoted by colonial authorities. Accordingly, the religious component of the protest movements in Malawi or Zaire, and the fact that most of the sovereign national conferences were headed by Catholic archbishops, is an indirect consequence of this European heritage.

Likewise, with regard to education more generally, European values and outlooks were transmitted through these schools into the consciousness of African students. In the cases of British, French, and Belgian colonies lessons included—inevitably, if contradictorily, given the weight of colonial rule—the notion that democracy was a superior political form to kingship or authoritarianism. European powers took great pride in their own cultural heritage even if they did not practice what they preached. Meanwhile, specific colonial powers naturally transmitted portions of their own historical experiences into the political consciousness of African subjects, which has had a lingering effect on political behavior in their former colonies. One specific bit of evidence for this in the case of France's former colonies can be identified in the comparisons between the sovereign national conferences and the Estates General of the French Revolution.[53] The idea that the francophone countries have a common political culture was vigorously argued earlier, and the conferences are only the most salient expression of that culture.

Finally, there is the "international factor" in democratization, pertaining not to how international contacts shape political culture but how they influence the transition to or consolidation of democracy.[54] It can hardly be an accident that the recent wave of democratization in Africa, which peaked in 1991 or 1992, ensued immediately after the collapse of Eastern Europe's communist regimes. Even if one prefers Marxian materialism to Hegelian ideals as the source of social mobilization, one cannot usefully deny the "demonstration effect" produced by the European events in 1989.[55] The World Bank only strengthened the prevailing zeitgeist of that fateful year with its call for improved "governance" in Africa. If declining economic prospects and deprivation alone were the only source of political tumult in Africa, then the recent revolutions would have occurred in 1985, or even 1980. Nonetheless, the chapters in this volume reveal the complexity of international and domestic factors in the reform processes, including many that identify well-established opposition movements articulating clear grievances long before the events of 1989.[56]

The revolutions of 1989 aside, though, wealthy states as well as organizations such as the IMF and the World Bank are well positioned to have some impact on the course of reforms. Przeworski's observation that transitions are a time of great uncertainty for political elites[57] reinforces the notion that international actors can serve as one source of reassurance for them. Unfortunately for would-be democratizers, many of the states now undergoing democratic reforms are simultaneously facing socially painful economic reforms, often imposed by the World Bank and the IMF. Yet, as Przeworski has argued in many works, economic decline represents one of the most serious threats to new democratic regimes. Few things bring the people out into the streets in anger more quickly than seeing the subsidies for food staples or other basic commodities slashed under a structural adjustment plan. More generally, if new regimes taking over collapsed economies do not bring rapid relief for economic deprivation, citizens usually have little patience for them, which in turn encourages military coups. External actors are thus important both for their rhetorical and their material contribution to reform movements.

Most importantly for the francophone African states, however, one cannot ignore the pervasive and deep influence of France itself on the subcontinent,[58] an international political reality that is not well appreciated in the United States. It is an assumption of this volume, however, that the policies of France, colonial, postcolonial and during the recent reform period, have lent a distinct quality to the reforms in francophone Africa. Most notably, President François Mitterrand's statement at the La Baule Conference in June 1990 in favor of democracy was an important catalyst for the reform movements. Similarly, France's recent return to its tolerance for authoritarianism, punctuated by the rise of President Jacques Chirac, has coincided with a stall in francophone African reforms. In the following chapters, we see how those seeking democracy in francophone Africa have grappled with the unique opportunities and constraints that they have faced.

Notes

1. See, for example, Robert Fatton, *Predatory Rule: State and Civil Society in Africa* (Boulder: Lynne Rienner, 1992).

2. Samuel P. Huntington, "Will More Countries Become Democratic?" *Political Science Quarterly* 99, no. 2 (1984):193–218. We use the term democracy in this introduction in the narrow sense, as opposed to a broader, social sense. For an elaboration of the broad (social)

sense of democracy compared to the narrow (strictly political), see John D. Martz, "Bureaucratic-Authoritarianism, Transitions to Democracy, and the Political-Culture Dimension," in Howard J. Wiarda, ed., *New Directions in Comparative Politics*, 2d edition (Boulder: Westview Press, 1991), pp. 204–207.

3. As Laurence Whitehead pointed out, authoritarian leaders frequently undertake to liberalize aspects of their governance during times of internal or external pressure with no intention of actually giving up power. Laurence Whitehead, "International Aspects of Democratization," in Guillermo O'Donnell, Philippe C. Schmitter, and Laurence Whitehead, eds., *Transitions from Authoritarian Rule: Comparative Perspectives* (Baltimore: Johns Hopkins University Press, 1986), pp. 8–9. This would appear to have been the strategy of Presidents Éyadéma, Mobutu, and Bongo since 1990.

4. It must be acknowledged, though, that some believe (1) that most societies in the developing world are not ready for democracy and (2) that, as a result, premature experimentation with democratic forms, through its economic disruptions, may only delay the development required for stable democratic governance. Such views can be inferred in Samuel Huntington's much-cited *Political Order in Changing Societies* (New Haven: Yale University Press, 1968).

5. Adam Przeworski, "Problems in the Study of Transition to Democracy," in Guillermo O'Donnell et al., *Transitions from Authoritarian Rule: Comparative Perspectives* (Baltimore: Johns Hopkins University Press, 1986), p. 48. Also consider the observation of Giuseppe Di Palma: "Political actors in a transition are not passive tools of history. If actors are aware of predicaments endemic to transitions and act in their own interests, then they *can* set in motion a process that, even under an unpromising start, may close (be it only in a few cases) with the adoption of appropriate democratic rules." Giuseppe Di Palma, *To Craft Democracies: An Essay on Democratic Transitions* (Berkeley: University of California Press, 1990), p. 46.

6. Bayart develops the idea of "historicity" in his monumental *The State in Africa: The Politics of the Belly* (London: Longman, 1993), especially pp. 1–37. "Historicity" refers to the uniqueness and autonomy of African societies in the face of Europe's efforts to stereotype and control them.

7. See the recent article by Samuel Decalo, "The Process, Prospects, and Constraints of Democratization in Africa," *African Affairs* 91 (1992):7–35, and John F. Clark, "The Constraints on Democracy in Sub-Saharan Africa: The Case for Limited Democracy," *SAIS Review* 14, no. 2 (Summer-Fall 1994):91–108.

8. Alfred Stepan, "Paths Toward Redemocratization: Theoretical and Comparative Considerations," in O'Donnell et al., *Transitions from Authoritarian Rule*, pp. 78–79.

9. As does, for instance, Fatton, in *Predatory Rule*, especially pp. 1–40.

10. As does Bayart, in *The State in Africa*.

11. For a survey of the problems of democratization and constitutionalism, see Jon Elster and Rune Slagstad, eds., *Constitutionalism and Democracy* (Cambridge, England: Cambridge University Press, 1988).

12. Przeworski, "Problems in the Study of Transition to Democracy," pp. 61–62, and Di Palma, *To Craft Democracies*, pp. 44–75. Cf. J. Samuel Valenzuela, "Consolidation in Post-Transitional Settings," in Scott Mainwaring, Guillermo O'Donnell, and J. Samuel Valenzuela, eds., *Issues in Democratic Consolidation: The New South American Democracies in Comparative Perspective* (Notre Dame, Ind.: University of Notre Dame Press, 1992), pp. 84–87.

13. Di Palma, *To Craft Democracies*, pp. 90–106.

14. See Harvey Glickman, "Issues in the Analysis of Ethnic Conflict and Democratization Processes in Africa Today," in Harvey Glickman, ed., *Ethnic Conflict and Democratization in Africa* (Atlanta: African Studies Association Press, 1995), pp. 1–31.

15. See Di Palma, *To Craft Democracies*, and Richard Joseph, "Zambia: A Model for Democratic Change," *Current History* 91, no. 565 (May 1992):199–201.

16. Huntington has called them "contextual" problems. See *The Third Wave: Democratization in the Late Twentieth Century* (Norman: University of Oklahoma Press, 1991), p. 209.

17. See René Lemarchand's discussion of the artificiality of the distinction between state and civil society in his "Uncivil States and Civil Societies: How Illusion Became Reality," *Journal of Modern African Studies* 30, no. 2 (1992):177–191. Nonetheless, the social scientist can scarcely survive without these distinctions, whatever their limitations. Naomi Chazan has similarly observed that "The contemporary African political experience defies the neat classificatory schemes devised to capture its multivariate texture. The message emanating from the continent in recent years is one of constant movement, of straddling the dichotomies of its observers." Naomi Chazan, "Patterns of State-Society Incorporation and Disengagement in Africa," in Donald Rothchild and Naomi Chazan, eds., *The Precarious Balance: State and Society in Africa* (Boulder: Westview Press, 1988), p. 122.

18. Larry Diamond, "Introduction: Political Culture and Democracy," in Larry Diamond, ed., *Political Culture and Democracy in Developing Countries* (Boulder: Lynne Rienner, 1994), p. 1.

19. On this methodological point, see Hugh Stretton, *The Political Sciences* (New York: Basic Books, 1969), chapters 1–3.

20. See, for example, Seymour Martin Lipset, "Some Social Requisites of Democracy: Economic Development and Political Legitimacy," *American Political Science Review* 53 (January–March 1959), pp. 69–75, and Larry Diamond, "Economic Development and Democracy Reconsidered," in Gary Marks and Larry Diamond, eds., *Reexamining Democracy: Essays in Honor of Seymour Martin Lipset* (Newbury Park, Calif.: Sage Publications, 1992), pp. 93–139.

21. Conway W. Henderson, "Population Pressures and Political Repression," *Social Science Quarterly* 74, no. 2 (June 1993):330.

22. Max Weber, *The Theory of Social and Economic Organization* (New York: Free Press, 1947), pp. 347–357. Also see the short discussion in Richard Sandbrook, *The Politics of Africa's Economic Stagnation* (Cambridge, England: Cambridge University Press, 1985), pp. 88–89, and the discussion of tributes, patronage, and prebends in René Lemarchand, "The State, the Parallel Economy, and the Changing Structure of Patronage Systems," in Rothchild and Chazan, eds., *The Precarious Balance*, pp. 151–154.

23. Michael Bratton and Nicolas van de Walle, "Neopatrimonial Regimes and Political Transitions in Africa," *World Politics* 46, no. 4 (1994):458.

24. Crawford Young and Thomas Turner, *The Rise and Decline of the Zairian State* (Madison: University of Wisconsin Press, 1985), pp. 330–356.

25. Sandbrook, *The Politics of Africa's Economic Stagnation*, p. 89. The classic argument for personal rule, and one of the seminal books on Africa of the 1980s, is that of Robert Jackson and Carl Rosberg, *Personal Rule in Black Africa* (Los Angeles: University of California Press, 1982).

26. Bratton and van de Walle, "Neopatrimonial Regimes."

27. On Eastern Europe and Latin America, see Luiz Carlos Bresser Pereira, Jose Maria Maravall, and Adam Przeworski, eds., *Economic Reforms in New Democracies: A Social-Democratic Approach* (Cambridge, England: Cambridge University Press, 1993); on Africa, see, for example, Nicolas van de Walle, "Crisis and Opportunity in Africa," *Journal of Democracy* 6, no. 2 (April 1995):128–140.

28. For one harsh assessment that is characteristic of academic analyses of structural adjustment, see J. Barry Riddell, "Things Fall Apart Again: Structural Adjustment Programmes in Sub-Saharan Africa," *Journal of Modern African Studies* 30, no. 1 (1992):53–68.

29. Ibid. See also John F. Clark, "Socio-Political Change in the Republic of the Congo: Political Dilemmas of Economic Reform," *Journal of Third World Studies* 10, no. 1 (Spring 1993):52–77, and the various contributions in the present volume.

30. See, for example, Ted R. Gurr, "On the Political Consequences of Scarcity and Economic Decline," *International Studies Quarterly* 29, no. 1 (March 1985):51–75.

31. For an excellent introductory survey, see Naomi Chazan et al., *Politics and Society in Contemporary Africa* (Boulder: Lynne Rienner, 1988), pp. 71–96.

32. Julius Nyang'oro and Timothy Shaw, eds., *Corporatism in Africa: Comparative Analysis and Practice* (Boulder: Westview Press, 1989).

33. Nevertheless, a good deal of "liberalization" has taken place in African societies where the free press has reemerged and civil associations have revitalized themselves, even when the state itself remains authoritarian. See John F. Clark, "The National Conference as an Instrument of Democratization in Francophone Africa," *Journal of Third World Studies* 11, no. 1 (Spring 1994):304–335.

34. For example, Mancur Olson, *The Rise and Decline of Nations: Economic Growth, Stagflation, and Social Rigidities* (New Haven: Yale University Press, 1982).

35. Irving Leonard Markovitz, *Power and Class in Africa: An Introduction to Change and Conflict in African Politics* (Englewood Cliffs, N.J.: Prentice-Hall, 1977), pp. 198–229. The "organizational bourgeoisie" is defined by its members' control over state offices, which allows them to extract wealth from the economy rather than from their ownership of the means of production.

36. Though the data are scant for the developing countries, compare Tables 18 and 40 in the *Human Development Report 1993* (New York: Oxford University Press, 1993), pp. 171–172 and 202, respectively.

37. Representative examples of the "instrumentalist" school include Aidan Southall, "The Illusion of Tribe," *Journal of Asian and African Studies* 5, no. 1 (January-April 1970):28–50; Nelson Kasfir, *The Shrinking Political Arena* (Berkeley: University of California Press, 1976); Joseph Rothschild, *Ethnopolitics* (New York: Columbia University Press, 1981); and Eric Hobsbawm and Terence Ranger, eds., *The Invention of Tradition* (Cambridge, England: Cambridge University Press, 1983).

38. One classic example of this approach is Clifford Geertz, "The Integrative Revolution, Primordial Sentiments, and Civil Politics in the New States," in Clifford Geertz, ed., *Old Societies and New States: The Quest for Modernity in Asia and Africa* (New York: Free Press, 1963), pp. 105–157. Also see Harold Isaacs, *Idols of the Tribe* (New York: Harper & Row, 1975).

39. For example, John S. Saul, himself a Marxian analyst, argued that "Marxist scientists and African revolutionaries can only make progress when they take ethnicity . . . seriously as a real rather than ephemeral and/or vaguely illegitimate variable." John S. Saul, "The Di-

alectic of Race and Class," *Race and Class* 20, no. 4 (1979):371, cited in Chazan et al., *Politics and Society in Contemporary Africa*, p. 124.

40. See—to cite only one of the classic works—Gabriel Almond and Sidney Verba, *The Civic Culture: Political Attitudes and Democracy in Five Nations* (Princeton: Princeton University Press, 1963).

41. Peter K. Bechtold, "More Turbulence in Sudan: A New Politics This Time?" in John O. Voll, ed., *Sudan: State and Society in Crisis* (Bloomington, Ind.: Indiana University Press, 1991), pp. 2–10.

42. Naomi Chazan, "Between Liberalism and Statism: African Political Cultures and Democracy," in Diamond, ed., *Political Culture and Democracy in Developing Countries*, pp. 69–76.

43. See, for example, John S. Mbiti, *African Religions and Philosophy* (New York: Praeger, 1970). No less a figure than Julius Nyerere has claimed that "Despite all the variations and some exceptions where the institutions of domestic slavery existed, African family life was everywhere based on certain practices and attitudes which together mean basic equality, freedom and unity." Cited in V. G. Simiyu, "The Democratic Myth in the African Traditional Societies," in Walter O. Oyugi et al., eds., *Democratic Theory and Practice in Africa* (Portsmouth, N.H.: Heinemann, 1988), pp. 49–70.

44. Chazan, "Between Liberalism and Statism," p. 70.

45. See Sahr John Kpundeh, ed., *Democratization in Africa: African Views, African Voices: Summary of Three Workshops* (Washington, D.C.: National Academy Press, 1992), pp. 9–10. Cf. the observation of Nyerere, note 43, *supra*.

46. For example, on the checks and balances in the political organization of the Yoruba (Nigeria), see Robert Smith, *Kingdoms of the Yoruba* (London: Methuen, 1976); on the importance of consultation among the Tswana (Botswana), see I. Schapera, *A Handbook of Tswana Law and Custom* (London: Frank Cass, 1970); and on the well-developed legal system of the Kuba (Zaire), see Jan Vansina, *The Children of Woot: A History of the Kuba Peoples* (Madison: University of Wisconsin Press, 1978), pp. 145–152.

47. Chazan, "Between Liberalism and Statism," pp. 70–71.

48. On the former, see David R. Morris, *The Washing of the Spears: A History of the Rise of the Zulu Nation Under Shaka and Its Fall in the Zulu War of 1879* (New York: Simon & Schuster, 1965), and on the latter, Alan Moorhead, *The White Nile* (Middlesex, England: Penguin, 1963), pp. 58–66, and Thomas Pakenham, *The Scramble for Africa, 1876–1912* (New York: Random House, 1991), pp. 301–302. Though the accuracy of these accounts may not be in question, they certainly feed the "heart of darkness" attitudes of common Western opinion about precolonial Africa.

49. Simiyu, "The Democratic Myth."

50. John D. Holm, "Botswana: A Paternalistic Democracy," in Larry Diamond, Juan J. Linz, and Seymour Martin Lipset, eds., *Democracy in Developing Countries*, vol. 2, *Africa* (Boulder: Lynne Rienner, 1988), p. 182.

51. And, one might add, since totalitarianism in some Western societies in the twentieth century, especially Nazi Germany and Stalinist Russia, reached depths of tyranny unknown anywhere in Africa.

52. On this point, cf. Sandbrook, *The Politics of Africa's Economic Stagnation*, pp. 42–62.

53. See Albert Bourgi, "Les états généraux de la démocratie," *Jeune Afrique*, no. 1591 (June 26–July 2, 1991):27, and Pearl T. Robinson, "The National Conference Phenomenon

in Francophone Africa," *Comparative Studies in Society and History* 36, no. 3 (July 1994):590–596.

54. For a general discussion, see Whitehead, "International Aspects of Democratization."

55. Douglas Anglin, "Southern African Responses to Eastern European Developments," *Journal of Modern African Studies* 28, no. 3 (September 1990):431–455.

56. In fact many, if not most, Africanists resist the idea that global political forces were the critical variable in the advent or timing of the 1989–1992 wave of African democratization. Douglas Anglin, for instance, downplays the importance of European events even while identifying them as part of the explanation. Anglin, "Southern African Responses." Pearl Robinson explicitly rejects the notion that the "Berlin example" was an important part of the African reform movements. Robinson, "The National Conference Phenomenon," p. 584.

57. See, for example, Adam Przeworski, *Democracy and the Market: Political and Economic Reforms in Eastern Europe and Latin America* (Cambridge, England: Cambridge University Press, 1991), p. 10.

58. In addition to David E. Gardinier's "The Historical Origins of Francophone Africa" in the present volume, see the recent work of Guy Martin, "Continuity and Change in Franco-African Relations," *Journal of Modern African Studies* 33, no. 1 (1995):1–20.

Part Two

Cases of Peaceful
Regime Change

Chapter Four

Benin: First of the New Democracies

SAMUEL DECALO

It is paradoxical that the third wave of global democratization affected Benin, of all African states, so immediately and totally that the country, already holding numerous dubious continental distinctions, was to become the pioneer of the "national conference" approach to the rollback of authoritarian rule, and ipso facto the first of Africa's new democracies.[1] This is even more perplexing when contrasted to the different evolution in neighboring Togo (which always invites comparison) where General Éyadéma brutalized the pro-democracy movement into submission and entrenched his military rule with a semblance of electoral sanction. Indeed, though the same winds of change—blowing from Paris, the World Bank, the International Monetary Fund (IMF), and Washington—shook all African autocracies, the contrast between the outcome in Lomé and that in Cotonou underscores how different results are likely in a process even now only half complete.

The opening up of political space in Africa came as a result of the interaction of many complex factors and pressures, internal and external, that have already been outlined in this book and elsewhere.[2] Many of these variables have affected the francophone African countries equally, though, as just noted, sometimes with different results. But more than in most other African states, an understanding of the remarkably smooth transition from military dictatorship to civilian rule in Benin—a country not hitherto known for smooth transitions of any kind—requires a deep appreciation of the unique domestic context that made anything except regime change impossible.

Years before the end of the cold war undermined the Marxist rationale of the Mathieu Kérékou regime, and before external pressures made military retreats from power inevitable in Africa, Kérékou was in an impossible quandary as to how to extricate Benin from the bottomless pit into which his policies had led it. The army was again deeply divided, restless, and bubbling with plots and power-grabs, much as in former years when Benin had held Africa's record for coups. France, which had always ultimately, though at times reluctantly, picked up the tab of Cotonou's deficits (regarding this a small price for the control of Benin), had served notice that the good old days were over. Moreover, Kérékou had never been able to extract much fiscal aid or other support from his new Arab and East Bloc allies. When civil society coalesced in 1989 in a concerted rebellion, the democratic option presented itself. Though at the outset Kérékou resisted the populist waves of discontent that engulfed his regime, democratization and withdrawal from power were not as unpalatable to him as they were to Éyadéma in neighboring Lomé, where quite different domestic and personal considerations played a role. Factors particular to Benin precluded a ruthless attempt by Kérékou to retain power, as Éyadéma did in Lomé, and hence a smooth transition to civilian rule was assured in Cotonou, giving democracy a chance to emerge and possibly to survive.

Prelude to the Kérékou Era

Kérékou, a northerner, seized power in 1972 after the country's first twelve years of independence had produced a series of debilitating and ineffective, ethnically skewed, musical-chair regimes punctuated by short bouts of military rule. None of the regimes that emerged in Cotonou had proved to be capable of centralizing effective national authority and providing political leadership or a coherent economic policy beyond a "public trough" for ethnic cohorts.

Dahomey, as the country was then known, was sharply polarized along ethnoregional lines, with animosities dating to the precolonial era when several competitive kingdoms such as Danhomé and Porto Novo were engaged in a dynamic tug-of-war in the south while the north was largely isolated from the rest of the country. With the onset of competitive politics in the French colony, an ethnic trio of political leaders emerged to dominate completely the political landscape and popular vote, making all secondary leaders or ideological parties virtually irrelevant. Justin Ahomadégbé, a prince of the royal Danhomé lineage, controlled the allegiances of southwestern Fon people; Sourou-Migan Apithy, of a somewhat lesser royal lineage, had a monopoly of power over the eastern Nagot-Yoruba people of the former Porto Novo kingdom; and in the north, Hubert Maga, though a commoner, forged behind his candidacy a powerful network of traditional chiefs/kings among the more decentralized and underdeveloped Bariba and other peoples.

The triumvirate completely dominated the electoral allegiances of their ethnic blocs from the 1950s on. As no single ethnic bloc or leader was able to rule alone, political alliances emerged (for example, in 1960–1963 and 1963–1965) which rapidly deteriorated into internal struggles for supremacy, leading to the military's intervention. So powerful was the stranglehold of the country's civilian bosses that in 1968, when precluded by the military from contesting the next presidential elections, their call for an electoral boycott from Paris, where they were in voluntary exile, was 80 percent effective. Then, when the triumvirate was finally allowed to compete for the presidency (after an equally brief army-elevated President Émile Zinsou interregnum), the percentage that each member of the trio garnered in "his" region in 1970 was exactly the same as they had obtained in 1960.

The armed forces were themselves polarized along similar ethnic and regional lines. During the 1960s and 1970s some 80 percent of the officer corps had been staffed by southerners (especially Fon), a function of this group's higher levels of literacy. By contrast, over 80 percent of the rank and file were northerners, and periodic ugly tensions between the two were barely papered over. Given society's polarization and efforts of the country's ethnic leaders to build up supportive civil-military power props, the army was itself highly politicized and was not a neutral bystander in the political conflict that periodically engulfed the country. Personal and ethnic loyalty pyramids coalesced across ranks within the armed forces in support of one or another of the triumvirate and, later, of the personal ambitions of specific officers. Indeed, though some of the coups that punctuated the country's early political life were overtly rationalized on political and economic grounds, covert personal and ethnic motives were never absent. By 1968 Dahomey had become a full-blown praetorian system within which individual officers and power cliques scrambled for supreme power.

The country's sharp ethnic divisions were mirrored in major social and economic disparities among Dahomey's regions. Regional statistics—on levels of education, literacy, per capita income, infant mortality, and so on—differed so sharply from one another as to resemble data drawn from completely different countries, with the north lagging far behind the south on all dimensions. Every leader who came to power utilized state resources, to the degree available, to reward his political cohorts and enhance his region to the exclusion of others, irrespective of possible resulting anomalies. A very telling quip in the 1970s on the always bone-jarring drive along the unpaved middle stretch—through Mahi country—of the country's otherwise tarred major north-south "National Road" was that the segment would only be paved under a Mahi president. This was an impossibility in light of the minority status of Dahomey's Mahi, and indeed, the segment remained unpaved for decades.

What has always greatly aggravated political strife and the ethnic tug-of-war in Dahomey is the fact that the country is one of Africa's least economically viable states. Though Dahomey has been known since colonial days for the large numbers of intellectuals, doctors, poets, and educated (southern) elites it produced—many migrating to France or other francophone countries in quest for employment—Dahomey was a typical client state. Producing only small amounts of agricultural goods—palm products, peanuts, and cotton—its balance of trade had been unfavorable since 1924. Since independence exports have covered as little as 15 percent of imports, and in most years French subsidies were needed just to balance the country's budget. The resultant fiscal stringency and budgetary austerity in Cotonou caused much unrest among the country's unionized urban workers, especially when contrasted with the blatant corruption and/or mismanagement of resources of the elite in power. Every political crisis in the country has had an economic dimension, since economic and political frustrations have been inextricably bound in this pauperized country.

By the time of Kérékou's coup d'état in 1972, Dahomey had experienced every conceivable kind of civilian rule, and all had been found wanting, including the government he overthrew, which was a unique Presidential Council in which all three of the country's ethnic leaders had agreed to take turns at the helm after the country had nearly disintegrated into civil war in 1970. Though Dahomey's first peaceful political succession had just taken place in 1972, with Maga handing over power to Ahomadégbé, the system was already beginning to creak as revelations of corruption, union unrest, and armed upheavals in the unruly and internally divided armed forces resurfaced. Kérékou, with the support of some of the middle-ranking officers who were untainted by prior association with the triumvirate and more nationalist and militant, though mostly southern, imprisoned the triumvirate and moved into the Presidential Palace. He was to remain there for seventeen years, by far the longest-lasting Beninese regime.

A Postmortem of the Marxist Experiment

The 1972 coup was seen at the time as nothing more than the latest of Dahomey's periodic military eruptions. But two years later Kérékou announced that the coup had actually been a socialist revolution. In December 1975 the country's name was changed to Benin (the old name, derived from the Fon kingdom of Danhomé, was anathema in two of the regions), and Marxism was declared as the state's ideology. Under the guise of a People's Republic, the regime adopted all the outward trappings of Marxism and began to nationalize the country's means of production.

Nothing better underscored the bizarreness of the "Marxist" upheaval in one of Africa's least viable client states than the fact that the first phase of the nationalizations amounted to only $8 million of assets. It was, moreover, France that provided bankrupt Benin with the funds to compensate French nationals whose property had been expropriated and to pay the salaries of Catholic priests teaching in church schools, who had hitherto offered tuition-free education to some 50 percent of the country's students. In addition, Paris later recruited "radical" technical assistants to guide the new People's Republic in consolidating the "Revolution."

Notwithstanding the red flag in due course unfurled in Cotonou, the ideological shift to the left was not primarily dictated by ideological convictions; though some of the officers in the junta that seized power were indeed radical, Kérékou himself was not—and several remained to the end ideologically conservative. Rather, there was a very urgent and pragmatic need to differentiate the new regime from all preceding ones in jaded Cotonou. Thus its raison d'être became Marxism, a class rather than ethnic ideology, with an anticolonial, nationalist, developmental thrust. Further, the junta needed a civilian constituency, some societal support, and some measure of legitimacy, given that Kérékou and his colleagues, disenchanted with the immobilism of the civilian era, intended to become an involved governing elite. Without some "rationalization" for their reign, the regime—a military one headed by a northerner to boot—could not expect to control society for long, especially in the hostile southern urban nerve centers, as ethnic divisions were still powerful in the country. But legitimation from society's modern strata—intellectuals, trade unionists, and students—was feasible. Concentrated in the coastal areas, these groups had, like the military, slowly become radicalized by the sterility of antecedent regimes, and their growing anti-French and anti-Western frustrations could be harnessed by the more nationalist postures offered by "Beninese Afro-Marxism".[3]

Also, the purge of all former civilian and military leaders (whatever their ethnicity) accompanying the "Revolution," attesting to a generational changing of the guard, was not unpopular in southern urban areas. Indeed, it was particularly symbolic in a country where a tightly knit group of ethnic civilian and military leaders had monopolized power since the 1950s. (Two of Benin's triumvirate—Apithy had just died—outlasted Kérékou and made a partial comeback in 1991.) And, finally, nationalization was a very popular policy in Cotonou. It not only satisfied long-suppressed resentments against French expatriates "in control" of the national economy but was also widely expected to lead to a proliferation of jobs and sinecure posts, materially assuaging youth and unionists alike in a hitherto destitute and moribund economy.

Despite some innovative policies, including the first efforts to develop the economy of the neglected north, Kérékou's reign was a disaster.[4] Though the clique that seized power started off ethnically balanced, every single southern officer—the real architects of the 1972 coup—fell by the wayside. The murder of the popular Captain Michel Aikpé in 1975, which triggered massive riots in Cotonou, drove the first wedge between the military and society. As power came to be concentrated in Kérékou's hands, factionalism—always a problem in the Beninese army—reemerged, demolishing the image it attempted to project of a cohesive non-ethnic regime. By the 1980s whatever legitimacy Kérékou may have garnered by his populist policies had shriveled. His main prop from that point onward—against both society and the army—was his heavily armed, elite 2,000-member all-northern Presidential Guard, which was fiercely loyal to him personally.

The regime was unable to develop any real constituency, even among groups it avidly courted. Old ethnic formations and leaders continued to attract support. (For that reason the civilian triumvirate was kept under house arrest until 1981.) As a centrist, Kérékou could never satisfy the true Left, which had discovered that, rhetoric notwithstanding, the regime was neither sincere about Marxism nor will-ing to share political power with its civilian ideological cohorts. (A cardinal tenet of Marxism is the supremacy of the party over all hierarchies, including the army.) At the same time, conservative elements as well as all those locked out of the new generational power hierarchy flocked out of the country, leading to both a decay in social services at home (education in particular) and the multiplication of opposition groups abroad. As legitimacy declined, the regime relied even more on brute force to remain in power, in turn alienating more and more groups in civil society. Though Kérékou constitutionalized and institutionalized his govern-ment in 1977—promulgating a constitution, setting up a sole Marxist-Leninist political party, Popular Party of the Revolution (Parti Populaire de la Révolution, PPR), and holding elections for a National Assembly—political space remained severely restricted. Only those judged reliable by the junta were permitted to par-ticipate, and the lopsided electoral "victories" (98 percent in 1984; 91 percent in 1989) were patently rigged.

More important, the economic policies espoused under the banner of Marxism brought Benin's weak economy very rapidly to its knees, threatening the liveli-hood of everyone in both the modern economy and in the informal sector. The country's perennially negative balance of trade deteriorated further under Kérékou, with exports falling to less than 15 percent of imports in 1988 (see Table 4.1), placing Benin at the mercy of the World Bank and other Western creditors. Nor did any amelioration take place in public finances with the shift from capital-ism to state ownership of the productive sectors of the economy. Just the reverse transpired, and with a vengeance. "[M]any of the 1970s reforms were at the least ineffective, and those responsible for administering them were all too often in-competent, indolent and corrupt."[5] The proliferation of state companies, market-ing boards, and monopolies—ideologically rationalized as instruments through which to regain control of the national economy and to rechannel middleman profits for the benefit of society at large—actually served to divert what few re-sources the state was still able to generate into the hands of those who had access to them. Few profits ever accrued to the state. Instead, the public sector became a cesspool of corruption, mismanagement, lack of accountability, and a feeding ground for predatory civil servants, bureaucrats, and military officers alike. A 1992 (postdemocratization) report on Benin's public finances noted that for thirty years fiscal irregularities, mismanagement, and budgetary disequilibrium had been the norm.[6]

New state companies were set up to cater to national pride, or else to provide new jobs to the regime's class cohorts, at times without any semblance of cost-benefit considerations. Others, such as the very costly Savé Sugar Society (69 bil-lion CFA francs), and the Onigbolo cement plant (37 billion CFA francs), were initiated on the basis of premises of success (exports to Nigeria) that never mate-rialized, since the companies, bloated with excess manpower costs and looted by their custodians, produced goods much costlier than European imports. Even

TABLE 4.1   Benin's Balance of Trade, 1987–1993 (in billions of CFA francs)

	1987	1988	1989	1990	1991	1992	1993
Exports	34.3	24.8	35.1	30.1	34.8	28.1	31.6
Imports	105.0	168.9	135.3	149.4	178.3	138.0	142.6
Trade balance	−70.7	−144.1	−100.2	−119.3	−143.5	−109.9	−111.0
Exports as % of imports	32.7	14.7	26.0	20.1	19.5	20.4	22.2

Sources: Jonathan Derrick, "Benin," *Africa Contemporary Record* 22, 1989–1990 (New York: Africana Publishing Company, 1995), pp. B3–B11; Samuel Decalo, "Benin," *Africa Contemporary Record* 23, 1990–1992 (in press), pp. B3–B11; Samuel Decalo, "Benin," *Africa Contemporary Record* 24, 1992–1994 (in press).

Benin's state purchasing organs favored and ordered lower-cost imports rather than the more costly locally produced state products. Totally uncompetitive, the Savé plant operated at 7 percent of capacity, and Onigbolo at 25 percent, levels inadequate to cover their operating costs, let alone their capital costs. To keep these firms afloat, Benin suffered large annual drains on its resources as well as large-scale borrowing abroad that added to a mushrooming national debt. (In mid-1993 both companies were finally privatized, at huge losses to the state's original investment.)

Nationalized private companies that had formerly been profitable also churned out losses for the state once production costs rose through the addition of layers of state administrators, phantom workers (their pay pocketed by managers), or rampant embezzlement that milked them dry. The state sector—slated to be the "engine of the revolution" by stoking a moribund economy—became a massive burden on the State, an anchor that sank the economy and Kérékou with it. By 1984 Benin's large national debt (two-thirds of its gross national product), accumulated during the 1970s dash towards socialism, could no longer be serviced. Despite negotiating concessionary interest rates, the regime, faced by a falling revenue base (reflecting a slowdown in all sectors of the economy) could not meet its fiscal obligations: Benin was bankrupt.

The first nationalizations had taken place in 1975, with the bulk of the takeovers complete by 1977–1978. A more viable economy might have survived the fiscal drain longer, but Benin's was not able to do so. Barely four years after the consummation of the "Revolution," Benin's Marxist phase was essentially over. In 1982 a painful "rectification" commenced—a rollback of all that had been erected at great cost and with much nationalist fanfare. But Kérékou was to discover that his radical rhetoric had scared off private entrepreneurs from investing in the country, just as many of the state enterprises were unsalable at any price and had to be closed down under lock and key.

With the economy at the brink of collapse, cost-accounting practices, previously eschewed as "capitalist" considerations irrelevant in socialist societies, began to play a role. Half of the country's fifty-three inefficient state companies were merged or closed down, to vociferous protests of die-hard Leftists (especially the radical communists) about the betrayal of Beninese socialism. By 1984 Cotonou was forced to start negotiations for a structural adjustment loan. It sent emissaries to the West, including two desperately to Washington, pledging that the regime was now granting "more importance to the national private sector and foreign investment"—which had formerly been attacked as the "blood-suckers of the people."[7] The government also promised—though not over its state radio—that any new capital arriving in Cotonou would be sacrosanct.

No risk capital was attracted to Benin, however. Indeed little new money ever flowed into Benin either before or after the "Revolution," just as very little investment enters the country today, for the simple reason that Benin's economy has few attractions for private entrepreneurs. It has neither exploitable resources nor valuable agrarian products; it possesses only a rudimentary infrastructure and a small population that cannot provide a market for much of a manufacturing sector either. Industry is minimal; accounting for 15 percent of the gross domestic product, it includes primarily the Sémé offshore oil deposits. After production began in the early 1980s, Sémé's meager royalties allowed the regime to limp along during its last years in power. Worse yet, an attempt to wring additional royalties from the Norwegian consortia brought instead their departure in 1985, along with a lawsuit, resulting in major shortfalls in production and royalties precisely when the regime was financially most hard-pressed.

The most dramatic illustration of how desperate the regime was for funds—which were needed to meet the state payroll, including the army's—came to light in 1988 when it was revealed that Cotonou had contracted with a foreign firm to dispose of 2 million tons of toxic chemical and radioactive waste per year. The regime had been so avid to land the contract that it agreed to premiums (US$2.50 per ton) that were a fraction of what tiny Guinea-Bissau had secured. The scandal led to the contract's falling through, much to the consternation of Cotonou, which had banked on the resultant revenues. The affair was to put another nail in the coffin of Kérékou's regime, for it also shattered the residual bonds of unity of the officer corps that had sustained him against escalating opposition in civil society; this in turn made the possibility of a continuation of stable military rule an unlikely one. (In the past when ethnic, programmatic, or personal cleavages had became unmanageable in the officer corps, the military had given up and invited back the formerly ousted civilian politicians.) The issue that polarized the Beninese army in 1988 was the site that Kérékou and his northern advisors had chosen for burial of the toxic waste. The site was populous Abomey, the historic capital of the Fon, a fact that kindled suspicions that such an unconscionable choice could only be a plot by northerners to poison their Fon rivals. The rift between Kérékou and the Fon, who were already incensed at the eclipse of their influence in the junta, burst into the open in several dangerous coup attempts in 1986.[8]

With no relief on the horizon for its many woes, a severe austerity program dictated by the IMF (dismantling of the state sector, cuts in the civil service, rollback on spending on social services, including education), and a military in disarray, the final blow to Kérékou came as the economy literally unraveled. The collapse of the economy ushered in the massive 1989 strikes that at inception were not over "democracy" but bread-and-butter issues—payment of salary and benefits arrears. From such modest demands suddenly developed a frontal attack on the legitimacy itself of a regime that had led the country to national bankruptcy.

The Decay of the State and the Rebellion of Civil Society

The decay of social and economic conditions in a society as proud and upwardly mobile as Benin's, coupled with the corruption and moral bankruptcy of the Kérékou regime, mobilized civil society against a regime already on its last legs long before the thrust for democratization was to appear in much of sub-Saharan Africa. All of the conditions were already in place in Benin for a massive upheaval calling for the withdrawal of the army from the political center stage, including a larger, more sophisticated, and grossly outraged civil society, now drawn into a confrontational stance vis-à-vis the regime.

Youth and university students had always been a thorn in the side of whoever was in office in Cotonou. They had challenged both conservative regimes (Maga's and Zinsou's) and progressive ones (Ahomadégbé's), and now challenged Kérékou. Student protests, demonstrations, and general unrest had punctuated the entire Kérékou era. Though the more radical youth were strongly attracted to the underground Communist Party of Dahomey (Parti Communiste du Dahomey, PCD) and conservative ones organized along informal ethnic lines (especially Fon, but also "Nordist"), students as a whole were more concerned with material issues—campus food, transport facilities, tardy tuition grants, employment prospects, and so on. Their commitment to Kérékou's brand of Marxism, even for those in whom it was more than superficial and/or opportunist, did not withstand the 1975 murder of Aikpé, to which many in the south had reacted with massive riots.

The university specifically was a hotbed of anti-Kérékou agitation, though primary and secondary schools alike were impregnated with political cells disseminating an array of handouts ranging from ultra-Left manifestos (favoring true radical change) to blatantly ethnic ones. As the economic morass deepened, student complaints swelled. They developed into an explosive boil that brought about the closure of the educational establishment in 1985 when the regime announced that it could no longer automatically hire all graduates (even those with needed skills such as doctors) in the civil service—at one stroke dashing the liveli-hood expectations of students in a society with few sources of employment other than the civil service. Ongoing student unrest was a feature of the last years of Kérékou's regime, and the January 1989 demonstrations that led to its demise began with student strikes.

In like manner much of Benin's large intelligentsia was ranged against the Kérékou regime. Many had actually gone into exile in France, either at the time of the "Revolution" or as economic hardship began to bite hard at home. (There was such an exodus at the time of the riots attending Aikpé's murder that the regime tried to stem the tide by imposing exit visas and confiscating the possessions of all who left illegally.) Many of those who remained in Benin were alienated by the rhetoric of the regime, its iron fist, its northern bias, and especially its unwillingness to integrate intellectuals—except sycophants and party hacks—into positions of authority. It also grated many Beninese—proud and urbane despite their country's modest global standing—to be treated as potential drug smugglers abroad, an inevitable outcome of Cotonou's becoming a transshipment center for drugs from Nigeria. That many of Kérékou's cronies had become immensely rich through drug trafficking and corruption epitomized to many citizens the utter moral bankruptcy of the regime.

Unionists were also hurting, with wages unaugmented since 1982 and eroded by inflation and the escalating cost of living. On top of a hiring freeze in the civil service there was an early retirement drive, and in 1987 the much-prized housing allowance was abolished. But this was just the tip of the iceberg. By 1988 the regime's dire fiscal straits resulted in salaries' being paid only every second month. Without other sources of income, civil servants suffered most as shoddy goods, produced by the state sector or imported from Eastern Bloc countries, were sold at ever-higher prices in Benin's nationalized stores. Both conservative and radical elements were straining within the single trade union federation into which they had been compressed by Kérékou. The union did not act on their behalf but as a control mechanism for the regime; it was headed by a Kérékou appointee who, ousted in a membership vote, had been reinstated by the president. With the federation's membership fragmented along ideological and ethnic lines, all pretense of partnership with the regime had long since disappeared. As the regime began to lag in the payment of salaries in 1987 and 1988 and government-nominated union leaders became less willing to press the regime with membership grievances, the movement began to dissolve into its original parts, starting with the October 1989 decision to disassociate from the country's sole party.

Finally, the shrinkage and eventual total collapse of the modern economy hurt everyone—salaried workers, civil servants, smugglers, traders, and the powerful coastal market women, the latter a major retail power in this part of West Africa. Trading and smuggling in particular (the latter of which had become a widespread activity by the 1980s for many Beninese) were threatened by new controls imposed by Nigeria in 1985 as well as by Beninese border police, who, chronically underpaid, began to exact higher "tolls" for turning a blind eye to the illicit trade across the border. As the austerity programs and delays in the government's meeting its payroll shrank demand, traders and smugglers not only could not pass on to customers the higher cost of their goods but also saw the market for their commodities shrink in absolute terms.

In 1988 Benin's banking sector collapsed. State banks, long ailing, had been especially plundered in 1987 and 1988, with huge illegal transfers abroad by state officials, including the Malian Mohamed Cissé, a security and sorcery aide to Kérékou. When banks literally ran out of banknotes and closed down, Kérékou's fate was sealed. The event ignited a veritable tinderbox and led directly to "democratization." It created an awesome national crisis no Beninese had witnessed before or could even have imagined. Just as the government could not meet its obligations or payroll, few individuals earning wages in the modern sector—private or public—could pay their bills; traders could neither sell nor buy; companies with liquid reserves in the banks that closed down, without access to their funds, could not operate. The immense liquidity crisis that ensued dramatically curtailed economic activity and created hardships and deprivations; it generated waves of prolonged, violent urban riots and demonstrations that the regime could neither appease materially nor quell with the force of its divided military. All of this served to tilt the balance towards a hitherto unthinkable option—convening a conclave of societal groups to seek unity in face of the country's profound crisis. This conclave, when it met, was hardly in a mood to ignore the fact that the ouster of Kérékou and the army from power had to be part of the solution to the country's problem.

Even before the onset of the crisis the regime had immense difficulties in meeting its 50,000-strong payroll as well as paying creditors. Salaries three months in arrears had become common by the late 1980s. Civil servants left work early to moonlight in the informal economy or to tend their garden plots. Many creditors refused to handle government orders without first being paid outstanding balances or to supply the government with new stock except against full prepayment. Soon some civil servants were owed twelve months' back pay; in "failing to pay salaries, the regime signed the death warrant it had drafted by its own gross corruption."[9] The host of grievances that had built up against Kérékou coalesced around this one issue that was capable of uniting all groups against the regime; even the military, itself unpaid for months, revolted and hijacked shipments of banknotes from abroad intended to assuage the worst-suffering civil servants.

Civil Society Triumphant: The National Conference of 1989

To tackle the massive national crisis Kérékou had no choice but to convene a conference in which all societal strata were represented, including political enemies in voluntary exile. Kérékou had hoped that such a conclave, which would grant advisory status to elements hitherto shut out of power, might lead to some sort of national reconciliation and unity on the bitter economic medicine called for by the 1989 structural adjustment program. But it was not to be. The National Conference of Vital Forces (Conférence Nationale des Forces Vives) met for nine days starting February 19, 1990, with 488 members, many representing the government, its ancillary organs, and the military. From the outset it was clear that Kérékou had totally misjudged the mood in the country, including of his own appointees to the conference. Rather than to accept his leadership and agenda, immediately the conference even rejected his role as chairman, electing instead Archbishop Isidore de Souza, and proceeded to make history.

The conference, broadcast live over radio and television, lashed out at the brutality, venality, and corruption of Kérékou's seventeen-year military reign. Hardline officers in the army (especially the northern and the ex-Marxist) several times urged Kérékou to disband the conclave, arrest the opposition leaders who had arrived from abroad, and ram through the needed reforms by force. But Kérékou was aware that Benin's problems were so monumental and the army's officer corps so internally divided that heavy bloodshed and probable internecine military fighting would ensue if he proceeded along this course. He was no doubt correct in this. Civil society was in a very ugly mood, much more so than in neighboring Togo, where an eighteen-month confrontation with Éyadéma was subsequently to erupt. Furthermore, senior southern military officers had warned Kérékou that they would not move against their kinsmen in Cotonou. On top of that, a World Bank delegation was at the time ensconced in a Cotonou hotel watching the conference proceedings and prodding Kérékou to compromise— hardly an audience that would take well to a bloodbath.

On February 25, in a monumental move to be imitated by many another national conference subsequently, Benin's national conference "solemnly declared its autonomy, and the executive power of its decisions," and assumed executive power, though prudently leaving Kérékou as interim head of state. Kérékou's heavily tarnished reputation was somewhat rehabilitated by his accepting that his time was up, resisting efforts by die-hard military elements to reinstate him by coup (some mutinies took place just the same), and eventually publicly requesting forgiveness for "the deplorable and regrettable incidents" during his reign.[10]

The interim government set up was a twenty-seven-member High Council of the Republic (on which sat all ex-presidents) charged with arranging a constitutional referendum and legislative and presidential elections. Nicéphore Soglo, a former World Bank officer strongly supported by both the World Bank and France, became executive prime minister.[11] Then there ensued a remarkably smooth transition that surprised the world. In a referendum in August and December 1990 Benin adopted and ratified a constitution (which included a clause that effectively precluded the aging triumvirate from running for office). Legislative elections followed in February 1991, and then in two rounds of presidential elections, on March 10 and 24, Soglo defeated the born-again democrat Kérékou with 67.73 percent of the vote. The maverick Benin thus became the first African state in which the army was forced out of power by civilians, and the first in which an incumbent was defeated electorally. (Mauritius, in 1981, was the first country to have seen a power transfer among parties.)

The manner in which Kérékou was ousted from power can be viewed as the functional equivalent of a civilian coup d'état: Kérékou was confronted with a fait accompli by a conference that had been convened to help defuse the crisis but that instead declared itself sovereign.[12] Then, to add insult to injury, it mounted the equivalent of a humiliating "trial of Kérékou by his opposition."[13] Such a "coup" was successful in Cotonou (unlike a failed attempt in Lomé) because (a) with Benin totally bankrupt, Kérékou had no options whatsoever; (b) the World Bank mission was present in Cotonou and the global spotlight was squarely on Benin, where the first such experiment was being conducted; (c) the bulk of the armed forces (apart from the ultra-loyalist northern Presidential Guard) could not be relied upon and would undoubtedly have divided into warring factions, an eventuality unacceptable to those who have been referred to as Benin's "intellectual" officers; and (d) unlike General Éyadéma in Togo, Kérékou was politically both more astute and patriotic and had much less personal culpability in the major crimes that had been committed during his reign. (He was in any case granted immunity from future prosecution for activities under his aegis.)

The events in Cotonou can also be seen as the revenge, or triumph, of Benin's long-suffering civil society against their prime tormentor—the predatory state.[14] Civil society, coexisting with state power, had flexed its muscles many times before, including against Kérékou, but over specific issues and with no a priori intent to topple the regime. But now, completely destitute as a direct result of the policies of a largely symbolic "People's Republic" that was fiscally paralyzed, and daily plundered of its remaining resources by the ruling elite, civil society lashed out with particular ferocity and with clear intent to rid itself of its tormentor. It was the magnitude of the upheaval of civil society in Benin and its ability to force a regime change in the absence of any military support—the purity of civil power, so to speak—that were most striking in Benin, especially since civil society had hitherto been viewed as a passive force in Africa. The events in Cotonou reverberated across Africa, and the model of regime change through national conference came to be inextricably associated with Benin; but poignantly, as events in Togo illustrated, civil society need not necessarily triumph, which underscored the unique domestic matrix of factors that coalesced in Benin to make change inevitable.

Civil society triumphed in Cotonou because the always upwardly mobile groups in the south had over time become even more major, sophisticated, and volatile forces capable of being drawn into confrontation and rebellion against the depredations of an arrogant military regime that was ideologically, socially, economically, and morally bankrupt. This revolt was in addition set against the backdrop of unequivocal political and economic conditionalities attached to the fiscal lifelines extended by global donor agencies. Moreover, France, hitherto the paterfamilias-savior of nearly all francophone countries, whether benevolent (Côte d'Ivoire) or brutal (Chad), could no longer be counted merely to look on benignly and with an open purse at the wasteful antics of her client states. Though Mitterrand's very specific counsel to francophone Africa at the Franco-African summit conference in June 1990 at La Baule, France, to democratize was greatly moderated in due time, France was no longer the *grand ami* of all Cotonou leaders. With an extremely viable replacement for Kérékou available, it could afford to dispense with him.

The transition from military rule to competitive civilian politics is not the end of the road for Benin but the beginning. This was especially true at outset, in 1990, since very little of substance actually changed with "democratization" in Benin. Even today, with the picture considerably rosier, assessments of the staying power of civilian authority only dramatically improved after the 1995 elections were concluded without hitch. Change is not, however, unidirectional, and there are too many pitfalls for weak countries such as Benin; the pressures on the Benin of 1990 as well as of 1995 are immeasurably greater than they had been in previous decades.

The country's legislative and presidential elections in 1991—the first truly free, multicandidate, multiparty contests since the colonial days (despite an incomplete poll in Borgou)—did produce a democratically chosen leader for Benin. But the elections also underscored the degree to which ethnicity provided the building blocks of power in the country. Though the old triumvirate's return to power was legally blocked by the constitution's age clause (voters had the option of ratifying the constitution with or without the clause, but the majority accepted the restrictive clause), this in no way discouraged ethnic voting.

The ethnic basis of all politics remained alive and well in Benin and, indeed, continues to play a role in all political contests. What changed was the emergence of a new generational elite of ethnic and regional power wielders. The hope for the future is (a) that there are many more ethnic political barons now in the legislative assembly than in the days of the triumvirate, and (b) that despite the splintered political party structure, these parties have proved, for five years now, to be capable of forming pragmatic power alliances, transcending the zero-sum game of ethnic politics.

The 1991 presidential elections were, as always, regional contests with very predictable outcomes. Kérékou's record of seventeen years of iron-fisted rule in Benin did not prevent him from assuming the northern leadership mantle. As with all previous ethnic leaders ousted from power, Kérékou's sins of omission and commission were forgiven and forgotten by his ethnic clientele, and he secured 94 to 98 percent of the vote in the second ballot in the two northern provinces, though little outside them. Soglo, who in the first round obtained 36.16 percent of the vote, again predictably sharing the south with other southern ethnic leaders, won the bulk of the southern vote (82 percent) in the second ballot, but little outside the south.[15] In like manner the twenty-four parties that competed for the new, small (sixty-four-seat) National Assembly were mostly ethnic/personal formations. Soglo won out over several southern ethnic leaders primarily because he was known to be France's choice and to have the ear of the World Bank as well (vital criteria for office at the time). In addition, he was able to cobble together a three-party coalition, Union for the Triumph of Democratic Renewal (Union pour la Triomphe du Renouveau Démocratique, UTRD), which in February 1991 had held only twelve of the assembly seats.

Though Soglo put together a technocratic cabinet and rapidly became the darling of the West, economic advances have been modest. This was a function of the low level from which the country began its recovery, notwithstanding French grants amounting to 17 billion CFA francs. In 1994, in the country's fifth year of its structural adjustment program, Benin remained at the lower end of achievement scales, at levels that cannot alleviate poverty, let alone lead to sustainable development. Though in public speeches Soglo has tried to emphasize the positive, including Benin's (modest) economic growth rate and the reduction of the deficit by 22.5 percent to 7 percent of gross domestic product, conflicting and less optimistic data cloud the record.[16]

But whatever the actual economic attainments of the new regime, the fact remains that for many civilian rule has been a disenchantingly harsh experience. That this could be otherwise in light of the pummeling the economy had received during the "Marxist" era is no longer accepted as valid justification by ever more impatient groups in civil society that helped to elevate Soglo to the political throne. Disenchantment, as usual, is deeper in the critical southern urban nerve centers of the country where economic deprivations are always felt more and societal needs and expectations are higher. With the state's legitimacy and capacity to govern deeply compromised during the Kérékou era, and development always an uphill battle in a country with an economic profile such as Benin's, it is not surprising that the new regime lost much early goodwill and has slowly come to be seen as incapable of ameliorating conditions in the country. As early as 1993 it was common to hear negative comments in coastal areas about "democracy" not having changed anything whatsoever in Benin.[17] Many southerners also comment that though political life is certainly more open and less repressive, the same elites (the word "crooks" actually crops up more often) are controlling everything as always. Such disparaging comments are being parroted in the north as well, where "democratization" is largely perceived in ethnic terms—namely, as the return of the hated southerners to the saddle.

Social disenchantment with the new regime and/or unwillingness to accept the new political order have been mirrored by a spate of military mutinies, mostly by northerners. Key members of the now disbanded Presidential Guard, unable to accept the eclipse of Kérékou and Bariba power, or else to adjust to civilian supremacy, have on several occasions rebelled. That they were given refuge and hidden by kinsmen illustrates the travails of trying to impose national law and order on societies where subnational legitimacy regards central authority as a form of alien colonialism. In the south student and civil service militancy have tested Soglo's administration virtually from its inception. Already in April 1991 university students were on strike, rejecting austerity, demanding speedier delivery of their scholarships and the resignation of the minister of education. Other demonstrations have followed, much as they erupted under Kérékou and all previous governments in Cotonou, at times to challenge the very legitimacy of the state. In February 1993, for example, a strike—ominously stated to be an unlimited one unless demands were met—called for "greater justice in the distribution of grants."[18]

The civil service has also taken to the streets on numerous occasions over various bread-and-butter issues, further complicating Soglo's efforts to attain a budgetary balance. Its members did so despite the fact that Soglo has gone out of his way to shield labor as much as possible from the massive cuts called for and periodically insisted upon by the IMF. Indeed, by mid-1992 organized labor was actually striking for increases in salaries and the indexing of pay scales to the rate of inflation. Labor also resisted Soglo's efforts to privatize the public sector—just as it had during the Kérékou era, and much for the same reasons: the implicit mass loss of jobs in enterprises slated to be taken over by more cost-conscious private entrepreneurs. The very name of American entrepreneur John Moore, famous throughout West Africa, who buys derelict bankrupt State industries (including in Togo and Benin) to turn them around in a matter of months, strikes terror in Beninese labor, aware that the turnarounds are accompanied by reductions in manpower complements of up to 70 percent and by the adoption of a Western work ethic.

Other groups in society have also progressively become disenchanted with Soglo. This was especially true with groups such as the Yoruba, who have kin across the border in Nigeria. They have flouted Soglo's government, in order to better survive, by a massive and total "disengagement" from the modern state and its authority, moving in large numbers into the informal sector, bypassing official institutions and regulations, and engaging in full-scale smuggling activities across the Nigerian border.

All these brought about a deflation of Soglo's authority in society, to which he has reacted with increased reliance on his powers to promulgate legislation by edict as well as through a measure of force and repression hardly befitting a consensual regime born in reaction to military dictatorship.[19]

Already in mid-1991 a pernicious de facto restriction was established on freedom of the press through rules punishing radio, television, and newspaper reporters found guilty of "excesses"; at the time, these were vaguely defined as offensive statements regarding "friendly" states (i.e., France). While this kind of censorship has long existed in the statute books of many countries, including the metropole's, slowly the censorship came to be applied to any kind of critical attack on state authority.

In like manner state repression and police action were originally applied mainly against the Communist Party of Dahomey, whose populist antitax and other disobedience campaigns were especially subversive in a country desperately attempting to stabilize itself financially. (The PCD later made an about-face, joining the presidential party alliance after the 1995 elections.) But in short order other forms of antiregime opposition—including, in 1994, the right to demonstrate publicly—came to be equated a priori with treason, especially if mounted by strata regarded by definition as suspect—youth, students, and unions.

Abroad, Soglo's main merits have been seen as steadfast resistance against societal and parliamentary pressures to moderate the harsh economic policies of fiscal stringency needed to stabilize Benin. But this has brought him into conflict not only with erstwhile National Assembly allies but also with the country's Constitutional Court when he tried to rule by decree in violation of his prescribed powers. Indeed Soglo's penchant to utilize his emergency powers and to rule by decree is seen in some quarters as the dictatorial "opening" in the constitution. A very serious conflict between Soglo and the assembly occurred in August 1994, when Soglo rejected a more moderate (i.e., free-spending) budget version from the National Assembly as incompatible with austerity pledges made to the IMF. Not having enough support in the assembly to pass his own budget, Soglo promulgated it by decree. The budget was thrown out by the Court as unconstitutionally passed, and Soglo drew the ire of parliamentarians who claimed that Benin was totally "under [IMF] control."[20]

All of this hardly seems to suggests that the transition from military to civilian authoritarian rule is about to be completed in Benin. Rather, it points to the fact that reconstruction has been painfully slow, as such tasks always are; that many of the hopes of yesteryear that led to the reestablishment of civilian authority have not yet been fulfilled; that a burgeoning and more aggressive civil society is increasingly impatient with its continued pauperization; that youth, unionists, and the civil service are tired of the "sacrifices" that each different regime, over thirty-five years, has called upon them to make. All these factors create societal tensions, political strains, and destabilizing tendencies.

Benin has never been economically viable, under any regime, and is not viable today. Yet in the 1990s it has a much larger urban and modern constituency to take care of and fewer resources or options because of the mismanagement of the past. Much debt forgiveness has been granted to African countries, including Benin, but there was never any Marshall Plan considered for the continent that could ease the pain of restructuring and reforming. Globally there is widespread donor weariness, especially with the only continent that has not succeeded in pulling itself up by its bootstraps. In addition, France, which had long been inclined to shield francophone African states from the effects of their errors or misfortunes, has been trying since the late 1980s to disengage itself from its former practice of intense preoccupation with every minutia of African affairs.

Since 1990 Benin has had the added distinction of being francophone Africa's pioneer New Democracy, and the country may indeed be a bellwether state. If Benin can weather the inevitable rough transition period until its slow economic growth begins to assuage the long-suffered frustration of national aspiration, and if the current system of modified presidential rule and fluid ethnopolitical alliances takes root, then Benin may have turned a very important corner: It would then become a successful New Democracy.[21] But if the old ethnic tug-of-war for supremacy returns, or the trade union–civil service–student coalition succeeds in derailing fiscal orthodoxy, or the Beninese military's penchant for mounting coups reemerges, Benin could score yet another continental distinction—that of the first of the new democracies to slide back into instability, authoritarianism, and possibly military rule.

Notes

1. Samuel Huntington, *The Third Wave: Democratization in the Late Twentieth Century* (Norman: Oklahoma University Press, 1991).

2. See, for example, Samuel Decalo, "The Process, Prospects, and Constraints of Democratization in Africa," *African Affairs* 91, no. 362 (January 1992):7.

3. See Samuel Decalo, "Ideological Rhetoric and Scientific Socialism in Benin and Congo/Brazzaville," in Carl G. Rosberg and Thomas M. Callaghy, eds., *Socialism in Sub-Saharan Africa: A New Assessment* (Berkeley: Center for International Studies, University of California, 1979), pp. 231–264; Samuel Decalo, "The Morphology of Radical Military Rule in Africa," *Journal of Communist Studies* 1, nos. 3–4 (September 1985):122–144; Samuel Decalo, "Benin," in *Coups and Army Rule in Africa: Motivations and Constraints* (New Haven: Yale University Press, 1990), pp. 89–132; Arnold Hughes, "The Appeal of Marxism to Africans," *Journal of Communist Studies* 8, no. 2 (June 1992):4–20; and Chris Allen, "Good-bye to All That: The Short and Sad Story of Socialism in Benin," *Journal of Communist Studies* 8, no. 2 (June 1992):62–81.

4. Chris Allen et al., *Benin, The Congo, Burkina Faso* (London: Pinter, 1989). See also Dov Ronen, "People's Republic of Benin: The Military Marxist Ideology and the Politics of Ethnicity," in John Harbeson, ed., *The Military in African Politics* (New York: Praeger, 1987), pp. 93–122.

5. Allen et al., *Benin*, p. 44.

6. Richard Aladjo, *La faillite du contrôle des finances publiques au Bénin* (Porto Novo: Éditions du Flamboyant, 1992).

7. "Trade Mission to US," *West Africa*, March 24, 1986, p. 647.

8. See "Benin: Going West," *Africa Confidential*, no. 25, October 31, 1984, pp. 1–8; Jonathan Derrick, "Benin," in Marion Doro, ed., *Africa Contemporary Record 1988–1989* (New York: Africana Publishing Company, 1989), pp. B3–B11.

9. Chris Allen, "Restructuring of an Authoritarian State: 'Democratic Renewal' in Benin," *Review of African Political Economy* 54 (July 1992):46.

10. "Benin: Test-Tube Democracy," *Africa Confidential* 31, no. 7 (April 6, 1990):4–5.

11. For biographies of Benin's leaders, see Samuel Decalo, *Historical Dictionary of Benin*, 3d ed. (Metuchen, N.J.: Scarecrow Press, 1996).

12. See Jacques Mariel Nzouankeu, "The Role of the National Conference in the Transition to Democracy in Africa: The Cases of Benin and Mali," *Issue* 21, nos. 1–2 (1993):44-45. See also Francis Laloupo, "La conférence nationale du Bénin: Un concept nouveau de changement de régime politique," *Année africaine 1992–1993* (Bordeaux: Centre d'Étude d'Afrique Noire, 1993), pp. 89–114; and John R. Heilbrunn, "Social Origins of National Conferences in Benin and Togo," *Journal of Modern African Studies* 31, no. 3 (June 1993):277.

13. *Africa Research Bulletin, Political Series,* March 1991, p. 10044.

14. For masterful development of the concept of the predatory state, see Robert Fatton, *Predatory Rule: State and Civil Society in Africa* (Boulder: Lynne Rienner, 1992).

15. For the results and analysis of the elections, see *Economist* Intelligence Unit, *Togo, Niger, Benin, Burkina Faso,* no. 2 (1991):31–36. See also the analysis of Chris Allen, "Restructuring an Authoritarian State."

16. *Africa Research Bulletin, Economic Series,* January 1994, p. 11586.

17. Interviews with Beninese citizens conducted by the author in Porto Novo and Cotonou, January 1993.

18. *Africa Research Bulletin, Political Series,* March 1993, pp. 10932.

19. In June 1992 thirty-four of the sixty-four deputies in the National Assembly formed a pro-Soglo coalition called Le Renouveau. In October 1993, fifteen of the thirty-four withdrew from the group as a result of dissatisfaction with Soglo's performance. See Pierre Englebert, "Benin: Recent History," *Africa South of the Sahara, 1996* (London: Europa, 1996), p. 166.

20. *Africa Research Bulletin, Political Series,* September 1994, 11574.

21. In the legislative elections of March 28 and May 28, 1995, National Assembly Speaker Adrien Houngbedji's Democratic Renewal Party (Parti du Renouveau Démocratique, PRD) and other parties opposed to President Soglo won forty-nine of the eighty-three seats. See Pierre Englebert, "Benin: Recent History," p. 166, and Afise D. Adamon, *La Conférence Nationale des Forces Vives et la Période de Transition* (Paris: Harmattan, 1995). On March 23, 1996, the Constitutional Court declared Mathieu Kérékou the winner in the second round of the presidential election. He received 52.5 percent of the votes and Nicéphore Soglo 47.5 percent. In the first round Soglo had received 35.7 percent, Kérékou 34.9 percent, Adrien Houngbedji 19.7 percent, and Bruno Amoussou 7.8 percent. Houngbedji and Amoussou gave their support thereafter to Kérékou. See Thernon Djaksam, "Benin's Election Drama," *West Africa,* April 1–7, 1996, pp. 497–498.

Chapter Five

Congo: Transition and the Struggle to Consolidate

JOHN F. CLARK

Among the francophone African states that have recently undertaken democratic reforms, Congo appears to be one of the few that have gone some distance in consolidating their new democratic institutions. In doing so, Congo has had to overcome an entrenched authoritarian regime and grapple with economic paralysis and ethnic confrontations; meanwhile, the French response to democratization in Congo has been ambivalent. During 1993 and 1994, under the pressures of pronounced economic contraction, Congo appeared headed for an ethnically oriented civil war. Since then public order has been slowly returning, and Congo now seems to be tentatively headed down the path of real, if imperfect, democracy. Perhaps Congo's favorable social features make it a good candidate for membership in the small club of stable, durable African democracies. Events thus far seem to indicate that the structural impediments to the continuing entrenchment of Congolese democracy are formidable but that they can possibly be overcome by sensitive national leadership.

Background to Congolese Society and Politics

Like most African states, Congo contains a multiplicity of ethnic groups, in this case including the Kongo, Téké, Vili, Bembe, Mbochi, Kouyou, and many others.[1] All of these groups may themselves be further broken down into other categories such as "tribe" or "clan." For instance, within the Kongo group, people of the Vili, "Bakongo," and Lari subgroups clearly distinguish themselves from one another. As in all African countries, ethnic identity in Congo has been in constant flux since the time of the first European contacts. As Samuel Decalo has suggested, however, competition among these groups and their subdivisions "forms the backdrop to all political conflicts in Congo."[2] While there is no reason to assume that such "primordial" ties doom Congo forever to some form of premodern politics, Congo's ethnic cleavages have hindered the process of effective governance in the past, and these cleavages have again proven to be the dominant sociopolitical feature of Congo during its recent experiment in democratization.

Other demographic features, however, distinguish Congo from its neighbors. For one, Congo is highly urbanized by African standards, with some 60 percent of its 2.3 million people living in cities of over 5,000; nearly half of the population lives in Congo's two largest cities, Brazzaville and Pointe Noire.[3] The state's agricultural and monetary policies have encouraged this urbanization by subsidizing foodstuffs and creating urban jobs.[4] Secondly, Congo's well-developed educational system has brought literacy to more than 60 percent of the people, making it one of Africa's more literate societies.[5] Brazzaville University produces hundreds of graduates each year, a disproportionate number of whom are trained in social sciences or the humanities rather than technical fields.[6] While these social features may serve to dampen ethnic conflict, they sometimes lend a political sophistication to Congolese society that makes governing there difficult.

Like many other French colonies, Congo began its independent political life as a nominal democracy in 1960. Congo's first president was the (defrocked) Abbé Fulbert Youlou, who was especially popular among the Lari in the Pool region (which surrounds Brazzaville). Youlou had been elected mayor of Brazzaville in 1956, and his party, the Democratic Union for the Defense of African Interests (Union Démocratique pour la Défense des Intérêts Africains, UDDIA), achieved a majority in Congo's new Assembly in 1958. The neocolonial Youlou regime is best described as mildly corrupt, directionless in domestic policy, and deferential to France. The ill-conceived, but high-profile development projects it undertook did little to improve the lives of ordinary Congolese, and its "pro-Katanga" foreign policy irritated many of Congo's progressive educated urban youth and bureaucrats.[7] Consequently, when Youlou began planning to make the UDDIA the sole legal party, the population resisted. Three days of street riots in August 1963, since then celebrated as "les trois glorieuses," led to the demise of Youlou's regime.[8]

Youlou was followed by a succession of leaders who were committed to some form of socialist development for Congo. Ironically, given the ostensible reason for Youlou's overthrow, all of them were committed to the one-party state. The first was Alphonse Massemba-Débat, a moderate socialist and the Speaker of Congo's National Assembly.[9] Under pressure from the leftist students, Massemba created the National Movement of the Revolution (Mouvement National de la Révolution, MNR) as the sole party and began to create a state sector. Congo's radical youth were partially co-opted into the Youth of the MNR (Jeunesse du MNR, JMNR), and Congo adopted its first Five-Year Plan in 1964. In August 1965 the state nationalized the schools, taking them over from Christian missionaries, many of whom subsequently left the country.[10] These state-run schools began training—and radicalizing—a new generation of Congolese, many of whom are now prominent social figures.

Despite Massemba's references to "scientific socialism" and his adoption of some radical measures, the new leader was more a technocrat than a committed ideologue, and most of Congo's economy remained in expatriate hands. Though Massemba did make some modest development gains and secured new foreign aid from the Soviet Union and China, he lacked a strong domestic base and was constantly buffeted by critics on both his "left" and "right." When he tried to suppress his increasingly vocal foes in mid-1968, he was forced to relinquish power to a charismatic young paratroop officer named Marien Ngouabi.

Ngouabi's ascent to power marked a fundamental reorientation in Congolese politics that endured until June 1991. Ngouabi was the first of three northern, military Congolese presidents; he was also the creator of the Congolese Labor Party (Parti Congolais du Travail, PCT), which institutionalized the commitment of the country's leaders to "Marxist" development over the next two decades.[11] The PCT formally came into existence on January 3, 1970, the same day that Ngouabi declared Congo a Marxist-Leninist state and announced the adoption of a new constitution. He also decreed a new flag (featuring crossed hammer and hoe on a red field) and a new national anthem.

Ngouabi thus went beyond the previous government's flirtation with Marxist-Leninist principles to a firm commitment to them. Initially Ngouabi was unable to implement a program instituting his views because of a simple lack of resources,[12] but this situation changed dramatically after the first "oil shock." Congo had been nurturing a nascent oil industry since the late 1960s, and its first major increases in production coincided with the dramatic rise in oil prices occasioned by the Organization of Arab Petroleum Exporting Countries (OAPEC) 1973 boycott and its aftermath. The windfall that resulted allowed Ngouabi to nationalize a large portion of the Congolese industry, create new industries, and organize several state-run farming cooperatives. When the 1973–1974 oil bonanza faded, however, Ngouabi had to struggle with the expectations that it had created in Congo's youth.

After seeing his popularity decline as the 1970s wore on, Ngouabi was murdered by gunmen in a dramatic shoot-out on March 18, 1977, outside his residence. Although a protracted trial implicated several senior Congolese politicians—including Massemba, who was subsequently executed—who the perpetrators were and the exact circumstances of Ngouabi's murder remain unclear.[13] Ngouabi was widely respected by many ordinary Congolese for his intelligence, incorruptibility, and hard work, and his murder left an indelible mark on the nation's political consciousness.

Ngouabi's successor was General Joachim Yhombi-Opango, whose reign marked a two-year relaxation in Congo's revolution, during which time the army gained at the PCT's expense.[14] As a northerner of mixed ethnicity and a weakly committed Marxist in a radical environment, Yhombi never consolidated his power and was forced to step down in favor of Colonel Denis Sassou-Nguesso in February 1979. The second oil shock of 1979–1980 was fortuitous for Sassou, providing him with the resources to consolidate his rule and continue socialist policies. As an Mbochi, Sassou had support in the Mbochi-dominated army, and as a hard-line Marxist, he was highly regarded among politically powerful southern intellectuals. In fact, Sassou's rise was widely regarded as a return to Marxist orthodoxy because of his radical credentials,[15] and he managed to keep the one-party state going for twelve more years.

We must be careful to make neither too much nor too little of Congo's putatively socialist course. For instance, large parts of the Congolese economy, especially rural agriculture, remained untouched by the official policies of Congo's "Marxist" era; indeed, the structure of Congolese political economy resembled that of many of Africa's other statist regimes, including rhetorically moderate ones. Like Ngouabi and Yhombi, Sassou by necessity spent as much energy co-opting or eliminating ethnic, party, and civilian-sector rivals as he did building a Marxist society. Nonetheless, the call for socialism was important in justifying the expansion of the state.

Perhaps surprisingly, Congo maintained relatively close relations with France throughout its twenty-eight-year socialist period. To be sure, Congo quickly established relations with the Soviet Union, China, Cuba, North Korea, and other communist states after Youlou's fall, and these relations blossomed over ensuing years. They included military training agreements, educational and cultural exchanges, trade accords, and economic and military assistance programs.[16] France nonetheless remained Congo's largest trading partner and a far larger source of foreign aid throughout the whole period. The socialist regimes satisfied their ideological needs by attacking the United States, with whom Congo severed relations between 1965 and 1977; indeed, French and Congolese anti-Americanism were complementary. Meanwhile, despite its anti-neocolonialist rhetoric, Congo allowed the French firm Elf-Aquitaine to become the chief exploiter of the country's petroleum,[17] the production and sale of which accounted for more than 90 percent of Congo's foreign earnings during the 1980s. Moreover, the influence of French culture in Congo remained strong during the 1963–1991 period. In 1987, the French even provided the Sassou regime with military assistance during a coup attempt,[18] as they have done so frequently in francophone Africa.

The Sources of Congo's Revolution

Both an economic crisis and a crisis of legitimacy were responsible for the collapse of the ancien régime in Congo, and naturally the former was partly responsible for the latter. As with former East bloc regimes, Congo's government justified its repression through the promise of material welfare. Hence, material deprivation exacerbated a psychological, even spiritual, disaffection in the Congo, and the collapse of Europe's communist regimes had a profound effect on sub-Saharan Africa's one-party states.[19] Meanwhile, Benin's stunning national conference in 1990, which promised transition to democracy through elections, strengthened the cries for *multipartisme* in francophone Africa specifically. As noted in Chapter 1, the statements by Mitterrand in favor of African democratization at the June 1990 Franco-African summit at La Baule, France, also had an impact.

The material crisis requires somewhat more detailed discussion because of its multiple dimensions. Congo faces the same structural impediments to economic growth as many developing countries: heavy reliance on a single commodity for income, declining terms of trade, and a neomercantilist relationship with its former colonizer. Congo's membership in the franc zone added to this structural burden, despite some positive effects.

Unable to meet its international obligations in the face of declining oil prices and economic crisis, Congo signed its first agreement with the International Monetary Fund (IMF) in July 1986, whereby it would undertake structural adjustments in return for debt relief the following year.[20] At that time Congolese officials agreed to cut the national budget in half, fight urbanization, reemphasize agriculture, and begin privatizing its parastatals and state-owned enterprises; in return, the IMF negotiated a ten-year repayment schedule with Congo's five major creditors. Despite the agreement, however, the economy continued to decline without real reforms taking place. Congo's entrenched bureaucrats and well-organized workers resisted cuts in government employment or wages and reductions in the retirement age, and the Sassou regime refused to give up on its ideal of state-led development. Thus the regime lacked both the will and the legitimacy to take the tough measures that the IMF had mandated.

Given their profligate spending habits, all former Congolese governments bear a share of the blame for Congo's debts. Congo's foreign debt first equaled its gross domestic product (GDP) in 1980 around $1.2 billion and increased to around $4.5 billion in 1990, or nearly twice its GDP.[21] The sources of this debt are to be found in the inability of Congo's governments to accept the severe limits that their meager resources put on socialist development. For instance, Congo's ever-expanding civil service grew from 3,300 in 1960 to 73,000 in 1986, or more than one-quarter of the work force.[22] In 1987 the civil service salaries alone absorbed 38 percent of the budget.[23]

Another burden on the Congolese economy was its numerous parastatals. By May 1978 there were "some sixty-odd" state enterprises in Congo, and by the mid-1980s their numbers peaked around eighty-five. These enterprises employed some 30,000 persons, representing another 16 percent or so of persons employed in the modern sector.[24] Useful as the parastatals were to create employment and promote industrialization, their cost to the Congolese economy has been high. As

Michael Radu and Keith Somerville observed, by 1987 "it was clear to everyone in Congo, excepting the most dogmatic radicals on the left, that the parastatal sector is one of the main reasons the country cannot pay its bills. . . ."[25]

While Congo's oil wealth might well have been expected to mitigate the country's economic problems (Congo being the subcontinent's fourth largest producer), it has actually been a bane as well as a boon to financial solvency. When Congolese production and oil prices increased in the early 1980s, the state's share of the annual oil receipts peaked around $900 million.[26] Instead of paying off its old debts with the windfalls, the Congolese government continued to borrow heavily on the assumption that these revenues would be permanent, but in fact world oil prices collapsed in 1985. During this time, other export sectors declined, so that by the late 1980s, 90 percent of foreign exchange was earned by petroleum revenues. Yet in 1991 Congo's oil revenues were only about $334 million, or 40 percent of their peak in the early 1980s.[27]

As a result of these economic factors, Congo was virtually bankrupt by 1990; it was over $1 billion in arrears on its debt payments,[28] and its national budget was again registering a huge deficit, as was its balance of payments. In December 1990 the World Bank suspended further loans to Congo because of its nonpayment of debt.

The Unfolding of Congo's Revolution

Congo's revolution began with subdued rumblings for political reform during the first half of 1990.[29] When the PCT Central Committee met at the end of June, the nation watched intently for news of reform, and the decisions of that meeting indeed marked the beginning of a process that would ultimately lead to the political demise of Sassou and the PCT. On July 4, 1990, the Central Committee announced that the PCT was abandoning Marxism-Leninism and that the regime would move toward a multiparty system; it also promised to make constitutional changes at an extraordinary PCT congress the following year. Sassou further fueled interest in political change by stating in several interviews that Congo needed a national debate on a new constitution and by freeing all of Congo's forty-odd political prisoners in August.

The events of the final four months of 1990 saw the crucial coalescence of Congo's antigovernment forces, including the urban left and Christian churches.[30] A general strike called by the Congo's sole legal union, the Congolese Labor Federation (Confédération Syndicale Congolaise, CSC) in mid-month finally forced the regime's hand. Until that point, Sassou was still trying to control the rampaging forces of democratization through intimidation even as he spoke of the need for political reform.[31]

The strike led the regime to acquiesce in a CSC Congress, which union leaders had been demanding for several months. This Congress, in turn, asserted CSC autonomy from the government, reiterated the call for a national conference, and demanded more benefits for workers; the government was left meekly to endorse the union's decisions. The tumultuous month of September 1990 ended with an unscheduled meeting of the PCT central committee that legalized the formation of other political parties "with immediate effect" but remained vague on the date and form of constitutional changes.

With pressure continuing to mount over subsequent months, Prime Minister Alphonse Poaty-Souchlaty announced his resignation on December 3. He and other major officials also decided to quit the PCT at the same time. Hence, when the PCT held an extraordinary congress between December 6 and 10, its decisions were virtually meaningless, despite an effort to revamp the party. On the last day of the year, again under pressure, Sassou announced that he was changing the date for the "conference of parties" from May to February 1991.

Once again, however, Sassou's concessions only led to more strident demands. A consortium of twenty-two new Congolese political parties formed during the previous fall rejected Sassou's proposed transitional regime and demanded an immediate national conference. Similarly, the CSC "deplored" the government increases of the minimum wage by 44 percent and the size of the civil service by 6,000 employees as too little. As the date for the scheduled opening of the national conference neared, Sassou struggled to keep the conference under his partial control by "stacking" its membership with PCT loyalists and by trying to intimidate the now-defiant Congolese media. The opposition maintained the upper hand, however, creating dozens of new political parties and opposition journals.

The opening of Congo's national conference on February 25 was marked by an immediate fight over representation and was briefly suspended, until March 4. As elsewhere in francophone Africa, the conference's strongest test was its early debate on whether its decisions would be "sovereign." When the provisional rule declaring the conference sovereign passed, the conference assumed the role of a constitutional convention, and President Sassou accepted this decision. Moreover, Congo's highest military commander also reaffirmed an earlier pledge that the army would not intervene in the political process.[32] The final blow to the regime came a few days later when the conference elected its officials: All eleven members of the governing presidium were from the opposition front, as were the four vice-chairpersons. The conference elected Monsignor Ernest Kombo, bishop of Owando, to be its supreme chairperson.

When the formalities of the conference were resolved, the delegates got down to the serious business of lambasting Sassou and the PCT. Sassou was repeatedly accused not only of corruption and mismanagement, but also of conspiracy in the assassinations of Ngouabi and several other political figures. Indeed, Sassou became a scapegoat for Congo's problems, "past, present and future."[33] With their confidence rising, the conferees banned any travel outside the country for all government officials, and some even called for Sassou's arrest. Sassou did not try to answer any of the charges until April 26, at which time his tone was repentant rather than defiant. Significantly, Sassou also noted that the conference debates signaled a renewal of ethnic strife.

At the end of the conference the delegates chose an interim government, headed by former World Bank official André Milongo, to rule for one year. Under this regime Milongo, with the title "Prime Minister," exercised executive powers, including control of the armed forces and economic policy, and the presidency was reduced to a largely ceremonial position, retained by Sassou. Bishop Kombo was selected to head Congo's interim legislature, the High Council of the Republic (Conseil Supérieur de la République, CSR). Legislative and Presidential elections were then scheduled for March and June 1992, respectively. Among the last acts of the 105-day conference was the replacement of Congo's Soviet-style flag and revolutionary anthem with traditional symbols and the dropping of the adjective "Populaire" from the country's official name ("République Populaire du Congo").

Congo's Transition Crises

Like the conference in Benin, and unlike those in Togo and Zaire, the Congolese national conference resulted in a widely accepted transitional government and the unequivocal commitment of the political class to establish a new order. At the same time, the leadership of the Congolese army, despite its high Mbochi representation, stated its intention to respect the political process. Nevertheless, a military coup was one of the principal challenges that the fragile Congolese democracy successfully faced during the subsequent year of transition. The other was the organization of free and fair elections.

After Milongo's installation, the rest of 1991 was spent preparing for Congo's upcoming elections. Unfortunately, the national census and the preparation of voter lists were fraught with difficulties, and the various elections were postponed numerous times.[34] A draft constitution, previously approved by the CSR, was put to a referendum in March 1992, some four months behind schedule. It was endorsed by 96 percent of the Congolese people in a vote that international observers declared to have been free and fair. Although the constitution does specify a strong, Gaullist-style presidency, it guarantees individual rights and accords citizens the right to associate freely in political parties.[35]

During these same months, however, Congo saw a foreboding struggle between Milongo's government and the Congolese army. Apparently, several members of Milongo's cabinet from the Pool region had plotted to bring the army under political control by spreading rumors of a future military coup.[36] In the midst of those rumors, Milongo appointed a new military chief, General Michel Gangouo, a sworn enemy of Sassou loyalists in the army. Milongo then began purging certain northerners of dubious loyalty from the military high command. This led to a tense standoff between Milongo's government and the army, which at one point involved a shoot-out causing six deaths and Milongo's seeking asylum at the

American Embassy.[37] Finally, a parliamentary commission that had been set up as the crisis began released its report, which indicated that Milongo's cabinet officers had fabricated the coup rumors. As a result, the CSR sided with the army, and Milongo was forced to dismiss Gangouo and reconstitute his cabinet according to a more regionally balanced formula. These steps ended the army revolt, though some army officers subsequently complained that the government was again spreading false rumors of military coups.

A second crisis erupted after the May 1992 local and municipal elections as a result of charges by virtually all parties of fraud and mismanagement.[38] These were attributed to the incompetence of the Milongo government and the manipulations of its interior minister, Alexis Gabou. This crisis was also mediated, allowing the election results to stand despite the improprieties—though Milongo again was forced to shuffle and reduce his cabinet. Another result of the crisis was that the CSR created an election commission to organize the upcoming legislative and presidential elections, stripping Milongo's government of this duty. These elections also had an ominous aspect, namely, the distinctly ethnoregionalist patterns of party support that emerged.[39]

By this point two major political coalitions had emerged in Congo, the Union for Democratic Renewal (Union pour le Renouveau Démocratique, URD) and the National Alliance for Democracy (Alliance Nationale pour la Démocratie, AND). The former supported the Milongo government and was led by Bernard Kolélas and his party, the Congolese Movement for Democracy and Comprehensive Development (Mouvement Congolais pour le Développement et la Démocratie Intégrale, MCDDI), which draws its strongest support from the Bakongo and the Lari. The dominant players in the AND coalition were Professor Pascal Lissouba, a former prime minister under Massemba-Débat, and his party, the Pan-African Union for Social Democracy (Union Panafricaine pour la Démocratie Sociale, UPADS). Lissouba, an Ndjabi, comes from Mossendjo district in the southwestern region of Niari, and his party draws the lion's share of its support from the southern regions of Niari, Bouenza, and Lékoumou (collectively known as "Nibolek"). Sassou and his reformed PCT were also in the AND camp, which made some ideological sense as the AND partners were viewed as being to the left of the URD. Another key Lissouba ally was Jean-Michel Bokamba Yangouma (from the northern region of Cuvette), the CSC leader who had been instrumental in Sassou's downfall and who had led the attack against Milongo in May 1992.

In two rounds of legislative voting in June and July 1992, the UPADS emerged with a plurality of thirty-nine seats, followed by the MCDDI with twenty-nine and the PCT with eighteen, the remainder (for a total of 125) being split among smaller parties.[40] As long as the AND alliance remained intact, it held a slim parliamentary majority of sixty-four seats. In the presidential elections in August, the order of the finishers was Lissouba (36 percent), Kolélas (20 percent), Sassou (17

TABLE 5.1   First Round of Congo's 1992 Presidential Elections:
Percentage of Vote, by Region

	Lissouba	Kolélas	Sassou	Milongo	Others
Brazzaville	17.2	29.9ᵃ	20.3	21.6	11.0
Pool	4.8	64.4ᵃ	3.3	16.5	11.0
Bouenza	80.6ᵃ	6.6	1.6	1.9	9.3
Lékoumou	91.7ᵃ	0.9	6.0	0.6	0.8
Kouilou	40.0ᵃ	16.6	5.3	4.7	33.4
Niari	88.7ᵃ	6.0	2.1	1.1	2.1
Plateaux	10.0	0.9	57.6ᵃ	0.7	30.8
Cuvette	13.5	0.8	47.9ᵃ	0.5	37.3
Sangha	30.8	3.4	41.9ᵃ	1.9	22.0
Likouala	24.7	1.1	58.5ᵃ	2.4	13.3

ᵃRegion's top finishing candidate.
Source: Congolese Ministry of State, untitled document.

percent), and Milongo (10 percent). In the runoff round between Lissouba and Kolélas later that same month, Sassou endorsed Lissouba, his coalition partner, while the Lari supporters of Milongo generally supported Kolélas. In the event, it was Lissouba who won a solid victory with 61 percent of the vote.

Once again, however, the ethnoregional character of the vote was notable (see Table 5.1). In the first round, Kolélas carried the Pool region easily, where the Lari and Bakongo predominate, and won a narrow plurality in Brazzaville, which, though ethnically mixed, contains a plurality of Lari and Bakongo. Milongo, a Lari, also performed best in Brazzaville and Pool. Lissouba, by contrast, did poorly in these areas but handily swept the vote in "Nibolek." Lissouba also won in Kouilou, the region containing Pointe Noire, Congo's "economic capital" and chief ocean port. The second-place finisher in Kouilou was Jean-Pierre Thystère-Tchicaya, a native of Pointe Noire and a former PCT stalwart, who garnered 28 percent of the vote there. Finally, Sassou won a majority or plurality in the sparsely populated northern regions of Cuvette, Sangha, Likouala, and Plateaux. Former President Yhombi, from Cuvette, finished a strong second with 27 percent in his home region. In the second round, Kolélas won only in Brazzaville, Pool, and (narrowly) Kouilou, with Lissouba carrying all other regions.

In all, the fourteen-month transition under Milongo was a trying but ultimately successful episode in Congo's struggle to establish a multiparty democracy, though Milongo's heavy-handed approach to bringing the army under civilian control nearly led to disaster. The favorable conclusion of the brief army revolt resulted from Bishop Kombo's sensitive leadership in forging a compromise in the CSR, from the restraint of General Jean-Marie Michel Mokoko in the crisis, and from France's sending clear signals that it desired a democratic outcome to the crisis.[41]

Ethnoregional Politics in Democratic Congo

Unfortunately for Congo, the struggle for democracy was still only beginning when Lissouba took office in August 1992. The next year and a half would see a frightening disintegration of the social peace in Congo, almost ending in civil war; it was not until late 1994 that relative calm returned. In this period, Lissouba's regime endured a series of crises, all related to the new rivalry that was emerging in the country between Lissouba and Kolélas. In each of these crises, the role of Sassou remained important.

The first crisis of the new regime began as Lissouba sought to form his first government. When the new government was announced in September, the PCT was awarded only three of twenty-eight cabinet posts, far fewer than expected. As a result, Sassou quickly abandoned Lissouba and went into alliance with Kolélas's opposition platform, the URD. Many Congolese regarded this alliance to be "against nature" because of Kolélas's long-standing hostility to the PCT during the 1970s and 1980s.[42] The URD and the PCT then collaborated in organizing the defeat of Lissouba's candidate for Speaker of the Assembly and elected instead André Moulelé, a PCT executive. At the end of October, Parliament voted no confidence in Lissouba's proposed government, headed by Stéphane Bongho-Nouarra. As one empathetic analyst put it, Lissouba had to adapt rapidly to the "cruel, Florentine practices of Congolese politics."[43]

Lissouba responded by dissolving the legislature and declaring that he would retain Bongho-Nouarra until new elections could be held. In turn, the opposition declared the dissolution of Parliament illegal and called for public resistance to the new government, leading to some violent protests.[44] With a severe national crisis brewing, the army interceded, offering mediation, calling for a neutral premier, and threatening further intervention to resolve the crisis. Accordingly, a compromise was reached whereby Lissouba agreed to form a national unity government that gave a majority of posts to the new (majority) URD-PCT coalition.[45] Nevertheless, the dissolution of Parliament stood, and legislative elections were eventually scheduled for May 1993.

Relative political peace prevailed in Congo over the four months leading up to the May elections. The result of these elections, though, was a solid victory for the Presidential Domain (Mouvance Présidentielle, MP)—as Lissouba's coalition had come to be known—in the first round. Again the ethnoregional nature of the voting was clear (see Table 5.2). Citing alleged "monstrous frauds and irregularities,"[46] the URD-PCT alliance refused to accept the results and announced a boycott of the second round of voting (which was to decide the eleven remaining seats), sparking the second crisis. Lissouba opted to go ahead with the elections on June 6, 1993, allowing the MP to capture seven more seats. In the aftermath of this vote, violence spread throughout Brazzaville, each camp beginning to fortify its part of the city, to collect arms, and to erect barricades.

TABLE 5.2   Performance of Parties in Congo's May 1993 Legislative Elections
(in seats won)

Region	AND Alliance		URD Alliance				
	UPADS	Other AND	MCDDI	PCT	Other URD	Independent	Total
Brazzaville	11	4	15[a]	4	2	0	36
Pool	0	1	11[a]	0	2	2	15
Bouenza	13[a]	1	0	0	0	0	14
Lékoumou	6[a]	0	0	0	0	0	6
Kouilou	0	2	0	0	5[a]	0	7
Niari	10[a]	0	0	0	0	0	10
Plateaux	0	1	0	3[a]	0	1	6
Cuvette	3	6[a]	0	2	2	0	13
Sangha	1	1	0	0	1	0	3
Likouala	1	1	0	0	2	0	4
Totals	45	17	26	9	14	3	114

[a]Region's top finishing party.
Source: Congolese Ministry of State, "Arrêté No. 1058 bis du 20 mai 1993."

After a month of bitter contestation and failed mediation, a new pro-Lissouba government was announced with former President Yhombi at its head; the opposition announced plans to set up its own government on the same day.[47] Meanwhile, the Supreme Court had ruled on the elections, stating that the results were published illegally, and voiding the second round.[48] Again barricades went up in the pro-Kolélas district of Brazzaville (Bacongo), and a new two-month period of violent disorder began. The division of Brazzaville along ethnic lines reflected the strong ethnoregionalism evident in the elections, indicated in Tables 5.1 and 5.2. There were a number of deaths in this period as the capital became the scene of numerous skirmishes among the Congolese militia and a variety of armed political forces representing Lissouba, Kolélas, and Sassou.[49] During this period Lissouba fired Mokoko, appointed General Raymond Damasse Ngollo to mediate the conflict, and declared a state of emergency.

The violence in Congo soon focused the attention of several international players on the situation there, including Gabon, the Organization for African Unity (OAU), and France. Through the mediation of these parties, particularly that of President Omar Bongo of Gabon, some civility was restored to relations between the two coalitions. On July 26 the two sides issued a joint statement pledging to remove the barricades, free kidnapped persons, disband private militias, and enter into negotiations, with Bongo and Ngollo as mediators.[50] On August 4 the two groups signed an accord in Libreville expressing confidence in and commitment to President Lissouba and the constitution and deploring the recent violence. It also established a mechanism to arbitrate the election dispute and set a new date (October 3) for a new second round of elections, allowing the state of emergency to be lifted a few days later.[51]

Following the October elections, in which the MP only won three more seats to the URD-PCT's seven (with one independent), it would have seemed that Congo's long, difficult transition was finally over. Unfortunately, a great number of arms had begun circulating in Brazzaville during the June–July violence, and unofficial militias loyal to Kolélas and Sassou continued to train in their respective quarters of the city. According to *Jeune Afrique*, each of the two opposition parties had created militias of some 1,500 combatants, including army deserters, village conscripts, unemployed urban youth, and, in the case of Kolélas's forces, Zairian mercenaries.[52] Kolélas's forces gathered in the Bacongo district, while those of Sassou organized in Talangai, Ouenze, and Mpila. In response to the kidnapping of two government officials and other unlawful acts, the Congolese army began an operation to root out the perpetrators in Bacongo and Makélékélé.[53] Meanwhile, militias in the opposition-controlled districts began killing or driving out Lissouba loyalists found there and conducting raids into other sections of town. The partisans of Lissouba from Nibolek responded in kind, creating mutual cases of ethnic cleansing within Congo's capital city. Although Lissouba arranged a summit meeting with the coalition leaders at the People's Palace on December 22, at which all sides appealed for calm,[54] the violence continued.

By the beginning of 1994 Lissouba had apparently resolved to move decisively to end the crisis. On January 5 he announced an expansion of the army, emphasizing that the new recruits would come from all regions.[55] Then, on January 17, Lissouba ordered the army to blockade the Bacongo section of Brazzaville, from which Kolélas's "Ninjas" were operating.[56] For the first time, the army used heavy weapons, causing serious damage to the "Ninja" stronghold. As a result, casualties during this episode were high. Nevertheless, the pressure seems to have succeeded in that another accord was reached on January 30, 1994.

The crises had taken a toll, however. Some 2,000 Congolese had died in the fighting between June 1993 and July 1994,[57] and many others were wounded, rendered homeless, or permanently traumatized. According to one first-hand source, "[t]he victims [of ethnic cleansing] were burned, buried alive, shot, thrown into the river, decapitated and/or slashed with machetes. Among the victims were men, women and children. . . . Women and very young girls, sometimes mother and daughters, have been gang raped. In fact, raping the enemy's women seems to have played as an important role here as in Bosnia. Infants have been placed in mortars and pounded to death."[58]

This violence represents perhaps the most severe ethnic violence in Congo's independent history and certainly the worst since the 1960s. The political fighting was accompanied by a general breakdown of order, which allowed criminal entrepreneurs to seize arms and use them to terrorize and rob their fellow citizens.

"Reconciliation" and the Advent of New Problems

After the January 1994 agreement the ethnic attacks and general violence gradually subsided over the following months, though the peace continued to be punctuated by occasional attacks by armed groups on civilians. The process was encouraged by a slow rapprochement between the MP and the Bakongo opposition. In June, Lissouba hosted Kolélas at a public reconciliation of the two rivals.[59]

The mayoral elections of July 1994 proved to be the next step in Congo's ethnopolitical reconciliation. Kolélas was elected mayor of Brazzaville and Tchicaya mayor of Pointe Noire. Lissouba, cognizant that his two opponents had a majority of support in their respective fiefdoms, had already declared himself sanguine about this outcome, even joking, "Let Kolélas show that he can govern one-third of Congo!"[60]

Representatives of the two major coalitions continued the process of reconciliation after mid-1994, even as sporadic incidents continued. On August 6, 1994, Kolélas and Christophe Moukoueke, speaking for the MP, actually embraced and observed a minute of silence for those who had perished in the violence.[61] In December UPADS and MCDDI members of Parliament undertook further discussion in continuation of this process,[62] and in January 1995 the two sides announced that they would create a public defense force, composed of some former militia members, to disarm civilians and restore public order.[63] Later in the month Lissouba took the next logical step by forming a new government that included four opposition members (three from the MCDDI and one from the Tchicaya's Rally for Democracy and Social Progress (Rassemblement pour la Démocratie et le Progrès Social, RDPS). Most significantly, Kolélas's own brother became the minister of the interior, a tremendous sign of Lissouba's trust and Kolélas's equanimity.[64] Nonetheless Kolélas and Tchicaya both insisted that they remained part of the opposition, and *Jeune Afrique* downplayed the significance of the new government, emphasizing that loyalists of the MP still dominated the cabinet.[65]

Paradoxically, this partial ethnopolitical entente between the Lissouba and Kolélas camps further alienated Sassou, despite the continuation of a nominal MCDDI-PCT alliance. Sassou's continuing opposition had both military and political aspects. In late May 1994, a large number of arms were stolen from the army training school at Gambona, which is near Sassou's hometown, Oyo.[66] It is suspected that these arms were taken by Sassou's 700-person militia, which now surrounds his Oyo estate. Loyal units of the Congolese armed forces then set up a watch over Sassou's estate from a discreet distance. Meanwhile, Sassou's "Cobra" militia in the Brazzaville districts of Ouenze, Mpila, and Talangai remained intact. On the political front, Sassou formed a new coalition of northern-based political parties, the United Democratic Forces (Forces Démocratiques Unies, FDU) in September 1994, which controls fifteen parliamentary deputies. Significantly,

Kolélas attended the founding of this organization, giving a tacit blessing to the group.[67] During the first half of 1995, accusations of slander and other bitter words flew back and forth between the MP and Sassou.[68]

The growing reconciliation of the two dominant southern players has also led to growing contestation *within* the two camps. Most notably, twelve parliamentarians in UPADS and another party, all from southern Bouenza region, announced their resignation from the party in January 1995 because of their "marginalization."[69] These deputies apparently felt that other citizens from the regions of Niari and Lékoumou were receiving more favorable treatment from the government. This group later formed its own party, the Union for the Republic (Union pour la République, UR). Deputies from Niari and Lékoumou had similarly complained that those from Bouenza were given too many important posts.[70] More recently, another rift between "reformers" and "conservatives" has opened in UPADS, causing one UPADS deputy to establish an opposition "current" within the party.[71] These schisms are typical in that political groups often stay united only as long as the threat from a perceived common enemy seems real. Meanwhile, in the MCDDI, Deputy Didier Sengha defected in April to form his own party, accusing Kolélas of being autocratic. The latter responded by pronouncing the former "a thief."[72] This intra-MCDDI dispute may reflect some of the ethnoregional tension among Kolélas's supporters.[73]

Economic Non-Reform

In the midst of these ethnoregional political traumas, only limited economic reforms have been undertaken in Congo.[74] The ruling group is caught squarely between the demands of Congo's active labor unions, one of which is now associated with the opposition, and those of the IMF. Other donors, including the World Bank and French Development Fund, take their cues from the IMF on further lending in support of reform. As in other African cases, Congo has been forced to accept the bitter pill prescribed by the IMF in return for bridging loans and help in rescheduling debt. Congo's relationship with the IMF, however, had been suspended since 1990 because of debt payment arrears. Only after making some modest progress towards implementation of reforms and clearing the arrears in 1993 did serious negotiations with the IMF begin anew. After much bargaining, the IMF approved a standby loan of some $33 million in May 1994, rescheduling some $1.5 billion of Congo's debt.[75]

IMF missions to Congo in November 1994 and March 1995 gave disappointing reports on Congo's structural adjustment program, however, and the IMF suspended its disbursements after the first of these visits. Specifically, the reports noted that tax and customs revenues were down sharply, and they pointed to massive fraud in the customs area.[76] Nevertheless, the IMF did sign another "letter of intention" in March, contingent on better performance. In April 1995 the government dismissed the tax collector general, Alphonse Mabiala, for "grave professional failings."[77] By May the state was again in arrears on its external debt, and the IMF made the decision not to renew Congo's structural adjustment program for another year, despite its March agreement. The perpetual negotiations between the IMF and Congo continue.

Meanwhile, strikes by public-sector workers were routine during 1994 and 1995, and the regime lacked the means, physical or financial, to control them. In November 1994 government workers were complaining that their salaries had not been paid in twelve months, but a last-minute accord in which the government promised some back pay headed off a strike for the moment.[78] When the government did not live up to the accord, however, a strike of most civil servants took place between February 20 and April 6, 1995. It should be noted that a new union grouping close to Kolélas, the Labor Confederation of Congolese Workers (Confédération Syndicale des Travailleurs Congolais, CSTC), has been most strident in its demands, but the old CSC, which is loyal to Lissouba, called for the 1995 action. The political loyalty of these workers and their leaders was thus overcome by the necessities of survival.

The government has resorted to mortgaging the state's future oil revenues and selling its stocks in lucrative industrial firms to pay its bills, particularly government salaries. When Congo was still out of compliance with the IMF in 1993 and could not acquire external funds from foreign lenders (including France), Lissouba desperately needed cash to pay arrears on these salaries. He became deeply irritated with Elf-Aquitaine, the French state oil company, when it refused to provide loans to Congo to pay civil servants. The situation was temporarily resolved at that time when Lissouba pulled off a secretly negotiated agreement with "Oxy" (Occidental Petroleum) in April 1993.[79] The $150 million that his government received up front (in exchange for future oil at bargain prices) allowed it to pay some of the back salaries owed the workers only days before the critical May 1993 elections, which the UPADS narrowly won. Besides costing Congo millions in lost oil revenue, this deal led to a major row with France that was not resolved until March 1994.[80] Similarly, the strike of April 1995 was ended by payments that the government made from the sale of its 25 percent stake in Elf-Congo. The sale raised some $50 million, but it may deprive the state of considerable future oil revenues.[81] In any case, much of the oil income generated by Elf-Congo and Agip-Recherches (an Italian firm) now goes to repay loans made over the last several years.

As for the more general effects of restructuring, the reforms undertaken so far have undermined the standard of living in Congo, without yet producing significant growth. With the infamous CFA franc devaluation of January 1994, for instance, Congo suffered higher inflation during 1994 (61 percent) than any other franc zone country.[82] Meanwhile, after years of delay, the government began taking the painful step of reducing the civil service (including "phantom" employees) in 1995; according to government sources, the number fell from 80,000 to 55,000 in the first half of the year, but it was actually only reduced to around 70,000.[83] The government also reduced sharply the salaries of the remaining employees.

Together, this rise in prices and loss of government jobs translated into a severe strain on the average Congolese budget and in some cases into malnutrition. The economic strain, which has been constant since 1990, also helps to explain Congo's recent ethnic violence. Many of the malefactors in the ethnic violence were unemployed urban youth who had little hope of finding jobs. Recruits to the ethnopolitical militia in Congo found not only adventure but also economic sustenance and a sense of belonging in the armed groups that they joined.[84]

Conclusions

Despite all of the difficulties, the very survival of Congolese democracy is impressive given the economic chaos that the new regime inherited from its predecessor and the severe international pressures it has faced. To be sure, Congo has stumbled from one crisis to the next since 1991. The Congolese example certainly suggests that political reform is likely to be fraught with great challenges and that democracy can only be consolidated over time, if at all. Moreover, the Congolese people are certainly no wealthier than they were in 1990 or 1991; thus the case of Congo, like those of Benin and the Central African Republic, serves to remind us that democratization is not necessarily linked with prosperity, especially in the short run.

Yet the Congolese have grown richer in their political culture and experience since 1991. Small signs of the slow institutionalization of democratic practice in the country may be discerned. For instance, the number of candidates in the legislative elections declined from 1,700 in the 1992 elections to only 386 in the 1993 elections.[85] Whether democracy has been worth the cost is something only the Congolese can judge, and their judgment will likely turn on whether democracy survives and whether the economy can now be put on a sound footing.

The "francophone" imprint in the nature of Congolese political reform is fairly clear. Congo's national conference was a prototypical example of the method of regime transition in francophone Africa. More generally, the social forces directing the "revolution" were overwhelmingly urban, educated elites, operating from the center, rather than "peasant masses" emerging from the periphery. Moreover, the role of France itself has been critical, as elsewhere in francophone Africa. The timing of the coalescence of the reform movement in 1990 reflects the influence of Mitterrand's La Baule statement. At other times the behavior of France, which has been involved in some contestation with Lissouba's regime, has had a more negative impact. French hostility to the Oxy deal, for instance, certainly encouraged Lissouba's opponents, who were at the time challenging his rule through nondemocratic means. While disturbing, France's clamoring to retain its economic stake in Congo can also be viewed as an obstacle overcome.

Yet the great challenge to Congolese democracy—indeed to any kind of public order—has been the severe ethnoregional strife of 1993 and 1994. Not surprisingly, this violence appears to have been linked to the country's severe economic crisis. If estimates that some 2,000 persons died in this strife are accurate, then one Congolese in a thousand perished in the fighting. While this fact is exceedingly disturbing, it may be said that the worst possibilities of such conflict were not realized; after all, at least *one in sixteen* Rwandans died in that country's ethnic war of 1994.[86] Thus Congo's 1993–1994 ethnoregional violence may be viewed both as a heart-wrenching tragedy and as an ugly social episode that could have been much worse.

What made these relatively positive outcomes in the Congo—democracy's survival and the limits of ethnoregional violence—possible? Part of the answer lies in the social demographics (e.g., education and urbanization, discussed earlier) and the political culture of Congo, which are more favorable to democratization than those of, say, Zaire. And more important still, the relative wealth of Congo's citizens, which is attributable to the country's modest petroleum endowment, renders the Congolese slightly more immune to appeals to violence based on allegations of ethnic favoritism in the government or society. Had Congo been poorer and less literate, it might have known the kind of bloodletting that Rwanda and Burundi have recently seen.

A second set of variables has been foreign influences. Besides France, various other foreign actors have interceded in Congo's troubles at crucial junctures. Notably, the help of Gabon's President Bongo and OAU mediator Mohammed Sahnoun in resolving the 1993 and 1994 crises was crucial, as was that of the international teams that observed Congo's many elections.

Yet the most important part of the explanation for Congo's relative success lies not in its "structural advantages" or the assistance of foreign players, but in the comportment of its leaders. While some analysts have insisted that "the prospects for democracy in African regimes depend on prior traditions of democracy," warning against too much emphasis on "individual agency,"[87] the outcome in Congo cannot be understood without considerable reference to the choices made by individual actors. For instance, the "call to arms" by the opposition after the 1993 elections nearly doomed the country. Yet all sides have also exhibited statesmanship at crucial moments, as we have seen.

The great challenge to continued political reform is the country's economic crisis, which has only been tentatively addressed thus far. Even the stabilization of ethnoregional peace may well depend on growing prosperity. The next milestone at which economic and social progress will be measured, in turn, is the 1997 presidential elections. Clearly, Lissouba is caught between the contradictory forces of Congo's still-strong labor movement and the IMF. Whether his regime has the political courage and skill and the determination and technical ability to escape this dilemma remains to be seen. Moreover, its chances are further conditioned by the behavior of Lissouba's opponents, who may choose to make his task either easier or more difficult. Finally, external forces such as the world price of oil, the pa-

tience of the IMF, and signals sent by France to would-be coup makers will determine the room for maneuver of the various Congolese actors. Yet the ultimate fate
of democracy in Congo still depends on the behavior the country's leaders.

Notes

1. For a brief background on Congo's ethnic groups and their leaders, see René Gauze,
The Politics of Congo-Brazzaville, translated, edited, and with a supplement by Virginia
Thompson and Richard Adloff (Stanford: Hoover Institution Press, 1973), pp. 1–8. For a
comprehensive discussion of Congolese ethnicity in which Congolese society is divided
into thirteen major ethnic groups, see Marcel Soret, *Histoire du Congo, capitale Brazzaville*
(Paris: Berger-Levrault, 1978), pp. 19–29.

2. Samuel Decalo, "People's Republic of the Congo," in Bogdan Szajkowski, ed., *Marxist
Governments: A World Survey,* vol. 1 (London: Macmillan, 1981), p. 214.

3. Bahjat Achikbache and Francis Anglade, "Les villes prises d'assaut: Les migrations in-
ternes," *Politique africaine,* no. 31 (October 1988):7. On the urbanization "problem," see
also Michael S. Radu and Keith Somerville, "The Congo," in Chris Allen et al., *Benin, the
Congo, Burkina Faso* (London: Pinter, 1989), pp. 206–207.

4. Achikbache and Anglade, "Les villes prises d'assaut," pp. 12–13.

5. Radu and Somerville, "The Congo," p. 150. On Congo's school system, see also Antoine Makonda, "Une école 'pour le peuple'?" *Politique africaine,* no. 31 (October 1988):
39–50.

6. Radu and Somerville, "The Congo," pp. 206–207. According to Makonda ("Une école
'pour le peuple'?" pp. 48–49), the secondary schools are also geared to the "production of
bureaucrats."

7. On politics in pre-independence Congo, see Gauze, Adloff, and Thompson, *Politics of
Congo-Brazzaville,* pp. 9–63. On the Youlou regime and its fall, see ibid., pp. 64–105,
125–150; Radu and Somerville, "The Congo," pp. 162–164; Decalo "People's Republic of
the Congo," pp. 214–215; and Apollinaire Ngolongolo, *L'assassinat de Marien Ngouabi, ou,
L'histoire d'un pays ensanglant* (Paris: Autoedition, 1988), pp. 45–57.

8. Emmanuel Terray, "Les révolutions congolaise et dahoméenne de 1963," *Revue
française de science politique* 14 (October 1964):918–925.

9. On Massemba-Débat's regime, see Gauze, Adloff, and Thompson, *Politics of Congo-
Brazzaville,* pp. 151–171; Radu and Somerville, "The Congo," pp. 164–168; and Ngolongolo, *L'assassinat de Marien Ngouabi,* pp. 59–62.

10. David E. Gardinier, "Schooling in the States of Equatorial Africa," *Canadian Journal
of African Studies* 8, no. 3 (1974):531–533. Also see Makonda, "Une école 'pour le peuple'?"

11. On the Ngouabi regime, see Radu and Somerville, "The Congo," pp. 169–181;
Gauze, Adloff, and Thompson, *Politics of Congo-Brazzaville,* pp. 172–185; Ngolongolo,
L'assassinat de Marien Ngouabi, pp. 63–65; and Decalo, "People's Republic of the Congo,"
pp. 216–218.

12. According to Decalo, "[the Ngouabi regime] *did not* bring about a redistribution of
economic power domestically or soothe domestic strife. For all its radical rhetoric and
Ngouabi's stress on ideological militancy and purity, only the superficial, trivial and structural aspects of Marxism were imposed on Congo" (emphasis added). Decalo, "People's
Republic of the Congo," p. 216.

13. For details on the trial of Ngouabi's alleged murderers, see especially Ngolongolo, *L'assassinat de Marien Ngouabi,* pp. 99–137.

14. Radu and Somerville, "The Congo," p. 181; Decalo, "People's Republic of the Congo," p. 218; and Colin Legum, ed., *Africa Contemporary Record 1978–1979,* vol. 11 (New York: Africana, 1980), pp. B552–B559. There was some dispute about Yhombi's ideological character at the time, owing to his short tenure in office. As prime minister in the current regime, Yhombi has proved himself to be thoroughly pragmatic.

15. See *Marchés tropicaux et méditerranéens* (Paris), February 16, 1979, pp. 457–458. It should be noted that some observers, including Radu and Somerville ("The Congo," p. 182), regard Sassou's putative return to orthodoxy more as post facto justification for his "coup" than genuinely serious commitment to Marxism-Leninism.

16. On the 1964–1973 period, see Gauze, Adloff, and Thompson, *Politics of Congo-Brazzaville,* pp. 193–196, and on the subsequent period, Radu and Somerville, "The Congo," pp. 219–224. Though China was the more important communist partner through the 1970s, the Soviet Union became more important after the Soviet-Congolese Treaty of Friendship and Cooperation was signed in 1981, just as China was refocusing attention on internal affairs.

17. In fact, the conventions signed between the Congolese government and the two major foreign oil companies, Elf-Congo and Agip-Recherches, were quite favorable to the oil companies. Instead of sharing the revenues from oil directly, the Congolese government merely imposed taxes and licensing fees. See Assou Massou, "Rente: La nouvelle donne," *Jeune Afrique,* no. 1803 (July 27–August 2, 1995):38–39.

18. Radu and Somerville, "The Congo," p. 225.

19. See Douglas Anglin, "Southern African Responses to Eastern European Developments," *Journal of Modern African Studies* 28, no. 3 (September 1990):431–455. As Gabon's President Omar Bongo colorfully put it, "The winds from the East are shaking the coconut trees." It is worth noting that one of the portraits on the wall of the museum-home of former President Ngouabi is that of former Romanian dictator Nicolae Ceaușescu.

20. Olivier Vallée, "Les cycles de la dette," *Politique africaine,* no. 31 (October 1988):20.

21. Cf. Vallée, "Les cycles de la dette," p. 18, and World Bank and UNDP, *African Economic and Financial Data* (Washington: International Bank for Reconstruction and Development, 1989), p. 89 (for 1987 debt). According to the *Economist* Intelligence Unit (hereafter EIU), the total debt in 1990 was $4.68 billion. EIU, *Country Report: Congo,* no. 4 (1992):17.

22. Radu and Somerville, "The Congo," p. 159. Note that this figure does not even include parastatal workers, university staff, party officials, or the Congolese National Army. The army included some 20,000 officers and soldiers in 1990 and had grown to some 25,000 in January 1995. See *Africa Confidential* 32, no. 2 (January 26, 1990):6–7, and *Marchés tropicaux et méditerranéens,* January 13, 1995, p. 95.

23. World Bank and UNDP, *African Economic and Financial Data,* p. 117.

24. The 1978 figure on parastatals is from Decalo, "The People's Republic of the Congo," p. 228. The U.S. Embassy in Brazzaville counted eighty-six parastatals in 1984, and the World Bank and UNDP counted ninety-four (including financial institutions) in 1986 (*African Economic and Financial Data,* p. 163). Figures vary not so much because new enterprises were created but because different sources include or exclude different kinds of institutions; marketing boards, national offices, utilities, banks, and so on are often lumped together with industrial enterprises in the parastatal category. Employment figures are an

approximation calculated from U.S. Embassy sources and from the World Bank and UNDP, *African Economic and Financial Data*, p. 163.

25. Radu and Somerville, "The Congo," p. 209. The debt of Congo's parastatals accounted for 28 percent of its total external debt in 1986. World Bank and UNDP, *African Economic and Financial Data*, p. 171.

26. *Bulletin quotidien* [official publication, Brazzaville], January 15, 1991, cited in *Foreign Broadcast Information Service–Sub-Saharan Africa* (hereafter *FBIS-SSA*), April 5, 1991, p. 3. On this point generally, see Vallée, "Les cycles de la dette," especially pp. 15–17.

27. Sean Moroney, *Africa: A Handbook*, vol. 1 (New York: Oxford University Press, 1989), p. 129; *FBIS-SSA*, April 4, 1991, p. 3. Congo earned an income of some $2.7 billion from its petroleum production in the 1982–1984 period ($900 million per year), but revenues have not surpassed $450 million since 1985. *Marchés tropicaux et méditerranéens*, February 19, 1993, p. 514.

28. *Africa Confidential* 31, no. 11 (June 29, 1990):8.

29. This section draws heavily on John F. Clark, "Socio-Political Change in the Republic of Congo: Political Dilemmas of Economic Reform," *Journal of Third World Studies* 10, no. 1 (Spring 1993):52–77. Notes documenting the events described in this section are not repeated except as necessary.

30. Abraham Okoko-Esseau, "The Christian Churches and Democratisation in the Congo," in Paul Gifford, ed., *The Christian Churches and the Democratisation of Africa* (Leiden, Netherlands: Brill, 1995), pp. 148–167.

31. This suggests that Sassou was seeking to follow the course of Houphouët-Boigny or Bongo, that is, to allow cosmetic reforms without giving up power. For instance, Sassou had two dissident journalists arrested for "subversion" on July 13 after they wrote a letter to the president calling for reform. See *FBIS-SSA*, July 16, 1990. He also banned the newly formed human rights organization of Congolese lawyer Martin Mberri. See Christine Coste, "A Breakdown in Democratization," *Jeune Afrique Économie*, October 1990, pp. 46–47 (reprinted in English in *FBIS-SSA*, January 3, 1991, p. 5).

32. See *FBIS-SSA*, November 20, 1990, p. 3, and March 12, 1991, p. 2. There was nonetheless a coup attempt on the night of May 18–19, though it was quickly quelled with Sassou's personal intervention. See Sennen Andriamirado, "Du mauvais usage de la démocratie," *Jeune Afrique*, no. 1588 (June 5–11, 1991):24–25.

33. See especially Patrick Girard, "La passion de Denis Sassou-Nguesso," *Jeune Afrique*, no. 1585 (May 15–21, 1991):22–23.

34. For a chronology of events through Lissouba's election in August 1992, see the International Foundation for Electoral Systems document, "IFES Observers' Report on Elections in Congo," September 1992. The voting lists scandal is also mentioned in "Characteristic Ambiguity," *Africa Confidential* 33, no. 5 (March 6, 1992):5.

35. "La constitution de la République du Congo," *Afrique contemporaine*, no. 162 (April-June 1992):35–59.

36. As noted earlier, Ngouabi, Yhombi, and Sassou, Congo's three "PCT Presidents," were all northerners and all military officers. There is, however, nothing to suggest that Army Chief of Staff Jean-Marie Michel Mokoko, also a northerner, would have supported Sassou personally, since (1) Mokoko had stood by and let his power be stripped away in 1991, and (2) Mokoko has had cold relations with Sassou since the "mysterious death of [Mokoko's] wife in 1990." See "Characteristic Ambiguity," pp. 5–6.

37. Ibid., p. 6.

38. On this episode, see "Testing the Waters of Democracy," *Africa Confidential* 33, no. 12 (June 19, 1992):6–7, and EIU, *Country Report: Congo*, no. 3 (1992):11.

39. *Marchés tropicaux et méditerranéens*, May 8, 1992, p. 1196. This problem is explored in more detail later.

40. "IFES Observers' Report on Elections in Congo," p. 9.

41. *Marchés tropicaux et méditerranéens*, January 31, 1992, p. 257.

42. "Que va faire l'armée?" *Jeune Afrique*, no. 1694 (June 24–30, 1993):15.

43. Zyad Liman, "Lissouba peut-il s'en sortir?" *Jeune Afrique*, no. 1682 (April 1–7, 1993):17. Sassou was apparently disillusioned with Lissouba because his first government did not contain enough PCT representatives.

44. Though the constitution is not as clear as it might be on the procedures for a presidential dissolution of Parliament, it seems to provide sanction for the action that Lissouba took. Article 80 states, "When the equilibrium of the public institutions is upset, notably in case of a sharp and persistent crisis between the executive and the Parliament, or if the Assembly twice rejects proposed governments in the space of a year, the President of the Republic may, after consulting the Prime Minister and the President of the National Assembly, pronounce the dissolution of the National Assembly."

45. The resulting new government, headed by a technocrat, Antoine Dacosta, included twelve opposition ministers, nine Lissouba supporters (the "Presidential Domain"), and two members of the Army. On these events, see Sennen Andriamirado, "Lissouba sous haute surveillance," *Jeune Afrique*, no. 1671 (January 14–20, 1993):10–11; "The Barons Mind the Shop," *Africa Confidential* 34, no. 7 (January 22, 1993):5–6; and *Marchés tropicaux et méditerranéens*, January 1, 1993, pp. 39–40. The mediation intervention of Omar Bongo, president of Gabon, was critical in this reconciliation. Despite his marriage to the daughter of Sassou-Nguesso, Bongo has developed a close relationship with Lissouba. (See the chapter in the volume on Gabon.)

46. Cited in *Marchés tropicaux et méditerranéens*, May 21, 1993, p. 1321.

47. *FBIS-SSA*, June 25, 1993, pp. 4–5.

48. "Congo's Political Foes Strike an Agreement," *Africa Report* 38, no. 5 (September-October 1993):5.

49. *FBIS-SSA*, July 12, 1992, pp. 5–6, and Francis Kpatindé, "Démocratie armée," *Jeune Afrique*, no. 1693 (June 17–23 1993):22–24. A total of at least twenty-eight people were killed during the June–July violence. *FBIS-SSA*, August 13, 1993, p. 1.

50. *FBIS-SSA*, July 27, 1993, p. 1.

51. *FBIS-SSA*, August 5, 1993, p. 1, and August 17, 1993, p. 1.

52. Francis Kpatindé, "Brazza comme Sarajevo," *Jeune Afrique*, no. 1725 (January 27–February 2 1994):21.

53. Zyad Liman, "Congo: Une tragédie programmée," *Jeune Afrique*, no. 1714 (November 11–17, 1993):7.

54. *FBIS-SSA*, December 23, 1993, p. 1.

55. Lissouba apparently felt that some members of the army, which had been dominated by northern Mbochis, were reluctant to obey civilian orders, especially those aimed at suppressing the opposition. On the reforms, see *FBIS-SSA*, January 6, 1994, p. 1.

56. *FBIS-SSA*, January 24, 1994, p. 3.

57. This widely used figure for the number of deaths is cited in *Le Monde*, February 2, 1995, p. 4. The precise number remains to be accurately determined.

58. Kajsa Ekholm Friedman and Anne Sundberg, "Ethnic War and Ethnic Cleansing in Brazzaville," unpublished manuscript, n.d. These Swedish scholars conducted research in Brazzaville in May 1994, and their report is one of the most detailed and authentic accounts of Brazzaville's 1993–1994 ethnic violence.

59. Francis Kpatindé, "Le retournement," *Jeune Afrique*, no. 1748 (July 7–13, 1994):26.

60. Quoted in his interview with Francis Kpatindé, "Lissouba dit tout . . . " in *Jeune Afrique*, no. 1729 (February 24–March 2, 1994):71.

61. Agence France-Presse, August 6, 1994, broadcast on the BBC, August 9, 1994 (transcribed by LEXIS/NEXUS).

62. *FBIS-SSA*, December 9, 1994, p. 1, and Faouzia Fékiri, "Lissouba prêche l'apaisement," *Jeune Afrique*, no. 1771 (December 15–21, 1994):22.

63. *Marchés tropicaux et méditerranéens*, January 13, 1995, p. 95.

64. The appointment of Philippe Binkinkita, a former leader of the "Ninjas," may prove to have been a brilliant stroke on Lissouba's part. Like Mandela's appointment of Buthelezi to the same post in South Africa, the presidents are effectively charging those who once disrupted the public order with restoring and maintaining that order.

65. Francis Kpatindé, "La montagne accouche d'une souris," *Jeune Afrique*, no. 1779 (February 9–15, 1995):34–35.

66. EIU, *Country Report: Congo*, no. 4 (1994):12.

67. EIU, *Country Report: Congo*, no. 1 (1995):6.

68. *FBIS-SSA*, May 26, 1995, p. 2. Cf. the statement of Sassou published under the title, "Sassou Nguesso: 'Il faut sauver le Congo,'" *Jeune Afrique*, no. 1797 (June 15–21, 1995): 36–38.

69. *FBIS-SSA*, January 31, 1995, p. 1, and *Marchés tropicaux et méditerranéens*, February 3, 1995, p. 265.

70. EIU, *Country Report: Congo*, no. 1 (1995):6.

71. *FBIS-SSA*, May 23, 1995, p. 3.

72. BBC broadcast, May 12, 1995, taken from Africa Radio No. 1, Libreville, broadcast on May 10 (transcribed by LEXIS/NEXUS).

73. For instance, there is a serious and long-standing rivalry between the Lari and the "Bakongo." On this rivalry and its roots, see Friedman and Sundberg, "Ethnic War and Ethnic Cleansing in Brazzaville," p. 1.

74. On the reforms that were undertaken in 1993, see the parliamentary address by Yhombi-Opango, reprinted in *FBIS-SSA*, August 2, 1993, p. 4. See also *Marchés tropicaux et méditerranéens*, January 22, 1993, p. 233, and February 12, 1993, p. 423; and "La lune de miel," *Jeune Afrique*, no. 1691 (June 3–9, 1993):22–23.

75. In July the World Bank announced that Congo had cleared its outstanding arrears. See EIU, *Country Report: Congo*, no. 4 (1994):17.

76. *Marchés tropicaux et méditerranéens*, December 2, 1994, p. 2534, and *FBIS-SSA*, June 7, 1995, p. 3.

77. *Marchés tropicaux et méditerranéens*, April 21, 1995, p. 838.

78. *FBIS-SSA*, November 9, 1994, pp. 8–9.

79. Francis Kpatindé, "La guerre du pétrole," *Jeune Afrique*, no. 1690 (May 27–June 2, 1993):12–15, and Zyad Liman, "La guerre du pétrole est-elle finie?" *Jeune Afrique*, no. 1705 (September 9–15, 1993):52–55.

80. In 1993 Elf-Aquitaine refused Lissouba's regime any new loans because of its delinquent status with the IMF. Lissouba pointed out, however, that Elf-Aquitaine had tradi-

tionally advanced millions to his dictatorial predecessor. (According to *Africa Confidential*, March 6, 1992, p. 6, both Jean-Christophe Mitterrand, the son of President Mitterrand and an important adviser to him on Africa, and Loïc le Floch-Prigent, president of Elf, were supporters of Sassou.) Lissouba took the French policy as a vote of no confidence in his government, and France in turn feared that it might lose its hold over the Congolese economy and face U.S. competition. Soon afterwards, Lissouba became so infuriated with French criticism that he suggested that the French ambassador should leave the country. Francis Kpatindé, "'Le mal du Congo s'appelle Sassou': Interview avec Pascal Lissouba," *Jeune Afrique*, no. 1697 (July 15–21, 1993):68. On the restoration of good relations, see *FBIS-SSA*, March 11, 1994, pp. 1–2.

81. *Marchés tropicaux et méditerranéens*, March 31, 1995, pp. 697–698.

82. *Marchés tropicaux et méditerranéens*, April 28, 1995, p. 871.

83. Cf. EIU, *Country Report: Congo*, no. 1 (1995):13, and *Marchés tropicaux et méditerranéens*, May 5, 1995, p. 944.

84. Friedman and Sundberg, "Ethnic War and Ethnic Cleansing in Brazzaville," pp. 8–9.

85. EIU, *Country Report: Congo*, no. 2 (1993):11.

86. Based on the very rough calculation that the country's population numbered about 8 million and those killed about one-half million.

87. Michael Bratton and Nicolas van de Walle, "Neopatrimonial Regimes and Political Transitions in Africa," *World Politics* 46, no. 4 (1994):488. For a contrary view, see John F. Clark, "Elections, Leadership, and Democracy in Congo," *Africa Today* 41 (1994):41–62.

Chapter Six

Niger: Regime Change, Economic Crisis, and Perpetuation of Privilege

MYRIAM GERVAIS

At the start of 1990 Niger possessed an authoritarian political regime similar to those that had ruled since independence from France in 1960. The most recent regime was headed by General Ali Saïbou, who had come to power with the backing of the military in November 1987 upon the death of General Seyni Kountché. Kountché had seized power in April 1974, replacing the civilian regime led by Hamani Diori that had governed since December 1958. General Saïbou had previously served as chief of staff of the armed forces under Kountché, who was his cousin. Few persons in early 1990 could have predicted that during the following year and a half the Saïbou regime would have to give way to a movement of political reform and democratization resembling in various ways those in other francophone African states.

To understand the course of this movement and the transition to democracy that took place, it is useful first briefly to review: (1) the economic and financial situation that helped to form the setting for political change; (2) key aspects of the political evolution of Niger between 1958 and 1987; and (3) the evolution of the Saïbou regime between 1987 and 1990.

David Gardinier and Laura Boudon translated this chapter.

Economic and Financial Situation

Nearly all of Niger's 9 million people inhabit a strip of land 150 miles wide along the southern border that comprises only 20 percent of the country's total area of 489,191 square miles. This Sahelian strip ordinarily receives ten to thirty inches of rainfall annually, which is sufficient to support agriculture and most of Niger's pastoralism. Farming and herding both sustain 80 percent of the population and provide the exports (groundnuts, cotton, livestock) that supply most of the state's revenues. These revenues are limited, for they rest upon a meager production sensitive to climatic hazards, including periodic drought. Most of the remainder of the state's revenues have derived since the early 1970s from the sale of uranium, of which there has been a glut on global markets with resulting low prices since the mid-1980s. As a consequence of these conditions and 3 percent annual population growth, per capita gross national product (GNP) fell from $440 in 1981 to $270 in 1993, making Niger one of Africa's poorest countries. A disproportionate share of personal income is enjoyed by the 80,000 wage and salaried workers, of whom half are government employees. Government spending represents nearly one-quarter of the total GNP. France, which is Niger's main trading partner, regularly provided assistance in dealing with budget deficits and debt servicing. Niger's financial difficulties led, beginning in 1983, to its reluctant acceptance of structural adjustment programs (SAPs) sponsored by the International Monetary Fund (IMF).[1]

Political Evolution from 1958 to 1990

In order to grasp the nature and extent of the changes that have taken place since 1990, it is necessary to review the political evolution of Niger since 1958. This recapitulation will shed light upon the groups that monopolized power, showing how the authoritarian regimes of Diori and Kountché were able to maintain themselves during three decades, and it will identify factors that made these regimes founder. This retrospective examination permits us to obtain a glimpse of the stakes and the power relationships that have conditioned the recent political life of Niger.

The 1958–1974 Period

The circumstances of Niger's rapid transition from French rule to independence brought the Nigerien Progressive Party (Parti Progressiste Nigérien, PPN) under Hamani Diori (1916–1989) to power in the legislative elections of December 12, 1958, and enabled the PPN during 1959 to destroy its rival, the African Socialist Movement (Mouvement Socialiste Africain, MSA), or Sawaba, under Djibo Bakary (b. 1922).[2] The PPN had been founded as the Nigerien section of the African Democratic Rally (Rassemblement Démocratique Africain, RDA), which

Félix Houphouët-Boigny had organized in October 1946. The RDA was an inter-territorial party that sought to end colonialism rapidly and to modernize society. The PPN was composed mainly of Jerma civil servants and teachers who had received a French education.

Following the lead of the RDA leadership, after 1951 the PPN decreased its militancy and showed a willingness to achieve its goals more gradually. Nevertheless, the PPN's hostility toward the French administration and the traditional chiefs had caused them to support rival parties, which had the result of keeping the PPN in a minority position in territorial affairs until 1958. At that time, after the MSA, which had formed the first Nigerien government in May 1957 under the terms of the *loi-cadre* of June 23, 1956, campaigned against Niger's membership in the French Community in the referendum of September 1958, the administration and a portion of the most influential chiefs abandoned the MSA in favor of the PPN. As a consequence, the PPN won the December elections for the new National Assembly, which elected the new government of an autonomous republic within the French Community. Thereafter the PPN used its control of the government and French support systematically to repress the MSA deputies and eliminate them from political participation. In May 1959 PPN nominees replaced the MSA deputies in the national assembly, and in October the MSA was legally banned.[3]

The elimination of the formal political opposition and the progressive suppression of resistance from the civil society permitted the PPN eventually to emerge as the sole political force in Niger. Hence from 1960 the Diori government ruled over a de facto single-party regime, though the laws authorizing multipartyism remained on the books. Thereafter, by filling all political space, the PPN became the sole interpreter of the constitution.

The control of the postcolonial state by an urban bureaucracy of Jerma ethnic stock shaped the nature of the relationships that would be maintained between the two principal ethnic groups in Niger. Following the colonial penetration, an implicit division of powers had been established. Politics devolved upon the Jerma, while most important economic matters remained in the hands of the Hausa. The geographic localization of the Jerma along the Niger River in the southwest favored a more intimate contact with the colonial system, which more profoundly affected their social structures. From the early colonial period, the Jerma constituted the core of recruits in the administrative and military structures. Few Hausa participated in the struggle for political power, and although they constituted the largest ethnic group in the country,[4] they, along with the other ethnic groups (Peul, Tuareg, Kanuri), would be dominated by the Jerma.[5]

During the colonial period the Hausa merchants had seen a fundamental part of their economic power undermined by the suppression of trans-Saharan trade. But this merchant class, which originated from the dominant families of Hausa society, succeeded in its conversion to other economic activities while maintaining privileged economic relationships based on ethnic and family ties with the commercial and industrial merchants of the Kano Region in Nigeria. This group gained influence with the colonial regime and was able to obtain favorable measures from the bureaucracy to protect its commercial activities.

Authoritarianism permitted the Diori regime to maintain itself in power and to control the functions of appropriation and distribution of state revenues to the profit of the political class. The cost of clientalism in a context of limited and varying state revenues led the state to ruin and left the peasant population completely destitute. It was the drought of 1973 that precipitated the fall of the Diori government, which was accused of having diverted the urgent aid in foodstuffs destined for the populations hardest hit by the drought. This created a propitious climate for the army, led by chief of staff Lieutenant Colonel Seyni Kountché (b. 1921), to take power in April 1974 and to see its action legitimated by both the population and international opinion.

The 1974–1987 Period

The army's seizure of power permitted the Jerma to dominate the political scene more than ever. Profiting from the growing revenues from uranium, functionaries and military officers collaborated to ensure the expansion of the public sector and promote the emergence of a bourgeoisie capable of counterbalancing the economic weight of the Hausa merchants.

The reinforcement of the state's role in the economy caused by the nationalization of the mining sector and the proliferation of parastatal firms required a growing number of high-level cadres. Consequently, the Kountché government granted priority to higher education and organized a generous system of scholarships in order to accomplish the training of these cadres. The rapid development of the private sector was made possible through preferential loans from financial institutions under state control.[6] The expansion of this state-generated sector turned out to be fragile, however. This stratum of entrepreneurs, which was the core of the modern private sector, was largely eliminated by the subsequent international economic recession.

Thanks to the uranium boom, the state was able to undertake transfers favoring specific social categories: private entrepreneurs, functionaries, university graduates, and mining workers; farmers, herders, and nomads were ignored, however. The rationale underlying this distribution of national resources was clear: Kountché's authoritarian government redistributed portions of the uranium revenues in such a way as to ensure the stability of its regime—that is, to those groups that could not easily be controlled if they were dissatisfied with the regime's practices. This mode of resource allocation was compromised, however, with the fall in revenues from uranium as well as the IMF restructuring program imposed on Niger later in part as a result. The drying up of state revenues had reduced the government's margin for maneuver; it was compelled, beginning in 1983, to seek loans from the IMF and to accept its first SAP in 1986.[7]

The deepening of the financial and economic crisis and its corollary, the adjustment program, revealed that the regime no longer possessed the mechanisms and financial means necessary for the maintenance of its system of appropriation and redistribution of revenue. The economic scarcity produced by these events sharpened the tensions and contradictions in society. The new transparency of public-sector management, the first derivative of the reforms undertaken under the framework of the SAP, threatened the privileges of the political class, while the rationalization of the public and parastatal sectors compromised the status of the organized social groups of the modern sector. The reforms required by the international financial institutions created important political stakes, including the very stability of the military regime. The crisis of political power that ensued was closely tied to the persistence of the economic decline in the country and to the attempts of the regime to maintain the status quo in its mode of allocating resources.

The 1987–1990 Period

Upon Kountché's death in November 1987, the Supreme Military Council (Conseil Militaire Suprême, CMS) that had helped him to govern elected General Saïbou (b. 1940) as his successor. While Saïbou had acquired a good reputation for his handling of drought relief in 1974 and 1985, he was otherwise undistinguished. Though a Kountché loyalist and a member of the same Jerma subgroup, he was a compromise candidate. Despite his election, he still had to contend with rivals who enjoyed the backing of powerful military factions. Because he lacked sufficient support from either the military or civilian elements to maintain himself in office over the longer term, Saïbou adopted a strategy that might increase his personal power and consolidate his regime. To these ends he undertook a number of conciliatory measures toward critics and rivals of the Kountché regime. He amnestied all political prisoners, including Hamani Diori (who left for Morocco) and Djibo Bakary. Saïbou urged all Nigeriens who were in exile to return and work for the good of their country. He replaced the military officers serving as prime minister and minister of finance with civilians. He announced proposals for elections to village, district, and regional councils that would permit increased popular participation in government.

Then, in July 1988, Saïbou commissioned the National Development Council (Conseil National de Développement, CND), which had functioned as an interim legislature under Kountché, to draft a new constitution to replace the National Charter adopted by national referendum in June 1987. The draft proposed by the CND was adopted by the Council of Ministers in July 1989 and then endorsed by 99.3 percent of the voters during a referendum in September. Thereby Niger regained a complete constitutional system.

Earlier, in August 1988, Saïbou had ended the fourteen-year ban on political organizations by announcing the formation of a new ruling party, the National

Movement for a Development Society (Mouvement National pour une Société de Développement, MNSD). Although Saïbou reiterated his opposition to the immediate reestablishment of a multiparty system, he declared that it was possible to have pluralism within a single party. In May 1989 the constituent congress of the MNSD elected a High Council of National Orientation (Conseil Supérieur d'Orientation Nationale, CSON) to replace the CMS, whose role Saïbou had already reduced in practice. After electing Saïbou as MNSD president, the congress decided that he would be the sole candidate for a national assembly that would replace the CND. Thus during the elections on December 10, 1989, 99.5 percent of the voters endorsed Saïbou as president for a seven-year term and a single list of ninety-three MNSD deputies. The president began the country's second republic by an extensive reorganization of the council of ministers under which he abolished the post of prime minister, thus becoming the head of government himself as well as head of state. At the same time, he relinquished the post of interior minister to a civilian appointee.

Saïbou's measures to conciliate rivals, to soften the harsher aspects of the regime inherited from Kountché (*décrispation* in current terminology), to promote popular participation, and to extend constitutional government, contain elements of liberalization and even democratization. Saïbou nevertheless was aiming primarily at increasing his grip on power within an authoritarian regime rather than changing its character. Moreover, for the time being, Saïbou and his associates within the MNSD controlled both the executive and legislative branches of government—but, as we shall see, not without serious challenges.

Another important aim of Saïbou's measures was improvement of his regime's standing with the international financial community so that he could obtain additional funds to offset the loss of income from uranium. An apparent liberalization thus represented an attempt to win the favor of the principal lenders and donors. The problem for Saïbou was that aid had strings attached. Key measures in the revised SAP of 1989 to restore financial health to the state were bound to encounter resistance from such organized social groups as civil servants, teachers, students, mine workers, and employees of parastatal organizations, who refused (and still refuse) to pay for the costs of adjustment. These measures included reduction of the numbers of government employees, salaries, and benefits; sale of most of the ten state corporations and eighteen parastatals and elimination of their redundant employees; cuts in the numbers of higher education graduates recruited for the civil service as well as the introduction of competitive examinations; and reduction in the percentage of the education budget spent for secondary and higher education in order to increase opportunities at the primary level, particularly in rural areas. Not surprisingly, the austerity measures that the regime adopted to satisfy the lenders led to strikes, violence, and loss of life on several occasions during 1990 (particularly in February and November). Whereas the Kountché regime had possessed the means effectively to repress these privileged groups when it considered their demands excessive, Saïbou did not.

Unable both to appease the protesters and to maintain the measures necessary for continued external assistance, Saïbou turned to political reform. In June 1990, following a new wave of strikes, the CSON announced that the constitution would be amended to permit a transition to political pluralism. In November, faced with renewed industrial action, Saïbou announced that, on the basis of the recommendations of a constitutional review commission, a multiparty system would be established. He also promised that less stringent austerity measures would be adopted in consultation with Niger's international creditors. Pending constitutional revision (which took place in April 1991), new political parties would be registered provisionally.

Following the example of other francophone African states in crisis, Saïbou announced that a national conference would be held during 1991 to determine the country's future political direction. In addition, municipal officials and development advisers would be elected by universal suffrage in late 1991, and multiparty elections would take place in early 1992. Saïbou would remain in office, but his powers would be reviewed.

These political reforms indicated that Saïbou had failed to obtain the popular backing for which he had hoped and that the armed forces could no longer be relied upon as they had under Kountché to repress protesters against the regime's policies and practices. Proof of the military's growing disunity was the announcement in March 1991 that military officers were being withdrawn from positions in the government, including the council of ministers and the administration of the seven regions (*départements*).[8]

Thus the tumultuous events of 1990 and early 1991 irremediably compromised the authoritarian regime of Ali Saïbou and brought about a major upheaval in the configuration of power in Niger. In these circumstances several questions may be asked. Did the process of political reforms that resulted give way to a new distribution of power? Have important new political actors emerged? Have these changes made Niger a genuinely more representative and democratic polity? For answers to these questions we may turn now to the national conference of 1991 and its aftermath.

The National Conference and the Elections of 1991–1993

The National Conference

The transition towards a democratic regime marked the emergence of the civil society on the political scene. After seventeen years of a military regime preceded by fourteen years of single-party rule, the national conference, held from July 29 to November 3, 1991, proved to be a powerful instrument for initiating political reforms, upsetting the long-standing distribution of power in Niger. To assess the scope of political change the conference accomplished, at least three questions must be addressed:

1. Did the representation of the various social and ethnic groups at the national conference reflect changes in the previous distribution of power among these groups?
2. To what extent was the distribution of political power that had been observable in the ancien régime affected by the outcome of the national conference?
3. Do the resolutions ratified by the national conference reflect a questioning of the inequitable distribution of revenues practiced by the former political regime?

The Representation of Groups. The national conference opened at the end of July 1991 in a climate of extreme political uncertainty stemming from a general sense that the Saïbou regime lacked legitimacy. The regime had lost its credibility through its repression of the student demonstrations in 1990 and through its socially devastating economic policies, which had evoked the wrath of the trade unions.

In fact, the Union of Nigerien Workers' Unions (Union des Syndicats des Travailleurs du Niger, USTN) and the Union of Nigerien Scholars (Union des Scolaires Nigériens, USN) were the main social forces to confront state power and to bring its legitimacy into question; these two social groups were the first to call for a political change,[9] and they constituted the sole organized opposition to an increasingly weakened state in Niger. The initiation of multiparty politics and the Saïbou government's conceding to the national conference therefore noticeably reinforced the credibility of this social "counterpower." Before 1990 the USTN had been an artificial institution created by the state to reinforce its own power rather than a union of protest.[10] At the time of the conference, however, both the trade unions and the student movement appeared as leaders of the rank-and-file protesters and as the uncontested leaders of the movement in favor of reformulating Niger's political institutions.

Indeed, the percentage of delegates loyal to the USTN and the USN in the national conference was far larger than the percentage of the general population that the two organizations represented.[11] While most of the members of the USTN are drawn from the 39,000 civil servants, the USN represented only 6.3 percent of the population of secondary school age and 0.7 percent of the population of university age.[12]

On the day after the promulgation of the Charter of Political Parties, a law defining their statutes and functions, in May 1991, there was a rapid multiplication of the number of parties.[13] Several of them undoubtedly owed their existence to the fact that, although only formally organized groups would be admitted to the conference, any accredited party had the right to participate.[14] The disappearance, at the end of the national conference, of at least nine of the twenty-four parties that participated in its proceedings lends support to this interpretation.

The number of delegates allotted to the parties (fourteen per party) did not correspond, in most cases, to their real importance in terms of electoral clientele.

Moreover, with the exception of the regional associations of party chiefs, a number of the parties relied on a single electoral base that included the union and student organizations. Unlike the old parties, including the PPN, the Democratic Union of Progressive Forces–Sawaba (Union Démocratique des Forces Progressistes–Sawaba, UDFP-Sawaba), and the MNSD, the parties of recent creation possessed a limited organizational embryo outside Niamey. In addition, at the time of the conference, these parties had not made their programs known or even established political platforms.

On the basis of the feeble number of delegates allotted to the rural population, it appears that this group, given its numerical weight in the country's population, was clearly underrepresented at the national conference. In effect, the rural population found itself represented only by the other group associations. The latter included notably the Association of Traditional Chiefs, the Women's Association of Niger, the Association of Nigeriens Abroad, and the cooperative associations. The government saw itself granted a hundred seats for members of the Council of Ministers, the judiciary, the National Assembly, and the administration. Finally, the workers of the informal sector, including agricultural workers, subsistence peasants, and herders, were also left out of the political reform process, despite the fact that their activities account for 80 percent of Niger's economy.

The elected members of the presidium charged with directing the proceedings of the conference came principally from the university, syndicalist, and student milieux, though a few functionaries and merchants were also included. The conference was presided over by Professor André Salifou of the University of Niamey.[15] The absence of members of the old political class from this body is noteworthy.

The rebalancing of the forces in favor of the opposition led by the unions and students was also accompanied by a transformation of the relations among Niger's ethnic groups at the political level. For example, the nine-member presidium contained six Hausa members but only one Jerma. This composition expresses an active participation of the members of the Hausa ethnic group in the process of constitutional revival in a country in which the Jerma have played the most decisive role in the direction of the country since independence. Likewise, the Democratic and Social Convention (Convention Démocratique et Sociale, CDS), which would obtain good results in the 1993 elections, was prominent in the deliberations of the conference. The CDS, in turn, had its principal seats at Zinder and Maradi, regions dominated by the Hausa.

A New Distribution of Power.   The army as an institution was kept out of the conference and, in practice, found itself removed from the political scene during the entire period of transition. After 1974, the Kountché regime had granted supremacy to the military over civilians in politics. For example, the posts of "prefect," a government representative at the territorial level,[16] were exclusively reserved for military men. As Niger is a vast territory, the prefects had charge of security issues in their departments and thus constituted one of the keys to the stability of the military regime. These posts proved to be strategic positions for the control of food aid and funds allocated by external lenders to promote rural development.

Despite the entry of civilians into the Council of Ministers and the designation of a prime minister beginning in 1983, however, the military presence in political circles was not immediately eliminated. Even when Saïbou began the process of liberalization, he evoked the main ideas of the constitution of the Second Republic, declaring: "From now on, we reject without appeal the principle of multipartyism in Niger as we affirm as irrevocable the presence of the military in the political and administrative apparatus."[17]

The status of the Nigerien Armed Forces (Forces Armées Nigériennes, FAN) at the conference thus reflected a profound change in the traditional distribution of power. Before 1991 it would have been unthinkable not to consider the FAN as a determining political force in any process of political reform. At the national conference, though, the army representatives found themselves in the category of observer delegates;[18] moreover, when the time came to vote, they were outnumbered by the minorities forming the group of associations. The muzzling of the army in the debates on constitutional revival was reaffirmed through Article Six of the Charter of Political Parties, which explicitly forbade the military from endorsing a specific party.[19]

In the period preceding the conference, the army was publicly disassociated from the process, but in face of the threats made by the USTN and the USN calling for civil disobedience, and in order to counter the danger of schism in its ranks, the headquarters of the FAN finally sent representatives. At the conference, these representatives had to reply publicly to charges concerning the responsibility of the army in the confrontation with students in February 1990 and in its actions in response to the uprisings of Tuareg rebels.[20] The testimony of those questioned in these two affairs, among whom were the president and the chief of staff, and the incrimination of those of high rank (in the killing of students and the summary executions of Tuaregs), drew attention to past abuses by the military. The revelation of serious crimes, including diversion of public funds and human rights abuses, served to undermine the myth of the integrity and the invincibility of military power.

The removal of President Saïbou was demanded with great insistence by the USN as well as by several marginal parties such as the Revolutionary Socialist Party (Parti Socialiste Révolutionnaire, PSR), the Union of the Masses for Democratic Action (Union des Masses pour une Action Démocratique, UMAD), and the Union for Democracy and Social Progress (Union pour la Démocratie et le Progrès Social, UDPS). The UDPS, whose leadership was composed largely of Tuaregs, sought to remove Saïbou from office for his role in the "affair of Tchintabaraden," whereas the USN wished to avenge the students killed during the 1990 demonstrations.

The position taken by the USN in concert with the smaller parties proved, however, to be the minority view. The other groups and parties preferred to keep Saïbou in office, serving in an essentially ceremonial capacity, until new elections could be held. In doing so the delegates at the conference recalled that President Saïbou had been the initiator of the first liberalization of the regime inherited from Kountché and that, after having conceded multipartyism, he had not sought to thwart the proceedings of the conference.

The decisions taken by the national conference, including the dissolution of the Saïbou government and of the National Assembly as well as the reduction of the powers of the head of state,[21] nevertheless illustrated the will of the participants to establish a break with the past. The delegates to the conference sought to strip the existing political class of its control and to avoid having individuals again utilize the prerogatives of power to preserve their offices or to ensure their reelection. Prudence in this regard extended to the point of forbidding the president of the re-public, the prime minister of the transition, and the president of the High Council of the Republic from offering their candidacies in the presidential elections.[22]

In these circumstances, the nomination of a prime minister became the first priority, eclipsing the debates on the lamentable economic situation and on the urgency of redefining the principles of social equity in public expenditures. Amadou Cheiffou,[23] a Peul from Maradi and a delegate of the Association of Nigeriens Abroad, quickly emerged as a strong compromise candidate between the two large ethnic groups. Another of his assets was his having had no previous involvement in Niger's politics. Cheiffou succeeded in gaining the support of the USTN, one of the most influential groups at the conference. He finally won the prime ministership with the support of five groups (the governmental group voted against him and the USN abstained).

The choice of an inexperienced individual with little knowledge of the affairs of the state demonstrated the opposition's suspicion toward the old political class, including every person suspected of having maintained relations with the government authorities or with the MNSD, the former single party. This sectarianism, however, despite its radical exterior, presented intrinsic limits, for it was difficult to find a competent replacement who had not directly or indirectly benefited from the largesse of the old regime.

The government of transition, though directed by Cheiffou, whose mandate was fixed at fifteen months, also included a High Council of the Republic elected by the delegates of the conference and presided over by Chairman Salifou. This body was designed to replace the dissolved Chamber of Deputies and to ensure that the tran-sition government conformed to the decisions taken by the national conference.[24] In effect, it was an organ of surveillance as much as interim legislature.

The Reorientation of Economic Policies. The national conference indulged in a detailed review of the events brought to its attention, sorting out the political and economic crimes that marked the preceding regimes with a fine-toothed comb. Though originally scheduled to last for thirty-eight days, the conference ultimately entailed ninety-eight days of proceedings. The technical files concerning urgent matters of economic policy were thus left aside for three months.

In September 1991 the budgetary situation of the state already appeared dire, the most urgent aspect of which was the payment of the monthly salaries of civil servants, for which insufficient funds were available. Yet the signs foreshadowing the near bankruptcy of the state were ignored. The identification of the various diversions and embezzlements of funds had led the national conference delegates to envisage the recovery of the goods and properties that had been obtained illicitly. This created the illusion in the minds of the majority of the delegates that the sums that would thus be recovered would resolve the budgetary problems of the state, enabling them to avoid the structural adjustment measures of the second SAP (1990–1993). The actual course of events, however, showed the inanity of such a solution.

The specialized commissions[25] created at the conference pursued their mandates vigorously, but often without the assistance of expertise in their domains. The conference produced a document called "List of Responsibilities" (*Cahier des charges*), recording the policies mandated by the conference and designed to serve as beacons for the future transition government. This document, which assumed rather the appearance of a list of demands, was adopted in the last ten days of the conference without any meaningful debate.

One month before the end of the proceedings of the conference, the delegates had heard a straightforward summary on the budgetary situation of the state. They learned that the funds available in the treasury amounted only to 58 million CFA francs, to which one could add the 7 million francs from the Office of Posts and Telecommunications (Office des Postes et Télécommunications, OPT). This sum fell far short of the state's financial needs as outlined in the proposals of the specialized commissions: These amounted to some 20 *billion* CFA francs in new expenditures, with only 6 billion in foreseeable new revenues.

The treasury representative emphasized that personnel expenses alone absorbed more than 60 percent of the fiscal receipts of the state. The total for salaries, along with the scholarships and the maintenance expenses of students (three budgetary items that the unions and the students judged untouchable) thus weighed heavily on the state budget. The representative also revealed the extent of the budgetary deficit, which had increased from 68.6 billion to 82 billion CFA francs due to the extra expenses added by the national conference. In short, the state had to reexamine the level of its expenditures or look for ways to generate new revenues.

Since the arrival of multipartyism and the conference's suspension of the second SAP in the face of strong union opposition, external donors had suspended all forms of budgetary aid. This external financing had proved vital during the first SAP (1987–1990) to maintain some semblance of a balanced budget[26] Needless to say, the suspension of such aid seriously affected the state's public finances. In cooperation with the World Bank and the IMF, France had provided substantial financial support to the budget of the Nigerien state.[27] Since the mid-1970s, French policies were determined by the desire to secure French access to uranium, which it bought in Niger for a higher price than on the world market. The fall of the world price of uranium and the end of the Cold War substantially changed the interests of France in Niger. In addition, the worsening of the deficit of public finances rendered France's budgetary support much more expensive. In these circumstances, and in spite of its support of the national conference (which it financed with the assistance of Germany), France aligned itself with the international lending institutions. This explains why during this period, unlike in the past, France was hesitant to supply additional credits. The figures divulged by the treasury to the conference revealed that civil service salary requirements and other treasury payments had been met only by recourse to forced borrowings from such public and parastatal concerns as the OPT since the start of the transition period. Meanwhile, the accumulation of arrears mounted.

If the delegates were little informed of these stakes at the start of the conference, the Treasury clearly demonstrated the need to revise the nature of state expenditures over the following months. The Treasury called on the conference delegates to reevaluate the degree of realism of the recommendations made by the specialized committees. To initiate such reforms, however, would have required that the two most influential groups within the conference agree to make concessions towards a more equitable reallocation of resources. Such a reallocation would have been in favor of the other social strata that had alone sustained the costs of the budgetary compressions: the workers of the informal sector, the unemployed, the peasants, and the stock raisers. Yet within the education commission, the students and teachers had already rejected every measure likely to lead to a longer vacation in the primary schools, a reduction of scholarships in higher education, or the abandonment of prerecruitment in the civil service. The members of this commission reiterated the state's support for a strategy of basic education for all on the condition that its implementation not be made to the detriment of secondary and higher education. The members of the commission also made explicit reference to the program of sectoral adjustment in education financed by the World Bank. If this reform had been ratified, it would have obliged the state to redirect a large part of the budgetary resources devoted to education to the primary level. Objection to this project was what had launched the student demonstration that ended tragically in February 1990.

Budgetary expenses per student at the university level in Niger were fifteen times greater than those devoted to pupils at the primary level.[28] Of these resources allocated to higher education, a large part was devoted to scholarships and maintenance costs. The level of enrollment at the primary level in Niger reached only 29 percent of those eligible to attend, compared with an average of 52 percent for the Sahel countries and 77 percent for the rest of Africa.[29] Consequently, taking account of the meager resources available for education, in particular for the rural population, these expenditures were benefiting the urban population and the most economically favored social strata to a greater degree.

Under the impetus of the unions and of the USN, which judged the expenditures for personnel and scholarships to be irreducible, the national conference refused to consider any reduction whatsoever in the salary total or any cutback in personnel.[30] Consequently, it endorsed the proposals expressed in the *Cahier des charges* on the maintenance of the existing distribution of state resources.

The adoption of the *Cahier des charges,* which sanctioned the rejection of any SAP and denied any cuts in certain state budgetary items, well illustrated the strength of the opposition. Antiregime parties, unions, and students all knew quite well how to secure their own interests and maintain the status quo in matters of state expenditures where it suited them. In this sense, the decisions made by the conference did not constitute a break with the old regime that had preserved the benefits and privileges of the civil service and organized social groups during the first SAP, even to the detriment of the majority of the population.[31]

In sum, the national conference reconfirmed the loss of political hegemony of the Jerma and accelerated the diminution of the role of the army that had begun in 1990 effectively stripping it of political power. But this shake-up in the political class was achieved in parallel with the maintenance of the status quo in basic economic policies.

The Elections

At the end of the national conference the configuration of power was noticeably modified; the members of the ancien régime were dispossessed of legislative power and ousted from executive power. At first glance, the replacement of the old political class seemed inevitable. Yet there was still cause to question the opposition's real capacity to confront the single party outside the structure of the national conference. The more or less representative distribution of delegates at the conference gave the illusion of an opposition more powerful than it actually was. A consensus seemed to exist in Niger on the need for political changes, but it was far from assured that one of the opposition parties could acquire the political strength to gain a majority of the vote in the legislative elections. All parties were to some extent victims of the limited size of their electoral clientele and their lack of widespread presence throughout the country; rather, each tended to defend the interests of only a tiny minority.

In these circumstances, the determining element that sealed the result of the electoral consultations in Niger was the schism occurring within the MNSD, the former single party. The election of Saïbou by universal suffrage in 1989 had muted the perceptible internal struggles since the death of Kountché. When a congress had been convened in March 1991 to reconfigure the MNSD in light of Niger's new multiparty system, rival factions appeared in full light for the first time. The first faction became identified with Mamadou Tanja, a lieutenant colonel of the FAN who had twice served as minister of the interior; he benefited from the support of powerful merchants of Maradi. The other faction aspiring to the party leadership was personified by Moumouni Djermakoye. A retired colonel and a dignitary of the ancien régime, Djermakoye had been minister of foreign affairs and a member of every government until 1988, at which time he was named ambassador to Washington and to the United Nations. Nonetheless, Saïbou, who had gained numerous supporters within the party and the army, where he enjoyed great popularity, was able to hold on and was renewed in his post. The length of the congress, however, which was initially scheduled for two days but actually lasted for a week, indicated the relentlessness of the other factions in seeking to draw advantage from the weakness of Saïbou's position.

The national conference's decision to prohibit President Saïbou from running in the presidential elections of 1993 put an abrupt end to his political ambitions and relaunched the struggle for the leadership of the MNSD. At a second congress held in November 1991, Tanja was elected to head the party, and the position of secretary-general was entrusted to the former minister of communications, Hama Amadou. The distribution of the positions within the MNSD reflected the electoral strength of the principal ethnic groups and demonstrated that the members of the MNSD were sensitive to the changing status of ethnic groups within civil society. The candidacy of Tanja, a Peul-Kanuri, constituted an asset in the race for power by symbolizing a form of renewal and a significant break with the past hegemony of the Jerma chiefs within the party.

Djermakoye, having been sidelined in an unequivocal manner, quit the MNSD in order to found his own party, the Nigerien Alliance for Democracy and Progress (Alliance Nigérienne pour la Démocratie et le Progrès, ANDP). Djermakoye's departure created an important breach in the electoral base of the MNSD in the western part of Niger.

After the legislative elections of February 1993, the Nigerien political landscape was defined largely by four large political formations out of the twelve parties that had solicited votes, as the number of seats obtained in the legislative elections testifies (see Table 6.1).

The MNSD succeeded in retaining twenty-nine seats and, without the defection of Djermakoye, doubtless would have obtained an absolute majority in the National Assembly. The distribution of seats tends to suggest that the customary chiefs, without whom no party could have hoped to gain support among the rural electorate in the past, preserved undeniable influence. The Kountché regime was sufficiently conscious of the decisive influence that the chiefs represented that it sought to control the mode of designating them.[32] The pitiful performance of the PPN-RDA and of the UDFP-Sawaba indicated that constituents had largely de-

TABLE 6.1   Nigerien Legislative Election Results, 1993 and 1995

Party	Seats in 1993	Seats in 1995
MNSD	29	29
CDS	22	24
PNDS	13	12
ANDP	11	9
PPN-RDA	2	1
UDFP-Sawaba	2	0
UPDP	2	1
PSDN	1	2
UDPS	1	2
PMT[a]	0	0
PUND	0	3
MDP[b]	0	0
TOTAL	83	83

[a]PMT = Parti des Masses pour le Travail.
[b]MDP = Mouvement pour le Développement et le Panafricanisme.
Sources: Niger, Commission de Supervision des Élections, *Résultats définitifs des élections législatives* (Niamey, March 18, 1993); *Marchés tropicaux et méditerranéens,* March 26, 1993, p. 814; "Niger: Élections législatives anticipées," *Marchés tropicaux et méditerranéens,* January 20, 1995, pp. 136–137.

fected to other parties and that these parties had became vestiges of the past. The CDS, and to a lesser extent the Nigerien Party for Democracy and Socialism (Parti Nigérien pour la Démocratie et le Socialisme, PNDS), effected an important breakthrough through the regional membership of their leaders and their ability to catalyze an anti-MNSD vote, which tilted the balance in several electoral districts. Nonetheless, had the ANDP not split from the MNSD, the opposition would not have been able to overcome its own limits and sweep the former ruling party from power.

After the release of the results of the first round in the presidential elections of February 27, 1993 (see Table 6.2), the opposition parties were obliged to forge an alliance to counter the advance of the MNSD candidate at the time of the second round, set for March 27, 1993.

In the event, nine of the twelve parties that presented candidates in the legislative elections united under the name Alliance of the Forces of Change (Alliance des Forces du Changement, AFC) and agreed to support the head of the CDS, Mahamane Ousmane, for the position of president.[33] In case of victory, the position of prime minister would fall to the head of the PNDS, Mahamadou Issoufou, and the position of president of the National Assembly to the head of the ANDP, Moumouni Djermakoye.[34] The opposition parties did not hesitate to ally with members of the old political class in order to ensure electoral success.

TABLE 6.2   Nigerien Presidential Election Results: First Round, 1993 (1,274,331 votes cast; voter turnout 32 percent)

Political Party	Candidate	Percentage of Vote
MNSD	Mamadou Tanja	34.39
CDS	Mahamane Ousmane	26.78
PNDS	Mahamadou Issoufou	15.59
ANDP	Moumouni Djermakoye	15.09
UPDP	Illa Kané	2.59
PPN-RDA	Oumarou Issoufou	2.01
PSDN	Omar Katselma Taya	1.85
UDFP-Sawaba	Djibo Bakary	1.71

Sources: Niger, Commission de Supervision des Élections. *Résultats provisoires: Présidentielles (1er tour)* (Niamey, March 1993); Canada, Ministère des Affaires Extérieures et du Commerce Extérieur (MAEC), *Rapport de la mission canadienne* (Ottawa, April 1993).

The victory of the coalition with the election of Mahamane Ousmane as president brought to a close a process that had lasted three years, putting an end to authoritarianism in Niger.[35] The acceptance by the members of the ancien régime of the electoral results seemed to confirm their willingness to carry on their political struggle in a pluralist framework from then on as well as their recognition of the principle of a loyal opposition capable of regaining power. In the opinion of international observers, the voting took place without constraint or intimidation at virtually all of the polling places.[36] In this sense, the electoral process in Niger indicated respect for democratic rules and a restored freedom of political expression, and the manner in which it took place could only reinforce the country's new democratic institutions.

Yet the strategy adopted by the opposition in the second round of voting for the presidency suggests that the changes that took place in the process of democratization had more to do with the reversal of alliances within the dominant class and the groups associated with power rather than with wholesale enfranchisement of previously excluded groups. The traditional and military elites were sidelined to the benefit of the technocrats and their allies. The enlargement of the numbers of groups participating that accompanied this rearrangement did permit some social groups to increase their influence. Yet these changes did not modify the relations of state power with the rest of the population, who remained marginalized in terms of political representation.

The 1993–1995 Period

The first priority for the coalition represented in the government of Prime Minister Issoufou was the economic crisis. In 1993 Nigerien state expenditures reached a total close to 100 billion CFA francs, or double the state's receipts of the time.[37]

This situation necessitated the resumption of negotiations with the World Bank and the International Monetary Fund for new loans, and these donors made the aid grants conditional upon the signing of a new SAP.

To become eligible once more for a confirmation agreement from the Bretton Woods institutions, the Nigerien government agreed to improve the collection of taxes and to limit public spending, including salaries. Niger had to satisfy these two prerequisites in order to transform the confirmation agreement into an economic and financial Policy Framework Paper. However, neither of the two objectives was attained by the government, and, as a result, the negotiations for ratifying this document were terminated. Significant overspending in the salaries category of the 1994 budget took place as a result of the increases of 5 to 12 percent granted to the employees of the public and parapublic sectors. Indeed, after the announcement of the devaluation of the CFA franc decided upon in January 1994, the government of Prime Minister Issoufou had to face a strong demand from the unions for salary increases of 50 to 70 percent as compensation for their loss of purchasing power. Judging the increases conceded by the government to be insufficient, the USTN in June 1994 launched a strike appeal. This strike, which lasted two months, together with periodic work stoppages throughout the rest of the year, paralyzed the Nigerien economy as well as the functioning of the state. These developments contributed greatly to the climate of political uncertainty that led the World Bank to break off the negotiations undertaken with the Nigerien authorities, thus depriving Niger of desperately needed sources of external financing.[38]

In this context, the outcome of the confrontation that had not ceased to develop between the USTN and the elected government was entirely predictable. The constant pressure applied by the unions throughout the whole year unsettled the regime and led to the calling of legislative elections in January 1995. But this destabilization of the new political class by the old opponents of the authoritarian regime was magnified by the attitude adopted by the elected representatives.

To comprehend fully the scope of this process, it is useful to review the political factors that precipitated the holding of new elections. In the first place, the opposition parties took advantage of the confrontations between the unions and the government in order to present, in September 1994, a motion of censure against the government. Even though this motion was defeated, it seriously undermined the credibility of Prime Minister Issoufou. His resignation a short time later obliged his party, the PNDS, to withdraw from the governing coalition. The isolation of the PNDS, which at its creation had been extensively supported by the unions, clearly shows the circumstantial nature of the regrouping of the coalition in 1993. It also illustrates the degree of opportunism shown by the representatives of the political parties sitting in the National Assembly.

The new prime minister named by President Ousmane, Abdoulaye Souley, who had been minister of commerce in the preceding cabinet, quickly found himself in a very difficult position when the PNDS, in October 1994, joined the parliamentary opposition rallied around the MNSD. As a result, the National Assembly was dissolved on October 17, 1994, by President Ousmane following another vote of censure against the government.

The campaign for the legislative elections of January 1995 occurred when the country was facing an economic and social crisis. But even in this atmosphere the campaign did not attract very much interest from the population as a whole. Neither the proposals made by the candidates nor the demands of the unions drew much of a response from the rest of the population. The opposition led by the MNSD gained a majority of the eighty-three National Assembly seats with forty-six elected; of this total, the MNSD had twenty-nine, the PNDS twelve, the Nigerien Party for Unity and Democracy (Parti Nigérien pour l'Unité et la Démocratie, PUND[39]) three, the Union of Democratic and Progressive Patriots (Union des Patriotes Démocrates et Progressistes (UPDP) one, and the PPN one. Table 6.1 shows that the vote was still polarized around the MNSD (the former single party) and the CDS of President Ousmane. But the game of the alliances in the 1995 election was played to the advantage of the MNSD, which was able to form a governmental coalition. The parties in the presidential camp are the CDS, the ANDP, the Social Democratic Party of Niger (Parti Social Démocrate Nigérien, PSDN), and the UDPS.[40] The sole significant element of the evolution of political habits concerned the Tuareg community, which had been politically marginalized since 1946; this group was now represented by the five deputies of the PUND and the UDPS.[41]

The return of the MNSD to power ought not be interpreted as a retreat from democratic life in Niger. The great volatility of alliances that resulted from these circumstances reveals the nature and composition of the Nigerien political parties. The members of these political formations are mainly from the dominant class, and their sole ambition is to accede to power. Taken as a whole, the political parties lack defined programs, do not respond in their actions to any precise electorate, and act only in terms of their immediate interest. One of the most enlightening examples of the inanity of partisanship that has characterized political life in Niger since the first legislative elections is the call for civil disobedience launched by the parliamentary opposition in April 1994.[42] This coalition, which was composed of thirty-three deputies of the MNSD, UPDP, and the UDFP-Sawaba, accused the government of discrimination against candidates belonging to their political groups when filling positions of responsibility. The boycott of the work of the National Assembly and the call for civil disobedience appear excessive in relation to the issue at stake.

This behavior on the part of the political parties may be explained in large part by the weakness of civil society and reminds us that democratic consolidation in Niger cannot be dissociated from its reinforcement. Only a more developed civil society can compel an elected government to govern in the general interest and furnish it with the means to face down group interests that pursue objectives contradictory to the interests of the majority of the population.[43]

Conclusion

In the Nigerien case, one of many in which new regimes have been brought to power in the wave of democratization that swept sub-Saharan Africa during the 1990–1993 period, the context in which a far-reaching transformation took place was closely linked to the economic crisis that this country had known since 1983. The financial crisis in Niger created an urgent need for economic reform in Nigerien state policies, which in turn started a growing opposition based on a debate about the nature of these reforms. In effect, however, the political stakes raised by the application of adjustment policies tended to compromise the benefits of the organized groups of the modern sector as much as the privileges of the traditional political class. Thus this struggle at the economic level gave rise in large part to the transition towards a pluralist system and the remaking of the political class in Niger.

The analysis in this chapter reveals that the political struggle that was initially carried on among opposing factions within the traditional political class evolved noticeably during the course of the national conference. Notably, at the moment of the elections the alliance among the members of these factions and the opposition parties played the key role in ousting the former single party from power.

The overhaul of the political class has certainly led to a new balance on the political scene and marks the attainment of power by some new social categories. At present, however, the power-holders in the regime do not seem to have distinguished themselves from their predecessors in matters of fundamental economic policies. In the case of Niger, then, democratization has not yet led to much greater social and economic equity.

Notes

1. Robert B. Charlick, *Niger: Personal Rule and Survival in the Sahel* (Boulder: Westview Press, 1991), pp. 3–6, 89–128; Edith Hodgkinson, "Niger: Economy," *Africa South of the Sahara, 1996* (London: Europa, 1996), pp. 694–698; Kathleen Mulligan-Hansel, "Niger: The Second Republic," *Africa Contemporary Record* 22, *1989–1990* (New York: Africana Publishing Company, 1994), pp. B94–B102.

2. The MSA was the result of the fusion in 1956 of the Nigerien Democratic Union (Union Démocratique Nigérienne, UDN), directed by the union leader Djibo Bakary, and the Nigerien Action Bloc (Bloc Nigérien d'Action, BNA), constituted around one of the traditional chiefs, Issoufou Djermakoye.

3. Mamadou Djibo, "Les transformations politiques au Niger (1958–1960)" (Ph.D. diss., University of Montreal, 1992); Charlick, *Niger*, pp. 33–52.

4. The percentages of the main ethnic groups in Niger are as follows: Hausa, 53.5 percent; Jerma, 21.2 percent; Peul, 10.4 percent; Tuareg, 9.3 percent; Kanuri, 4.3 percent; and Toubou, 0.5 percent.

5. Finn Fuglestad, *A History of Niger, 1850–1960* (Cambridge, England: Cambridge University Press, 1983), p. 191.

6. Myriam Gervais, "Les enjeux politiques des ajustements structurels au Niger, 1983–1990," *Canadian Journal of African Studies* 26 (1992):231.

7. Ibid., p. 236.

8. Pierre Engelbert, "Niger: Recent History," *Africa South of the Sahara, 1996,* pp. 687–693; Charlick, *Niger,* pp. 72–88; Mulligan-Hansel, "Niger," pp. B94–B102.

9. Union des Syndicats des Travailleurs du Niger, *Lettre du Secrétaire Général à Son Excellence le Président de la République du Niger,* Niamey, February 25, 1991.

10. The National Union of Nigerien Workers (Union Nationale des Travailleurs du Niger, UNTN), which would later become the Union of Nigerien Workers' Unions (Union des Syndicats des Travailleurs du Niger, USTN), did not resort to striking before 1990, unlike the national union, which formed a common front with the students to demand multipartyism and the holding of a national conference.

11. The numbers of representatives from the various groups present were as follows: Union of Nigerien Workers' Unions (Union des Syndicats des Travailleurs du Niger, USTN), 100 delegates; Union of Nigerien Scholars (Union des Scolaires Nigériens, USN), 100 delegates; Nonaffiliated unions (two per union), 20 delegates; Patronat, 100 delegates; 24 political parties (fourteen per party), 336 delegates; 69 associations (two per association), 138 delegates; government, 100 delegates. In addition, observers were present from the Central administration, the Nigerien Armed Forces (Forces Armées Nigériennes, FAN), International financial institutions, the League of Human Rights, Amnesty International, and the Association of African Attorneys (Association des Juristes Africains).

12. Institut de Recherche en Éducation (hereafter IREDU), *Document de référence pour la réunion des Ministres de l'Éducation des pays du Sahel, Bamako, 15–18 janvier 1990* (Paris: IREDU-CNRS, 1990), p. 6.

13. As of June 1992, of forty parties originating during the democratization process, only sixteen were officially recognized and permitted to present candidates for the legislative and presidential elections.

14. Djibril Abarchi, *Caractérisation politique: Caractérisation du droit de la personne* (Montreal: Centre Canadien d'Études et de Coopération Internationale, 1993), p. 14.

15. André Salifou is one of the founders of the Union of Democratic and Progressive Patriots (Union des Patriotes Démocrates et Progressistes, UPDP), which was authorized to participate in the national conference.

16. The administrative map of Niger is made up of seven departments—Dosso, Tillabery, Tahoua, Agadez, Maradi, Zinder, and Diffa—as well as the urban community of Niamey.

17. Abarchi, *Caractérisation politique*, pp. 9–11.

18. Niger, "Acte fondamental nos I et II de la conférence nationale: Statuts et règlements intérieurs," *Journal Officiel* (Niamey), August 1, 1991.

19. Niger, "Acte fondamental n° XXIV/CV (Portant Charte des partis politiques)," *Conférence nationale* (Niamey), November 3, 1991.

20. Sporadic attacks fomented by Tuareg groups had as targets administrative positions or the sites of projects in the regions of Tahoua and Agadez in northern Niger. The conference paid particular attention to a bloody confrontation at Tchintabaraden in May 1990, in which a subprefecture was targeted and sixty-three people, including eleven policemen, were killed. Though it is unknown how many Tuaregs died in the reprisals, the figure 200 was widely circulated. The Tuaregs who went before the courts in April 1991 were acquitted.

21. Niger, *Conférence nationale*, 1991.

22. Niger, "Projet de constitution de la IIIᵉ République," Haut Conseil de la République (Niamey, 1991).

23. Before his nomination to the position of prime minister of the transitional government, Amadou Cheiffou, trained as an engineer, was a regional representative in Dakar of the Organization of International Civil Aviation (Organisation de l'Aviation Civile Internationale, OACI) for Central and West Africa.

24. Abarchi, *Caractérisation politique*, p. 2.

25. The seven specialized commissions were: the Commission of Political Affairs, the Commission of Economic Affairs, the Sociocultural Commission, the Commission of Crimes and Abuses, the Commission of Education, the Commission of Rural Development, and the Commission of Communication.

26. Gervais, "Les enjeux politiques des ajustements structurels au Niger," p. 240.

27. Myriam Gervais, "Structural Adjustment in Niger: Implementations, Effects, and Determining Political Factors," *Review of African Political Economy* 63 (1995):38.

28. D. Berstecher and R. Carr-Hill, *Primary Education and Economic Recession in the Developing World Since 1980* (Paris: UNESCO, 1990).

29. IREDU, *Document de référence pour la réunion des Ministres de l'Éducation des pays du Sahel*, p. 4.

30. The money spent on wages increased during the transition period from 34.5 billion CFA francs in 1989 to 38.99 billion CFA francs in 1992, as the number of state employees went up from 36,979 to 39,000. This increase weighed heavily on the state budget, since the wages, which already represented 69 percent of the tax revenues in 1989, represented 94 percent of the tax revenues in 1992. Niger, Ministère des Finances, *Loi des finances* (Niamey, 1992).

31. Gervais, "Les enjeux politiques des ajustements structurels au Niger," pp. 237–239.

32. Souleymane Abba, "La chefferie traditionnelle en question," *Politique africaine*, no. 38 (June 1990):57–58.

33. A native of Zinder, Ousmane was adviser to the prime minister's cabinet from 1986 to 1990 and became known in the realm of activities of the Committee of Coordination of Democratic Struggles (Comité de Coordination des Luttes Démocratiques, CCLD), which included the unions and the militant parties in favor of democratic change. His party, the CDS, had an important regional base. During the national conference, he was reproached for being too close to the state.

34. "Niger: Moumouni Djermakoye, président de l'Assemblée Nationale," *Marchés tropicaux et méditerranéens*, April 16, 1993, p. 1008.

35. Niger, Cosupel, *Résultats définitifs transmis à la Cour Suprême: Élections présidentielles (2ᵉ tour)*, Niamey, March 29, 1993.

36. Canada, Ministère des Affaires Extérieures et du Commerce Extérieure, *Rapport de la mission canadienne*.

37. Niger, Ministère des Finances, *Lois des finances*, 1993.

38. Gervais, "Structural Adjustment in Niger," p. 39.

39. Though one might expect the acronym for the Parti Nigérien pour l'Unité et la Démocratie to be PNUD, Nigerien usage is PUND.

40. "Niger: Élections législatives anticipées," *Marchés tropicaux et méditerranéens*, January 20, 1995, pp. 136–137.

41. In October 1994 the Nigerien government concluded a peace agreement with the Coordination of Armed Resistance (Coordination de la Résistance Armée, CRA), the representatives of the Tuareg rebellion.

42. "Niger: Appel de l'opposition à la désobéissance civile," *Marchés tropicaux et méditerranéens,* April 22, 1994, p. 822.

43. In February 1995 the National Assembly elected Hama Amadou of the MNSD as prime minister. A year of conflict and deadlock between his government and President Mahamane Ousmane contributed to a military coup on January 27, 1996. The new regime, headed by Colonel Barre Mainassara Ibrahim, arrested the president and the prime minister, banned political parties, suspended the constitution, and created a temporary national council to govern the country. Thereafter, the new regime scheduled new presidential and legislative elections for July 1996. See *Britannica Book of the Year* (Chicago: Encyclopaedia Britannica, 1996), p. 450; Christel Caupin, "Le Niger à la veille de l'élection présidentielle," *Marchés tropicaux et méditerranéens,* June 21, 1996, pp. 1236–1239.

Chapter Seven

The Central African Republic: Political Reform and Social Malaise

THOMAS O'TOOLE

Meaningful political reform in the Central African Republic (CAR), a potentially rich, landlocked country at the heart of the continent, is probably not possible at present. Before democratic reform can actually begin, the country's peoples must first develop a coherent political form that has some relevance to their own historical and cultural realities. The long list of failures of twentieth-century governance in the country suggests that new institutions created whole-cloth out of "imported" principles are distrusted by the people on whom they are imposed.

With the collapse of the authoritarian regimes of Eastern Europe and the Soviet Union and the growing cries from Africa for "democracy" in the late 1980s, some reworking of the system of governance in the CAR seemed possible to a small group of urban, Western-educated Central Africans. A number of professionals, civil servants, and academics began to herald a "renewal" as though democratic institutions had ever really been tried before in the CAR. A little more than a generation earlier, the French had bequeathed the forms of democratic institutions to the country as they ended their direct political control, but democratic institutions were never really established. The history of failure of those "imported" institutions, along with the failure of the other projects and institutions imposed on the people of Central Africa during the past hundred years, makes the prevailing cynicism in the CAR toward political or governmental reform understandable.

If "government" is defined simply as "a group of people having the power, legitimate or not, to govern within the state which consists of both a demarcated territory and a population," then, from independence to the present, the CAR can be said to have had a government.[1] It should not be supposed, however, that a democratically chosen government with accountability of the rulers to their subjects has ever existed. In spite of superficial trappings of constitutional democracy, with rituals of elections patterned on Western models, the government of the CAR has never been democratic. The official political arena in the CAR remains very small. Even with the more open politics of recent years, most decisionmaking of direct importance to most Central Africans occurs within local ethnically based communities rather than in the formal political sectors. The hegemonic groups that control the government in the capital, Bangui, actually play only a small role in the lives of the 80 percent of the population that does not live in this urban center. Though subject to various extortions from lower-level bureaucrats and soldiers, most of the people in the rural areas and small towns avoid contact with the official political system as much as possible.

Simply describing the various CAR governments since 1960 as "one-party," "military," or "authoritarian" regimes, however, has little value. In general, the political bureaucracies, the formal political institutions (where they existed), and the court system in the CAR have always been subjugated to the whims of a small elite.[2] Highly fluid, these ruling cliques were fundamentally variable in membership, incohesive, and haphazard, with idiosyncratic behaviors substituting for coherent programs. Political principles of negotiation, reciprocity, or even ideological preferences were largely lacking. Ranging from neopatrimonial to personal-coercive regimes, the governments of the CAR have always rested on a mixture of clientalism between the heads of state and powerful French patrons on one hand, and similar bonds between the CAR ruling cliques and their ethnic group supporters on the other.[3] A Central African variety of patriarchal patrimonialism that suppressed class conflict and ethnic competition, with the assistance of personalized French support, became the dominant pattern whether specific regimes were military or civilian. To describe the political systems of this country prior to 1993 as "democratic" in any standard sense of the word would have been ludicrous. The ruling elites in all the post-independence regimes paid lip service to democratic forms, but the actual processes and patterns of government were seldom, if ever, democratic.

Moreover, it is unlikely that the end of any given military regime or single-party system in the CAR will usher in an era of democratic legitimacy in any but a most gradual, evolutionary way. The current political culture of the nation has deep roots that are not going to change easily.[4] The ethnic cleavages that have largely been suppressed since the onset of the colonial era have not been eliminated as potent and potentially important political factors. Economic and social development as well as long-term political stability in the CAR requires social and political structures very different from those that have evolved in the country thus far. All the regimes in the CAR, including the present one, it would appear, have been incapable of initiating the long process of sustainable participatory develop-

ment needed to bring about a different, less alienating, more peaceful, and productive Central African Republic.[5] The end of what Jean-François Bayart has
termed the "hegemonic state" is not achieved by one relatively honest election.
Liberal democracy does not, of itself, eliminate patrimonial corruption as an ongoing process, though it may, in time, limit the negative impacts of such corruption and allow the growth of alternative social groups.[6] In time some of these alternative groups could lead to changes in the style of governance, which may be a
first step on a long path toward political systems that are more democratic.

Background: Independence and Neocolonialism

In 1894 France created the territory of Ubangi-Shari out of lands that it had occupied in the forests and grassy plateaux north of the Congo Free State (today's
Zaire). Ubangi-Shari was first administered as a part of the French Congo, which
also included the Middle Congo, Gabon, and, after 1900, Chad.[7] In 1920 Ubangi-
Shari became one of the four territories of French Equatorial Africa, an administrative federation under a governor-general at Brazzaville established to parallel
the federation of French West Africa. Resistance by local populations was brutally
suppressed as European and southwest Asian concessionaires exploited the local
human and natural resources through the 1920s and 1930s. During this period
the French introduced the mandatory cultivation of cotton in order to fund their
administration and limited services.[8]

During World War II Bangui was the Central African headquarters of General
Leclerc's Free French forces. On November 10, 1946, as citizens of the Territoires
d'Outre Mer (French Overseas Territories), the approximately 20,000 Africans allowed to vote in the Ubangi-Shari colony elected the first Ubangian deputy, a
Roman Catholic priest, Barthélémy Boganda, to the French National Assembly
with 9,000 votes. In his first term, though, Boganda became aware that little could
be accomplished in the French assembly for the people of Ubangi-Shari.

While back home in 1948, he consolidated support among African teachers
and truck drivers, and attempted unsuccessfully to set up a marketing cooperative
among African planters of his own ethnicity. His marriage in 1950 to Michelle
Jourdain, a parliamentary secretary of Popular Republican Movement (Mouvement Républicain Populaire, MRP), the French political party, cut him off from
the support of the Catholic hierarchy and left him free to found the Movement
for the Social Evolution of Black Africa (Mouvement pour l'Évolution Sociale de
l'Afrique Noire, MESAN).

Never really a political party in the usual sense, MESAN was a quasi-religious
movement and a rallying point for Ubangian self-identity and pride in response
to white settler racism. Like Leopold Senghor's negritude, MESAN was an affirmation of black humanity.[9] In the MESAN appeal to the population (issued in
Sango, the national lingua franca) for the referendum on membership in the
French Community on September 28, 1958, the major message remained simply

that Africans must be fully accepted as worthy human beings. The affirmation of black humanity for which MESAN leaders called was not African nationalism, but it did include requests for civil rights within the French Community.

Like Leopold Senghor in Senegal, who sought to retain ties between the territories of French West Africa as they moved towards self-government in 1957 and 1958, Boganda campaigned for similar arrangements among the territories of French Equatorial Africa. But his plans were defeated—above all, by the refusal of Gabon, which had seen its revenues transferred for the development of the Middle Congo. Thus Boganda was forced to consider the future of a self-governing CAR linked only to France.[10] From 1946 until his death in an air crash in March 1959, Boganda played a major role in the politics of his country and remained firmly committed to the idea of assimilation; he sought reform within the French Union, rather than independence, up to 1958.[11] The constitution of 1958, creating the Fifth French Republic, provided for the free association of autonomous republics within the French Community, with France as the senior partner. France would retain jurisdiction over international relations, defense, currency, economic and financial policy, policy on strategic raw materials, and, unless specifically excluded by agreement, over higher education, internal and external communications, and supervision of the courts. The president of the French Republic was to be the president of the community's executive council, composed of the prime ministers of the member states and the French ministers concerned with community affairs. A senate composed of members elected indirectly by each community member in proportion to its population and a common high court of arbitration were to complete the government.

As Boganda had feared, the independence granted on August 13, 1960, came to an Ubangi-Shari that was a separate state, with its own government and constitution; the already established administrative entities of French Equatorial Africa were bypassed. This explains many of the difficulties that the leadership of the Central African Republic—and of other individual countries formed from French Equatorial Africa and French West Africa—had in establishing viable state structures. The colonial system had been established with highly centralized administrations directed through Brazzaville and Dakar, with the governments of individual territories having very little actual authority. As a result, the individual states had virtually no autonomous governmental institutions established before independence.[12]

Geographical and historical factors had placed such riverine ethnic groups as the Banziri, Mbaka (Ngbaka), and Yakoma in close contact with the French colonial establishment at the end of the nineteenth century. This gave these riverine or "Ubangian" groups the most continuous contact with the French colonial establishment. Such proximity offered them, in turn, access to external commercial, educational, and political advantages which have persisted to the present.[13] In the nineteenth century these groups had also developed political mechanisms, often based on trading (including slaves) contacts that allowed them quickly to establish networks of patronage-based alliances throughout those areas of the region nominally controlled by the French.[14]

Until 1993, all the country's most prominent twentieth-century public figures were from such riverine groups. Included were Barthélémy Boganda, the "father" of the country; David Dacko, who became the first president of the independent Central African Republic in August 1960; Jean-Bédel Bokassa, who controlled the government from the time of his coup on January 1, 1966, until the French returned Dacko to power on September 21, 1979; and General André Kolingba, who assumed control of the government from Dacko on September 1, 1981. (Kolingba was Yakoma, a group known for its military abilities; the other three leaders were Mbaka.) Even the most persistent opponent of the ruling cliques, Dr. Abel Goumba, who was born and grew up among the Banda at Grimari, is a Banziri. The riverine Banziri, who specialized in fishing, canoeing, and trading, traditionally maintained close ties with the more numerous Banda of the interior. After the explorer Paul Crampel signed a protectorate treaty with the principal Banziri leaders in 1890, various Banziri entered French service. Among them later would be Goumba's father, who served as an interpreter-scribe in the colonial administration in Banda country.[15]

From time to time some members of the urban, Westernized elite refused to belong to the CAR's ruling political cliques. Usually these outsiders challenged the ruling patrimonial cliques as much for reasons that might be labeled "ethnic" as for political and economic reasons. Nevertheless, to be a political power in the CAR throughout the past century one's "white" contacts for economic support were as important as one's "black" supporters to demonstrate at least some semblance of legitimacy. Until 1993, other outsiders—those who were not from the "privileged" riverine groups, such as Ange-Félix Patassé (a Kaba-Souma, or Sara from the northwest) or even Goumba, who had much Banda support—could only challenge the riverine-based patron-client systems but could not dominate them.

The French government was quite content to let these local client-patron networks function as the government of the CAR as long as they did not represent too great a threat to French commercial and military interests or pose too much of an embarrassment to the French government. When a populist government might challenge French commercial interests, as Goumba and his Movement for the Democratic Evolution of Central Africa (Mouvement d'Évolution Démocratique de l'Afrique Centrale, MEDAC) appeared to do in 1960, the French stepped in to support Dacko. Lacking popular support and any firmly established nationwide political party despite the backing of MESAN in March 1959, President Dacko was highly dependent on France for economic and military support. When Dacko's total mismanagement and corruption made it apparent that his regime was coming apart, the French were prepared to assist Commander Henri (also known as Jean) Izamo, a Sara and the head of the gendarmerie, to assume power on New Year's Eve in 1965. But Colonel Jean-Bédel Bokassa ambushed Izamo and seized power for himself.

Even though the French had not chosen Bokassa to replace Dacko at the heart of their client regime, Bokassa's preemptive takeover did not greatly upset French plans. Only after allegations that he had been personally involved in the murder of schoolchildren did he become too much of an embarrassment for the French. Long before that, he had become increasingly corrupt and dictatorial, making himself "Life President" in 1972 and crowning himself emperor at an extravagant coronation—which, incidentally, made a number of French people very rich—in December 1976. Finally, while the emperor was out of the country in September 1979, French paratroopers put Dacko back in power.[16]

From the time of Central Africans' first involvement with the world capitalist system with the slave trade, through the imposition of direct economic intervention by European powers in the late nineteenth century and up to the present, the standard of living for the majority has declined. The pattern has been one of a continual erosion of village economies and a decline in the people's ability to meet basic needs. As the involvement of the Republic in the world economic system grew, so too did the degree of inequality within the society.[17]

Despite its relatively small population (somewhat less than 3.75 million) and a considerable resource base, the CAR is both absolutely and relatively poorer than most other countries.[18] In 1993 the CAR ranked 156th out of 173 nations on the United Nations Development Programme (UNDP) Human Development Index.[19] Less than 13 percent of the population had access to health care facilities and safe water. The per capita GNP has actually declined since independence, and the outlook for the immediate future holds little hope of improvement even if the new political leadership plays a far more positive role in solving problems of mass poverty and increasing employment than any of the previous regimes have. The annual per capita GNP in 1993 was less than US$400, and most Central Africans, living in rural areas at subsistence level, are not even considered in most formal economic calculations.

The Contemporary Political and Economic Crisis

At the end of the 1993 growing season the market system was so disrupted that farmers were unable to sell the relatively small amounts of coffee and cotton they produced. Export crops were rotting in place. Government employees and military personnel had not been paid. Merchants, mostly of Lebanese, Yemenite, Portuguese, and Greek ancestry, were no longer paying taxes and owed the government huge sums.[20]

To understand this crisis, one has to look back to the early 1990s when the World Bank, the International Monetary Fund (IMF), and other Western agencies controlling the CAR economy were continuing to emphasize free-market theories of development and accommodation to capitalist world economies as the solution to the country's economic problems. These theories suggest that the chronic and ever-growing government deficits and mismanagement of the country's key export-earning economic activities are the reasons the country is so poor rather than the inequities of the world system, which impoverish countries like the CAR.[21] The small patrimonial elite, which held political power from the early 1950s until the early 1990s, was largely alienated from the grass roots. This co-opted urban elite became the rather inept political administrators of a neocolonial state.[22] After independence the continued expansion of government expenditures for administration and the spiraling costs of maintaining this African bureaucratic bourgeoisie at ever-higher levels of luxury drained off what little direct investment capital might have been available after the vast majority of profits had been expatriated.[23] Hence the structural adjustment measures mandated by external funding agencies in the early 1990s could not be fully implemented. More radical analysts maintain that critical economic conditions such as those that exist in the CAR have deeper structural causes that transcend internal difficulties. From this perspective, the predominance of France and other Western nations, working behind the scenes in virtually all areas of economic endeavor, has locked the CAR into an ever-worsening downward spiral. Those arguing from these viewpoints suggest that the basic obstacle to economic and political development in the CAR remains the persistent, parasitical subservience of the Central African economy and political elite to French and other Western entrepreneurs and commercial interests. The political and economic ineptness of the Central African leadership into the 1990s is thus understood simply as a symptom of the deeper structural problems of dependency.[24] Little headway has been made in the CAR since independence in overcoming French preponderance and cultural conditioning.

Faced with pressures from financial and political leaders in the United States in the late 1980s, leaders of the World Bank and the IMF increased their mandates for economic restructuring and austerity measures on the CAR government leaders so that the state could achieve solvency and begin to repay debts. IMF, World Bank, and other donor bureaucrats showed only limited sensitivity to the minimum survival needs of the people of the CAR.

Earlier, in the 1980s, the French government had found that it could no longer afford to subsidize the inefficiency, poor management, and lavish lifestyles of the ethnically based and military-dominated government of André Kolingba, which had been in power with little popular support since 1981. Responding to French pressure, Kolingba offered a new constitution calling for a prime minister nominated by the president and ratified by the presidentially appointed Council of Ministers. This constitution was adopted by referendum, and Kolingba was elected president of the republic for six years under a single-party format on November 21, 1986. The Central African Democratic Assembly (Rassemblement Démocratique Centrafricain, RDC) was the vehicle of his control. On July 31, 1987, for the first time in twenty years, legislative elections were held.[25]

The decline of Cold War mindsets allowed the fragile alliances between France (and other Western patrons) and the ruling elite to loosen in the early 1990s.

Rather than to be seen as supporters of authoritarian regimes in Africa, the French began to pressure their African clients to stay ahead of the growing U.S. and German pressure for economic and political liberalization.[26] Kolingba's opponents were emboldened by the 1988 declaration of French President Mitterrand indicating that he was no longer committed to defending African dictators. When Mitterrand went further and tied French aid to democratic reform at the 1990 Franco-African summit at La Baule, opponents of the Kolingba regime realized that French intervention to maintain Kolingba in power was becoming highly unlikely. Non-Yakoma members of the small urban elite, small businesspeople, teachers, and some civil servants became more outspoken in their demands for political and economic reforms.[27] Some students and a few workers also supported these demands.

The Acceleration of Reform

Faced by this small but persistent coalition of opposition forces and considerable external pressure from France, Germany, the United States, the IMF, the World Bank, and even the Roman Catholic Church for political liberalization and democracy in the early 1990s, General Kolingba was forced to take some token steps in the direction of liberalization. Committed, in theory, to inclusive political participation and political freedom, the external patrons, upon which the virtually bankrupt Kolingba regime had previously depended, began to demand that Kolingba participate in the near-universal movement in francophone countries to organize national conferences. With little grassroots support and eroding support from the military, Kolingba was obliged to bend to these pressures.[28]

In the CAR, as in many other places in francophone Africa, popular protests played a role in the initial steps toward democracy, though these were largely unfocused and with rather unclear goals. In 1991 the Coordinating Committee for the Convocation of a National Conference (Comité Coordonnateur pour la Convocation d'une Conférence Nationale, CCCCN), an umbrella opposition group, began demanding a national conference in the CAR. Opposition parties whose leaders were already prominent in the CCCCN formed a new alliance of political groups, the Permanent Council of Opposition Parties (Conseil Permanent des Partis de l'Opposition, CPPO) late the same year. During 1992 General Kolingba faced continual strikes. French-influenced officers and even rank-and-file members of the military began to distance themselves from Kolingba, and the shadow support of Kolingba's puppet party, the RDC, began to unravel as well. As French subsidies declined, student protests and strikes continued, as much over grants and fees as over political issues.[29]

Despite almost unanimous opposition by the elite-based opposition in January 1992, Kolingba appointed Alphonse Blague to set up special committees to prepare a new electoral law, redraw constituencies, and fix rules for all-party talks.

Anxious to keep the process of reform under his control, Kolingba persisted in calling the national conference a "national debate" and arbitrarily arrested opposition leaders. Unwilling to accept the limited participation permitted by Kolingba, opposition forces pushed for a full, sovereign national conference. In the first months of 1992 leaders of the Alliance of Democratic Forces (Concertation des Forces Démocratiques, CFD) and its trade union allies refused to participate in the "national debate" scheduled for August 1–20, 1992.

Only about 100 delegates, mostly Kolingba supporters, attended this stage-managed political event. Peaceful demonstrations by the CFD were met by police brutality, resulting in the deaths of some attendees, including a prominent CFD member. Though the debate continued and some major constitutional proposals were made, the debate gained the Kolingba regime little credibility. With France and the United States adopting a hard line on democratization as a prerequisite for budget aid, opposition groups gained increasing leverage throughout 1992 in pushing for relatively open elections. Rather than to accept the meaningful dialogue and possible reform that might have come from a truly open national conference, Kolingba pushed for elections while he still controlled the media and could count on his eroding patronage-seeking supporters.

At the end of his term in October 1992 Kolingba faced almost certain defeat in the hastily organized first round of presidential and legislative elections. Claiming irregularities and inadequate preparation, Kolingba canceled the elections. Many observers suggested that the cancellation might also have been specifically designed to thwart the one candidate who had not publicly called for the elections, Dr. Abel Goumba. It should also be noted that under Goumba's leadership, the CFD had become a broad coalition of parties and interests, which clearly challenged the narrow ethnic and personal bases of support of all other parties and groups.

In the following months Kolingba scrambled to create an interim government with enough credibility to allow him to stay in power until the elections he had rescheduled for February 1993. In early December 1992 General Timothée Malendoma, a French-trained veteran who, like Jean-Bédel Bokassa, had fought in Indochina and served as minister in both the Bokassa and second Dacko governments, agreed to serve as interim prime minister. A leading figure in the CFD and one who had served six months in prison for opposition to Kolingba, Malendoma had considerable credibility, though he was called upon to head a cabinet in which Kolingba supporters held most key posts. The main opposition groups were wary of a cabinet in which Kolingba supporters held ten portfolios whereas members of opposition parties only held nine. The leaders of the CFD and other parties refused to participate in the government, though members of Malendoma's Civic Forum (Forum Civique, FC) and some other splinter groups did accept posts. A televised speech by General Malendoma on December 28, 1992, in which he complained that Kolingba was trying to run the government through his supporters, put Malendoma back in the good graces of the CFD. Forced to choose between resigning in protest or continuing the struggle, Malendoma was asked by the CFD to remain in office until elections.[30]

Scrambling to avoid a defeat, Kolingba first postponed the elections until April 1993, then tried to put them off until October, but ultimately scheduled them for August. In this way Kolingba hoped to continue avoiding substantive dialogue yet keep protest from reaching a crisis point. But the handwriting on the wall signaling the end of the Kolingba regime was already clear in June.

On June 3, French Minister of Cooperation Michel Roussin, a former paratrooper, withdrew French officials who were helping to maintain the Kolingba regime in power. Among them were Colonel Jean-Claude Mantion, a former commander in chief of Kolingba's mostly Yakoma presidential guard, from his position as Kolingba's special adviser (*conseiller spécial*). Roussin then sent Mantion, who was an officer of the French Direction Générale de la Sécurité Extérieure (DGSE), back to France. Four days later Alain Pallu de Beaupuy, another former DGSE colonel and the French ambassador to the CAR, who had arrived in October 1992 to take charge of this sensitive region (including Chad and Sudan), was also removed. A month before, Pallu's colleague, Lieutenant Colonel Cazemayou, another DGSE officer, who had replaced Mantion as head of the presidential guard, had been embarrassed when his troops held Kolingba hostage until they received long overdue pay.[31]

By the deadline for filing, August 2, 1993, nine candidates had paid the 45 million CFA franc deposit and registered for the August 22 election. Kolingba presented himself as a candidate along with four old hands at the game—François Bozize, David Dacko, Abel Goumba, and Ange-Félix Patassé. The two interim prime ministers, Timothée Malendoma and Enoch Derant Lakoué, were joined by the only woman candidate, the perennial Ruth Roland, and a total unknown, Benoît Likiti.

When provisional results showed Patassé well in the lead and Kolingba eliminated from the second round, the incumbent announced that he would change the electoral law, seemingly preparing to overturn the results. The French reacted within hours and suspended bilateral aid. Even though Patassé had been prime minister under Bokassa for some months in 1976 and had remained in the government until the despot dissolved the cabinet and declared himself emperor in 1978, he was obviously a more popular choice than Kolingba. By the late afternoon Kolingba backed down, abandoned the proposed changes, and said that he would not make any modifications that would upset the peace and friendly ties with Paris.[32]

Patassé received strong support among Sara populations in the northwest of the country along the border with Chad. Many of these votes were cast by Sara refugees from Chad whose language and body markings are identical with those of members of the Sara ethnic group whose homes are in the Central African Republic. With the aid of these votes and those of urban student and worker followers, who continued to perceive him as progressive in spite of his erratic political career, Patassé received 37.32 percent of the votes cast.[33]

Abel Goumba made a strong showing and, with a strong base in Bangui and supported by Nestor Kombo-Naguemot's Liberal Democratic Party (Parti Libéral Démocratique, PLD) in Berberati and Joseph Bendounga in Bossangoa, finished with 21.68 percent of the vote. Former President David Dacko received 20.11 percent of the vote, garnering almost all Mbaka votes in the southwestern part of the country. Kolingba polled only 12.1 percent of the vote and failed to qualify for a second-round ballot in the September presidential elections. The remaining 8.79 percent of the vote was scattered among the other candidates.

Carefully shepherded by the French (with 1,400 troops stationed in the country) and, to a lesser extent, the governments of Germany and the United States, a second round of elections was successfully conducted on Sunday, September 19, 1993. Pitting the top two finishers in the first round of elections, Ange-Félix Patassé and Dr. Abel Goumba, against each other, these elections achieved a 68 percent turnout from the 1.2 million Central Africans eligible to vote. Patassé was declared by Edouard Franck, the president of the Supreme Court, to be the winner of these elections on Monday, September 27. Running for the third time in the country's history, Patassé won just over 52 percent of the vote against Goumba, who took just over 45 percent. The French foreign minister immediately declared French satisfaction that the voting had been done in an acceptable fashion. The next day the French cooperation minister promised to resume aid to Bangui once President-elect Patassé was installed.[34]

Born at Paoua (Ouham-Pende), Ange-Félix Patassé had completed advanced studies in agriculture in France before he was appointed minister of rural development by Bokassa in 1966. In September 1976 Bokassa appointed him prime minister. In December 1976 Patassé was made the president of the first imperial government, though he fell out of favor and was replaced in July 1978. In semi-exile in Paris, Patassé had become the head of the Front for the Liberation of the Central African People (Front de Libération du Peuple Centrafricain, FLPC) and joined Dr. Abel Goumba and others in opposition to Bokassa. After the French returned David Dacko to power, Patassé returned to Bangui only to be imprisoned from October 24, 1979, to November 27, 1980. Running against Dacko in the seriously flawed elections of March 1981, he received 238,739 votes of the total of 744,689 votes cast. Patassé fled to Paris in September 1981, and then returned to Bangui in February 1982 after Dacko had resigned and attempted a putsch against the Kolingba government on March 3, 1982. Though his attempt to overthrow Kolingba had been thwarted by the presidential guard commanded by Colonel Mantion, Patassé took refuge in the French embassy. After mediation by Guy Penne, President Mitterrand's adviser, Patassé was flown to a French-supported asylum in Togo in a French military plane. After returning to the CAR after ten years of exile in Togo, Patassé at last achieved his longtime goal. In September 1993, the fifty-seven-year-old Patassé was elected president of a bankrupt country.

Conclusion: Prospects for the Patassé Regime

Taking office in mid-September 1993 with a fair degree of goodwill, Patassé was forced to create a coalition government, since his Movement for the Liberation of the Central African People (Mouvement pour la Libération du Peuple Centrafricain, MLPC) gained only 40 percent of the legislative seats. Government workers were on strike for most of 1993, schools had been closed since 1990, and social services had virtually collapsed. It would appear that the French are reluctant to supply enough support to enable Patassé, whom they had rescued in 1982, to preserve the appearance of the stable democracy that the French had long claimed as their heritage in this former colony. Patassé, the first democratically elected president of the CAR, has failed to deliver on promises of a clear-sighted, efficient government. He has yet to secure a permanent return of public services to normality and to create durable political stability.

Patassé may not be authoritarian or repressive, as yet, and the present constitution, unlike that introduced by General Kolingba during the era of the one-party state in the 1980s, does include specific safeguards for democracy and human rights. Patassé's regime, however, resembles those of his predecessors in at least two important ways. It relies upon members of his own ethnic group (the Sara of the Ouham-Pende region of the north) who were his friends and allies during his years of exile. Secondly, like previous regimes, it has little relative importance in the daily lives of most of the ordinary people, who seek to avoid contact with it.

Genuine pluralism remains a fragile flower in the CAR. Patassé was already voicing fears of coups in late 1994 and appears able to do little about the rampant banditry, smuggling, and poaching of elephants and other game in northern regions near the war zones of southern Sudan and near areas of rebel activity in southern Chad. On November 27, 1994, by-elections were held in six constituencies to fill seats where results in the 1993 general election had been declared invalid. Patassé's MLPC lost one seat and saw two others go to deputies who were reelected as independents. In response, Patassé speeded up the process of instituting a new constitution for the CAR to replace the one introduced by General Kolingba. The new constitution, drafted in August 1994, provides for the creation of new regional authorities and decentralization, both long-standing items on Patassé's personal political agenda. After it had been submitted to a national panel of representatives of political parties, trade unions, churches, local councils, and interest groups in October, the constitution was presented to a referendum on December 28, 1994. This constitution was fiercely opposed by the RDC as a threat of the balkanization of the CAR and by the Alliance for Democracy and Progress (Alliance pour la Démocratie et le Progrès, ADP) because it allows the president to serve three six-year terms, to appoint the presiding and assistant judges of the Constitutional Court, and to have considerable power over the prime minister. Dr. Abel Goumba, the leader of the Patriotic Front for Progress (Front Patriotique pour le Progrès, FPP), pointed out that opponents to this constitution had not been given fair access to the media, that no neutral commission was available to monitor the vote, and, finally, that the constitution was a creation of the president and the prime minister. André Tchpaka, the director general of the national television station, was sacked because he campaigned against Patassé's new constitution.

The results of the constitutional referendum were not an overwhelming victory for Patassé. Although 82.06 percent of those who voted cast yes ballots, only 45 percent of the 1,247,290-strong electorate voted. The constitution means little to most people. Support may have been somewhat stronger in the rural areas, probably because farmers saw Patassé as someone who boosted their living standards by raising farm prices in the wake of the French devaluation of currency in the former African colonies rather than because of any real support for constitutional changes. Deputies in the National Assembly forced Prime Minister Jean-Luc Mandaba to resign on April 11, 1995, under accusations of "scandalous behavior characterized by corruption, wheeler-dealing, nepotism, and idleness."[35] Though Patassé chose Gabriel Kyoyambounou, a member of the Yakoma ethnic group, as the new prime minister, several key ministers are members of Mr. Patassé's own ethnic group. The government banned a peaceful march on May Day 1995 organized to press Patassé to allow a national conference of the kind that had occurred in many of the CAR's francophone neighbors. More than 100 years since the French foundation of Bangui, more than three decades since the death of Barthélémy Boganda, and more than ten years since the fall of Emperor Jean-Bédel Bokassa, the Central African people, who have suffered through colonization and decolonization, have yet to see democracy function in their poor, chaotic nation.

Though Ange-Félix Patassé once emphasized his connections with the masses and championed the struggles of the poor, neither his pronouncements nor his government organization offers much ideological clarity or even coherence. The very real problems of rural poverty and marginalized urban populations, of exploitative relationships with Western companies and individuals, and of stagnant production do not lend themselves to easy solutions. With few major industries to tax and little surplus to extract from the overwhelmingly subsistence-based economy, Patassé has, like his predecessors, continued to negotiate agreements with multinationals and their Western government supporters to generate enough economic growth to allow him to maintain a presidential patronage system. He has not yet resorted to the worst abuses of personal dictatorship.[36]

A neocolonial future premised upon some increase in productivity in export agriculture, reduction of diamond smuggling, revival of gold production, possible exploitation of uranium and oil discoveries, and the continued destructive cutting of the tropical rain forests would seem to be the most likely scenario for the rest of this century in the CAR. At best the country can hope to be led by a relatively benign bureaucratic oligarchy rather than an increasingly abusive regime.

Central Africans must have a terrible sense of déjà vu. Since independence the people of the CAR have been governed under eight constitutions. All of these constitutions have been drawn up by professors of French law, all have been highly theoretical, and all have been violated by the very heads of state who had taken oaths to support them. There is little evidence to suggest that the Patassé regime will turn out much differently. Yet the CAR possesses greater economic potential than many other francophone African countries. The humid savannas of the country are well suited to cultivation and animal breeding. The country is not overpopulated, and diamond and gold production continue to produce considerable revenue. Its dense forest is one of the richest in the world and has only recently begun to be overexploited. Given a reasonable increase in export revenue from gold, diamonds, and timber products as well as robusta coffee, cotton, and, possibly sisal, tobacco, and rubber, the persistent balance of payments problems facing the CAR could be improved. Increased revenue from taxes, less fraud on customs dues, and, above all, better administrative management and a reduction in embezzlement of public funds could address the budget deficit of currently more than 40 billion CFA francs and begin to reduce the national debt, which is almost 200 billion CFA francs. In the long run, though, the balkanization of French Equatorial and West Africa may have created nations that are economically nonviable. Like Barthélémy Boganda, the agronomist René Dumont believed that only a union of territory stretching from Cameroon to Rwanda would form a viable economic unit.[37] It is highly unlikely that the small numbers of Central Africans who actually participate in processes of liberalization or democratization, splintered into a variety of heterogeneous groups composed of students, teachers' unions, new political parties, and government officials, have the capacity to institutionalize democracy in their country. Why should the majority of the Central African people support regimes based on values and forms imposed from outside and built on principles that are not related to their needs? Real democratization in the CAR may require a return to the politics of Boganda, which demarginalized the large masses of people—women, youth, workers, poor cultivators— all the sectors of the population whose identity is ignored by externally based liberal democratic theory.[38] For a few brief years, Boganda's efforts did unleash the creativity of the people of the CAR and placed them center stage in history making for their country. Obviously Boganda's approach to democratization raised new problems related to the multiplicity of sites of political struggle and the need for institutions that could link them. Given the continuing political and economic crisis in the country, clearly "business as usual" is not adequate. Different approaches, including those sketched out by Boganda, are badly needed.[39]

Notes

1. Dov Ronen, "The State and Democracy in Africa," in Dov Ronen, ed., *Democracy and Pluralism in Africa* (Boulder: Lynne Rienner, 1986), p. 195.

2. The general discussions of these groups in *The New Elites of Tropical Africa*, edited by P. C. Lloyd (London: Oxford University Press, 1966), are still valid today, informed as they are by attention to kinship and ethnic affinity and the extractive view of politics that still

dominates the national scene in the Central African Republic and many other African countries.

3. On neopatrimonialism, see S. N. Eisenstadt, *Traditionalism, Patrimonialism, and Modern Neopatrimonialism* (Beverly Hills, Calif.: Sage Publications, 1975). See Naomi Chazan et al., *Politics and Society in Contemporary Africa* (Boulder: Lynne Rienner, 1988), pp. 142–143, 171, for a description of personal-coercive regimes such as that of Jean-Bédel Bokassa, where the entrenchment of the regime is predicated on the connections between strong leaders and coercive government apparatuses.

4. The use of this term is a reminder that the social, historical, economic, and cultural realities of the people of the Central African Republic must be given greater emphasis in any attempt to understand the political realities of the country than has yet been done. On this problem as a general African phenomenon, see Irving Leonard Markovitz, *Power and Class in Africa* (Englewood Cliffs, N.J.: Prentice-Hall, 1977). On the problem for the CAR, see Didier Bigo, *Pouvoir et obéissance en Centrafrique* (Paris: Karthala, 1989).

5. See Guy Gran, *Development by People: Citizen Construction of a Just World* (New York: Praeger, 1983).

6. Jean-François Bayart, *L'État en Afrique: La politique du ventre* (Paris: Editions Fayard, 1989).

7. Pierre Kalck, *Central African Republic* (Oxford: Clio Press, 1993), pp. xxvi–xxvii.

8. Thomas O'Toole, *The Central African Republic: The Continent's Hidden Heart* (Boulder: Westview Press, 1986), pp. 24–25.

9. Pierre Kalck, *Histoire Centrafricaine: Des origines à 1966* (Paris: L'Harmattan, 1992), pp. 276–278.

10. Irving Leonard Markovitz, *Leopold Sedar Senghor and the Politics of Negritude* (New York: Atheneum, 1969).

11. Pierre Kalck, "Barthélémy Boganda: Tribun et visionnaire de l'Afrique centrale," in Charles-André Julien et al., eds., *Les africains,* vol. 3 (Paris: Éditions Jeune Afrique, 1977), pp. 103–137.

12. O'Toole, *Central African Republic,* p. 36.

13. Robert W. Harms, *River of Wealth, River of Sorrow: The Central Zaire Basin in the Era of the Slave and Ivory Trade, 1500–1891* (New Haven: Yale University Press, 1981).

14. William J. Samarin, "Bondjo Ethnicity and Colonial Imagination," *Canadian Journal of African Studies* 18 (1984):345–365.

15. Personal correspondence in March 1994 with Pierre Kalck, a French overseas administrator in the Ubangi-Shari territory between 1949 and 1959, and thereafter an economic adviser to the Central African Republic government.

16. Bigo, *Pouvoir et obéissance,* p. 289ff.

17. Geraldine Faes, "Centrafrique, riche . . . et pourtant," *Jeune Afrique Économie,* no. 137 (November 1990), pp. 121–125; Denis Paye, "Facteurs socio-économiques de l'insuffisance du développement: L'exemple de la République Centrafricaine," *Revue française d'études politiques africaines* 20 (April-May 1985):68–80, 97–99; and Laurent Zecchini, "Une économie sous perfusion," *Le Monde,* November 30, 1984, pp. 13–14.

18. Kalck, *Central African Republic,* pp. xx, xxxvi.

19. United Nations Development Programme, *Human Development Report 1993* (New York: Oxford University Press, 1993).

20. *Economist* Intelligence Unit (hereafter EIU), *Country Report: Cameroon, Central African Republic, Chad* (hereafter *Country Report: CAR*), no. 1 (1994):28.

21. See Yarisse Zoctizoum, *Histoire de la Centrafrique,* vol. 2, *1959–1979* (Paris: L'Harmattan, 1984), for a specifically Central African–focused Marxist rebuttal of the World Bank perspective such as that found in the World Bank's publication, *Adjustment in Africa: Reforms, Results, and the Road Ahead* (New York: Oxford University Press, 1994).

22. For an adequate working definition of neocolonialism, see Richard Sandbrook, *The Politics of Basic Needs: Urban Aspects of Assaulting Poverty in Africa* (Toronto: University of Toronto Press, 1982), pp. 83–90.

23. Markovitz, *Power and Class in Africa,* pp. 204–229.

24. See, for example, Yarisse Zoctizoum, *Violence du développement: Domination et inégalité* (Paris: L'Harmattan, 1984).

25. Kalck, *Central African Republic,* p. xxxi.

26. Ibid.

27. Personal correspondence with Pierre Kalck, March 10, 1994.

28. "Central African Republic," in Arthur Banks, ed., *Political Handbook of the World: 1992* (Binghamton, N.Y.: CSA Publications, 1992), pp. 135–136.

29. Kalck, *Central African Republic,* p. xxxv.

30. EIU, *Country Report: CAR,* no. 1 (1993):21–23.

31. See articles in *Le Monde,* September 6 and September 25, 1993.

32. See Reuters reports, September 22, 1993.

33. The information on Sara votes is from personal correspondence with Pierre Kalck, March 10, 1994.

34. EIU, *Country Report: CAR,* no. 4 (1993):21–24.

35. This quotation is taken from EIU, *Country Report: CAR,* no. 2 (1995):22. Many other details for events from late 1993 to the present have been gleaned from EIU Country Reports for that period.

36. See the allegations of fraud and corruption in Vincent Thierry, "Patassé dans la tourmente," *Jeune Afrique,* no. 1728 (February 17–23, 1994):20–23.

37. René Dumont, "Le difficile développement agricole de la République Centrafricaine," *Annales de l'Institut National Agronomique* 4 (1966):1–85.

38. Kalck, "Barthélémy Boganda."

39. On April 18, 1996, 400 soldiers at Bangui mutinied to protest nonpayment of long-standing salary arrears. During the ensuing violence 10 persons were killed and 40 wounded. The mutiny ended on April 21 when the government paid the soldiers three months' arrears. Then on May 18, a second mutiny broke out among 200 soldiers, who seized the armory. They accused the government of wanting to disarm them and of arresting some of the earlier mutineers despite a presidential amnesty. The extensive disorders that took place led President Patassé to seek French help. On May 22 France provided 2,300 troops, who assisted in restoring order. Between May 18 and 23, 32 CAR civilians were killed and 212 injured; 8 mutineers died and 5 were wounded, as were 5 French soldiers. Minister of Cooperation Jacques Godfrain denied that France intervened in order to prop up Patassé. He declared that the French troops were maintaining a democratic state, with all its attributes, and that the intervention had the support of neighboring states. (*West Africa,* April 29, 1996, p. 667; *West Africa,* May 27, 1996, p. 812; *West Africa,* June 3, 1996, p. 852.)

Part Three

Old Faces, Moderate Reforms

Chapter Eight

Burkina Faso: The "Rectification" of the Revolution

LAURA E. BOUDON

The wave of political reforms and democratization moving across the African continent since 1989 has affected landlocked and poverty-stricken Burkina Faso as well as its wealthier neighbors. Since President Thomas Sankara's assassination in 1987, the former Upper Volta has undergone significant political changes under the leadership of President Blaise Compaoré. The primary topic of this chapter is Compaoré's "Rectification of the Revolution" in the context of political reform movements.. The key question to be addressed is whether Compaoré's reforms represent a turning point in the political history of Burkina Faso or merely another episode in the periodic political shifts for which the country is known. Hence it is necessary first to review the postcolonial history of Burkina Faso, with particular emphasis on the social revolution undertaken by Sankara, and then to focus on the events in the country since the beginning of Compaoré's administration in 1987.

Independence, the Onset of Autocracy, and Political Turmoil

The history of the territory constituting today's Burkina Faso has generally been turbulent. Established as a French colony in 1920, the territory was dismembered and reunified several times, alternating between status as a colony in its own right and attachment to several adjacent French colonies, including the French Sudan

(Mali) and Côte d'Ivoire. The country then known as Upper Volta finally stabilized as a single political unit in 1947 and gained independence from France on
August 5, 1960. (It acquired the name Burkina Faso in May 1984.)

At independence, Burkina Faso signed numerous cooperation agreements with
France relating to the diplomatic, economic, monetary, and technical assistance it
would receive thereafter. Although Burkina Faso refused to sign defense agreements with France, it did allow French troops to overfly, transit, and encamp on
its territory en route to a neighboring country but not to remain on Burkinabè
soil for a prolonged period of time.[1] Generally, however, relations with France did
not help to promote stability to the degree achieved in Côte d'Ivoire or Gabon.

As elsewhere in Africa the lack of national consciousness was one source of instability. Before independence, the various ethnic groups that comprise Burkina
Faso were geographically separate and lacked regular intercommunication. As
René Otayek has bluntly put it, however, "the state is the prerogative of the Mossi
Empire."[2] The Mossi have historically been, and continue to be, the ruling group
in the country; they are concentrated in and around the capital city, Ouagadougou, and represent 45 percent of the country's population. The other 55
percent is composed of some sixty other ethnic groups, the most important of
which are the Birifor, Bobo, Bwa, Dioula, Gourounsi, Lobi, Senoufou, and Peul.
These groups are mostly concentrated in the more fertile western portion of the
country.

The country's profound underdevelopment has been another source of instability. Burkina Faso's situation in the post-independence era has been quite bleak
and its prospects limited. It has long been among the poorest of the poor countries in the world. According to the United Nations Development Programme's
1993 *Human Development Report*, of 173 countries surveyed Burkina Faso ranked
170th on a scale of human development (a combined index of income, education,
and health indicators). Ninety percent of the population lives in rural areas and
depends on the land, despite the poor quality of the soil. In 1960, salary and wage-
earners comprised only 3 to 4 percent of the male labor force, most of whom
worked for the Burkinabè state. The particularly long dry season as well as the
lack of good farming land and irrigation resulted in the underemployment of
people in the countryside. Together, these economic realities implied limited options for development.

Maurice Yaméogo, the first elected president under Burkina Faso's original
constitution, began the difficult task of creating a national identity for the country among peoples who had not had, and may not have desired to have, much
contact with one another. Although Yaméogo was reelected in 1965, his rule
brought about strained relations between the new state and Burkinabè society.
These tensions were the background for the country's first military coup in 1966,
in which General Sangoulé Lamizana assumed the presidency. This proved to be
only the first in a succession of numerous military coups. In 1970, following four
years of "restricted political activity," Lamizana orchestrated a return to civilian

rule under a new constitution. Dissent among left-wing political groups, however, led the military, and consequently Lamizana, to halt these reforms at an early stage. Another stillborn attempt at civilian rule was made in 1977, when yet another new constitution reestablished multiparty rule.

In 1980, however, Lamizana was overthrown by his own officers, and Colonel Saye Zerbo became head of state. Zerbo in turn was replaced in a coup two years later by Jean-Baptiste Ouédraogo, another Mossi military officer, in November 1982. This last coup d'état, however, broke the Burkinabè tradition of military takeovers in three ways: It was the first coup that resulted in any deaths, civilian or military; its leaders were of particularly low rank in the military; and the putsch was the first to be met with public indifference.[3]

Throughout this period in Burkinabè history, the various leaders and their governments maintained close ties with France; there were no major disagreements between the two countries. Burkina Faso was economically quite dependent on French aid, which it used primarily to counter fiscal deficits. Between 1960 and 1972, for example, French aid to Burkina Faso reached US$2 billion, the equivalent of five times the country's government budget for 1972.[4]

The Populist Revolution of 1983

The removal from power and imprisonment of Thomas Sankara, then prime minister under Jean-Baptiste Ouédraogo, marked the beginning of the "revolution" in May 1983. Thousands of soldiers and youths took to the streets in the following months demanding that Sankara be freed. When the demonstrations failed to gain Sankara's release, 250 soldiers marched into the capital on August 4, 1983. They then freed Sankara and overthrew Ouédraogo in what at the time appeared to have been just another military coup.

Sankara, however, was a self-proclaimed Marxist revolutionary and was only superficially similar to other Burkinabè military leaders; he was a Mossi just like many of them were, but there most resemblances ended. He believed that the underdevelopment of the country was caused by two factors: French exploitation and the "forced-labor phenomenon,"[5] or the regular employment of one million Burkinabè men on the plantations of Côte d'Ivoire. This "forced labor" was a consequence of the imbalance between Burkina Faso's meager natural resources and its sizable population. Sankara was also convinced that autarky would enable Burkina Faso to solve some of its economic problems.[6] In addition, Sankara held an unconventional position regarding women. He believed them to be dominated and exploited by men, and he was not shy about expressing his opinion on this subject: "[W]omen are exploited like dairy cows in our society; they are made to bear children, give milk, work themselves to the bone and then provide a source of pleasure for their husbands."[7]

Sankara spelled out the direction of his populist[8] revolution in his Political Orientation Speech (Discours d'Orientation Populaire) on October 2, 1983. Peasants were to be the primary beneficiaries of what he considered a revolution.[9] In theory he was eager for his fellow citizens, men and women, to engender revolutionary social and political change in their country. His stated intent was to create structures that would allow them to take charge of the country's development and to eliminate corruption. As Elliott Skinner put it, Sankara "was determined to head a clean and honest regime, to exclude all former politicians from power, and to finally deprive the Mossi chiefs, who were survivors of a decadent feudal past, of the power they had held over the centuries."[10]

The key institution that Sankara's revolutionaries created to govern the country was the National Council of the Revolution (Conseil National de la Révolution, CNR), "the power that plans, leads, and oversees national political, economic and social life."[11] The Council was made up of Sankara, Compaoré, and two other military officers, Captain Henri Zongo and Commandant Jean-Baptiste Boukari Lingani. The Committees for the Defense of the Revolution (Comités pour la Défense de la Révolution, CDRs) were to be the local representatives of the revolutionary power in the villages, neighborhoods, and workplaces. They were to restructure solidarity networks and social space in their entirety and to provide the bases for health and education services.[12] In other words, the revolutionary state was attempting to co-opt certain segments of civil society and create new civic organs.

The revolutionaries also transformed the judicial system by replacing the customary resolution of disputes by traditional leaders with Popular Tribunals of Conciliation (Tribunaux Populaires de la Conciliation, TPC). These tribunals were created to resolve conflicts and were given considerable leeway in issuing judgments, which ranged from "the seizure of land and livestock, up to collective punishment inflicted upon villages."[13] These changes were meant to organize judicial affairs and render adjudication more equitable and just.

On the first anniversary of the revolution, the CNR renamed the country Burkina Faso, or "The Land of Men of Integrity," and changed the flag and the national anthem. These symbolic gestures were intended to indicate the birth of a new country, spiritually and politically different from the one that existed previously.

Along with the transformation of Burkinabè political consciousness, the CNR also aimed to reform the country's economy and to delink it from international capitalism.[14] A Popular Program of Development (Programme Populaire du Développement, PPD) was implemented to carry out the economic and social policies of the CNR. Its priorities were to fulfill the basic needs of the Burkinabè people through better health and education programs and to increase the agricultural production of the country with the hope of attaining self-sufficiency.[15] Agriculture was to be reformed by improving the management of water resources, the implementation of large-scale irrigation projects and programs to halt environmental degradation.[16] The source of funding for these agricultural reforms remained unclear.

In an interview with *Africa Report*, Sankara laid out the revolution's economic goal: "[A] nationally independent economy, one that is free from the domination of international capital."[17] Sankara also clarified his position on foreign assistance by saying that Burkina Faso was still willing to accept foreign aid, as long as it was not a threat to the sovereignty, dignity, and honor of the Burkinabè people. In other words, he was unwilling to accept aid on a conditional basis.

In the realm of foreign policy, Sankara sought to separate his country politically and economically from what he considered to be the imperialist Western powers and their financial institutions, while bringing it closer to other revolutionary regimes around the world. For Sankara, Burkina Faso's enemies included France, the United States, and Côte d'Ivoire, and its allies were Libya, Nicaragua, Cuba, and Ghana, though Sankara maintained that Burkina Faso was, in principle, nonaligned.[18] He was quite outspoken in these views, berating French President François Mitterrand for his policies towards South Africa, Angola, and Chad, when the latter visited Ouagadougou during the summer of 1987.[19] In turn, Mitterrand, exhibiting some equanimity, attributed Sankara's earnest attitude to his youth. In fact, it is interesting to note that France had not reacted particularly negatively to the coup that had brought Sankara to power. Though the French Socialist government was perplexed at events in Ouagadougou, it did not reduce its assistance to the impoverished country.[20]

Reactions to the revolution among Burkinabè citizens were diverse but, on balance, negative. First, the Mossi leaders, whom Sankara specifically wanted to remove from power, felt alienated by Sankara's leadership, despite the fact that in many situations they were able to neutralize the CDRs and pursue their personal goals.[21] Second, trade unions and Marxist political groups such as the Patriotic League for Development (Ligue Patriotique pour le Développement, LIPAD), which had originally supported the CNR, viewed the creation of the CDRs as an attempt to marginalize them, and they separated themselves from the populist state before the end of its first year in power.[22] The tension between the state and elements of civil society escalated following the arrest of union and political party leaders in 1986. This tension, however, subsided in 1987 because of a more moderate attitude on both sides of the dispute. Union leaders, for example, were to be chosen by the unions in conjunction with the CNR.[23] Third, during the CNR's first year in office, an important resurgence of both the Islamic and the Catholic faiths took place, providing people with a psychological refuge from the CDRs and undermining the popular energy Sankara sought to infuse into the revolution.[24]

Whatever Sankara's intentions, his policies alienated many of those groups whom he wanted to exclude and failed to satisfy those whose cause he wanted to advance. His revolution in the end did not advance the cause of democracy in Burkina Faso; on the contrary, it may have hindered it. Otayek notes that the revolution came to a dead end because it had failed in its most crucial project: the restructuring of society.[25] Although Sankara was quite serious about popular participation, the revolution remained, in Richard Sandbrook's judgment, a "largely top-down affair."[26]

From an economic standpoint, Sankara's revolutionary policies were not able to eradicate, or even significantly reduce, Burkina Faso's poverty levels, despite a 120 percent increase in public spending between 1984 and 1987. In 1987, foreign debt stood at 350 billion CFA francs, while international sources of support had fallen sharply because of Sankara's confrontational attitudes toward the West and the International Monetary Fund (IMF).[27] This lack of funding was the impetus for the import bans on fruit and manufactured products in April 1987, which Sankara expected would lower Burkina Faso's trade deficit. In fairness, one should also note that the lack of rain during the revolutionary years diminished the possible benefits of Sankara's policies.

The general uneasiness created by these developments served as the main justification for Sankara's assassination on October 15, 1987. According to one major group of Africanists, Sankara's policies brought his regime to an end.[28] At the same time, the exact circumstances of Sankara's death are not known. As Skinner wrote, "it is not yet known if the President was killed by a grenade even before leaving the car which drove him to the housing complex of the Conseil d'Entente, or if he resisted arrest and killed one guard before being himself gunned down."[29]

Compaoré claimed that Sankara was killed because he was plotting against the other members of the CNR, yet no proof was ever brought forth to substantiate this claim. Ouagadougou remained surprisingly calm in the days and months following the revolutionary leader's death despite the passionate feelings stirred by Sankara, positive and negative. Sankara has continued to haunt Burkinabè politics, however. His death and his unfulfilled vision are still discussed today as a crucial part of Burkinabè history and politics. For many Burkinabè, Compaoré is to this day important mainly as the man who killed their national hero.

Compaoré's "Rectification of the Revolution"

On the very day of Sankara's death, Compaoré, who had been Sankara's closest associate, became head of state and embarked on a "Rectification of the Revolution." Compaoré explicitly compared his project to the glasnost taking place in the Soviet Union under Gorbachev.[30] In order to remain in power, Compaoré had to be very cautious. He was conscious of the malaise in Burkinabè society following Sankara's assassination and recognized its existence occasionally in public speeches, as did several of his top associates.[31] One of the symptoms of this social crisis was a distinct rise in the crime rate in Ouagadougou.[32]

Compaoré, a member of the Mossi ethnic group, was obliged to demonstrate respect to his Mossi elders, whom Sankara had shunned, while continuing to use the rhetoric of the revolution, which many younger leaders still favored. Not easily placated, however, the Mossi were the first to create an opposition party at the end of 1987, in the form of Hermann Yaméogo's Movement of Progressive Democrats (Mouvement des Démocrates Progressistes, MDP). To satisfy those who wanted the revolution to continue, Compaoré maintained the CDRs but changed their name to Revolutionary Committees (Comités Révolutionnaires, CRs) in March 1988.

Another reason for Compaoré's caution was his lack of confidence in himself, according to Ike Onwordi, journalist for *West Africa*.[33] His self-confidence increased dramatically over the first year of his administration, however, and became even greater following a purported coup attempt against him in September 1989, in which the two other former leaders of the CNR, Jean-Baptiste Boukari Lingani and Henri Zongo, were killed.[34] Hence, two years after Sankara's assassination, Compaoré had consolidated power sufficiently to begin carrying out his reforms.

Political Reform and Political Opposition

The social and political goals Compaoré set out for his administration in 1988 had much in common with Sankara's agenda; after all, Compaoré did not argue that he had abandoned the revolution that he and Sankara had started. His agenda included, in addition to economic development and political reform, a reduction of unemployment, a reform of the educational system, literacy campaigns, the integration of marginal groups into society, and the further empowerment of women.[35]

Compaoré originally designed the Popular Front (Front Populaire, FP) to replace the CNR in the process of rectifying the revolution, but in mid-1989 he announced that the FP would be a forum for all major political groups to ensure the unity of the Burkinabè people and the future of the country. His intention is reflected in the official definition of the Popular Front as a "regrouping of political organizations, of democratic, anti-imperialist mass organizations of Burkina Faso, convinced of the necessity of uniting people in the fight against imperialism and all forms of internal domination in view of economic and social development for the veritable profit of the popular masses."[36]

Wishing to emphasize the democratic nature of the Popular Front, Compaoré allowed the legal creation of opposition political parties, such as the MDP. Another of the newly formed opposition groups is the Sankarist movement, which came into existence following the revolutionary leader's assassination and is organized around the actions and thoughts of Sankara and pursues the emancipation of Burkinabè people from Western imperialism. In 1989 alone, approximately forty parties were legally created, including several environmental parties such as the Ecological Party for Progress (Parti Écologique pour le Progrès, PEP). Its agenda includes a healthy environment, development, and social progress.[37]

The major opposition parties to be included in the Popular Front were the MDP and the anti-Marxist National Convention of Progressive Patriots/Social

Democratic Party (Convention Nationale des Patriotes Progressifs/Parti Démocrate Social, CNPP/PDS). When the MDP and the CNPP/PDS joined the Popular
Front, they were led by their respective founders, Hermann Yaméogo, son of the
country's first president, and Pierre Tatsoba, both of whom tended toward the
right wing of the political spectrum.[38] Both leaders were quite enthusiastic about
the Popular Front, Yaméogo claiming, in June 1989, that "this democratization effort is not for show."[39]

The two opposition leaders, however, were eventually expelled from the Front.
Yaméogo was ousted in the fall of 1990 and created a new party, the Alliance for
Democracy and Federation (Alliance pour la Démocratie et la Fédération, ADF),
which garnered most its support from former MDP members. The ADF favors
democracy, a redefinition of the role of the state, and decentralization of the political institutions in Burkina Faso.[40] The MDP is still officially part of the Popular
Front, but it is basically an empty shell. Tatsoba, for his part, was expelled from
the Front in March 1991, along with his party and his supporters, because of basic
ideological differences with other groups in the Popular Front. Many of the party
members of the FP are Marxists and favor maintaining Sankara's program. Tatsoba and his followers refused to go along with the Sankarist quasi-Marxist program and were therefore expelled.[41]

The ADF and the CNPP/PDS agree that Compaoré's party, the Organization
for Popular Democracy/Movement of Labor (Organisation pour la Démocratie
Populaire/Mouvement du Travail, ODP/MT), wanted to impose its hegemony on
the Front.[42] According to Russell Geekie, this party "likes to take credit for engi-
neering the return to multiparty rule, but critics charge that the party's conversion to ballot box politics and political reform over the last two years has been
carefully managed to allow it to keep its hold on power."[43]

Although the Popular Front appeared to be a way for its leader to maintain
power, reform did create a more open society in Burkina Faso. An independent
radio station was set up and an independent daily newspaper, *L'Observateur
Paalga*, began publication in 1989.[44] Even the state newspaper, *Sidwaya*, was operating more autonomously from the government. The citizens of the country no
longer felt as limited in their actions or thoughts, due to either the CRs or the
state itself, as they had previously.

At the end of 1989, as political reform got underway in neighboring Benin,
Compaoré evoked the need for institutional changes in Burkina Faso, which
would be presented to Burkinabè citizens for democratic choice. By March 1990
the Front had begun writing a new constitution. According to Compaoré, there
were two main reasons, one internal and the other external, for a new Burkinabè
constitution.[45] Domestically, Compaoré claimed—rather cryptically—that the
"insufficient regulation" of the social and political aspects of civil society was a
problem. In his view, the absence of norms signified that neither the collectivities
nor the individuals knew their roles, duties, or rights. Abroad, the collapse of

Eastern European communist regimes and the emphasis placed on democracy by the Western powers reinforced the need for reform.

The structure and content of the new constitution closely resemble those of the French Constitution of the Fifth Republic. There are several noteworthy sections in this constitution. First, the constitution calls for the separation of power between the executive, legislative, and judicial branches of government. Second, it creates a second chamber in the legislative branch, the Chamber of Representatives (Chambre des Représentants), in addition to the existing Assembly of Deputies (Assemblée des Députés). This second legislative body was designed to be mostly consultative. Third, the new constitution does not allow military personnel to hold office.[46] This clause was critical because it meant that Compaoré would have to give up his military affiliation in order to run for president. More generally, it marked the beginning of the separation between the military and the state apparatus in Burkina Faso.[47] Finally, multiple political parties are allowed, as long as they are not tribal, regional, religious, or ethnic. In other words, they must have a cross-local constituency. Opposition parties called for the support of the constitution, as it represented a significant step toward multiparty rule and would be preferable to the existing document. However, they were dissatisfied with the sections of the draft that dealt with the electoral code, which did not provide sufficiently for fairness and transparency.[48] Following the referendum, Compaoré's response to them was essentially that, since the people had voted for the constitution, it now had to be implemented as adopted.

However, the constitution has still not been completely implemented. Specifically, the second chamber called for by the constitution has not been established. When Compaoré was asked about this in December 1992, he replied only that "[T]his is certainly one item of unfinished business in our democratization process."[49]

Both before and after the adoption of the new Burkinabè constitution, Compaoré refused to convene a sovereign national conference as called for by the opposition parties and as had taken place in many other francophone African countries. In demanding such a conference, the opposition aimed to create a dialogue among the various political, social, ethnic, and religious groups of the state and of civil society so that the processes of development and democratization could move forward.[50]

In an attempt at reconciliation with the opposition, Compaoré called for a national forum to begin on February 11, 1992. The forum lasted only one week, as Compaoré and the forty-two opposition parties could not agree on media coverage. The ADF lost several of its key leaders, including Hermann Yaméogo, when they were offered senior governmental positions. Thus Compaoré proved his ability to dismantle and co-opt the opposition when necessary.

Following the 1992 legislative elections, a new cabinet was formed, including all of the political forces that participated in the elections. The CNPP/PDS was given three cabinet portfolios, the MDS two, and the other parties that had been elected to a seat one ministry each.

At the end of 1992 and the beginning of 1993, a strike and a sit-in were organized on the university campus in Ouagadougou. Student discontent stems primarily from overdue grant payments but is rooted in the employment crisis that many university graduates are facing. The Burkinabè state can no longer provide jobs for all the university graduates, whose numbers have mushroomed from 523 in 1974 to 7388 in 1992. The main task of the Burkinabè state in educational policy has been to adapt the structure and content of the educational system inherited from the French to the needs of the Burkinabè productive sector and society.[51] Also in January 1993, unrest began among civil servants, who were demanding wage increases following the lifting of a wage freeze that had lasted several years.

On January 22, 1994, a new opposition political grouping, the Convention of the Forces of Progress (Convention des Forces du Progrès, CFP), was formed to bring together several of the smaller groups that participated in the election—the Union of Social Democrats, the MDP, the Group of Democrats and Patriots, the Alliance for Progress and Freedom, the Popular Movement for Freedom and Development, the League for Progress and Development, and the Revolutionary Workers' Party as well as some other new parties, whose goals are not yet clear.[52] The CFP's goals are to promote consultations among these opposition parties and, more generally, to strengthen democracy in Burkina Faso by providing an opposition forum for the discussion of ideas.

On March 16, 1994, Prime Minister Youssouf Ouédraogo resigned as a result of the failure of wage negotiations between civil servants and the state. An agreement had been signed between the government and the unions on a small salary increase, but it was rejected later in the day by several of the union leaders who had signed it.[53] A new prime minister, Marc-Christian Roch Kaboré, was chosen and an entirely new cabinet was named. However, changes in the personalities involved were not enough to avert the three-day general strike called for by the General Labor Confederation of Burkina Faso, which began on April 6. The unions demanded a 40 to 50 percent salary increase.[54] Though the government said it understood the workers' frustrations, it argued that it was limited in its actions by rigid budgetary constraints. It is noteworthy, however, that the strike was not put down forcibly and was allowed to take place without any major incidents.

In July 1994 legislators authorized the government to privatize nineteen public companies, including those providing public transportation and stable agricultural prices. Other enterprises to be sold off included a sugar producing plant, an oil company, and the national printing company.[55] Less than one month later, eleven had been privatized; the others are pending.

At the beginning of 1995, in preparation for the municipal elections, the opposition parties and the unions stepped up their activities. They did so in part by taking to the streets.

Elections

Since 1991 the citizens of Burkina Faso have run what Augustin Loada and René Otayek have called an "electoral marathon."[56] They went to the polls four times in three and a half years, which for sub-Saharan Africa is quite a record.

On June 2, 1991, 93 percent of those who voted approved the constitution presented to them by Compaoré; however, only 49 percent of registered voters actually cast a ballot,[57] despite the military's apparently having pressured people to vote.[58] The abstention rate was high for several reasons. First, June 2 was at the very beginning of the agricultural season. Second, the outcome was already known, since most groups were campaigning for the adoption of the constitution. Finally, although no boycott of the vote had been called, it is probable that some voters stayed home because no national conference had been conducted or scheduled, and they therefore viewed the election as a fraud.[59]

Compaoré's unwillingness to allow a national conference to take place resulted in an opposition party boycott of the December 1991 elections, in which Compaoré was elected president. Demonstrations began in October and outlasted the presidential election. No candidate registered to oppose Compaoré. Burkinabè bishops met with Compaoré in mid-November, requesting a deferment of the elections, renewed dialogue with the opposition, and a change in the electoral code; a few days later, the national human rights organization rejected the status of observer that the government had offered it.[60] On December 1, 1991, Compaoré was elected with 86 percent of the vote; however, only 25 percent of registered voters went to the polls. For many observers of Burkinabè politics, this boycott meant that Compaoré's attempt to democratize had failed miserably.[61]

The national legislative elections of May 24, 1992, were another major test for democratization in Burkina Faso. Compaoré's ODP/MT won the majority of the 107 available seats in the Assembly of Deputies. Table 8.1, which summarizes the results of the elections, shows that the Popular Front received seventy-nine seats (seventy-eight for the ODP/MT and one for the MDP), and the outspoken opposition parties received sixteen seats (twelve for the CNPP/PDS and four for the ADF). The other parties listed are quite small; though they are not members of the Popular Front, they have not vigorously opposed it either.[62] The overwhelming victory of the FP came as a surprise to those following the elections closely, including the independent newspaper of Burkina Faso, *L'Observateur Paalga*. Foreign observers thought that the elections had been fair.[63]

In the February 1995 municipal elections, Compaoré's ODP/MT sought to confirm its overwhelming victory in the legislative elections and increase its political hegemony. Among the key issues in the election campaign were campaign financing and election transparency. The ODP/MT obtained 65 percent of the votes and 1,112 seats of 1,710. According to Loada and Otayek, these local elections proved that power in Burkina Faso is centralized in Ouagadougou, and that

TABLE 8.1   Results of Burkina Faso's 1992 Legislative Elections

Party	Seats
ODP/MT	78
CNPP/PDS	12
African Democratic Rally	6
ADF	4
African Independence Party	2
MDP	1
Burkinabè Socialist Party	1
Movement for Social Democracy	1
Union of Independent Social Democrats	1
Union of Social Democrats	1

Source: *Foreign Broadcast Information Service–Sub-Saharan Africa,* "Supreme Court Releases Final Election Results," June 11, 1992, p. 22.

decentralization is necessary for real democracy to take root in the Burkinabè countryside.[64]

Economic Reforms

Although the institutional political reforms that Compaoré initiated seem quite substantive, the more significant changes have been in the realms of economic and foreign policies. For the Western policy analysts keeping an eye on events in the country, as well as for many within, these shifts represent a return to realism and moderation, leaving behind the radical ideas and policies of Sankara. In the economic sphere, Burkina Faso has been pursuing a policy of state capitalism.[65] Compaoré "pledged allegiance to the capitalist system"; he wanted economic growth and the development of capitalism, but "not at the expense of the Burkinabè people."[66]

Burkina Faso is pursuing both economic liberalization and democratization at the same time. The relationship between the two and their influence on each other is not entirely clear, but some scholars worry that the adverse impact of neoliberal policies on employment and public services could jeopardize democratic gains.[67]

In March 1991 Burkina Faso signed a structural adjustment agreement with the IMF, including a standby loan of US$31 million, in order to pursue the liberalization of the economy. The goals of the program included a deep restructuring of public spending, a growth rate of 4 percent per year, the limitation of inflation to less than 4 percent, and the reduction of current account deficits to 14.6 percent.[68]

The much-debated and long-feared devaluation of the CFA franc took place in January 1994. In its response to this new economic challenge, and in comparison to some of the larger francophone African countries, Burkina Faso is actually doing quite well. For the president, the solutions to the devaluation crisis lie in increased production and exports, and decreased imports. As a result, local production and consumption of food and goods are being strongly encouraged.

Foreign Relations

Compaoré decided at the beginning of the Rectification that Burkina Faso could not move forward if it remained isolated from the Western world and its capital. The "Beau Blaise," as Compaoré has been nicknamed, improved Burkina Faso's relations with such capitalist neighbors as Côte d'Ivoire, while still maintaining fairly close relations with its former allies, such as Libya. Relations with the United States, however, worsened following the U.S. downing of two Libyan planes on January 4, 1989. Compaoré's description of the episode as an "act of terrorism" resulted in a temporary recall of the American ambassador.[69]

It is interesting to note that the democratization process began in Burkina Faso prior to the Franco-African summit at La Baule in June 1990. For Burkina Faso, this meeting only reemphasized the direction in which it had already started to move. Relations with France at this point were fairly warm. French aid to Burkina Faso increased during the "Rectification of the Revolution," although Mitterrand had personally expressed regret over Sankara's death.[70]

The relationship with France in the postrevolutionary period has been a much improved one, and Compaoré has gone to Paris several times. In June 1993, during one of Compaoré's trips to Paris, Prime Minister Edouard Balladur presented France's perspective on developments in Burkina Faso: "[W]e have viewed with great satisfaction the way Burkina Faso has tackled the difficult situation it was facing so we have reassured the president we will assist him in every possible way whenever he wants us to."[71]

Following the devaluation of the CFA franc, the French government continued to praise Burkina Faso. The minister of cooperation, Bernard Debré, and the minister of the economy, Edmond Alphandéry, both visited Burkina Faso in December 1994. They viewed Burkina Faso's situation as quite favorable and sided with Burkina Faso against what they saw as the excessive demands of the World Bank.

On July 14, 1995, Jacques Chirac's first Bastille Day celebration as president, Compaoré was the only foreign dignitary present and invited. This gesture on Chirac's part was meant both as a compliment to Burkina Faso's political and economic achievements and as a sign of the good existing relations between France and African nations in general and Burkina Faso in particular.[72]

Conclusions

Is Burkina Faso a democracy today? Has it even moved in that direction since 1987? If not, has the groundwork at least been laid in the civil society for future democratization?

It is important at this point to distinguish between a limited, procedural democracy and deeper, social democracy. Rueschemeyer, Stephens, and Stephens provide one such minimalist definition: In their view, democracy "entails, first, regular, free and fair elections of representatives with universal and equal suffrage, second, responsibility of the state apparatus to the elected parliament, and third, the freedoms of expression and association as well as the protection of individual rights against arbitrary state action."[73] Others argue as strongly that no democracy merits the name unless it embraces its citizens more fully and provides for minimal economic needs. John Clark argues, however, that expecting African countries to provide comprehensive social welfare for their citizens is unreasonable and would only cause them to return to political instability.[74]

The available evidence suggests that though Burkina Faso still falls short of even the minimalist ideal, it is finally moving in the right direction—and the path toward democracy is quite a radical change from the types of state and society that the CNR was trying to create. In terms of the criteria set forth by Rueschemeyer et al., Burkina Faso is at least on course. In the electoral arena, the legislative elections that took place in May 1992 were, by most accounts, fair. There were no complaints, either from human rights activists, or even from the opposition, which is usually the first to cry foul. As for the state's responsibilities, it appears that Compaoré is willing to take responsibility for his policies and actions before the people and their representatives. And as for the requisite civil liberties, citizens of Burkina Faso are once again legally allowed to participate in the organizations of their choice as well as to demonstrate or strike for better living conditions and wages. An independent press operates freely but with self-restraint. Moreover, Halidou Ouédraogo, the leader of the national human rights movement, claimed in 1993 that there were no more political prisoners in Burkina Faso.[75]

The next question is whether Burkina Faso will continue on its path of reform. Goran Hyden has proposed several considerations that might very well determine the likelihood of democratic consolidation in African countries. Is discretionary money available from natural resources with which the state can improve the social and economic conditions of the people? What types of state mechanisms are in place to deal with potential ethnic and religious conflicts? Has a middle class developed sufficiently in the country in order to provide economic stability? Is civil society dynamic, yet nonconfrontational? Do the elites of the country have a unique agenda? Is the military subordinate to civilian authority?[76]

In responding to this set of questions, it becomes apparent that the basic problem for Burkina Faso is its poverty. There is little discretionary income from natural resources, of which Burkina Faso has precious few. There is only a tiny middle class, since the potential for large-scale production is so small; and there is little prospect for capital accumulation. Thus, in the case of Burkina Faso, there is "even less [chance] for class formation" than in other African states.[77] As Clark has argued, the primary impediment to democratization in Africa is underdevelopment itself, which creates a range of more proximate constraints on democracy.[78] In short, the lack of economic resources will be an impediment to further democratic change.

Burkina Faso does, however, have several positive characteristics in its favor. First, despite the existing Mossi dominance within the state apparatus, it does not suffer from chronic ethnic or religious strife. The various ethnic groups are mostly dispersed around the country and do not clash in urban centers (Burkina Faso's population remains 80 percent rural). Second, its civil society is comparatively dynamic and active. Unions, associations, and religious groups abound and express themselves regularly through strikes and demonstrations. Sandbrook goes one step further than Hyden in suggesting that the strengthening of civil society will take place with the democratization of the associations that constitute it.[79] This proposition is hard to assess in Burkina Faso without further research into the actual associations. Third, the elites of the country no longer have an agenda that is separate from that of the state. During Sankara's administration, many fled the country, but after the beginning of the Rectification they began to return. They approved of Compaoré's decision to return to capitalism. Lastly, the military's role has been declining in Burkina Faso since the adoption of the 1991 constitution. Although Compaoré was a member of the military for many years, he has given up his military affiliation and to a certain degree has cut his links to it.

In Pascal Zagré's view, the Burkinabè culture is genuinely democratic. He discusses the fact that open debate was always a part of Mossi tradition and that historically the chief was elected. Although scholars disagree on whether or not a democratic culture is necessary, these background traits do appear to enhance the prospects for democracy in Burkina Faso.[80]

In conclusion, it appears that the future of Burkina Faso's democracy depends on three key factors. First of all, for Burkina Faso to continue its path toward liberal democracy, the military must remain on the sidelines. The country must be able to leave behind its history of repeated military coups and begin to provide a more stable environment for the advance of democracy and of development. In addition, the first elections in which power is transferred from Compaoré to another president will be a key indicator of democratic consolidation, especially if the new president is from a different party. The transfer itself as well as the way in which it takes place will help analysts to assess the depth of the democratization process. Since Compaoré is permitted to run for a second seven-year term, any such transfer of power presumably would not take place before 1998.

Third, and maybe most important for a country as poor as Burkina Faso, its economic situation must improve so that the fragile fabric of civil society does not fray in the process of building this democracy. For this, the Burkinabè state will require much appropriate international assistance. France, in particular, will have to contribute significantly, in order to keep Burkina Faso on the right path. Chirac's administration seems quite positive about Burkina Faso's progress and interested in participating in its political and economic development.

Laura E. Boudon

It is important to remember how far Burkina Faso has come in the process of democratization. From a populist/military/Marxist-Leninist regime, it is moving toward a liberal democracy. As Larry Diamond has pointed out about democratization in general, "if progress is made toward developing democratic government, it is likely to be gradual, messy, fitful and slow, with many imperfections along the way."[81] Burkina Faso faces a long and difficult road ahead. There is room to hope, however, that the "fits" are few and that the progress towards real democracy can be steady.

Notes

1. Anton Andereggen, *France's Relationship with Sub-Saharan Africa* (Westport, Conn.: Praeger, 1994), p. 63, and I. William Zartman, *Europe and Africa: The New Phase* (Boulder: Lynne Rienner, 1993), p. 28.

2. René Otayek, "Burkina Faso: Between Feeble State and Total State, the Swing Continues," in Donal B. Cruise O'Brien, John Dunn, and Richard Rathbone, eds., *Contemporary West African States* (New York: Cambridge University Press, 1989), pp. 13–30.

3. These three reasons were discussed in "Upper Volta," *Africa Contemporary Record* 15 (1982–1983):B584.

4. Claude Wauthier, *Quatre présidents et l'Afrique: De Gaulle, Pompidou, Giscard d'Estaing, Mitterrand* (Paris: Éditions du Seuil, 1995), p. 247.

5. Michael Wilkins, "The Death of Thomas Sankara and the Rectification of the People's Revolution in Burkina Faso," *African Affairs* 88, no. 352 (1989):376.

6. Ibid., p. 385.

7. Ibid., p. 383.

8. The term *populist* has been used to describe Sankara's regime by Otayek, "Burkina Faso," as well as by Richard Sandbrook, *The Politics of Africa's Economic Recovery* (New York: Cambridge University Press, 1993).

9. Sandbrook, *Politics of Africa's Economic Recovery,* p. 130.

10. Elliott P. Skinner, "Sankara and the Burkinabè Revolution: Charisma and Power, Local and External Dimensions," *Journal of Modern African Studies* 26, no. 3 (1988):445.

11. *Thomas Sankara Speaks* (New York: Pathfinder Press, 1988), p. 42.

12. Otayek, "Burkina Faso: Between Feeble State and Total State," p. 22.

13. Ibid., p. 21.

14. For more on delinking, see Talata Kafandi, "Burkina Faso: August 1983—The Beginning of Delinking?" in Azzam Mahjoub, ed., *Adjustment or Delinking? The African Experience* (Atlantic Highlands, N.J.: Zed Books, 1990), pp. 109–127.

15. Mike Speirs, "Agrarian Change and the Revolution in Burkina Faso," *African Affairs* 90 (1991):101.

16. Ibid., p. 101.

17. Interview of Thomas Sankara by Margaret Nowicki, *Africa Report* 29, no. 4 (July-August 1984):5.

18. Ibid., p. 9.

19. Skinner, "Sankara and the Burkinabè Revolution," p. 448.

20. *Africa Contemporary Record* 15 (1982–1983), p. B588.

21. Otayek, "Burkina Faso: Between Feeble State and Total State," p. 24.

22. Ibid., p. 27.

23. Ibid., p. 28.

24. Ibid., p. 24.

25. Ibid., p. 23.

26. Sandbrook, *Politics of Africa's Economic Recovery,* p. 130.

27. Economic figures are from Wilkins, "The Death of Thomas Sankara and the Rectification of the People's Revolution," p. 385.

28. Naomi Chazan et al., eds., *Politics and Society in Contemporary Africa* (Boulder: Lynne Rienner, 1988), p. 145.

29. Skinner, "Sankara and the Burkinabè Revolution," p. 454.

30. "The rectification process," *West Africa,* no. 3707 (1988):1572.

31. Ernest Harsch, "How Popular is the Front?" *Africa Report* 34, no. 1 (January-February 1989):58.

32. *African Contemporary Record* 20 (1987–1988):B13.

33. "The Compaoré Enigma," *West Africa,* no. 3716 (1988):2028.

34. "Compaoré and the Coup Attempt," *West Africa,* no. 3763 (October 2–8, 1989):1636.

35. Gabi Waibel, *Frauen in Burkina Faso: Lebensverhaltnisse, Handlungsperspektiven und Organisationsformen* (Saarbrücken: Verlag Publishers, 1992), p. 36.

36. Joan Baxter and Keith Somerville, "Burkina Faso," in Chris Allen et al., *Benin, Congo, and Burkina Faso: Politics, Economics, and Society* (London: Pinter: 1989), p. 253.

37. *Economist* Intelligence Unit (hereafter EIU), *Country Report: Burkina Faso,* no. 2 (1991), p. 41.

38. "From Left to Right," *West Africa,* June 12–18, 1989, p. 962.

39. Ibid., p. 963.

40. *Africa Research Bulletin, Political Series,* September 15, 1990, p. 9790.

41. *Africa Research Bulletin, Political Series,* February 1991, p. 10019, *Africa Research Bulletin, Political Series,* August 1991, p. 10227.

42. Russell Geekie, "Compaoré's Campaign," *Africa Report* 36, no. 5 (September-October 1991):55.

43. Ibid., pp. 55–56.

44. Ibid., pp. 56–57.

45. On these reasons, see Marc Aicardi de Saint Paul, "Présentation de la constitution du Burkina Faso," *Afrique contemporaine,* no. 159 (1991):74–101.

46. Sandbrook, *Politics of Africa's Economic Recovery,* p. 131.

47. The new constitution explicitly declares that coups are illegal, stating: "All power that does not emanate from this constitution, namely, that following a coup or putsch, is illegal." *La Constitution du Burkina Faso adoptée par le référendum du 2 juin 1991 et promulguée le 11 juin 1991* (Ouagadougou, 1991), Article 167, p. 50.

48. Geekie, "Compaoré's Campaign," p. 58.

49. *Foreign Broadcast Information Service Daily Report–Sub-Saharan Africa* (hereafter *FBIS-SSA*), December 28, 1992.

50. For more information on this topic, see John F. Clark, "The National Conference as an Instrument of Democratization in Francophone Africa," *Journal of Third World Studies* 11, no. 1 (1994):304–335.

51. "Université cherche raison d'être," *Jeune Afrique* (June 17–23, 1994):38.

52. *FBIS-SSA,* January 24, 1994, p. 3.

53. *FBIS-SSA,* March 18, 1994, p. 1.

54. *FBIS-SSA*, May 16, 1994, p. 2.

55. "Privatisation en projet," *Marchés tropicaux et méditerranéens,* July 15, 1994, p. 1505.

56. Augustin Loada and René Otayek, "Les élections municipales du 12 février 1995 au Burkina Faso," *Politique africaine,* June 1995, pp. 135–143.

57. EIU, *Country Report: Burkina Faso*, no. 3 (1991), p. 40.

58. The charge was made by the president of the Burkinabè Movement for Human Rights. See "Nous devons rester sur nos gardes," *Jeune Afrique* (June 17–23, 1993), p. 36.

59. EIU, *Country Report: Burkina Faso*, no. 3 (1991), p. 40.

60. EIU, *Country Report: Burkina Faso*, no. 1 (1992), p. 40.

61. See, for example, Sandbrook, *Politics of Africa's Economic Recovery,* p. 132.

62. These small parties have created little controversy and have not been mentioned in international weekly magazines such as *Jeune Afrique, West Africa,* and *Africa Report.*

63. EIU, *Country Report: Burkina Faso*, no. 2 (1992), p. 42.

64. Loada and Otayek, "Les élections municipales," p. 125.

65. Baxter and Somerville, "Burkina Faso," p. 259.

66. *Africa Contemporary Record* 21 (1988–1989), p. B17.

67. Barbara Grosch, "Through the Structural Adjustment Minefield: Politics in an Era of Economic Liberalization," in Jennifer A. Widner, ed., *Economic Change and Political Liberalization in Sub-Saharan Africa* (Baltimore: Johns Hopkins University Press, 1994), pp. 29–47.

68. Pascal Zagré, *Les politiques économiques du Burkina Faso: Une tradition d'ajustement structurel* (Paris: Éditions Karthala, 1994), p. 193.

69. *Africa Contemporary Record* 21 (1988–1989), p. B17.

70. *Africa Contemporary Record* 20 (1987-1988, p. B15.

71. *FBIS-SSA,* June 16, 1993, p. 1.

72. Frédéric Dorce, "Chirac-Compaoré: Reconnaissance de la France," *Jeune Afrique Économie,* no. 201 (1995):48–51.

73. Dietrich Rueschemeyer, Evelyne Huber Stephens, and John D. Stephens, *Capitalist Development and Democracy* (Chicago: University of Chicago Press, 1992), p. 43.

74. John F. Clark, "The Constraints on Democracy in Sub-Saharan Africa: The Case for Limited Democracy," *SAIS Review* 14, no. 2 (Summer-Fall 1994):107.

75. "Nous devons rester sur nos gardes," p. 37.

76. Goran Hyden, paper presented at the Colloquium for Democratization and Development in Africa, Florida International University, Miami, March 1992.

77. Patrick Chabal, *Power in Africa: An Essay on Political Interpretation,* 2d ed. (Blasingstoke, England: Macmillan, 1992), p. 259.

78. Clark, "The Constraints on Democracy in Sub-Saharan Africa," p. 97.

79. Sandbrook, *Politics of Africa's Economic Recovery,* p. 146.

80. Zagré, *Les politiques économiques du Burkina Faso,* p. 222.

81. Larry Diamond, "Beyond Autocracy: Prospects for Democracy in Africa," in *Beyond Autocracy in Africa* (Atlanta: Carter Center of Emory University, 1989), p. 24.

Chapter Nine

Gabon: Limited Reform and Regime Survival

DAVID E. GARDINIER

The limited reforms resulting from a prolonged upheaval in Gabon during the first half of 1990 ended the single-party regime and created a new political framework for the following years. Though the tumultuous events left President Omar Bongo and his associates in the ruling Gabonese Democratic Party (Parti Démocratique Gabonais, PDG) in control of the state and the government, thereafter they had to contend with a legal opposition that enjoys strong support in the coastal provinces and in the north. They also had to permit much greater public scrutiny of their actions. At the same time, the Bongo regime, through a combination of fraud, force, and external assistance, managed to retain a sometimes shaky grip on state power and to block further reforms.

In this chapter these developments are explored with a view to providing a better understanding of their significance as well as that of the course of political reform in Gabon. The chapter is organized into three sections. The first examines the rise of a single-party system under Bongo's leadership after November 1967 during a period in which the development of the country's oil and minerals was irrevocably changing the economy and society. The second focuses upon the circumstances that destabilized the regime between January and May 1990 to the point of forcing Bongo and his associates to accept the restoration of multipartyism and the freer exercise of civil liberties. The third deals with the course of political life, including the regime's tactics for perpetuating itself in power, during the subsequent four and a half years.

I wish to thank the Scarecrow Press for granting permission to incorporate portions of the Introduction to my *Historical Dictionary of Gabon* (Metuchen, N.J.: Scarecrow Press, 1994) into this essay.

The Rise of the Single-Party System

Gabon achieved independence on August 13, 1960, as a result of decolonizing forces elsewhere in the French Union that had contributed to the collapse of the Fourth Republic in May 1958 and then to the demise of Charles de Gaulle's French Community, which had limited the African territories to autonomy or self-government. Although anticolonialism had developed among the Gabonese elite, some of whom had held office in the representative institutions of the Fourth Republic, the country had never produced what one might call a national-ist movement. Ethnic diversity and rivalry (particularly between the Myènè and the Fang, as well as intra-Fang), the geographical barriers to the establishment of linkages between the political elite and the masses dispersed throughout the forested interior, limited economic development (mainly the timber industry and the cash crops of cocoa and coffee), the small numbers with an education beyond the primary grades—all were factors inhibiting the rise of a nationalist movement that might have mobilized popular energies for securing freedom from foreign rule, the creation of national unity, and modernization of the economy and soci-ety. Independence arrived with the vast majority of the population remaining po-litically unaware while retaining patterns of subsistence activity and social rela-tions not terribly different from the previous decades and perhaps centuries.

At independence Gabon possessed neither the resources nor the personnel to operate its administration and economy, let alone to develop them, without con-tinued outside aid and assistance. Much of this support was forthcoming from France and was institutionalized in the fifteen cooperation agreements signed a month before independence. At the same time, private investors from France, other Common Market countries, and the United States continued the develop-ment of the country's mineral resources begun during the late 1950s. The early 1960s saw the first significant exports of manganese and uranium as well as the successful prospecting and construction of facilities that would lead to the ex-ploitation of petroleum in the late 1960s and early 1970s.[1]

In the meantime, within three years after independence, the political institu-tions modeled upon those of the French Fifth Republic had broken down, victim to the rivalries among the politicians and parties. Central to the collapse was the determination of President Léon Mba (1902–1967) to provide a strongly authori-tarian leadership, taken with the increasingly repressive measures necessary for him to do so. His actions provoked a military coup against his regime in February 1964. French military intervention, which restored Mba to office, allowed him to eliminate the restraints on his power represented by a multiparty National As-sembly and to establish an authoritarian regime. It enabled him also to transfer his power intact to a successor selected on the advice of agents from the office of President Charles de Gaulle—Albert-Bernard (later Omar) Bongo (b. 1935). Bongo would face the difficult task of maintaining political stability while trying to establish a less repressive and more broadly based regime.

For these tasks Bongo possessed a number of assets. As a member of the numerically small Téké people of the far interior, he stood outside the ethnic rivalries that had troubled political life for two decades. Though young, Bongo possessed a good education in business administration and a decade of governmental experience, including several years in the president's office.[2]

In March 1968, with the agreement of a National Assembly that by then included only deputies from Mba's party, Bongo proceeded to abolish all existing parties. He created a single new one, the PDG, which for the next twenty-two years would be the only legal party. Bongo justified the establishment of a single party mainly on the grounds that the older parties represented competing ethnic and regional interests that hindered stable government and national unity. Yet he recognized the persisting strength of such interests by creating a cabinet of some fifty members and an unnecessarily large civil service in which elements of these interests could be included. As a result, the ethnic and regional backgrounds of appointees often carried far greater weight than their professional qualifications and experience. Bongo particularly favored appointees from his own Haut-Ogooué Province, including Téké and Obamba people who were his relatives or those of his wife, Joséphine Kama Dabany, to whom he was married from 1959 to 1988.

It was Bongo's ability and willingness to consult and engage in dialogue with the political elite and, to a lesser extent, the latter's cooperation that enabled the political system to function. His control of opportunities for lucrative public employment—and hence for personal enrichment—made it possible for him to incorporate the bulk of the educated elite into the system and to obtain their support for or acquiescence to his policies. Most of those unwilling to work within the system withdrew from political activity and sought private employment or lived abroad, either in France or in other francophone countries. Those who criticized the Bongo regime or who showed opposition risked severe repression. As early as 1972, the regime suppressed what the press called a "professors' plot" by Marxists at the newly opened university in Libreville. After being held in a Libreville jail for three and a half years, four professors and several students were sentenced in 1975 for an alleged plot against the security of the state. Eventually the professors were allowed to return to their teaching positions. But they refused offers of government posts that would have required them to join the PDG, and, until the upheaval of 1990, they stayed out of politics. Their refusal to join the PDG enhanced their standing among the opponents of the regime, particularly those on the Left.[3]

The single-party system provided Gabon with a new stability. But not surprisingly, it also gave the president and the ruling class the means to perpetuate themselves in office with little regard for the wishes of the people. Those in power held the key positions in the PDG and thus influenced the selection of candidates for office, who ran unopposed. Revolt would have been futile because the France of Presidents Charles de Gaulle, Georges Pompidou, and Valéry Giscard d'Estaing

(1958–1981) was prepared to intervene militarily to support Bongo under the terms of the defense cooperation agreement. Gaullist agents aided Bongo in erecting a security apparatus that relied on mercenaries to protect those in power.[4]

In April 1969 Bongo curbed the independence of organized labor by requiring workers to join a single union, the Confédération Syndicale Gabonaise. In 1973 this union became a special organ of the PDG with officially appointed officers. Wildcat strikes and work stoppages periodically reflected workers' dissatisfaction with these arrangements, which they lacked the power to alter. The large role of foreign workers in the economy further weakened the ability of the Gabonese workers to protect their interests.[5]

Nevertheless, the economic growth linked to the development of the country's mineral resources, particularly petroleum, from the late 1960s to the mid-1980s, tended to mute popular criticism of the regime. The greatly increased mineral revenues permitted Bongo to undertake such development projects as the Transgabonais Railway, to create two dozen parastatals, and to expand facilities for education and health care. But the production of foodstuffs for local markets languished because of low controlled prices and the failure of the regime to maintain a system of roads. As a result, by the late 1980s Gabon was importing 85 percent of its food.

Industrialization promoted urbanization and a more rapid rate of population growth. Between 1960 and 1990 the population of Gabon doubled to one million, with at least 20 percent of the increase resulting from immigration. Whereas only 15 percent of the population was urban in 1960, by 1990 close to three-quarters resided in towns and cities, particularly Libreville with over 400,000 and Port-Gentil with 70,000. At least half of the population now earned its living from salaries and wages. The much larger industrial working class that had emerged was vulnerable to changing international market conditions.

At the same time the extension of educational opportunities had produced a much larger literate population. Nearly all persons over the age of fifteen years could now speak French, and 60 percent of them could also read it. As a result, the speakers of the country's more than forty Bantu languages now possessed a medium for communicating with one another and for receiving news in both local and international radio and television broadcasts. They were acquiring a heightened political awareness through access to information about Gabon and the world that the regime could no longer control or censor.[6]

Gradually, through the years since 1968, the Bongo regime had amended the constitution of 1961 to increase the power of the executive and to institutionalize a role for the PDG. The National Assembly became a rubber stamp for the executive, and the congresses of the PDG superseded the Assembly in the expression of ethnic and regional concerns. The party was structured hierarchically in the manner of Marxist-Leninist parties, with local, provincial, and national committees. At the summit was a Political Bureau headed by Bongo as secretary-general. During the 1980s, the party functioned increasingly through a kind of democratic centralism involving less dialogue than during the 1970s. This situation probably contributed to the increased amount of grassroots dissatisfaction over misman-agement, corruption, and multiple officeholding expressed at extraordinary con-gresses summoned to deal with particular problems—for example, the economic crisis in July 1979 and the challenge of the Mouvement de Redressement National (MORENA) in March 1983.[7]

MORENA was an opposition group first formed among Gabonese exiles and students in France. The election of Socialist President François Mitterrand in May 1981 and a Leftist majority in the National Assembly, which supported policies fa-voring human rights in African states, encouraged MORENA to come into the open in Gabon itself. In November 1981, it surfaced in Libreville among intellec-tuals and civil servants, who were mainly of Fang and Punu origins. They sought a more equitable distribution of wealth among provinces and individuals, a restoration of multiparty democracy, and a curb on abuses and corruption in government. In light of the French Socialist government's position that it would not intervene militarily to protect the Bongo regime against domestic opponents, the president moved quickly to crush MORENA. In November 1982 twenty-nine of its supporters were given long prison sentences at hard labor despite the lack of evidence to prove the regime's accusation that they were seeking to overthrow the government. Thereafter, Bongo greatly increased the size of the Presidential Guard (PG), which was commanded by privately employed French officers.

After the suppression of MORENA within Gabon, MORENA-in-exile was or-ganized in Paris. Its members were led by a Catholic priest, the Reverend Paul Mba-Abessolé (b. 1939), who emphasized that the group would work peacefully and through dialogue with those in power to achieve its goals.

The Socialist government in France, much to the consternation of the Bongo regime, allowed MORENA-in-exile to hold public meetings and press conferences reported in the media, including television broadcasts into Gabon. Thus Father Mba became known to both French and Gabonese viewers. He probably had a ready-made audience among the 40 percent of the population that are Fang (their numbers had been increased by 60,000 Equatorial Guinean refugees from the Ma-cias regime during the 1970s). But he had a particular appeal for two other rea-sons. He possessed the ability to communicate directly with the ordinary people in simple and straightforward terms. Further, he sought to bring about changes through nonviolent means. As a result, he acquired a considerable reputation and moral stature as a courageous opponent of the Bongo regime.[8]

The Upheaval of the First Half of 1990

In the meantime, the country's prolonged economic downturn, which had begun after 1985, was having serious effects. Falling prices for oil in the world market and the weakness of the dollar were continuing drastically to reduce the govern-ment's revenues. Whereas before 1985 oil had provided 65 percent of the budget resources and 85 percent of export receipts, in 1988 oil generated only 30 percent and 18 percent respectively. During the late 1980s income from manganese, timber, uranium, cocoa, coffee, and palm oil remained barely stable or declined slightly. Thus the 1987 and 1988 national budgets dropped to half of those of 1984 to 1986. Development projects, in particular, were cut back severely. Whereas the investment budget had totaled 400 billion CFA francs in 1985 (FF8 billion [French francs]), it fell to 60 billion CFA francs in 1988. At the same time higher interest rates increased the expenses of government. In these circumstances unemployment grew to the point that domestic consumption dropped by one-third. Schools lacked books and supplies, hospitals medicine and equipment, and the roads deteriorated further. In mid-1989 the secretary-general of the Confédération Syndicale Gabonaise announced that 50,000 workers had lost their jobs since 1985, one-third of them in the private sector. Altogether, 200 companies had closed down. The public sector had been hard hit, particularly since the completion of work on the Transgabonais Railway in 1987.[9]

In February 1989 the country learned through the columns of Le Monde that during the 1970s and 1980s one-fourth of public revenues had been diverted into private hands. During a decade in which the annual salaries of all 40,000 government employees totaled FF2 billion, top officials had transferred some FF28 billion to foreign bank accounts. This was nearly double the national debt of 1990 that the country was struggling to repay. It was reported that Bongo and his associates had amassed personal fortunes that collectively totaled FF30 billion, with Bongo's alone estimated at FF500 million, making him one of the wealthiest men in the world.[10] The following month, the same newspaper reported that only 2 percent of Gabon's population, mainly the ruling class and their extended families, had received 80 percent of all personal income.[11]

A series of austerity measures that the government introduced between 1987 and 1989 in order to qualify for international loans reduced the income of employees in both the public and private sectors. During 1989 the ordinary people had reason to hope for the return of good times as the onshore oil fields at Rabi-Kounga began to produce, though the increased revenues would not become available to the government until 1990. As 1989 wore one, it became evident that the austerity measures were hitting hardest the portion of the population least capable of supporting them while allowing the ruling class to maintain its affluent lifestyle on only a slightly reduced scale.

MORENA circulated tracts in Libreville identifying President Bongo as the "Gabonese evil." News of events in Europe, relayed into Gabon by international radio and television, also had an impact. The celebration of the 200th anniversary of the French Revolution throughout 1989 drew attention to a historic popular revolt against privilege. Focus on the rights of man and the citizen served to remind the Gabonese of the restraints on the exercise of such rights under the Bongo regime. The disintegration of the repressive communist regimes throughout Eastern Europe encouraged the dissatisfied to think of the possibility of replacing long-entrenched regimes and rather quickly.

Bongo himself recognized the latter influence several months later as it began to affect several formerly French states in West Africa when he observed: "The winds from the East are shaking the coconut trees." To help defuse popular discontent, Bongo encouraged a week-long visit in May 1989 by Father Mba, whose proposals for reform he promised to consider. Mba was treated more as a visiting dignitary than the leader of a suppressed political party, much to the consternation of some of the PDG's less flexible leaders.[12]

In September and October 1989 the government announced that it had discovered and suppressed two related plots to assassinate Bongo and to overthrow the government. They were led by Punu elements including civil servants and military men in league with foreign business interests and a religious sect led by a Malian trader. Bongo was reportedly much shaken when he learned of the involvement of three trusted officers, one of them formerly from the PG and another currently heading the PG at Franceville, the chief executive's hometown. In mid-December, after new austerities provoked a strike by electricity and water workers that brought industry and commerce to a standstill, Bongo observed that the austerity measures had reached the limits of the supportable.[13]

Then began the wave of strikes and demonstrations that shook the foundations of the Bongo regime. On January 16, 1990, students at the Omar Bongo University who had been boycotting classes went on strike over the shortage of professors and library works, which diminished the quality of the education they were receiving. The students, most of whom received financial support from the government, were also concerned about the impact of the austerity measures, which were eroding their purchasing power and limiting the expansion of the overcrowded and inadequate educational facilities. The following day, the police forcibly evicted the students from the law and economics faculty who were occupying the campus. On January 18, high school students took to the streets to demonstrate their solidarity. They were joined by adults who were not students and who the government claimed were mainly immigrant Africans; the latter were blamed for the rioting that involved looting of Lebanese properties in the humble quarters and other criminal damage. Police firing at the feet of demonstrators killed five persons and injured at least seventy. Two hundred fifty people were arrested. Bongo met with student representatives on January 22 to permit them to air their grievances and to defuse their discontent.[14]

Following the riots of January 18, and despite government measures to curb protest, demonstrations intensified in Libreville and strikes spread to workers in both public and private sectors, bringing the capital almost to a standstill. Demands focused upon higher wages, fairer distribution of the country's wealth, and democratic reforms. Neither Bongo's concessions to particular groups between February 14 and 24 nor his banning of all strikes and demonstrations on February 22 succeeded immediately in halting the protests. The crisis peaked on February 26 when airport personnel, telecommunication workers, and gas station attendants joined teachers and physicians striking for better pay and working conditions. Workers also demanded the creation of free trade unions not under government control and Gabonization of jobs. By the end of the month most strikers had returned to work after obtaining presidential promises to establish committees to consider their grievances and demands.

By that time, the events were pressuring the government to undertake changes in the political system that would move it away from the one-party regime. From a commission on democracy created in January came the recommendation that the PDG be dissolved in order to pave the way for a new political grouping, the Gabonese Social and Democratic Assembly (Rassemblement Social et Démocrate Gabonais, RSDG), which would be open to various currents of opinion. The commission intended the RSDG to provide an apprenticeship for political pluralism over a five-year period. For Bongo the RSDG constituted a means of permitting wider participation while maintaining his control over the nation's political forces. Thus he summoned a national conference that, after unexpected delays, began to meet on March 27 to discuss the new arrangements.

On February 26 Bongo announced a new provisional government replacing that of August 1989. Though he brought into office several younger and better qualified ministers with well-educated or experienced advisers, he retained most of the previous ministers who had held key posts. Among them as prime minister was Léon Mébiame, known to have little sympathy for democratic reform.

On March 21, amid continuing popular economic and social unrest, the government granted legal recognition to seventy-four political associations so that they might participate in the national conference. Though the conference's name was taken from the national conference assembled in Benin the previous month, Bongo did not intend it to possess sovereignty or to have the power to bring his holding of the presidential office into question. His view was that its decisions would be only advisory, to be implemented as he considered appropriate.[15]

Although Bongo would have preferred to keep all parties under his control within the proposed RSDG, the opposition rejected such incorporation. They urged the immediate return to multipartyism. While the opposition was splintered into many groups, there were broadly two tendencies among them. MORENA under Father Mba represented Christian democracy with a strong populist bent. MORENA had strong support from both Catholic and Protestant elements, including some who were troubled by the influences of Masonry and Islam in the Bongo regime, and it was most extensively implanted in the north and among the Fang people.

The secularist and socialist tendency was represented by the Gabonese Progress Party (Parti Gabonais du Progrès, PGP), which had its strongest support among workers and the Myènè peoples of the coastal regions. Its leaders were respected professionals of aristocratic background, mainly Nkomi and Orungu from Port-

Gentil, and included professors at the university who had been imprisoned during the 1970s as a result of the "professors' plot." Among them were Joseph Rendjambe, professor of economics and a successful businessman, and his close relative, Pierre-Louis Agondjo-Okawe (b. 1936), former dean of the law and economics faculty at the university and currently head of the bar in Gabon. Because the PDG also included reformist elements, led, among others, by Ali Bongo (b. 1959), forces favoring reform had a majority in the national conference. The reformism of Ali Bongo and his associates had a generational dimension in that they wished to replace longtime PDG stalwarts of little education and meager ability with younger people from their own group.

The national conference asked Omar Bongo to serve out the rest of his term (until the end of 1993) but to resign as head of the PDG and to put himself above parties. It also called for the return of a multiparty system, which was reestablished through constitutional amendment on May 22.[16]

On April 27, following the end of the national conference, Bongo named a new government headed by Casimir Oyé-Mba (b. 1942), from the Fang of the Estuary Province. Oyé-Mba, who had not previously been involved in politics, had been serving as governor of the Bank of the Central African States at Yaoundé. Oyé gave minor posts to some opposition party members, but the PDG retained firm control over the government. Elections for a new National Assembly, which had been postponed pending the outcome of the national conference, were scheduled for September 1990.[17]

In the meantime, also on May 22, the death of PGP leader Rendjambe in suspicious circumstances in a Libreville hotel owned by the government set off an explosion of violence in the main cities and towns the following day. The inability of the government to control the violence and destruction at Port-Gentil, which threatened French lives and property (including the oil installations), led on May 24 to a French military intervention to restore order. France intervened, it would appear, without prior consultation with the Gabonese government and without the intention of restoring the authority of the Bongo regime. Intervention nevertheless had the effect of propping up the government until the PG could regain control of Port-Gentil. Thereafter, French officials played an important role in reestablishing communications between the Bongo regime and the leadership of the PGP and to calming the tense situation. France urged Bongo to proceed with reforms that would enable the opposition parties to compete fairly in the coming elections for the Legislative Assembly.[18] By this time France was encouraging democratic reform in accordance with Mitterrand's pronouncement at the Franco-African summit at La Baule, France, in June 1990.[19]

The Bongo Regime's Perpetuation in Office

The circumstances of the assembly elections in September and October, which involved many irregularities, intimidation, and fraud, above all on behalf of PDG candidates, allowed that party to retain a slight majority of the seats. When it became clear to Father Mba that the government would not allow him to win the second round of voting in a Libreville constituency where the government claimed he won only 49.44 percent of the ballots in the first round, he withdrew his candidacy. He also urged MORENA members not to participate in any of the second-round voting, which enough of them did to aid indirectly the survival of the PDG government. Thus, whereas Agondjo-Okawe, whose election the Bongo forces did not seek to prevent, won a seat from Port-Gentil, Mba-Abessolé had to pursue his opposition outside of the legislative body. As a result of the balloting, the PDG held 63 of the 120 seats in the National Assembly; 27 went to the two factions of MORENA, 18 to the PGP, and 12 to other, mainly socialist, parties. Oyé-Mba gave minor cabinet posts to some opposition deputies in the new PDG-dominated government that he headed.

On March 5, 1991, the National Assembly unanimously adopted a new constitution that restored multipartyism and contained strong guarantees concerning civil liberties. The constitution provided for a strong president, as in the past, but it added some strength to the office of the prime minister.

Though the upheaval of 1990 restored multipartyism and a freer exercise of speech, press, and assembly, it left President Bongo and his associates of the PDG in control of all branches of government. However, their actions were henceforth open to greater public scrutiny in the National Assembly and in the media. While the pro-government daily, *L'Union*, continued to represent the PDG's views, opposition groups founded a number of weekly papers and two radio stations.

The regime had a strong political base only in the president's own Haut-Ogooué Province and among PDG officeholders in other provinces and the capital who have benefited from arrangements that gave them both power and wealth. If the seats in the National Assembly had been distributed more strictly according to population, the PDG would not have retained its majority in that body or control of the government.

The increased revenues from the Rabi-Kounga oil fields during the early 1990s permitted the Bongo regime to secure the international loans to keep the government afloat. But its unwillingness or inability to institute a financial discipline that would lessen the privileges of the ruling class delayed needed economic restructuring and the restoration of adequate levels of services in education and health care as well as road maintenance. As a result, chronic unrest continued among the urban population, taking the form of periodic strikes, work stoppages, and demonstrations by both public and private sector employees. During 1993 rural populations barricaded the roads to protest the consequences of governmental neglect.

In the face of the unrest, Bongo himself at one point noted: "The PDG controls the government but the opposition controls the streets." Proof of this statement came in June 1991 when a general strike organized by the opposition parties forced Bongo to implement the changes provided by the new constitution. But in general, the divisions within the opposition parties often made joint action difficult, as did disagreements on the strategies for dealing with the regime. Thus the period between the election of a multiparty parliament and the reelection of Bongo as president in December 1993 was largely one of stalemate. During these years the opposition sought to find the best strategies for unseating Bongo while the latter aimed to perpetuate himself in office.[20]

During the late 1980s and early 1990s the French Socialist regime was undertaking a reassessment of France's relations with sub-Saharan Africa, linked in part to serious financial difficulties within the franc zone, of which Gabon is a member.[21] Encouragement of democratic reform in a climate of economic downturn seemed likely to promote instability that might threaten French interests. In the case of Gabon, France wondered whether a government composed of opposition parties (provided it could be achieved) would be as willing as the Bongo regime to continue the arrangements that had brought so many benefits to France and its citizens.

The return to power in France of a Center-Right coalition as a result of the parliamentary elections of March 1993 placed primary responsibility for dealing with these problems in the hands of a government headed by Prime Minister Edouard Balladur, a protégé of President Pompidou. That government's minister of cooperation, Michel Roussin, indicated that it was easing off on the pressures for further democratic reform. On June 23, 1993, he declared that the movement towards democracy in Gabon would be allowed to follow its own rhythm.[22] At the same time, France continued to work with the Bongo regime to deal with its economic and financial problems. Its task was complicated by Gabon's suspension of its International Monetary Fund (IMF) structural adjustment program (SAP) in early 1992. But France refused to cancel Gabon's debt as it was doing in the case of the poorest of the francophone African states.[23]

Throughout most of the remainder of 1993, the Balladur government undertook steps, in cooperation with the government of Gabon, to ensure fairness in the presidential elections of December 1993. It contributed funds and personnel for the taking of a national census, which was a prerequisite for the establishment of updated voter rolls. The census, the breakdowns by province and prefecture of which were not made public but some of which leaked out, indicated that the Estuary (Libreville) and Ogooué Maritime (Port Gentil) Provinces, which had elected mainly opposition deputies in 1990, now had over half of the country's population, while the interior provinces dominated by the PDG had lost population. Along with other European governments, France aided in the preparations for the voting in such matters as identity cards, indelible ink, transparent urns, and so on.[24]

The system of election required a second round of voting if no candidate won an absolute majority in the first round. Thus each of the opposition groups ran its own candidate, with a view to uniting behind the leading one among them in a second round against Bongo. All of them were convinced, as were French observers, that Bongo could not win a majority in the first round. The position of his party had been weakened when such stalwarts as Léon Mébiame, Jules Bourdès-Ogouliguendé (former president of the National Assembly), Jean-Pierre Lemboumba-Lépandou (former finance minister and a notable from the Haut-Ogooué Province), and Alexandre Sambat (former ambassador to Washington) entered the contest against him. As the electoral campaign heated up, Bongo increasingly worried about his chances. Thus in mid-September he used a pre-1990 press law to prevent publication of most of the opposition newspapers for many weeks and sought to jam the airwaves of the opposition's radio stations.[25]

As the elections drew closer, the Balladur government altered its stance of favoring fair elections, quite likely influenced by the approaching necessity of devaluing the CFA franc. France's new stance permitted Minister of the Interior Charles Pasqua to send electoral experts to Gabon to help Bongo falsify the results of the voting in the Haut-Ogooué and Ogooué-et-Lolo Provinces,[26] the provinces in which the PDG retained its strongest grip over local administration. Bongo at this point barred the National Democratic Institute for International Affairs of Washington, D.C., from entering the country to train election personnel as previously agreed, thus preventing arrangements that might have ensured greater honesty and fairness in the balloting. During the balloting in the two provinces just mentioned, the official results showed the numbers voting to have exceeded the voting-age population by 40 percent and Bongo receiving huge majorities, even in precincts where the forces of Lemboumba-Lépandou had voted in large numbers for their candidate. In the Estuary Province (Libreville) there were all sorts of irregularities in the balloting that brought the results into question. To make matters worse, Bongo did not await completion of the counting of the votes in a central headquarters dominated by his supporters to announce that he had won reelection with 51 percent of the vote. In the course of the counting, a leak to a Reuters correspondent indicated that Bongo was leading with 37 percent but that Mba-Abessolé had 32 percent, with the remainder divided among the nine other candidates. But the official results gave Father Mba only 27 percent.[27]

The Balladur government immediately endorsed the results of the election, even though both former Prime Minister Jacques Chirac and Louis Dominici, the French ambassador and a Bongo partisan, urged him to hold a second round; they, like nearly everyone else, knew that Bongo had not really won a majority in the first round. But Bongo feared that he would be defeated in a second round, and so none was held. He stationed units of the PG about the capital to repress protests against this electoral fraud, which Mba-Abessolé called "an electoral coup."[28]

Following the death in December 1993 of Côte d'Ivoire President Félix Houphouët-Boigny, who had strongly opposed devaluation, France moved, on January 12, 1994, to devalue the CFA franc by 50 percent, as international financial institutions had been urging it to do for many years. A key reason that Balladur gave support to Bongo's electoral coup was the certainty that Bongo would acquiesce to devaluation despite his vehement opposition. Balladur was unsure how Mba-Abessolé, the possible winner in a second round, would respond.[29]

Even before the devaluation, France, in cooperation with the IMF, had been preparing a new SAP for Gabon. Few believe that Gabon can live up to its terms without provoking unmanageable social unrest. Especially difficult to implement are provisions requiring the restructuring and possibly the sale of many of the seventeen public companies and twenty-nine parastatals. The severe reduction of their budgets and the dismissal of several thousand superfluous employees could increase social unrest. France has sought to facilitate cooperation by arranging a postponement of the repayment of much of Gabon's international debt for several years and by canceling portions of the debt that Gabon owes to it, with further cancellations likely in the future. France has also loaned funds to cushion the impact of devaluation through the reduction of Gabon's import duties.[30]

This kind of assistance arrived too late to ease the consequences of the rising cost of living following the devaluation, which led to the worst outburst of violence in Libreville since the 1964 military coup. In late February 1994 a strike was launched by the Gabonese Confederation of Independent Unions (Confédération Gabonaise des Syndicats Libres, CGSL) in cooperation with some opposition parties, particularly the National Assembly of Woodcutters (Rassemblement National des Bûcherons, RNB), the majority segment of MORENA, headed by Mba-Abessolé. The demonstrations and rioting that ensued and their suppression by the PG cost nine lives according to official sources and thirty-seven according to opposition sources, and scores were injured. The PG destroyed the RBN's Radio Liberté as well as the humble residence of Mba, who took refuge in an embassy and then slipped out of the country for several weeks to Paris to avoid possible detention.[31]

The Bongo regime spent the rest of 1994 trying to find a way to incorporate more of the opposition into the government but without abandoning its control.[32] By its attempts it underscored the illegitimacy of the presidential election. It now found the opposition parties much more solidly united against it than they had been before the elections. To try to end the stalemate, it agreed to formal negotiations with the opposition parties in Paris in September in the presence of international observers. Because Mba-Abessolé refused to participate unless Bongo also did, leadership of the opposition passed to Agondjo-Okawe. Jean-François Ntoutoume-Emané headed the PDG delegation. The resulting Paris Accords were signed by representatives of the government and opposition parties at Libreville on October 7, 1994, in the presence of Minister of Cooperation Michel Roussin, who promised France's cooperation in implementing them.[33] The arrangements led to a so-called transition government that included several opposition ministers. But both Mba and Agondjo-Okawe declined to serve, just as they had on all previous occasions when offered portfolios in a PDG-dominated cabinet. Heading the new government was a PDG stalwart of Fang origin, Paulin Obame Nguema, M.D.; the former prime minister, Oyé-Mba, became minister of foreign affairs. Whether the government will implement the various measures agreed upon in Paris to ensure honesty and fairness in future elections remains to be seen. The next Assembly elections have been postponed until late 1996.

Whether the opposition parties, if victorious, could organize a viable government, is a real question. Bongo's electoral coup in December 1993 deprived the country of a runoff with Mba-Abessolé that would have indicated to what extent non-Fang might vote for a Fang president in preference to Bongo and the PDG. The role of Mba-Abessolé and his Fang supporters in the February 1994 disorders in Libreville intensified the fears of some Myènè and other small ethnic groups for their security if a regime dominated by Fang came to power. These feelings are particularly strong among the supporters of the PGP.

At the same time, Agondjo-Okawe's poor showing in the presidential contest (in which he won only 5 percent, according to official figures, and in which he was surpassed by Bongo in his home city of Port-Gentil) may reflect more than electoral manipulation. It may also show a shift of some Nzabi support to Bongo as a result of the establishment in October 1992 of a close relationship between the president and Congo President Pascal Lissouba, who has considerable influence among his Gabonese kinsmen. Whether the PGP can retain its Assembly seats and its status as a major opposition party remains to be seen.

On July 23, 1995, a national referendum amended the constitution to permit full and complete implementation of the Paris Accords. The terms also include establishment of the rule of law and the transformation of the PG into a Republican Guard no longer under direct presidential control. Bongo is likely to avoid compliance with these provisions.[34]

Much will depend upon France, which elected Jacques Chirac as president in May 1995; he appointed a new Center-Right government headed by the former foreign affairs minister, Alain Juppé, as prime minister. The new French regime is unlikely to be receptive to a change in regime in Libreville that might serve its interests less well than does Bongo's. There may be limits to its support, however, if Bongo's grip on the country should show signs of weakening. A good deal will depend upon his ability to balance French insistence on compliance with the terms of the SAP with sufficient expenditures to prevent increasing levels of social unrest. But what is clear, in any case, is that the future of political reform in Gabon depends at least as much on events in France as on developments within Gabon.[35]

Notes

I wish to express my gratitude to François Gaulme of *Marchés tropicaux et méditerranéens* and Sennen Andriamirado of *Jeune Afrique* for sharing their insights into recent Gabonese history during my sabbatical in Paris in 1993 and 1994. The bibliographical sources for the study of history and politics in Gabon are discussed in my reference work, *Gabon* (Oxford: Clio Press, 1992).

1. Gardinier, *Historical Dictionary of Gabon* (hereafter *HDG*), pp. 14–15, 27. The economic development and politics of the period of the Fourth French Republic are discussed in Virginia Thompson and Richard Adloff, *The Emerging States of French Equatorial Africa* (Stanford: Stanford University Press, 1960), and in Brian Weinstein, *Gabon: Nation-Building on the Ogooué* (Cambridge, Mass.: MIT Press, 1966). For political evolution, including during the Mba era and relations with France, see John A. Ballard, "Four Equatorial States," in Gwendolen Carter, ed., *National Unity and Regionalism in Africa* (Ithaca: Cornell University Press, 1966), pp. 231–336. For the development of the oil economy, see Douglas A. Yates, *The Rentier State in Africa: Oil Rent Dependency and Neocolonialism in the Republic of Gabon* (Trenton, N.J.: Africa World Press, 1996).

2. Gardinier, *HDG*, pp. 15–16, 64–65. The best introductions to the eras of Mba and Bongo are found in François Gaulme, *Le Gabon et son ombre* (Paris: Éditions Karthala, 1988), and James F. Barnes, *Gabon: Beyond the Colonial Legacy* (Boulder: Westview Press, 1992). For the French role in selecting Bongo as Gabon's president, see *Foccart parle: Entretiens avec Philippe Gaillard* (Paris: Fayard and Jeune Afrique, 1995), pp. 65–67.

3. Gardinier, *HDG*, pp. 253–254, 279; Robert H. Jackson and Carl G. Rosberg, *Personal Rule in Black Africa* (Berkeley: University of California Press, 1982), pp. 156–159. Essential for understanding the evolution of the PDG are François Hervouet, "Le processus de concentration des pouvoirs par le président de la République au Gabon," *Penant* 93 (January-March 1983):5–35, and *Penant* 93 (April-June 1983):200–215 (article in two parts); and N'Dong Obiang, "Le Parti Démocratique Gabonais et l'état," *Penant* 93 (April-June 1983):131–152.

4. Pierre Péan's *Affaires africaines* (Paris: Fayard, 1983), despite a certain failure to control its sources, provides generally accurate accounts of the involvement of French interests in Gabon and their relations with the notables of the Bongo regime. See also Martin Edzodzomo-Ela, *De la démocratie au Gabon* (Paris: Éditions Karthala, 1993), pp. 5–22.

5. Gardinier, *HDG*, pp. 200–201.

6. Ibid., pp. 3–5, 19–20, 201–202. An analysis of the 1993 census may be found in Albert Ondo Ossa, "Le phénomène d'urbanisation dans les pays sub-Sahariens: Le cas du Gabon," *Mondes en développement* 22, no. 85 (1994):75–81.

7. Gardinier, *HDG*, pp. 253–254, 267–268.

8. Ibid., pp. 218, 225–232.

9. Ibid., pp. 21–22. For the origins of the economic crisis, see Hugues-Alexandre Barro-Chambrier, *L'économie du Gabon. Analyse: Politiques d'ajustement et d'adaptation* (Paris: Économica, 1990); Gabriel Zomo Yebe, *Comprendre la crise de l'économie gabonaise* (Paris: L'Harmattan, 1993).

10. *Le Monde*, February 25, 1989.

11. *Le Monde*, March 20, 1990.

12. David Gardinier, "Gabon," *Africa Contemporary Record* 22 *1989–1990* (New York: Africana Publishers, 1995), p. B109.

13. Ibid., pp. B110–B111.

14. *Marchés tropicaux et méditerranéens*, January 26, 1990.

15. Gardinier, "Gabon," pp. B112–B113.

16. François Gaulme, "Le Gabon à la recherche d'un nouvel ethos politique et social," *Politique africaine*, October 1991, pp. 50–62; Charles M'Ba, "La 'conférence nationale' gabonaise: Du congrès constitutif du Rassemblement Social et Démocrate Gabonais

(RSDG) aux assises pour la démocratie pluraliste," *Afrique 2000,* no. 7 (November 1991):75–90; J.C. Dady Bouchard, *La longue marche de la démocratie gabonaise* (Libreville: Éditions Gabedip, 1992), pp. 3–15.

17. Gardinier, *HDG,* p. 25.

18. *Jeune Afrique,* June 4, 1990, pp. 5–8; *Jeune Afrique,* June 11, 1990, pp. 11–13; *Jeune Afrique,* June 13–19, 1990, pp. 25–26; *Jeune Afrique,* July 4–10, 1990, pp. 28–29; *Le Monde,* June 2, 1990, p. 30; *Le Monde,* June 3–4, 1990, p. 29.

19. *Politique étrangère de la France: Textes et documents* (May-June 1990), pp. 125–130. For the evolution of French policy, see also François Gaulme, "France-Afrique: Une crise de coopération," *Études,* no. 3801 (January 1994):471–486.

20. Gardinier, *HDG,* pp. 25–26.

21. A significant body of evidence suggests that the present arrangements in the franc zone permit the francophone African states to avoid economic reforms that might lessen the benefits currently being derived by their ruling classes. Restructuring might well contribute to a more broadly based and possibly more democratic system. See Nicolas van de Walle, "The Decline of the Franc Zone: Monetary Policies in Francophone Africa," *African Affairs* 90, no. 4 (October 1991):383–405.

22. *Afrique-Express,* no. 5 (June 24, 1993):23.

23. *Economist* Intelligence Unit, *Country Report: Gabon* (hereafter cited as EIU, *CR Gabon*), no. 4 (1993):6.

24. EIU, *CR Gabon,* no. 3 (1993):9; EIU, *CR Gabon,* no. 4 (1993):18.

25. *Jeune Afrique,* December 2–8, 1993, pp. 36–40 (includes biographies of the candidates); EIU, *CR Gabon,* no. 4 (1993):6–10; James F. Barnes, "Adieu, Système Bongo," *Africa Report* 38, no. 6 (November-December 1993), pp. 66–69; Barnes, "The Tainted Win," *Africa Report* 39, no. 2 (March-April 1994), pp. 67–69; "Gabon's President Wins Contested Election," *Africa Report* 39, no. 1 (January-February 1994), pp. 8–9; African-American Institute, *Gabon: A Report on the Presidential Elections, December 5, 1993* (New York: African-American Institute, 1994).

26. Confidential interview by the author, Paris, June 22, 1994. Stephen Smith attributes the electoral fraud in the two provinces specifically to the Direction Générale de la Sécurité Extérieure (DGSE, the counterespionage service within the French Interior Ministry), Elf-Aquitaine, and French Ambassador Louis Dominici. Stephen Smith, *Libération,* December 18, 1993.

27. *Marchés tropicaux et méditerranéens,* December 17, 1993; *Jeune Afrique,* December 23, 1993–January 5, 1994, pp. 36–37; EIU, *CR Gabon,* no. 4 (1993):6–10. EIU, *CR Gabon,* no. 1 (1994):7–9; "Gabon's President Wins Contested Election," *Africa Report* 39, no. 1 (January-February 1994), pp. 8–9; Barnes, "The Tainted Win."

28. EIU, *CR Gabon,* no. 1 (1994):10–11; J.-J. Nambo, "Parodie d'élection présidentielle au Gabon," *Politique africaine,* no. 53 (December 1994):133–139.

29. Ibid., p. 13.

30. EIU, *CR Gabon,* no. 4 (1993):18; EIU, *CR Gabon,* no. 1 (1994):14; EIU, *CR Gabon,* no. 2 (1994):9; *Le moniteur du commerce international,* July 18, 1994, pp. 43–45; "IMF Approves Credits for Gabon," *IMF Press Release* no. 94/22, March 30, 1994, p. 2; *Le Monde,* October 11, 1994.

31. *Libération,* February 25, 1994; *Africa Confidential* (London), vol. 35 (March 4, 1994):8; EIU, *CR Gabon,* no. 1 (1994):11–12; EIU, *CR Gabon,* no. 2 (1994):9.

32. According to Nancy Lawler, "Reports that some members of the army and the government were thinking of joining with the opposition may have prompted Bongo to participate in a peace conference in Paris between the government and opposition parties." *Britannica Book of the Year, 1995* (Chicago: Encyclopaedia Britannica, 1995), p. 408.

33. The text of the Paris Accords may be found in *Documents d'actualité internationale,* January 1, 1995.

34. EIU, *CR Gabon,* no. 3 (1994):6–9; EIU, *CR Gabon,* no. 4 (1994):6–11; *Jeune Afrique,* September 15, 1994; *Jeune Afrique,* September 22–28, 1994; *Jeune Afrique,* October 6, 1994; *Marchés tropicaux et méditerranéens,* October 7, 1994; *Le Monde,* July 25, 1995.

35. *Jeune Afrique Économie,* June 5, 1995, pp. 9–21; *Jeune Afrique,* May 18–24, 1995, pp. 78–89.

Chapter Ten

Cameroon: Biya and Incremental Reform

JOSEPH TAKOUGANG

Although it is generally agreed that developments in Eastern Europe contributed to increased demands for political reforms, including the introduction of multiparty politics in most African states beginning in the late 1980s, the situation in Cameroon[1] was different. In fact, it could be argued that the reform process in Cameroon started as early as November 1982 following the peaceful transfer of power from President Ahmadou Ahidjo to his prime minister and constitutional successor, Paul Biya. As Pius Njawe, editor of the weekly newspaper *Le Messager* and one of President Biya's most ardent critics, has pointed out: "Cameroon is a country where Perestroika was discussed well before Mikhail Gorbachev came to power in the Soviet Union. Cameroon's President Paul Biya talked about change, democratization, the liberalization of political life—if acts had followed the political discourse, Cameroon would have been the vanguard of the great movement in Africa."[2] According to Njawe, although President Biya preached about changes (and despite the fact that he may have instituted certain reforms), his actions fell far short of his words. Consequently, Cameroon could not escape being swept up in the winds of change that engulfed the continent beginning in the late 1980s.

It is against the background of Biya's early political reforms that later demands for greater political reforms in Cameroon are examined in this chapter. Several questions present themselves in the case of Cameroon. Were the original reforms a prelude to further democratic changes or were they intended to win the support of the Cameroonian people and help establish Biya in power? How did the people react to the reforms? Why did Cameroonians who seemed to appreciate the president's reforms suddenly turn against him? To what extent were external factors and domestic problems responsible for demands for further political reforms? Finally, how has Biya managed to remain in power since the introduction of multi-party politics in December 1990? These are the central questions that will be addressed as we examine the transition from single-party rule to the legalization of multiparty politics in Cameroon.

Early Political Reforms Under President Biya, 1982–1990

On November 4, 1982, President Ahidjo stunned the Cameroonian people when he announced his decision to resign from the presidency of the republic. Two days later, on November 6, he was succeeded by Paul Biya, his prime minister and constitutional successor. Although Biya had promised to follow in the footsteps of his predecessor when he took over the presidency,[3] it soon became evident in his speeches and from his actions that the new president was also determined to create a more liberal and "democratic" society in which there would be more tolerance, greater individual freedom, and the free exchange of ideas.[4] Evidence of the new society that President Biya hoped to create was apparent with the proliferation of more than half a dozen independent newspapers by the end of his first year in office. Even often critical foreign magazines, including *West Africa* and *Jeune Afrique*, were allowed in the country without the excessive government censorship that had been exercised in the past to eliminate "subversive" articles or passages.

Moreover, unlike the Ahidjo days, when Cameroonians were restricted from making critical political statements, a greater degree of individual freedom and freedom of expression was tolerated as part of the president's early political reforms. For example, Cameroonians could now make "constructive criticisms" of the administration and its policies without having to fear persecution. Another significant change early in his administration was Biya's attempt to open up the Cameroon National Union (Union Nationale Camerounaise, UNC), the country's sole legal party, by making elections more competitive. Unlike his predecessor, Biya believed that the party could be both democratic and an effective instrument of national development if free discussions and choices were allowed in the party.[5] One way of achieving the latter was by encouraging multiple candidates in party elections. Similar to the system in Tanzania under President Julius Nyerere, this new form of one-party participatory democracy[6] would allow more than one candidate to run for various party posts in a constituency. The objective of the new system was to infuse new blood into the party by giving voters the opportunity to decide who should represent them within the party structure and in the legislature. If Biya's proposal had been accepted, it would have been implemented in the legislative elections scheduled for May 29, 1983.

Not surprisingly, the proposal was initially rejected by party officials because the Political Bureau and the Central Committee of the UNC were still controlled by members of the ancien régime who owed their political fortunes to the former president and feared that the new system would threaten their continued stay in power. In fact, although President Ahidjo had resigned as head of state, he maintained the almost equally powerful position of chairman of the UNC. The bicephalism in leadership between the head of state and the chairman of the party led to a series of conflicts between the former president and his successor.[7] This struggle culminated in a failed military coup d'état in April 1984, in which Ahidjo, who was in self-imposed exile in France, and who had earlier resigned as chairman of the party, was implicated.[8]

Soon after the failed coup, Biya moved quickly to consolidate his power by either replacing or transferring from important positions in the government and party those suspected of loyalty to the former president. Later, at the party congress in Bamenda in March 1985, President Biya orchestrated the replacement of the UNC with the Cameroon People's Democratic Movement (Rassemblement Démocratique du Peuple Camerounais, RDPC) as the new sole legal party in the country. By 1986, Biya had securely established himself as head of state and chairman of the party, which allowed him to implement the new electoral procedure he had proposed in 1983.

The policy was first implemented in the election of party officials in 1986, and later in the municipal and legislative elections in 1987 and 1988, respectively. The new electoral system appears to have been successful in its intended goal. For instance, about 70 percent of the officials elected in the cell and branch organs of the party in the 1986 elections were new. At the section level, only twenty-four of the forty-nine previous presidents (less than 50 percent) were returned to office. At the same time, 57 percent of the officials elected to the women's wing of the party were new, and *all* of the elected presidents of the youth wing were new.[9] Similarly, in the 1988 legislative elections, 85 percent of those elected to the National Assembly were new members. The change in the electoral process also saw an increase in the number of women's representatives from 1 percent in the previous assembly to 22 percent in the 1988 assembly.

Earlier, in November 1983, in another apparent demonstration of his commitment to democratic reforms, Biya modified Article 7 of the constitution by allowing several candidates to run in future presidential elections of the country. Thereafter, anyone wishing to challenge the president in an election could do so if he or she met certain conditions. But, as we will see shortly, the conditions were so difficult that they practically eliminated the chances that anyone could run against Biya.

For a people who had survived more than two decades of Ahidjo's autocratic rule, Biya's reforms were welcome. Commenting on the changes brought about by the new electoral process, a high-ranking party official in Fako Division (South-West Province) noted that the new democracy had made it possible for Cameroonians to run for office in any part of the country.[10] Another party official, noting that the new changes were the final realization of true democracy in Cameroon, declared, "[D]emocracy has been the cry of every Cameroonian. Today, it is a dream come true. It has been received with warmth because every citizen can contest elections everywhere in the country."[11] Though these comments were primarily from party and government officials, they seemed to reflect the opinion of most Cameroonians. Even Cameroonian students, both at home and abroad, who had often been critical of Ahidjo's repressive policies, praised the new president for his openness and candor.

Although Biya was highly praised and credited with early reformist inclinations prior to the wave of "democratic fever" that gripped the continent beginning in the late 1980s, it was also apparent that the reforms were tailored to ensure his continued rule. Later events confirmed that the open discussions of the first years of his administration were tolerated only because of their indictment of the Ahidjo era. As one administration critic noted, the freedom of the press in Cameroon "starts where condemnation of the Ahidjo regime is concerned and ends where criticism of the Biya era begins."[12]

Meanwhile, even though multiple candidates were allowed in party and legislative elections, the Political Bureau was still involved in selecting the lists of candidates who ran in legislative elections. The Bureau's involvement was not necessarily undertaken to ensure that candidates were acceptable to their various constituencies but rather that they were good party militants who respected the laws of the land and the party.[13] In other words, no one who was outside of the party or whose ideas were not in concert with those of the party could hold any important political office or be elected to the National Assembly. Therefore, since there was no possibility of electing a nonparty candidate to the National Assembly, the institution remained largely a rubber stamp for presidential policies.

Another indication that the reforms were more for public consumption than to effect real political change was in the wording of the constitutional amendment allowing challengers in presidential elections. As noted earlier, the conditions for becoming a candidate were nearly unattainable. For example, a potential candidate was required to present a petition with 500 signatures—fifty from each of the ten provinces in the country—from important officials such as parliamentarians, governors, and municipal councilors. Additionally, a five-year continuous residency within the national territory was required.

One of the problems with the first condition was that under the single-party system, every state institution was related to the party or the government. At the same time, almost all important nominations to important government positions were made either by the president or approved by him. It would have been a sign of disloyalty to the president and political suicide for any of those qualified to sign the petition of a potential presidential challenger. The five-year residency requirement was seen by many analysts as an attempt to disqualify exile groups such as the Union of the Peoples of Cameroon (Union des Populations du Cameroun, UPC), which had a strong base of support in France, from presenting a presidential candidate.

A further indication that Biya was more interested in consolidating his hold on power than in introducing genuine democratic reforms in Cameroon was his retention of some of the very repressive laws and institutions that his predecessor had used in suppressing individual and political freedoms. Typical of these laws were the March 12, 1962, and June 19, 1967, decrees restricting freedom of expression and the organization of political associations, respectively. Under the guise of the 1962 antisubversion decree, for example, journalists and other Cameroonians who were critical of the administration were dealt with severely. Article 3 of the decree called for a fine of 200,000 to 2 million CFA francs or imprisonment for a period of one to five years, or both fine and imprisonment, for anyone who "publishes or reproduces any false statement, rumor or report or any tendentious comment or any statement or report which is likely to bring into hatred, contempt or ridicule any public authority."[14]

The fact that Biya's political reforms were more symbolic than real became even more apparent in the late 1980s when he steadfastly resisted calls for the introduction of multiparty democracy in Cameroon. Although he had encouraged competition within the party, he opposed demands by Cameroonians for the creation of a multiparty system, which he dismissed as simply a "distasteful passing fetish."[15] Like his predecessor and leaders elsewhere on the continent, the president perceived multipartyism not only as a threat to his authority but also as politically divisive and detrimental to social and economic development. Thus he declared:

> At the national level, the one-party system appears today to be the only suitable institutional framework for bringing together Cameroonians of all origins. It should, therefore, give birth to a new brand of Cameroonians devoid of any tribal or regional allegiances. . . . It is also necessary for the mobilization of human resources, especially intellectual resources, which, though so invaluable, are still scarce in our country. For, how could we ensure the efficient running of the state machinery if the political leanings of the few senior officials Cameroon now has were to be torn between several opposition parties, thus creating for any ruling regime an insurmountable crisis of power?[16]

Biya also reminded those clamoring for multipartyism that he had initiated glasnost and perestroika in Cameroon before Gorbachev did so in the Soviet Union.[17]

Hence, because of Biya's opposition to a multiparty system in Cameroon, those who advocated it were severely punished. In February 1990, for instance, ten Cameroonians, including Yondo Mandengue Black, a former president of the Cameroon Bar Association, were arrested in Douala (the economic capital of Cameroon) for attempting to form an alternative party. Later, on May 26, 1990, six people were killed when troops opened fire on crowds that had gathered in Bamenda (North-West Province) for the launching of an unauthorized party, the Social Democratic Front (SDF; Front Social Démocratique).

The Birth of Multiparty Politics in Cameroon

Although President Biya tried to muffle further demands for multiparty democracy in Cameroon, 1990 brought an intensification of the efforts of various groups to implement change. It appears that Cameroonians, who only a few years earlier had praised the president for introducing "democratic" reforms, were no longer satisfied with his brand of change. Now they demanded "genuine" political reforms, including the legalization of multiparty politics. Several factors may account for this change in attitude.

First, corruption by government officials, patronage, and nepotism continued almost unabated. For example, the anglophone population, which had expected better treatment than it had received under President Ahidjo,[18] became increasingly disenchanted with Biya's administration. The frustration apparently reached a boiling point in 1986, when, in an open letter addressed to all English-speaking parents, anglophone students from the North-West and South-West Provinces detailed what they perceived as a series of unfair treatment endured by anglophones since reunification in 1961.[19] (This simmering discontent may account for the fact that the first serious opposition party in the country, the SDF, was formed in the anglophone North-West Province and that the anglophone provinces became hotbeds of opposition politics.)

At the same time, northerners and Muslims (who comprise 15 percent of Cameroon's population and are concentrated in the north), who had enjoyed a privileged position when Ahidjo, himself a northern Muslim, was president, saw their political influence gradually eroding in favor of members of Biya's ethnic group, the Beti. The declining fortunes of the Muslims and northerners became even more apparent after the failed April 1984 coup, which the minister of armed forces, Gilbert Andzé Tsoungui (a Beti), alleged was "99.9 percent northern-inspired."[20] On the other hand, most Bamiléké businessmen, who remain the dominant indigenous economic group, felt that their economic interests were increasingly threatened by what some of them perceived as special privileges given to businessmen from the president's ethnic group.[21]

Though the sociopolitical climate may have created an excuse for change, the worsening economic situation reflected in the high rate of unemployment created further discontent. Early in his administration, Biya had been able to address the unemployment problem and also carry out many of his social and economic programs from revenue derived from the sale of Cameroon's exports at favorable prices. Additional funds came from the extrabudgetary accounts in foreign banks that had accumulated from the sale of Cameroon's oil under Ahidjo. In 1985, for example, 180 billion CFA francs were withdrawn from this source to supplement the national budget.[22]

Beginning in 1986, however, Cameroon, like many of its African counterparts, began experiencing a decline in its foreign earnings as the prices for its exports fell. The price of oil, which by 1984 contributed about 40 percent of the country's export earnings,[23] declined from US$29 a barrel in 1984 to $10 in 1986. This price drop contributed to a fall in revenue for the state, from 694 billion CFA francs in 1984/1985 to 243 billion in 1986/87.[24] Compounding the problem was a decline in the value of the dollar for which oil was sold, from 500 CFA francs to the dollar in 1985 to 300 francs in 1987. In real terms, therefore, the proceeds from oil were far less than what they had been in 1985. Similarly, the price for cocoa fell from 940 CFA francs per kilogram in 1985 to 700 francs in 1986. Other export crops underwent a similar fall in prices. Altogether, the value of Cameroon's exports, which had exceeded 1,000 billion CFA francs in 1984/85, dropped to 575 billion francs in 1986/87.[25]

Though domestic problems were the most significant factor in the demand for political reforms in Cameroon, political developments in the Soviet Union and Eastern Europe in the late 1980s served as catalyst for change in most African countries, including Cameroon. Motivated by the end of the Cold War and the change of governments in most of the former communist states of Eastern Europe, Cameroonians intensified their demands for multiparty democracy throughout 1990. President Biya would later acknowledge during a visit to the United States that the crumbling of communism in Eastern Europe had contributed to challenges to one-party rule in Cameroon and throughout Africa.[26]

Also important in the demand for change in Cameroon were pressures exerted by France (Cameroon's major trading partner) and other Western capitalist nations and financial institutions. During the Cold War, it was politically expedient for the major Western democracies to support (financially and otherwise) authoritarian regimes as a means of preventing the spread of Soviet influence in Africa. But with the end of the Cold War and the collapse of the Soviet empire, it was no longer necessary to support such regimes.[27] At the Franco-African summit at La Baule, France, in June 1990, for example, President François Mitterrand threatened African leaders who did not implement political reforms with economic retribution.[28] One year later, at the fourth Conference of Heads of Francophone States held at the Chaillot Palace in Paris, November 19–21, 1991, democracy was again an important topic of discussion. The final resolution of the conference, known as the "Chaillot Declaration" declared its support for human rights and the democratic process.[29]

Beyond the general policy statement, France is believed to have placed additional pressure on President Biya to institute many of the political reforms that were necessary. At the same time, however, France still saw Biya's administration as the pillar of political stability in Cameroon. In other words, any reform had to be under Biya's leadership. France's preference for Biya was clarified at a meeting between the French ambassador to Cameroon, Yvon Omnes, and representatives of the SDF party in which the ambassador described Biya's administration as a force for peace, stability, and unity, whereas the SDF was seen as violent and disruptive.[30] In fact, to demonstrate further its support for President Biya, France not only endorsed Biya's reelection in the highly controversial October 1992 presidential elections but also granted the government US$100 million in aid to ward off sanctions by the World Bank and the International Monetary Fund.

Nevertheless, with increasing domestic and foreign pressure, and with nearby countries such as Gabon, Benin, Zaire, and the Congo conceding to demands for multiparty democracy early in 1990, President Biya was finally forced to do the same. In December 1990 he engineered passage of a law by the National Assembly authorizing the formation of other parties in the country. Except for minor restrictions,[31] the new law also allowed all prospective parties to start functioning within three months even if their applications had not been approved by the minister of territorial administration.[32]

By July 1991, more than half a dozen parties had been legalized, including the SDF, the UPC, the National Union for Democracy and Progress (Union Nationale pour la Démocratie et le Progrès, UNDP), and the Liberal Democratic Party (LDP).[33] But even after the president had been pressured to legalize multiparty politics in Cameroon, his main concern was how to manipulate the "new" political environment to his advantage rather than how to win a legitimate term in office.

Resistance and Change, 1991–1994

Despite serious challenges from the opposition parties since the legalization of multiparty politics in Cameroon, Biya has managed to remain in power. He has done so by manipulating the political system to his advantage and by implementing a "carrot-and-stick" approach. The "stick" included the use of the security forces and other repressive measures to intimidate leaders of various opposition parties, their supporters, and other critics of his administration. For instance, from December 19, 1990, to the first multiparty presidential election on October 11, 1992, soldiers and other security forces were often used to disperse antigovernment demonstrations in towns and cities across the country, resulting in the deaths of about 300 people in 1991 alone.[34] Commenting on the political climate in Cameroon since the introduction of multiparty politics in December 1990, one observer noted:

> Since the advent of multi-party politics in Cameroon, many citizens who have dared to take sides with opposition political parties have always had it rough from the CPDM [the English abbreviation for RDPC] government or the so-called presidential majority who are doing everything to stay in power. It has not only been mere arrests and torture with flimsy or no explanation at all, but also deaths, a situation which has forced many Cameroonians to flee the country to strange lands for safety.[35]

Meanwhile, because of their apparent support for the opposition and criticism of the administration, many journalists and independent newspapers also became victims of government intimidation. On December 19, 1990 (the same day that multipartyism was legalized in the country), the administration issued Law No. 90/052 regulating the independent press. Among other provisions, the new law required all newspapers to submit each edition for review by the prefect (administrative head of the division) where the paper was published before it could go on sale. Section 4 (17) of the law also stipulated that the minister of territorial administration had the right to seize or ban any publication or issue that did not follow the review process.[36]

Though Biya was prepared to use repression measures to intimidate the opposition, he was also ready to offer them the "carrot." This included granting the opposition parties certain concessions without necessarily giving them the opportunity to undermine his control of the instruments of power. For example, he opposed calls by the opposition parties for a sovereign national conference (SNC), which had already achieved some measure of success in resolving the political stalemates in Benin and Congo, to discuss the political future of the country.[37] In rejecting the call for an SNC, Biya argued that such a conference was "*sans objet*' and had no legal foundation" in Cameroon, since the constitution already allowed political pluralism in the country.[38] At the same time, he promised early legislative elections in 1992 instead of the scheduled 1993 date. He also authorized his prime minister, Sadou Hayatou, to organize what became known as the "Tripartite Conference" to end the political deadlock in late 1991.

Even though the concessions fell short of the opposition's call for an SNC, they created the appearance that the president was prepared to respond to opposition demands. In the event, however, neither the Tripartite Conference nor the decision to call early legislative elections made any significant difference. In fact, after almost two weeks of deliberations, from October 30 to November 13, 1991, some of the major opposition leaders, including heads of the SDF and the Progressives' Movement (Mouvement des Progressistes, MP) refused to sign the final report (the Tripartite Accord) of the conference, describing it as "a masquerade" and "an act of treason."[39] Their main objection to the accord concerned its failure to address seriously the issue of constitutional reforms.

While promising early legislative elections, Biya had also indicated that he would appoint the next prime minister from the party that won the majority in the new Assembly. Two points are worth noting about his pledge, however. First, by promising to appoint the next prime minister from the party with the majority in the National Assembly, the president was perhaps making it clear to the opposition parties that he would remain president even if his party, the RDPC, did not win the majority of seats in the legislature. Secondly, the fact that the new prime minister would be appointed by the president of the republic, and not by the leadership of the party that won the majority, was an indication that whoever got the position would still be responsible to President Biya and therefore subject to removal by him. After all, Article 8 (Sections i and ii) of the constitution stipulated that the president appoints his ministers and may also terminate their appointments at will.

Fortunately for the president, such maneuvering was not necessary. In the first multiparty legislative election in Cameroon since the creation of a single-party state in 1966, held on March 1, 1992, the RDPC was able to win 88 of the 180 seats in the legislature. Although the victory did not give the RDPC a ruling majority in the National Assembly, it allowed Biya to select the new prime minister from his party, and it placed him in a stronger position to form a parliamentary majority.

The latter was achieved soon after the elections when the RDPC moved quickly to form a parliamentary alliance with the Democratic Movement for the Defense of the Republic (Mouvement Démocratique pour la Défense de la République, MDDR), a small party led by Dakolé Daïssala, which had won all of its six seats in the Far North Province. Perhaps in appreciation for his willingness to form an alliance with the RDPC, Daïssala was subsequently rewarded with the position of minister of state in charge of Posts and Telecommunications.

Another strategic move taken by the president soon after the legislative elections to ensure his hold to power was the appointment of Simon Achidi Achu (an anglophone from the North-West Province) to the post of prime minister and head of government. Achu thus became the first English-speaking Cameroonian to hold the position since the creation of the unitary constitution in 1972. Many political observers saw his appointment as likely to serve two purposes: First, it could be seen as an attempt by the administration to weaken the SDF, which enjoyed tremendous support among anglophone Cameroonians, particularly those from the North-West Province; secondly, it could help to consolidate the president's support among English-speaking Cameroonians. By the same token, many critics saw Achu's appointment as merely symbolic and insignificant to anglophones because, for the first time since 1972, two vice prime ministers (Gilbert Andzé Tsoungui and Hamadou Moustapha, both francophones) were also appointed. As one opposition member would later comment: "Achu . . . remains a lame duck prime minister. He has no real power. Real power still resides in the hands of Andzé Tsoungui and Hamadou Moustapha. After all, if the post of prime minister was so powerful, why would he need two vice prime ministers, if not to monitor him and report back to Biya?"[40]

The president's effort to divide the opposition continued throughout 1992 in anticipation of the October 11 presidential election. On September 28, 1992, only two weeks before the election, for example, Biya signed an agreement with the parliamentary wing of the opposition UPC, led by Frédéric Kodock, which had won eighteen seats in the legislative election. Apart from the prospect of improving his chances for reelection, the alliance with Kodock had other implications; it was seen as an effort by Biya further to consolidate his control of the legislature and to cause more friction between the parliamentary wing and the other factions of the UPC. For supporting the president, Kodock was appointed minister of state in charge of Planning after the presidential election.

Later, in another move that was likely to consolidate further his hold on the presidency as well as to divide the UNDP, which had won sixty-eight seats in the

March legislative elections, Biya appointed to his November 1992 cabinet the UNDP's president, Hamadou Mustapha, and its secretary-general, Issa Tchiroma Bakary, apparently without the consent of the UNDP leadership.

Besides co-opting some of his political opponents into his administration, Biya was also able to manipulate the electoral process to his advantage. On February 16, 1992, just two weeks before the March legislative elections, the administration made available 500 million CFA francs to be divided among all parties that participated in the elections. Although this seems to have been a generous gesture by the administration, it appears that the real motive of the offer was to improve the chances of electing RDPC candidates by encouraging as many opposition candidates as possible to run. After all, at the time, the RDPC was still the oldest legal and best organized party in the country. In fact, it was reported that some opposition candidates had been forced to run in the election after government authorities threatened to prosecute them for corruption.[41]

Additionally, the electoral code for the legislative and presidential elections had been drawn up by a National Assembly composed of mostly RDPC representatives, which raised questions regarding their fairness and objectivity. Similarly, the Ministry of Territorial Administration, rather than an independent body, was responsible for overseeing both the legislative and presidential elections—which raised more questions. One of the reasons cited by SDF President John Fru Ndi for refusing to participate in the March legislative elections was his charge that the minister of territorial administration had divided the electoral districts in a manner that gave the RDPC an advantage. Moreover, the fact that eleven of the thirteen members of the Vote Counting Commission in the presidential election were either RDPC members or from the president's ethnic group did not help to create an atmosphere of trust. Finally, a delay of twelve days before the final election results were announced led to widespread suspicion that the vote count had been manipulated in favor of the president.

Although Biya was reelected by a slim majority—39.9 percent of the votes cast, compared with 35.9 percent for Fru Ndi (SDF) and 19.2 percent for Bouba Bello Maigari (UNDP)[42]—the opposition parties and some international observer groups, including the Washington, D.C.–based National Democratic Institute for International Affairs (NDI), that had monitored the elections, accused the president and the RDPC of fraud and other election improprieties that might have contributed to the incumbent's victory.[43]

In its final report on the election, the NDI placed the overwhelming responsibility for many of the election irregularities on the administration. Among the charges was that the government had nearly exclusive access to the public media during the campaign, through which they promoted Biya's candidacy without giving equal time to the various opposition parties. The NDI report cited television coverage on October 7, 1992, when a total of 142 minutes were spent promoting Biya's candidacy, while only twelve minutes were assigned on the coverage of all the other opposition party candidates. The report also alluded to the arbitrary change of polling sites, especially in areas where support for the incumbent president was weak.[44]

Even the nation's Supreme Court, which was charged with proclaiming the results of the presidential election, acknowledged that the election had been fraught with irregularities. At the same time, however, it announced that it was required by the electoral code and the constitution to announce the results it had been given by the Electoral Committee and not to investigate any irregularities. Commenting on the Court's deliberations, a newspaper columnist noted that even its president, Mouelle Bipanda, admitted to many shortcomings and irregularities of the election, but, like Pontius Pilate, "washed his hands and handed out the dangerously controversial verdict."[45]

More credence to the charges of fraud by the administration and the ruling party came in statements by George Achu Mofor, former governor of the East Province and brother of Prime Minister Achu. In his letter of resignation to the president, Achu Mofor cited unequal treatment of voters and opposition candidates in his province and instructions by the minister of territorial administration to all the governors to do everything "fair and foul" to ensure at least a 60 percent victory of the RDPC party candidate in their respective provinces:

> Let me draw your attention to the fact that I did not find it in accordance with my conscience to implement the instructions of the Minister of Territorial Administration given during the extraordinary Governor's Conference of 28 September 1992. By these we were instructed to do everything fair and foul to ensure at least a 60 percent victory for the CPDM [i.e., RDPC] party candidate in our provinces. . . . To assist us in this task a six-page document issued by the UDC [Union Démocratique du Cameroun, or Democratic Union of Cameroon] party on Techniques of Electoral Fraud was distributed to us. As another example of blackmail and influence, he issued to us a second document entitled MAJORITE PRESIDENTIELLE by which the prison staff, about 5,000 strong, was requested to support your candidature to show gratitude for the recent regulation you adopted relating to better working conditions for them, and that in case of your victory the disciplinary measures taken against some of them during the last strike would be reviewed.
>
> We have been instructed to execute the exceptional security measures taken by government to ensure that all citizens accept the results and to severely repress any acts of violence resulting from discontent following their declaration.[46]

A Divided Opposition

Though President Biya, like many of his counterparts in Africa, may be charged with manipulating the electoral process to his advantage, it should also be pointed out that the inability of the opposition parties to organize a sustained and well-coordinated strategy against the administration may have contributed to his continued stay in power. For example, if the other opposition parties, particularly the UNDP and the faction of the UPC that had participated in the legislative elections,

TABLE 10.1 Cameroonian Legislative Elections, March 1992: Provincial Distribution of Seats Won by the Major Parties

Province	Party				Total
	RDPC	UNDP	UPC	MDR	
Adamawa	0	10	0	0	10
Center	23	1	4	0	28
East	7	4	0	0	11
Far North	13	10	0	6	29
Littoral	4	5	10	0	19
North	0	12	0	0	12
North-West	20	0	0	0	20
South	11	0	0	0	11
South-West	1	13	1	0	15
West	9	13	3	0	25
Total	88	68	18	6	180

Sources: Compiled from detailed results of the elections in the *Cameroon Tribune,* March 11, 1992, and *Le Messager,* March 7, 1992.

had joined the SDF in boycotting the elections, serious questions would have been raised, both domestically and internationally, on the validity of such an election and on the legitimacy of the regime. Alternatively, had the SDF participated in the election, it is unlikely that the RDPC would have won all twenty seats in the North-West Province where the SDF enjoyed tremendous support. In other words, because support for the various parties appeared to be based more on ethnic and regional loyalties than on any clearly defined ideological differences, most analysts believe that the SDF (whose leader, John Fru Ndi, hails from the North-West Province) would have won all or most of the twenty seats in the province had the party participated in the legislative elections. However, because the SDF boycotted the elections, the RDPC victory was seen more as an expression of loyalty to many of the "Fons" (Superior Chiefs) who supported the RDPC and to northwesterners in the administration like Simon Achidi Achu, Akum Fomum, Francis Nkwain, John Niba Ngu, and Lawrence Fonka Shang, the Speaker of the House of Assembly, who were still RDPC party members, rather than for the party itself.

Ethnic loyalty may also account for UNDP victory in the "Grand North," where the party won all twenty-two seats in the North and Adamawa Provinces and ten of the twenty-nine seats in the Far North Province. Although the UNDP also won thirteen of the fifteen seats in the South-West Province and did better than the RDPC in the West and Littoral Provinces, most of the seats in the latter were won by the UPC candidates because of the province's historic association with that party. (See Table 10.1.)

Thomas Melone, a former RDPC parliamentarian who was reelected in the March legislative elections as a UPC candidate from the Sanaga-Maritime Division, noted that one of the reasons for the strong support for the UPC in the Lit-

TABLE 10.2   Cameroonian Presidential Election, October 1992: Results by Province (in percent)

| | Candidate and Party | | | | |
Province	Biya (RDPC)	Fru Ndi (SDF)	Maigari (UNDP)	Others[a]	Total
Adamawa	26.13	6.38	64.04	3.45	100
Center	71.03	18.57	9.05	1.35	100
East	68.50	6.60	21.59	3.31	100
Far North	47.65	4.24	42.88	5.23	100
Littoral	14.31	67.60	14.44	3.65	100
North	42.87	3.15	50.42	3.56	100
North-West	9.60	86.30	3.03	1.07	100
South	94.82	3.55	1.23	0.40	100
South-West	21.36	51.60	24.13	2.91	100
West	11.86	67.78	1.98	18.38	100

[a]The "Others" category is made up of the three other presidential candidates: Jean-Jacques Ekindi (MP), Adamou Ndam Njoya (Union Démocratique du Cameroun, UDC), and Hygin René Philippe Williams Emah Ottou (Rassemblement des Forces Patriotiques, RFP). Together they won less than 5 percent of the ballot. The parliamentary wing of the UPC supported Biya, while its other factions backed other candidates.
Source: Cameroon Tribune, October 27, 1992, pp. 10–11.

toral Province, particularly in the Bassa areas of Nkam and Sanaga-Maritime Divisions, was that the UPC carried the colors of Um Nyobé and the struggle for independence.[47] It is also likely, as the results of the presidential elections would later demonstrate, that the SDF would have won most of the seats in the West, South-West, and Littoral Provinces, where the party enjoyed strong support.

The opposition parties' failure to support a consensus candidate against the incumbent president in the October presidential election also contributed to Biya's reelection. For example, he won convincingly among his co-ethnics in the South, Center, and East Provinces with over 94, 70, and 68 percent of the votes, respectively, but performed poorly in five of the other seven provinces. (See Table 10.2.) Conversely, SDF leader John Fru Ndi did well in the North-West, South-West, West, and Littoral Provinces, and Bouba Bello Maigari, leader of the UNDP and a northern Muslim, won in the Adamawa and North Provinces.[48] It is therefore safe to conclude from the results that a consensus opposition candidate supported by the two major opposition parties—the SDF and the UNDP—could have led to Biya's defeat.

The Post-Election Period

President's Biya's effort to cripple the opposition parties continued after his reelection. Shortly after the results were announced, John Fru Ndi and more than one hundred of his supporters were placed under house arrest for protesting what they viewed as a "stolen election." Additionally, under the pretext of national security, a three-month state of emergency was imposed in the North-West Province, the major stronghold of the SDF. Other reports indicate that as many as 5,000 troops were deployed in the North-West, West, South-West, and Littoral Provinces, where the opposition parties also enjoyed strong support.[49]

The administration has also continued to implement other measures to restrict freedom of expression and other activities that the administration deems threatening to state security—that is, Biya's hold on power). On October 29, 1992, for example, three English-speaking journalists of the government-owned radio and television station (CRTV) were reprimanded by the Director of Information for attending a press conference and asking questions that "embarrassed the Minister of Communication."[50] The administration has also kept a close watch on the activities of the various opposition parties. On September 24, 1993, the prefect (administrative head) of Bafoussam issued an order forbidding a conference by the UPC that had been scheduled in the city for October 1–3.

Although intimidation and harassment by the administration have certainly made it difficult for the opposition parties to function effectively, their internal bickering and inability to form a well-coordinated opposition against the government continued to plague them as well. As indicated earlier, division within the UNDP, the largest opposition party, with sixty-eight seats in the legislature, culminated in the dismissal of two members of the party's executive committee for accepting appointments in Biya's government despite objections from the party's leadership. Even the SDF, unquestionably the largest opposition party in the country (even though it is not represented in the National Assembly) and whose leader had won 35.9 percent of the votes in the presidential election, has also been plagued by internal discord. This became evident with the dismissal of Siga Asanga, the party's secretary-general, for allegedly extending an olive branch to the RDPC-controlled government with a view to including the SDF in the administration.[51] Later, in 1995, some members of the executive committee resigned from the SDF, charging the party with having a "regionalistic view" and accusing its president, Fru Ndi, of embezzling party funds.[52]

Meanwhile, efforts by some of the opposition parties to develop a common strategy against the administration and the ruling RDPC resulted in the creation in October 1994 of the Allied Front for Change (AFC), an alliance of sixteen parties, including the SDF, the MP, and Samuel Eboua's Movement for Democracy and Progress (Mouvement pour la Démocratie et le Progrès, MDP). However, the AFC has been ineffective in achieving its objective. For one thing, the alliance has been plagued by ideological differences and rivalry among the leaders of the various parties. At the same time, two parties, Adamou Ndam Njoya's UDC, and Maigari's UNDP (whose representation in the legislative assembly could be helpful to the alliance) refused to join it, claiming SDF domination of the group.[53] The ineffectiveness of the AFC (and the opposition in general) has led one analyst to characterize their opposition to the government as the bark of a toothless bull-dog.[54]

Although one of the main objectives of the government has been to contain any challenges from the opposition parties, it has nevertheless been concerned with developments in the two anglophone provinces (the North-West and South-West Provinces), where many prominent English-speaking Cameroonians have since 1990 been demanding a return to the pre-1972 federal structure, which had allowed a certain degree of autonomy to the former West Cameroon.[55] In arguing the case for a federation, one observer noted that the struggle was not against any group of people or single individual but against a corrupt system:

> [T]he narrow-mindedness of our society has given our struggle an image that looks like a struggle of Anglophones against Francophones or just one to drive the president from power. No! Our struggle is against a system, not against a person or people. We are struggling to change a system that has led to fatal moral consequences as the main criterion for success is based on personal acquisition of wealth, thus allowing a feverish scramble for money and a false respect for those who acquire it.[56]

Meanwhile, more radical anglophone groups have called for secession and the creation of a separate English-speaking Cameroon to be renamed "Ambazonia." While the latter may not represent the view of most anglophones, it certainly reflects the frustration and disappointment with the way English-speaking Cameroonians have been treated since reunification. At the All Anglophone Conference (AAC) held in Buea April 2–3, 1993, for example, members cited the exploitation of the resources of the two anglophone provinces for the economic development of the francophone provinces, the oppressive form of government perpetrated by the predominantly francophone ruling class, and the fact that anglophone Cameroonians were treated as "second-class citizens" in their country.[57]

A second All Anglophone Conference (AAC II), held in Bamenda from April 29 to May 2, 1994, to review the progress made since the first conference in Buea, also reiterated the plight of English-speaking Cameroonians. In its final report, known as the "Bamenda Proclamation," the conference participants noted that "any union between Francophone Cameroon and Anglophone Cameroon would not last, develop and prosper, unless it was built on a solid foundation and was sustained by a greater degree of openness, trust, mutual respect, and a sense of belonging by all."[58]

On November 6, 1994, President Biya announced—perhaps in an effort to address demands for a return to the federal structure and other constitutional reforms—the formation of a constitutional committee to review the constitution that had been drafted by a committee of experts appointed by the administration in March 1993 as part of the Tripartite Accord of November 1991. Because the fifty-seven-member constitutional review committee (appointed by President Biya) was dominated by RDPC supporters, it is expected that the new constitution will bear the stamp of presidential and RDPC approval. In late November

1995 Biya presented a constitutional reform bill to the National Assembly providing for restoration of decentralized local government and for creation of a Senate
and a Constitutional Court separate from the present High Court. Biya stated that
the bill embodies a commitment to a liberal and democratic society that guarantees respect for human rights and freedoms.[59] The president will determine
whether the final text will be submitted to a referendum.

Conclusion

Even though President Biya may have introduced reforms after taking office in
November 1982, his measures did not reach far enough to shield Cameroon from
the "winds of change" that blew across the continent beginning in the late 1980s.
In fact, despite his professed quest for freedom and democracy, President Biya has
been reluctant to allow any changes that went beyond the limited political framework he envisioned for the nation, especially if they threatened his continued stay
in power. Ultimately, most Cameroonians saw the reinstitution of multiparty politics as possibly the only means of attaining a truly free and democratic society.

Since the restoration of multiparty politics in December 1990, however, Biya
has managed to remain in power. He has been able to do so for a number of reasons. First, he has rendered the opposition less effective by co-opting some of its
members into his administration or by using various state institutions to intimidate them. Secondly, he has been able to manipulate the electoral process, especially in the October presidential election, to his advantage. Finally, because of
philosophical and strategic differences rather than any clearly defined political
differences, the various opposition parties have failed to sustain a well-coordinated challenge to Biya.

Notes

1. Unlike most of the countries in this study, which were formerly French colonies, the
Republic of Cameroon is a bilingual country (English and French), created in 1961 from a
reunification of the former British Southern Cameroons and the former French
Cameroons. Both territories were previously under United Nations trusteeship.

2. Pius Njawe, *World Press Review*, January 1992, p. 51.

3. See President Biya's speech to the National Assembly when he took the oath of office
in Cameroon National Union, *The New Deal Message* (Yaoundé: Éditions Sopecam, 1983),
p. 329.

4. For example, see Paul Biya, *Communal Liberalism* (London: Macmillan, 1987), pp.
36–38.

5. *Africa Research Bulletin, Political Series*, September 1983, p. 6976.

6. R. L. Sklar, "Democracy in Africa," in Patrice Chabal, ed., *Political Dominance in Africa*
(Cambridge, England: Cambridge University Press, 1986), p. 23.

7. In a series of moves after resigning from office, the former president attempted not
only to undermine the authority of his successor as president but even tried to subject the

head of state to the authority of the party. For a detailed discussion of these moves, see Henri Bandolo, *La flamme et la fumée* (Yaoundé: Éditions Sopecam, 1985).

8. For a detailed discussion of the conflict between the two men and the April 1984 coup, see Victor Julius Ngoh, *Cameroon 1884–1985: A Hundred Years of History* (Limbe, Cameroon: Navi Group Publications), pp. 310–325.

9. Tikum Mbah Azonga, "Cameroon in 1986: Four Years of Biya," *West Africa*, January 5, 1987, p. 13.

10. ESSTI, *Paul Biya, 5 ans après . . . Les camerounais jugent leur président* (Yaoundé: Impression ESSTI, 1987), p. 13.

11. Ibid., p. 23.

12. David Achidi Ndifang, "The Eclipse of Ahidjo," *West Africa*, September 5, 1983, p. 2049.

13. Asonglegac Nkemleka, "Party on the Move," *West Africa,* April 28, 1986, p. 873.

14. Cited in Philippe Lippens and R. A. Joseph, "The Power and the People," in Richard Joseph, ed., *Gaullist Africa: Cameroon Under Ahmadou Ahidjo* (Enugu, Nigeria: Fourth Dimension Publishers, 1978), p. 114.

15. Chris Simpson, "The Carnage Continues," *West Africa*, April 29–May 5, 1991, p. 653.

16. ESSTI, *Paul Biya*, p. 44.

17. Akwanka Joe Ndifor, "A Political Turning Point," *Africa Report* 6, no. 4 (July-August 1991):18.

18. For a discussion of the anglophone problem under the Ahidjo regime, see Frank M. Stark, "Federalism in Cameroon: The Shadow and the Reality," in Ndiva Kofele-Kale, ed., *An African Experiment in Nation Building: The Bilingual Cameroon Republic Since Reunification* (Boulder: Westview Press, 1980), pp. 101–132; and Jean-François Bayart, "The Neutralisation of Anglophone Cameroon," in Joseph, *Gaullist Africa*, pp. 45–92.

19. For details on the grievances, see "Open Letter to all English-Speaking Parents of Cameroon from the English-Speaking Students of the North-West and South-West Provinces, August 20, 1985," and "Foncha's Brief Account of the Events Which Took Place in Bamenda Township on Saturday 26th May 1990 Culminating in the Shooting and Killing of Five Innocent Young Men and One Girl," mimeographed documents.

20. "Cameroon Coup Attempt: '99.9 Percent Northerners,'" *West Africa*, April 23, 1984, p. 865.

21. For example, see Jean-François Bayart, "Cameroon," in Donal B. Cruise O'Brien, John Dunn, and Richard Rathbone, eds., *Contemporary West African States* (Cambridge, England: Cambridge University Press, 1989), p. 40.

22. Mark W. DeLancey, *Cameroon: Dependence and Independence* (Boulder: Westview Press, 1989), p. 141.

23. Nancy C. Benjamin and Shantayanan Devarajan, "Oil Revenue and the Cameroonian Economy," in Michael G. Schatzberg and I. William Zartman, eds., *The Political Economy of Cameroon* (New York: Praeger, 1986), p. 165.

24. "Committed to Efficiency," *West Africa*, June 27, 1988, p. 1158.

25. Ibid.

26. *Washington Times*, May 8, 1991.

27. Jennifer A. Widner, "Kenya's Slow Progress Towards Multiparty Politics," *Current History* 91 (May 1992):217.

28. *Africa Research Bulletin, Political Series*, July 15, 1990, p. 9713.

29. *Africa Research Bulletin, Political Series*, November 16–December 15, 1991, p. 10610.

30. *Africa Confidential*, December 4, 1992, p. 6.

31. The only restrictions were that all new parties were to be neither ethnically nor regionally based and that members of any new parties had to be residents within the national territory. The first restriction was probably aimed at preventing the creation of the kinds of parties that had led to political turmoil in most postcolonial African nations. The second restriction, however, was most likely aimed at preventing the UPC and the Cameroon Action Movement (CAM), which had large followings abroad, from functioning effectively or even participating in the political process.

32. *Jeune Afrique*, January 9–15, 1991, p. 26.

33. About seventy parties had been legalized in the country by the time of the presidential election on October 11, 1992.

34. *Le Messager*, October 28, 1992, p. 15.

35. *Cameroon Post*, February 24–March 3, 1994.

36. *Africa Watch*, February 12, 1991, p. 5.

37. Because of the president's refusal to call a sovereign national conference, the various opposition parties in May 1991 called for the nonpayment of taxes and other dues to the government by private businesses as a means of putting additional pressure on the government to call the conference. This action, which was known as "Operation Ghost Cities," also involved the voluntary shutting down of private businesses as well as the suspension of taxi and bus services except on Saturdays and Sundays. Although the boycott did not include government workers, it was almost impossible for them to go to and from work, especially in larger cities like Douala, because of the lack of taxi services. According to one source, the government was losing as much as 4,000 million CFA francs a day in revenue during the six months or so that the boycott was in place.

38. *Cameroon Analysis*, April 23, 1991, p. 3.

39. "Agreement Row," *West Africa*, November 25–December 1, 1991, p. 1980.

40. Cited in Tikum Mbah Azonga, "Biya Reshuffles Cabinet," *West Africa*, August 15–21, 1994, p. 1430.

41. *Africa Confidential*, March 6, 1992, p. 4.

42. In its own results of the elections announced two days earlier, on October 21, 1992, the SDF declared its candidate, John Fru Ndi, the winner in the presidential elections with 38.67 percent of the votes against Biya's 36.86 percent.

43. For details on the electoral problems, see the National Democratic Institute for International Affairs, *An Assessment of the October 11, 1992, Elections in Cameroon* (Washington, D.C.: National Democratic Institute for International Affairs, 1992), pp. 2–4 (hereafter cited as NDI, *An Assessment*).

44. Ibid.

45. *The Herald* (West Cameroon), October 26, 1992, p. 2.

46. NDI, *An Assessment*, p. 110.

47. *Cameroon Tribune*, March 12, 1992. Um Nyobé was the secretary-general of the UPC who had been assassinated on September 13, 1958, by government troops while he was in hiding near his hometown of Boumnyebel.

48. For details on the October presidential election results, see the *Cameroon Tribune*, October 27, 1992, pp. 10–11.

49. "Election Results Controversy," *West Africa*, October 26–November 1, 1992, p. 1836; Tikum Mbah Azonga, "The Fru Ndi Factor," *West Africa*, November 9–15, 1992, p. 1914.

50. This information is from a mimeograph by Boh Herbert, editor-in-chief of *Post-watch Magazine,* on human rights abuses in Cameroon following the October presidential election.

51. *Africa Research Bulletin, Political Series,* May 1994, p. 11445.

52. *Africa Research Bulletin, Political Series,* April 1–30, 1995, p. 11821.

53. "New Opposition Alliance," *West Africa,* October 17–23, 1994, p. 1798.

54. Tikum Mbah Azonga, "A Toothless Bulldog?" *West Africa,* February 27–March 5, 1995, p. 303.

55. Under the federal constitution, the former British Southern Cameroons became West Cameroon, while the former French Cameroons, which became the Republic of Cameroon at independence on January 1, 1960, became East Cameroon.

56. *Le Messager,* July 13, 1992, p. 8.

57. For more on the All Anglophone Conference, see *The Buea Declaration* (Limbe, Cameroon: Nooremac Press, 1993).

58. Cited in Tikum Mbah Azonga, "The Anglophone Problem," West *Africa,* June 20–26, 1994, p. 1090.

59. *West Africa,* December 4–10, 1995, p. 1868.

Chapter Eleven

Côte d'Ivoire: Continuity and Change in a Semi-Democracy

ROBERT J. MUNDT

Democracy, whether defined as limited government or some minimal level of pluralism, is rarely given freely to a country by an authoritarian regime. For the incumbent rulers, there are always many good reasons why democratization is "not in the nation's best interest at this moment." This rationale actually rings true to many observers because democracy is often (and perhaps by definition) associated with uncertainty and instability.[1] For whatever reason, democratization is generally the product of an authoritarian regime's failure to maintain effective control; it usually grows out of a situation in which none of several contending elites has the resources to achieve complete control, and in which agreement to limit and to share is the best available option for those contenders who collectively can impose a new order. In short, democratization grows out of erosion of power and stalemate.

Guided by these general principles, one can identify the factors explaining the gradual loss of control by President Félix Houphouët-Boigny and the Democratic Party of Côte d'Ivoire (Parti Démocratique de la Côte d'Ivoire, PDCI); these factors, in turn, provide a context for understanding the actions of Houphouët's successor, Henri Konan Bédié, to retard change. The loosening of control began in the late 1970s and proceeded through the first competitive elections in 1980, the first multiparty elections in 1990, the first minimally pluralist power sharing that came with the post-Houphouët consolidation of power by Bédié, and finally the activities of the PDCI and its opponents in the 1995 elections. We shall find sufficient causes in the widening range of contestation for power that, notwithstanding Bédié's authoritarian tack in 1995, has left no one individual or group in a position to govern alone.

Ivoirian Politics During the Struggle for Independence

The political history of Côte d'Ivoire was, from the emergence of indigenous political forces until the 1990s, intertwined with the political career of President Félix Houphouët-Boigny.[2] Houphouët became a political presence when he was elected first president of the Syndicat Agricole Africain (SAA). The SAA was an organization of African planters formed in reaction to racial discrimination in the white-dominated planters' organization and the price-support policies of the colonial government. About the same time, Houphouët also took the lead in organizing the Association of Customary Chiefs, thus extending his influence among traditional leaders throughout the colony.[3] Finally, Houphouët's medical training in Dakar and experience as a government employee gave him access to the small but influential Ivoirian administrative cadre.

Ivoirians participated in competitive elections for the first time in August 1945 when residents of Abidjan were allowed to select a municipal council. European and African citizens, along with some subjects (Africans who had not satisfied the conditions for French citizenship), were chosen on a common roll among slates composed of nine subjects and nine citizens each. Some slates included both Europeans and Africans, while some African contenders put forth lists dominated by a single ethnic group. Houphouët proposed an innovation that was radical in the context: an exclusively African slate distributed among major ethnic groups. Most African contenders then withdrew, and European voters abstained in protest. Houphouët's African Bloc won an overwhelming victory.[4]

The first election to the French Constituent Assembly in which Africans participated was held in October 1945, with separate electoral colleges for citizens and noncitizens. Houphouët was the SAA candidate in the second, noncitizen, college. He failed to get an absolute majority in a first round, which was crowded with candidates, and his large plurality became only barely a majority against an Upper Volta candidate in the runoff. In these early experiences, Houphouët showed great skill in coalition building, but he was frustrated by the fragility of such coalitions in the context of electoral politics.

In Paris, Houphouët introduced a bill calling for abolition of the colonial practice of forced labor. The proposal attracted little attention in a still-disorganized France, and it passed with neither a floor debate nor a roll-call vote. In Africa, however, its impact was enormous, for it consolidated Houphouët's political fortunes. Forced labor was the most hated aspect of subject status among colonial populations, and Houphouët was the person responsible for its removal.[5] He was reelected overwhelmingly under a new constitution in June 1946 running under the banner of the PDCI, associated in the Constituent Assembly with the French Communist Party (PCF).

Houphouët was a member of the French National Assembly for fourteen years, ultimately holding ministerial positions in four Fourth Republic governments (including the final, transitional government with de Gaulle as prime minister) and the first government under the Fifth Republic (headed by Michel Debré).[6] His was a major role in this confused period: He was a minister-delegate to the presidency when the *loi-cadre* of June 1956 was worked out, which first provided Africans with universal suffrage on a common roll.[7] In the last government of the Fourth Republic and the first of the Fifth Republic he was one of four ministers of state, each of whom represented one of the main political tendencies. These four were part of the "Matignon Team," which regularly met in de Gaulle's office "and played a fundamental role in initiation and amendment" as the new constitution was shaped.[8] Thus Houphouët, as a close and careful observer of the last floundering Fourth Republic governments, was profoundly impressed by the strong leadership of de Gaulle. Furthermore, Houphouët is reputed to have developed considerable skill in negotiation and logrolling in Paris, which carried over into his later leadership style.[9]

The alliance between the African Democratic Rally (Rassemblement Démocratique Africain, RDA), of which the PDCI was the Ivoirian branch, and the PCF, however, was to cause Houphouët and other associated African leaders great difficulty. Houphouët saw the alliance as politically expedient when the PCF participated in the French government. However, when the Communists moved permanently into opposition and took an active role in the stridently ideological politics of 1947–1948, the alliance became a handicap. Now Houphouët became an apparent threat to conservative colonial interests. The PDCI entered into a period in which it was constantly harassed, with its activists disenfranchised and jailed by the colonial administration. Houphouët was protected from arrest by his parliamentary status, but his immunity was popularly attributed to his own special powers and prestige. At the same time, he became less sanguine about the benefits presumed to flow from continued involvement with the PCF, and as a result, in 1950 he made the decision to break with the Communists and reconcile with the French government.[10] Thus, at the same time as the PDCI organization was battered and disrupted by colonial persecution, Houphouët's personal position became more secure. By the early 1950s he was the undisputed head of the party and to the colonial administration seemed the obvious choice to speak for the Ivoirian population in the move toward self-rule. He had rebuilt the party under his firm control in the classic style of a political machine, managing over time to combine overwhelming personal popularity among Ivoirians with the respect and trust of the colonizers—on reflection, a rather remarkable achievement.

Britain's grant of independence to the Gold Coast in March 1957 met with a cool reception in Abidjan. Houphouët's vision for the future was largely that of de Gaulle: a federal community of equal francophone states. He proclaimed that

African countries had little to gain from "nominal independence." As other francophone colonies, particularly neighboring Guinea in 1958, pushed for complete
independence, Houphouët saw the likelihood that continued opposition to independence would erode his political support. Accordingly, he participated in the negotiations through which, on August 7, 1960, Côte d'Ivoire became an independent
republic. In November of that year Houphouët was elected the country's first president, without opposition. He was reelected in the same fashion in 1965, 1970, 1975,
1980, and 1985. The first years of independence were marked not only by spectacu-
lar economic growth but also by several challenges to the party and its leader. The
most serious of these still looms large in the country's political history, the "events"
of 1963. There is still no consensus on the sequence of these events, including
whether there really was an attempted overthrow or whether the whole scenario was
staged by Houphouët himself. The outcome, in any case, was clear: There were
120–200 arrests and a series of secret trials in Yamoussoukro. Although none of the
thirteen death sentences issued was carried out, Ernest Boka, then president of the
Supreme Court, died in detention in what was described as a suicide. Jean Baptiste
Mockey, one of the PDCI's cofounders, was also implicated; he was arrested and was
kept in detention for four years.[11] Most observers mark 1963 as the point at which
Houphouët consolidated all government responsibilities in himself.[12]

Authoritarian One-Party Rule: 1963–1980

From 1963 until his death in 1993 Houphouët's dominance of Ivoirian politics
had no serious challenges. In this respect the Ivoirian case is singular. Houphouët
astutely controlled the party and the country by keeping possible contenders off
guard. From independence through the mid-1970s he delegated limited powers to
three lieutenants: August Denise, Jean Baptiste Mockey, and Philippe Yacé. He assigned responsibilities and honors in a way that kept aspirants in a state of tension, never sure if one or another was favored. However, as noted earlier, Mockey
had fallen from grace in 1963, and although he was later rehabilitated, he never
fully regained the president's trust.[13] Denise, although always a faithful lieutenant,
was growing old. Faced with Yacé's growing influence relative to the other second-
echelon leaders, Houphouët removed him from his positions as PDCI secretary-
general and president of the National Assembly; he created a new nine-member
Executive Committee for the PDCI, bringing in a new generation of politicians
but promoting no one to second place. Though the post of vice president was created in 1980, it was never filled, and it was abolished again in 1985 because of
Houphouët's annoyance at the unseemly competition that its existence evoked.
Article 11 of the Constitution was again modified in 1990 to specify that the president of the Republic would be succeeded by the president of the National Assembly, who would hold office until the next regularly scheduled election.

Houphouët's reign has been characterized as benevolent authoritarianism. Indeed, if democracy is defined not by process but by the maintenance of a govern-

ment that is *responsive* to citizen demands, there was something to be said for democracy *à l'Ivoirienne*. The president remained attuned to his constituents' problems through the process of *dialogue*, "a combination of palaver and chiefly audiences under a tree."[14] Houphouët, who was respectfully identified as *"le Vieux"* ("the Old Man") by most of his compatriots, used the dialogues to respond to disturbances such as ethnic clashes, dissatisfaction with schools, or labor unrest. It is arguable that his rule was in fact institutionally bounded not by the country's constitution but by the chiefly traditions into which he was born.[15] Of course, the president was also co-opting potential sources of opposition in this process, but he did emphasize accommodation rather than repression,[16] and could do so provided the economic resources were available. For example, substantial investments were made in the north of the country in the sugar and cotton industries. While the economic rationale for them was questionable, these policies showed a clear willingness on the part of the Houphouët regime to distribute wealth for political purposes.[17] A political machine requires fuel, which the thriving economy of the 1960s and 1970s provided in abundance.

In 1983 Jean-François Médard offered a thumbnail sketch of the Ivoirian state as it had evolved under Houphouët:

> We certainly do not pretend that Côte d'Ivoire is a pluralist, liberal democracy on the Western model; moreover, it does not pretend to be that. The absence of judicially protected civil liberties, the state monopoly of the press, the absence of institutionalized opposition and, until recently, of free elections, permit us to speak of an authoritarian political regime. But that is true of the overwhelming majority of political systems present and past. Yet, there are immense differences among different authoritarian regimes. . . . The Ivoirian regime achieves a strange combination of authoritarianism and liberalism, of authority and benevolence, of firmness and moderation: in short, it is a paternalistic regime.[18]

In addition to domestic supports, however, Houphouët continued to benefit from close ties with the metropole. He served as France's most reliable and knowledgeable intermediary in Africa, and France's support of his position as Ivoirian leader and as African elder statesman was clear and unswerving.[19] The French presence in Côte d'Ivoire was more evident than in any other African country.[20] French expertise built an administrative infrastructure of unequaled quality in Africa; though in recent years French expatriates have gradually been departing, they leave behind them a great depth of indigenous administrative and technical expertise.[21]

Still, control in a clientalist system is always tentative. The PDCI had limited the potential for the development of local political power bases by requiring the at-large election of its entire slate of delegates to the National Assembly. On the model of Louis XIV, Houphouët had created a political class that was largely dependent on him personally for influence. He was aided in this achievement by the absence of large-scale precolonial political systems in most of the forest zone.[22] There was thus no officially recognized "boss" in any local area, although Houphouët eventually encouraged the development of linkages between urban elites and their hometown associations, "as long as it was done in such a way that it did not allow any overt manifestations of ethnicity."[23] In any case, ambitious politicians found other means of accumulating political resources. For example, in creating parastatal enterprises, Houphouët had allowed the growth of "segments" in a previously hierarchical system.[24] The "barons" who controlled the parastatals warred with one another throughout the 1970s, creating a situation that, according to the model presented at the start of this chapter, could be the precondition for liberalization.

Solid ethnic or regional bases of power that might have threatened the stability of the Ivoirian political system were thus absent or weak. Rather, there was a persistent competition among individual power seekers that Houphouët tried constantly to quell. Henri Konan Bédié's rivalry with Mohammed Diawara (as well as with such other powerful contenders as Philippe Yacé and Emmanuel Dioulo) evolved ultimately into the conflict between Bédié and Houphouët's first and only prime minister, Alassane Dramane Ouattara.[25]

If 1963 marks the beginning of consolidated authoritarian rule, 1977 may mark its apogee. Most notably, this was the year that three senior ministers were dismissed from government as a result of unsatisfactory economic performance. Yves-A. Fauré interprets the clampdown that year as a successful effort by Houphouët to reassert his exclusive authority over the distribution of wealth.[26] It appeared then that there would still be wealth to distribute, as Côte d'Ivoire had become the world's largest single producer of cocoa that year.

Factors in the Liberalization of Ivoirian Politics

1978 was a disastrous turning point for the Ivoirian economy. Coffee and cocoa prices collapsed, prices of imported goods rose (reflecting the second "petroleum shock"), interest rates and the value of the U.S. dollar increased. Because of the International Coffee Accord, Côte d'Ivoire could not sell all the coffee it produced. All this came on the heels of massive government borrowing on international markets and spending on questionable capital projects in the preceding years.[27] Between 1979 and 1984 modern-sector employment dropped 30 percent, and gross domestic product declined more than 1.5 percent each year. Côte d'Ivoire was reclassified by the World Bank from middle-income to low-income. Cocoa and coffee prices continued to decline through the 1980s. Because by 1987 coffee export receipts had dropped 40 percent, the country was forced to stop interest payments to its principal international creditors.

Also by the late 1980s, the country's forest reserves had been nearly depleted. A bright hope in the previous decade, the off-shore oil fields, did not prove to be sufficiently productive for their exploitation to be pursued. Finally, a severe drought struck in 1983 (perhaps related, according to some authorities, to the removal of the rain forest), which not only affected agriculture but also severely reduced hydroelectric production. As a result, Ivoirian cities began experiencing power outages.

The first constitutional provision for meaningful popular participation in Côte d'Ivoire since independence came in 1980, through competitive National Assembly elections within the single party. This was the model first implemented by Julius Nyerere in Tanzania in 1965. As in the Tanzanian system, presidential elections were not affected; Houphouët was reelected unopposed to his fifth term as president. Although there had been demands for liberalization before that time, Fauré is persuasive in his explanation that Houphouët was not simply ceding to such demands but had calculated that popular discontent with the venal behavior of high-level officials at a time when most incomes were dropping would turn out younger contenders.[28] This result would both deflect some of the popular disapproval and increase the distance between the president and the nearest contenders for power. The election, according to Fauré, was in fact a "purge," as 82 percent of incumbents in the National Assembly were replaced. The 1985 election produced a similar effect, with 65 percent of seats turned over.[29]

Besides a few trusted old lieutenants, the members of Houphouët's later cabinets were newcomers who owed him their positions. This was the ultimate expression of "democracy from above," in Tessy D. Bakary Akin's phrase.[30] Still, the local-level competition for office in 1980 awakened political instincts and gave new value to home-base popularity. In many instances, it also politicized the *indigène*-"stranger" hostility that is particularly localized in Côte d'Ivoire by that country's encouragement of peasant farmer migration into the homelands of other ethnic groups to develop the plantation economy.[31]

Enter political dissident Laurent Gbagbo, who was to become the principal opponent to Houphouët in the presidential election of 1990. Gbagbo was a university lecturer (formerly director of the Institute of Art History and African Archeology) who in 1982 circulated a suppressed speech he had intended to deliver on the advantages of multiparty democracy. These thoughts were expanded in his monograph *La Côte d'Ivoire: Pour une alternative démocratique.*[32] He had first been detained for his political activities in 1969 and had endured two years in prison from 1971 to 1973. To avoid a repeat performance, Gbagbo fled the country for France in 1982, and remained there for six years. During his absence, however, his works were widely circulated among Ivoirian elites and he became the first widely known opposition leader in the country's history. His arguments for the multiparty state were moderate compared with the widely circulated works of another Ivoirian writing under the pseudonym Marcel Amondji. Since these authors' works were published by Harmattan and Karthala in Paris, their proposals were widely available in the francophone world. The Ivoirian regime could not prevent the spread of these bitterly critical perspectives, which in the light of the economic disaster of the 1980s struck a responsive cord.

In 1988 Gbagbo returned from exile, having founded the Ivoirian Popular Front (Front Populaire Ivoirien, FPI) as an opposition party during his exile. He ran into difficulty almost immediately in trying to assert his pluralist role, being briefly detained and given a lecture by President Houphouët-Boigny and the entire cabinet.

Although these internal critics attempted to politicize the country's economic distress, international financial institutions paid no attention to democratic political reform in their prescriptions for Ivoirian recovery. In fact, in abolishing the various fiefdoms that supported the rival "barons," Houphouët was slimming down the government apparatus in accordance with the wishes of the International Monetary Fund (IMF), even as he reconsolidated his own power. The international lending agencies were latecomers to the movement toward political liberalization, as we shall see.

At the time that France granted independence to its African colonies, it had shown no interest in the promotion of pluralism in the form of opposition parties. Rather, it looked for leaders who demonstrated overwhelming support and who could then negotiate independence and the subsequent relationship. At a conference of francophone mayors in Abidjan on February 26, 1990, former French prime minister and mayor of Paris Jacques Chirac cited Côte d'Ivoire as a one-party system that respects democracy; he called multipartyism a luxury that may impede economic growth.[33]

Indeed, France showed little interest in democracy until the June 1990 meeting of heads of francophone states at La Baule, France, at which President Mitterrand announced that henceforth France would link its aid "to the efforts of those heading toward more freedom."[34] The return to party pluralism in Côte d'Ivoire had been announced two months earlier.

The economic downturn of the 1980s had multiple political effects. First, urban dwellers have "returned to the land," only to encounter land saturation due to massive in-migration in the rich agricultural regions. Because a private land-tenure system has never been developed, interethnic relationships in many rural areas are volatile. At the elite level, the Ivoirian political machine, which had functioned so well since independence, found its resource base dried up by the economic downturn. Particularly affected was the ability of the party to co-opt younger political aspirants.

Of more immediate political concern, however, was political activity in Abidjan, where, especially beginning in 1987, there had been strikes and protests by workers, students, and teachers. Several members of the teachers' union were arrested following disputes among rival leaders. This was followed by a governmental shake-up rumored to have resulted from a coup plot. More serious disturbances followed the announcement of economic austerity measures; the government's structural adjustment program of early 1990 involved cuts of 15 to 40 percent in civil servants' salaries. The ensuing demonstrations caused the government to shift the cuts away from the lowest-level employees, but unrest continued and the whole plan was postponed. Strikers included bus drivers, dock workers, police, soldiers, and even doctors and dentists.[35] "Dialogue" no longer seemed to be working, and shortly thereafter Houphouët decided to allow the legal formation of new political organizations and parties.

Though students and teachers may have been influenced by events in Eastern Europe, they were much more influenced by local issues, and the grievances of other groups were almost purely economic.[36] Since the legalization of competition predated by several months the La Baule meeting, the French position (at least as publicly stated) had not played a role. Indeed, Jennifer Widner suggests that Houphouët was more shaken by Sékou Touré's rapid loss of status after his death on March 26, 1984, followed by a military coup on April 3, and warned his colleagues "not to overestimate the government's popularity with its citizens."[37] This occurred five years before the disintegration in Eastern Europe.

In the Ivoirian case, one is led to an almost single-cause explanation for the beginning of reform: The economic downturn of the 1980s reduced Houphouët's political and economic options and led him to approve multiparty elections as the only way left to buy time.

The Ivoirian military contributed significantly to the general discontent in 1990, when conscripts demanding higher pay occupied Abidjan–Port Bouët International Airport, invaded the Plateau (Abidjan's business district), wounded several civilians, and confiscated automobiles.[38] However, they have generally remained apolitical, and top officers have been co-opted into higher-level positions in the government and in the prefectoral service.[39] Nevertheless, in the African context, their political role has been uniquely marginal.

The Pluralist Situation

Côte d'Ivoire is among the few countries covered in this volume that have not experienced military rule, and it has not even seen the breakdown of the dominant party's control of movement toward pluralism. Thus the situation never existed that would favor the calling of a national conference. Opposition leaders Francis Wodié and Laurent Gbagbo seemed to favor a national conference; when Gbagbo was asked, "How do you see the immediate future of democracy in Côte d'Ivoire?" he answered:

> I propose that as soon as possible, the present National Assembly be dissolved, that parties be established and begin to live, that a provisional government be formed to conduct constitutional debates, that this government convene a constituent assembly charged with giving Côte d'Ivoire a new fundamental law. I propose that after the vote on this constitution, after its approval by the people, if possible by referendum, the new institutions be put in place.[40]

Gbagbo gave no specifics as to how such a procedure might be implemented, and his FPI pushed rather for the restoration of multiparty democracy already promised in Article 7 of the 1960 Constitution: "Parties and political groups compete for the expression of the suffrage. They form and conduct their activities freely, on condition that they respect the principles of national sovereignty and of democracy, and the laws of the Republic."[41] On April 30, 1990, President Houphouët-Boigny announced a return to the multiparty system so described in the Constitution, and thus agreed to run in a competitive election for the presidency for the first time since independence.

Campaigns and Elections in 1990

An FPI document of May 1990 implicitly accepted the dominant party's challenge and invited the Ivoirian people to support them in the coming elections. Gbagbo soon emerged as the FPI candidate for president; he managed to put together a presidential coalition with three other parties: Bernard Zadi's Union of Social Democrats (Union des Sociaux-Démocrates, USD), Francis Wodié's Ivoirian Worker's Party (Parti Ivoirien des Travailleurs, PIT), and Moriféré Bamba's Ivoirian Socialist Party (Parti Socialiste Ivoirien, PSI). However, a total of twenty-one parties were formed, with little cooperation in the National Assembly contests.

The process of certifying opposition parties took up a large part of the six months between the constitutional change and the elections, thus leaving little time to mount campaigns. Nor were the state-controlled media easily converted to the role of neutral reportage. Inexperience with contested elections also contributed to bad faith in the confusion concerning the location of polling places, the distribution of ballots, and the like. There were charges of vote-buying and the sponsorship of intimidating *loubards* (thugs) by both the PDCI and the opposition. Opposition parties were denied permits to build headquarters and had difficulty obtaining telephones and getting access to printing presses. There was even the charge that the PDCI was encouraging the proliferation of opposition parties. Yet, while Houphouët's candidacy benefited from all the advantages that a long-dominant party could muster, most observers believe that the PDCI would have prevailed over its fragmented opposition even in a completely fair election.[42]

Official results of the presidential election were announced on November 7, 1990: Of 4,408,809 registered voters there had been a turnout of 3,048,964 (69.2 percent). Houphouët had won a seventh term with 81.7 percent to Gbagbo's 18.3 percent. Although unsuccessful in the presidential contest, Gbagbo was elected to the National Assembly the following month.

There were 486 candidates in the series of legislative elections, 237 from the PDCI and 214 from the opposition (including 35 running as independents). The turnout was a low 40 percent of registered voters, reflecting, according to Fauré, the confusion of rural voters about the meaning and purpose of multiparty voting.[43] The PDCI won 163 of 175 seats, the FPI nine (including Gbagbo), and the PIT one (Wodié); two independent candidates were elected. Despite this victory, the PDCI experienced a significant turnover; while 234 of the 490 legislative candidates were PDCI, only 61 of 175 incumbents were reelected. The municipal election results were equally lopsided, with opposition candidates winning control in only six of 135 localities.

The End of the Houphouët Era

The outcome of the 1990 election established the presence of a parliamentary opposition for the first time in the country's history. Three FPI deputies were even named to the National Assembly Bureau (the Assembly's executive committee) of thirty-six members. Clearly, however, Houphouët had not been converted to power sharing, especially on matters that concerned him most personally. Hence, even in the election year, he pushed ahead with his prize project, the consecration of the Basilica at Yamoussoukro, with the determination of an authoritarian leader not to be swayed by unfavorable public opinion. In addition, a major constitutional change was implemented by decree: Houphouët created the post of prime minister, to which he appointed a technocrat, Alassane Dramane Ouattara.

More importantly, the regime did not show consistency in its willingness to tolerate political pluralism or dissent. Twelve opposition leaders, including Laurent Gbagbo, were convicted of inciting a violent demonstration in 1992 and were imprisoned, Gbagbo himself receiving a two-year sentence. Although the facts in the violent episode were confusing, it is hard to dispute Gbagbo's own statement that the trial was political, because the ties between the perpetrators of the violence and the politicians were not defined. The opposition leaders' trial was followed by the arrests of student activists and the banning of all further marches. Although an amnesty was announced for all persons convicted of political crimes since 1990, opposition members staged a boycott of the National Assembly because those convicted had not been allowed to appeal their sentences, and because members of the security forces had not been called to account for excesses in their reactions to political protest. It was clear that the norms of a parliamentary, limited government were far from institutionalized.[44]

Widner reminds us that:

> On the other side of the balance sheet, by the third quarter of 1992 the government had not only released Gbagbo, but it also had allowed him to speak at length on state-run television. It tolerated a flourishing opposition press as well as criticism in official newspapers and from technocrats who voted against the PDCI, and it conferred legal status on new, autonomous syndicates. Opposition members of the national assembly worked side by side with members of the long-established PDCI, their jokes attracting laughter and their comments taken seriously.[45]

The equivocal attitude of the government toward its new parliamentary structures finally brought international attention to Ivoirian politics. In 1992, the imprisonment of opposition leaders was condemned by the European Parliament (under French Socialist leadership), and a U.S. State Department official called for an official inquiry into the violence by soldiers against a student demonstration.[46] Yet it was already clear that the relatively mild forms of Ivoirian repression were unlikely to be objects of attention from abroad. Only some dramatic event such as a sudden crackdown or coup would have serious repercussions. The interest of the Ivoirian regime in a favorable investment climate argues powerfully against harsh suppression of opposition—unless that opposition is sufficiently strong and united to pose a serious threat of electoral victory.

Houphouët's vision and his physical strength began to deteriorate in the late 1980s. He was hospitalized with prostate cancer in Paris in June 1993 and returned to Côte d'Ivoire in November on life-support systems. According to official sources, his death came on December 7 after he had ordered his support system to be turned off on the same day of the month that the country had achieved its independence.

Within hours of *le Vieux*'s death, Henri Konan Bédié announced his succession to the presidency, a decision confirmed by the Supreme Court two days later. Alassane Ouattara then resigned as prime minister, thus signaling the beginning of a prolonged power struggle. On December 11, Bédié named Finance Minister Daniel Duncan Kablan as the new prime minister.

Although it was widely anticipated that political unrest would break out in this time of transition, Bédié declared a two-month mourning period (in accordance with Baule tradition), with burial scheduled for February 7, 1994, in the Basilica at Yamoussoukro. The opposition movements remained largely quiet, and there were no demonstrations, not even over the devaluation of the CFA franc.

In September 1993, French Prime Minister Edouard Balladur had informed African leaders that France would henceforth provide structural adjustment aid only to countries that had signed agreements with the IMF and the World Bank. This was interpreted as an admission that France was unable to cope alone with francophone Africa's economic problems and had turned those responsibilities over to the Washington-based organizations.[47] Shortly after Houphouët's death the French announced the 50 percent devaluation of the CFA franc. (Some in Africa argued wistfully that it would never have happened if Houphouët were alive, and the timing of this decision was hardly coincidental: Mitterrand and Balladur used the gathering of leaders at the funeral to announce France's next steps.) Though the devaluation clearly poses difficulties for the fragile democratic structures in the poorest francophone African countries, it has mixed effects in wealthier ones like Côte d'Ivoire, where exports are more competitive and government revenues stronger; the 1994 Ivoirian national budget was much lower in dollar terms than that of 1993. In the Ivoirian context, the political effect of devaluation (muted for the short term by a price freeze) must be seen in contrast to the alternative, namely, the continued deterioration of the economy with an overvalued currency.

At a special congress of the PDCI in April 1994, Bédié was named president of the party "by acclamation and unanimously," according to state television. At least one dissenting delegate complained that he was not allowed to address the congress and, borrowing a term from the debate in Europe on political unification, stated that the party was experiencing a "democracy deficit." Bédié now holds the same combination of state and party positions as Houphouët did at the time of his death.

The Bédié administration continued the ambiguous policy of the PDCI toward those who attempt to practice multiparty pluralism. Within a few months of Houphouët's death three journalists were arrested, including the secretary-general of the FPI and publisher of that party's newspaper, *La Voie*, Abou Sangare Dramane. Dramane was sentenced to three years in prison at hard labor for incitement to violence. In support of the charges, the state prosecutor cited an editorial in which Dramane wrote: "[T]he PDCI must be restrained. Legal means exist, among them the general strike, civil disobedience, demonstrations, etc." Meanwhile, Laurent Gbagbo told a BBC reporter that he has tried to maintain the organizational structure of the FPI, meeting with grassroots activists in the Abidjan area. He had also held discussions with President Konan Bédié at the latter's request concerning the arrest of Dramane and the others.[48]

The 1995 Campaigns

It was widely believed that the PDCI was greatly advantaged in 1990 by the short time for organization and campaigning between the sudden and unanticipated restoration of the multiparty system and the first election under that regime. The buildup to the 1995 elections was much longer, and several differences from the previous situation were especially encouraging to the opposition.

There was, first, the presence of a potentially formidable opponent, in the person of Alassane Ouattara, who moved from the post of prime minister to that of deputy managing director of the International Monetary Fund in Washington. A head-to-head battle between Bédié and Ouattara would have been a much more even match than the Houphouët-Gbagbo contest had been in 1990. Secondly, largely as a result of Ouattara's presence as a possible opponent, the PDCI suffered a serious split for the first time in its history. In mid-1994, a number of PDCI officials defected and announced the formation of the Republican Rally (Rassemblement des Républicains, RDR). Djény Kobina, the deputy mayor of Cocody, emerged as its secretary-general in June 1994 and has generally been its spokesman since then. Its roster also includes former ministers Henriette Diabaté (Culture), Grah Claire (Women's Promotion), and Amadou Coulibaly (Transport and Tourism). Even Philippe Yacé has been identified as an "undeclared" RDR supporter. According to Kobina, thirty-one Assembly delegates support the new movement.[49]

At least publicly, Laurent Gbagbo welcomed these events and even agreed to identify joint assembly candidates. He also proposed cooperation in the presidential race: The opposition's assumption was that none of the three major candidates (Bédié, Ouattara, and Gbagbo) would win a majority outright in the first round in October 1995. However, private polls showed that Bédié and many PDCI Assembly candidates could have been defeated in October—if the opposition had united behind the same candidates and had been allowed to compete freely. Côte d'Ivoire now has the two-round election system of France's Fifth Republic. Hence all candidates could have run in the first round, as long as the opposition agreed to support their strongest candidate in the runoff. The RDR has strong support in the north and northwest, and the FPI has been popular among segments of the urban population hard hit by the currency devaluation.[50] All seven major opposition parties joined forces as the Republican Front (Front Républicain, FR) to combat unpopular aspects of the electoral code.

This would appear to be a formidable coalition. But not all trends favored the opposition. There was, first of all, the economy. Houphouët's decision to liberalize may be attributable largely to the economic downturn, which left him unable to nourish his political machine, but economic forces have been kinder to Ivoirian cultivators recently. The producer price for one kilogram of coffee went from 200 CFA francs (4 French francs) in 1993 to 650 CFA francs (6.5 French francs after devaluation) in 1994. Prices for cocoa, pineapples, and food crops (notably rice) reached record highs in 1994.[51] Moreover, international agencies, acting on the belief that "if devaluation cannot be made to work in Côte d'Ivoire, it will not work anywhere," have given special support to the Ivoirian transition through the devaluation. Though France canceled development loans to various CFA countries, the French Development Fund (Caisse Française de Développement, CFD) also pledged US$280 million to Côte d'Ivoire in 1994.[52] Thus, without overly distressing the lending agencies, Bédié was able to announce salary increases for civil servants on May 1, 1995 (a date timed to blunt opposition use of the traditional labor holiday). The raise, affecting over 105,000 public workers—a crucial voting bloc—was 3 percent for those with salaries over 300,000 CFA francs, and 15 percent for those below 100,000 francs.[53]

Building on this favorable turn in the economy, the PDCI under Bédié showed its willingness to employ all the means at its disposal to maintain its position, and it has demonstrated skill at doing so. Its biggest weapon has been its majority in the National Assembly, which adopted an electoral code that requires that both parents of a presidential candidate have Ivoirian nationality and that any candidate have resided in the country for the previous five years. Both measures were seen as direct and personal attacks on the candidacy of Alassane Ouattara.

The PDCI has a long tradition of co-opting opponents with offers they can hardly refuse. Both Kobina and Gbagbo have been offered important positions if

they would join the government, and Ouattara had to weigh his chances of success against the leverage he had with the government as long as he remained non-
committal on his candidacy. Most of those engaged in political life in Côte
d'Ivoire have government positions. A small pay raise may not be important to
high-level officials, but the threat of losing their positions commands instant attention. The government has been diligent in identifying opponents to PDCI rule
and in purging them from the ranks of the civil service and parastatal enterprises.[54] Thus, in managing his political capital, Ouattara had to decide how
much to invest in maintaining his supporters in positions of influence. A decision
on his part to cooperate with the regime would protect them, whereas a declaration of candidacy would force them into a position of high risk.

The PDCI also benefited from the lack of interest shown by France and the
West in the "details" of the Ivoirian electoral process. On a day when Ivoirian security police had killed two demonstrators, Jacques Godfrain, the French minister
for cooperation, reflected Chirac's sentiments of five years earlier when he assured
Bédié that "France will be by your side, Mr. President, for the long period that lies
ahead of you."[55]

Finally, the PDCI played a trump card that Houphouët would never have advised. It stimulated ethnic conflict, both among groups within the Ivoirian population and the large number of foreigners in the country. Houphouët had preached
"dual nationality" as early as 1964 for the citizens of other member states of the
Organisation Commune Africaine et Malgache (OCAM), although the idea was
dropped because of highly unusual overt opposition to it at home. He had even
made it possible for foreign residents to vote, and foreign nationals were an important support base for the PDCI, especially in the 1990 election. Indeed, after that
election Widner was able to conclude that "the prospect of increasing levels of ethnic division as a result of the legalization of opposition parties was minimal.
. . . The Côte d'Ivoire case proved a counter-example to the often-heard argument
that competitive politics necessarily brings ethnic division."[56]

But tensions around the large foreign population have led to political manipulation of nationality: The new electoral code provides that both parents of a candidate must have Ivoirian nationality; the PDCI position is that Ouattara's father
was Burkinabè (from Burkina Faso). The opposition hit back in the same vein,
claiming that Bédié's father was Ghanaian; two journalists were prosecuted for in-
vestigating the latter story. It might just be impossible to prove parents' nationality, in any event, since all candidates were born before independence and before
the creation of a vital statistics registry system. However, the PDCI and its opponents agreed on one point in the electoral code: Foreigners should be disenfranchised.

The PDCI used both ethnic tensions and anti-Muslim fears to stir up tension
among domestic groups as well. State television played up fundamentalist Muslim
extremism in North Africa, and two journalists from the Muslim *Plume Libre*
were prosecuted for sedition. Muslims have been prominent among senior civil

servants dismissed for their opposition leanings. Finally, the president of the National Islamic Council, Idriss Koudoss Koné, was kidnapped in January 1995 by unknown persons.[57] Because Muslim generally means "Dyula" (itinerant Muslim traders) in the Ivoirian perspective, these activities raise both religious and ethnic tensions.

Of course, the mosques have been used for anti-Bédié and pro-RDR statements, and the Muslim press is militant at times, which in many eyes justifies the PDCI campaign, and which prompted Bédié to speak in March 1995 of his fear of a renewal "of tribalism, of exclusion, of religious fanaticism," and of his desire to preserve "peace and national unity."[58] Bédié and the PDCI hope that this issue will strain the Republican Front's shaky alliance of northerners and urban southerners.

The president met with opposition leaders in April 1995. They had requested the session to express their displeasure over the electoral code. Hoping to create a truly independent electoral system, they also proposed a system whereby a representative from each party would sign an affidavit on the result at each polling station, which was to be available to the Constitutional Court to decide challenges.[59] Because the government was not ready to negotiate away these advantages, the opposition increased the ante by calling for a massive demonstration in Abidjan. On May 4, 1995, the Republican Front rally marched through central Abidjan. Its organizers estimated the crowd at 60,000, though the government put the number at 3,000.[60] However, on July 8 there was another FR demonstration, focusing once again on withdrawal of the election code; a Reuters report estimated the number of participants at this one to be more than 20,000.[61]

The central question in mid-1995 was whether Ouattara would be a candidate for the presidency. Secretary-General Kobina met Ouattara in Paris in late June 1995 and reported his words to be, "My suitcase is prepared, I'm ready to join you."[62] The RDR then held its first party congress and formally petitioned Ouattara to be its candidate. As it became clear that the government would not agree to opposition demands for revising the electoral laws, Ouattara and his followers decided to boycott the election.[63] Gbagbo and the FPI followed suit, leaving only Francis Wodié in the position of challenger. Demonstrators in support of the boycott clashed with police and PDCI personnel, and sporadic violence occurred, with at least thirty-five deaths in the period leading up to and just after the elections.[64] The boycott, along with fears of violence, reduced registration from 4.4 million in 1990 to 3.8 million in 1995, and voter turnout even in that reduced electorate dropped from 69 to 56 percent. Consequently, although Bédié was reported to have won the presidency on October 22 with 96 percent of the vote, that figure represented total support of only 2 million votes—a substantially smaller proportion of the electorate than the nearly 3 million votes for Houphouët in 1990. The outcome announcement set off ethnic violence, especially by "indigenous" people against Baule planter-settlers around Gagnoa.

Bédié recovered some legitimacy in the parliamentary elections of November 26, 1995, in which both the FPI and RDR participated, and which took place in

relative calm. The PDCI won 147 of the 175 seats, down from its 163-seat majority in 1990 but still showing its solid control. The outcome called into question
the administration's strong-arm tactics, since it seems clear that Bédié could have
won simply on the basis of the PDCI's patronage and propaganda machine and
did not need to confront the opposition with electoral law manipulations. In the
short term at least, improvements in the economy gave the government the resources it needed to tempt opposition leaders back to the fold. The PDCI leadership appears to have a real fear that the opposition might eventually unite behind
candidates capable of defeating them. Even in its defeat, the opposition was successful through its boycott in demonstrating the limits of citizen support for
Bédié and the PDCI.

Conclusion

Henri Konan Bédié seems to have consolidated his position rather well, having
managed the 1995 campaigns and the situations leading up to them about as
shrewdly as one could imagine. The transition from Houphouët to Bédié has
nonetheless strengthened the position of PDCI opponents, since Bédié was forced
to be conciliatory toward them in his bid for control. Even as his government continues to harass opponents, it is clear that the regime lacks the means to reestab-
lish the authoritarian system of the Houphouët era. Under present circumstances,
the regime in fact benefits from the release of pressure provided by the presence
of a limited opposition (Wodié's presence on the presidential ballot was extremely
useful to the PDCI), even as the regime must respond to demands for improved
economic conditions.

There is no simple dichotomy between democracies and dictatorships. As the
Mexican one-party-dominant experience demonstrates, semi-democratic systems
can achieve long-term stability and may provide the basis for an evolutionary path
toward true pluralist democracy. The similarities between post-1990 Côte d'Ivoire
(and other liberalized African states) and Mexico are more than superficial.

There remains, however, the difficulty of achieving stable pluralist democracy
in a multiethnic state. Ethnic rivalries were quite effectively controlled by the
"ethnic arithmetic" of the one-party state. Even in the post-1990 government, it
was clear that PDCI Secretary-General Laurent Dona Fologo and Prime Minister
Ouattara represented the north. As in the past, the various important ministries
covered different ethnic interests and generations. But now, as real pluralism
emerges, the Ivoirian experience is looking less and less unique: A government
under threat will always be tempted to draw the weapon of ethnicity, and no
leader is likely to emerge who feels secure enough to rule without it. The opponents have found common ground in their resentment of Baule dominance, while
the government pushes the northern/southern (or Muslim/non-Muslim) division. These conflicts may have unprecedented effects on the country's stability, as

in other states where the configuration of parties around ethnic or regional identities has been the norm. Côte d'Ivoire remains singular, however, in the degree to which ethnic groups have been geographically mixed, even down to the village level. Though this means that secession is unlikely ever to be a threat to Ivoirian statehood, this local-level mixture could be explosive if agitated. At the very least, under true pluralism, and assuming that ethnicity will be politically significant even if violence is prevented, it introduces the problem of how to achieve equitable representation under a system of single-member districts. Such constitutional issues are several steps away, but they will inevitably arise if the more immediate tensions are contained.

Another unique feature of Ivoirian society among the African francophone states is the high proportion of nonindigenous population. Richard Crook has pointed out that although 30 percent of the total population is foreign, the proportion rises to 41 percent of those between fifteen and sixty years of age.[65] In some parts of the southern region, the proportion of the total population that is foreign exceeds 50 percent. Thus Côte d'Ivoire is in a situation comparable, perhaps, only to some of the Persian Gulf states in the degree to which questions of democracy will be tied up in the definition of citizenship. Here again, authoritarian rule offered possibilities of control that are becoming more difficult under pluralism.

At the start of this chapter, it was postulated that democracy is at best reluctantly granted by authoritarian leaders. The evidence in the Ivoirian case is that the earliest liberalizing moves were in the Bonapartist tradition: a rather cynical use of the franchise to erode the standing of challengers. As economic resources shrank, however, true defensive democratization began to occur; now movement continues in that direction, even with some amelioration in the economy.

Many ordinary citizens have little specific interest in the reluctance of political elites to let go of power. It is an open question what proportion of the crowds cheering the arrival of elections is enthralled by the process, as opposed to the ends they hope to achieve through the process. The Ivoirian case supports the recent literature on democratization suggesting that successful liberalization results from economic failure under authoritarian government. It is equally true, however, that the failure of a *democratic* regime's economic policy can easily destroy the legitimacy of an open electoral process, civil liberties, and other essential features of democratic politics. In Africa, and especially in Côte d'Ivoire, the *conjuncture* forced the hand of authoritarian elites, but it is not clear how much liberalization will be achieved before democratic institutions are called to account for their failure to unravel the tough economic dilemmas challenging them.

Notes

1. Adam Przeworski, *Democracy and the Market: Political and Economic Reforms in Eastern Europe and Latin America* (New York: Cambridge University Press, 1991), pp. 11–14.

2. Aristide R. Zolberg, *One-Party Government in the Ivory Coast,* rev. ed. (Princeton: Princeton University Press, 1969). This work remains the authoritative source on Houphouët's early career and his role in Ivoirian politics through the 1960s. See also Barbara Lewis, "Félix Houphouët-Boigny," in Harvey Glickman, ed., *Political Leaders of Contemporary Africa South of the Sahara: A Biographical Dictionary* (Westport, Conn.: Greenwood Press, 1992), pp. 87–94. The work by Lewis provides a good brief contemporary biography of Houphouët.

3. Zolberg, *One-Party Government,* pp. 73, 287.

4. Ibid., p. 69.

5. Ibid., pp. 74–75.

6. Philip Maynard Williams, *Crisis and Compromise: Politics in the Fourth Republic* (Hamden, Conn.: Archon Books, 1964), p. 182; Serge Berstein, *The Republic of de Gaulle, 1958–1969* (Cambridge, England: Cambridge University Press, 1993).

7. Philip Maynard Williams and Martin Harrison, *De Gaulle's Republic* (London: Longmans, 1960), p. 30.

8. Berstein, *The Republic of de Gaulle,* pp. 4, 6.

9. Zolberg, *One-Party Government,* pp. 92–93.

10. Negotiations with the French government were made easier by the presence of François Mitterrand, then of the Union Démocratique et Sociale de la Résistance (UDSR) as Minister of Overseas France. Mitterrand had replaced ministers from the more right-wing Mouvement Républicain Populaire (MRP).

11. Aristide R. Zolberg, "Political Development in Ivory Coast Since Independence," in Philip Foster and Aristide R. Zolberg, eds., *Ghana and the Ivory Coast: Perspectives on Modernization* (Chicago: University of Chicago Press, 1971), pp. 15–21.

12. Jean-François Médard, "The Historical Trajectories of the Ivoirian and Kenyan States," in James Manor, ed., *Rethinking Third World Politics* (New York: Longman, 1991), pp. 185–121.

13. This situation fueled speculation that Mockey's death in 1981 was not an accident, as was officially announced.

14. The dialogue process is described at length in Michael Cohen, *Urban Policy and Political Conflict in Africa* (Chicago: University of Chicago Press, 1974).

15. Jean Maddox Toungara, "The Apotheosis of Côte d'Ivoire's Nana Houphouët-Boigny," *Journal of Modern African Studies* 28, no. 1 (1990):23–28.

16. The events of 1963, the bloody repression of ethnic unrest in Gagnoa in 1970, and more recent actions against students in Abidjan demonstrate, of course, that the regime did not hesitate to use force where accommodation seemed risky. The fact remains, however, that these were exceptional and not the response of first resort.

17. On allocations designed to redress the economic lag in the north, see Bastiaan A. den Tuinder, *Ivory Coast: The Challenge of Success* (Baltimore: Johns Hopkins University Press, 1978), pp. 145–148; Nguessan Zoukou, *Régions et régionalisation en Côte d'Ivoire* (Paris: L'Harmattan, 1990), pp. 131–132; and Dwayne Woods, "Ethno-Regional Demands, Symbolic and Redistributive Politics: Sugar Complexes in the North of the Ivory Coast," *Ethnic and Racial Studies* 12, no. 4 (October 1989):485–486.

18. Jean-François Médard, "La régulation socio-politique," in Y.-A. Fauré and J.-F. Médard, eds., *État et bourgeoisie en Côte d'Ivoire* (Paris: L'Harmattan, 1983), pp. 61–62.

19. F. O. Alalade, "President Félix Houphouët-Boigny: The Ivory Coast and France," *Journal of African Studies* 6, no. 3 (Autumn 1979):12–131; Jacques Baulin, *La politique*

africaine d'Houphouët-Boigny (Paris: Eurafor-Press, 1980). Baulin, recounting Houphouët's success at preventing a rapprochement between France and Guinea, wrote: "[C]ould the influence of Houphouët be so great with the President of the French Republic [de Gaulle]? To the point of having a role in the African policy of France? The answer to these questions is affirmative" (p. 83). Houphouët's relationship with France seems to have been not only extremely close but also more reciprocal than those of other African leaders.

20. I. William Zartman and C. Degado, eds., *The Political Economy of Ivory Coast* (New York: Praeger, 1984). In this work, it is noted that Côte d'Ivoire had "the largest French population in any country outside of the metropole . . . the highest number of French technical assistants . . . the highest number of students in French universities, and the highest number of large French firms . . . " (p. 13).

21. Richard Crook, "Patrimonialism, Administrative Effectiveness, and Economic Development in Côte d'Ivoire," *African Affairs* 88, no. 351 (April 1989):205–228.

22. Catherine Boone, "The Social Origins of State Liberalism in Côte d'Ivoire" (paper delivered at the annual meeting of the American Political Science Association, Washington, D.C., September 1993).

23. Dwayne Woods, "Elites, Ethnicity, and 'Home Town' Association in Côte d'Ivoire: An Historical Analysis of State-Society Links," *Africa* 64, no. 4 (1989):469.

24. Yves-A. Fauré, "Côte d'Ivoire: Analyzing the Crisis," in Donal B. Cruise O'Brien, John Dunn, and Richard Rathbone, eds., *Contemporary West African States* (Cambridge, England: Cambridge University Press, 1989), pp. 59–73.

25. On this rivalry, see Jacques Baulin, *La succession d'Houphouët-Boigny* (Paris: Eurafor-Press, 1989).

26. Fauré, "Analyzing the Crisis," p. 71.

27. Ibid., pp. 59–62.

28. Ibid., pp. 63–66.

29. Ibid., pp. 67–72. For a detailed discussion on the decision to have competitive elections in 1980, see Jacques Baulin, *La politique intérieure d'Houphouët-Boigny* (Paris: Eurafor-Press, 1987), and for an update on electoral practices, see Tessy D. Bakary Akin, *La démocratie par le haut en Côte d'Ivoire* (Paris: L'Harmattan, 1992).

30. Bakary Akin, *La démocratie par le haut.*

31. Jean-Pierre Chauveau and Jean-Pierre Dozon, "Au coeur des ethnies ivoiriennes . . . L'état," in Emmanuel Terray, ed., *L'état contemporain en Afrique* (Paris: L'Harmattan, 1987), pp. 221–296.

32. Laurent Gbagbo, *La Côte d'Ivoire: Pour une alternative démocratique* (Paris: L'Harmattan, 1983).

33. In 1987 Chirac was quoted as "being not at all convinced that pluralist democracy is the best system for Africa. His preference leans rather toward the 'multitendency' single party." *Jeune Afrique*, May 27, 1987, p. 32.

34. Kay Whiteman, "The Party's Over," *Africa Report* 39, no. 2 (March-April 1994):12–18. It may be that Houphouët was not present at the La Baule summit, Whiteman suggests, because he had "no desire to be lectured."

35. Richard C. Crook, "State, Society, and Political Institutions in Côte d'Ivoire and Ghana," in Manor, *Rethinking Third World Politics*, p. 239.

36. Laurent Gbagbo, in *Côte d'Ivoire: Histoire d'un retour* (Paris: L'Harmattan, 1989), referred frequently to events in the Soviet Union, Eastern Europe, and Algeria (where the Front de Libération Nationale had just decided to hold multiparty elections). He also casti-

gated the French for their lack of support for African democracy: "They judge events differently, depending on whether they occur in Eastern Europe or in Black Africa. They think that it is already good that we can find a bowl of rice to eat; while as concerns the countries of Eastern Europe, the democrats of Western Europe mobilize to help these countries achieve democracy" (p. 59). It seems clear that the movement toward reform was already much discussed and well under way in Côte d'Ivoire at this time and can be explained without reference to this outside stimulus. Student unrest leading to the February demonstrations was sparked when "electricity cuts . . . deprived university students of their ability to study for exams." See "Africa Rights Monitor: Côte d'Ivoire," *Africa Today* 37, no. 2 (1990):86. According to the *New York Times* (March 3, 1990), the initial student grievances were school fees, cuts in scholarships, and the announced reduction of government wages. Political overtones and slogans followed quickly, however.

37. Jennifer A. Widner, "The 1990 Elections in Côte d'Ivoire," *Issue* 20, no. 1 (Winter 1991):36.

38. Elements in the military have been restive since 1990. In March 1993 forty-five members of the Republican Guard revolted in Abidjan and Yamoussoukro, taking three officers hostage. The mutineers were demanding special payment because they guard the president; Houphouët managed to solve the problem peacefully.

39. Crook, "State, Society, and Political Institutions," p. 239.

40. Gbagbo, *Côte d'Ivoire: Histoire d'un retour,* pp. 63–64.

41. Antoine Séry, *Côte d'Ivoire: Après la faillite, l'espoir?* (Paris: L'Harmattan, 1990), p. 117.

42. *New York Times,* March 3, 1990; Widner, "The 1990 Elections in Côte d'Ivoire," p. 34.

43. Yves-A. Fauré, "L'économie politique d'une démocratisation: Éléments d'analyse à propos de l'expérience récente de la Côte d'Ivoire," *Politique africaine,* no. 43 (October 1991):37.

44. Mark Huband, "Silencing the Opposition," *Africa Report* 37, no. 3 (May-June 1992):55–57.

45. Jennifer A. Widner, "Two Leadership Styles and Patterns of Political Liberalization," *African Studies Review* 37, no. 1 (April 1994):151–174.

46. Huband, "Silencing the Opposition."

47. Whiteman, "The Party's Over."

48. *Summary of World Broadcasts* (London: BBC, April 24, 1994).

49. *Africa Confidential,* no. 39 (July 15, 1994):6; *Africa Confidential,* no. 39 (October 21, 1994):3; *Jeune Afrique,* May 18–24, 1994, p. 53.

50. *Africa Confidential,* no. 39 (March 31, 1995):7.

51. *Jeune Afrique,* March 16–22, 1995, pp. 18–19.

52. *Africa Confidential,* no. 39 (February 3, 1995):6.

53. *Jeune Afrique,* May 18–24, 1995, p. 52.

54. *Africa Confidential,* no. 39 (March 31, 1995):7.

55. *New York Times,* October 23, 1995, p. 8.

56. Widner, "The 1990 Elections in Côte d'Ivoire," p. 39.

57. *Africa Confidential,* no. 39 (March 31, 1995):7.

58. *Jeune Afrique,* March 16–22, 1995, p. 21.

59. *Africa Confidential,* no. 39 (March 31, 1995):7.

60. *Jeune Afrique,* May 18–24, 1995, pp. 52–53.

61. *Reuters Information Service,* July 8, 1995.

62. *Reuters Information Service*, June 30, 1995.

63. Géraldine Faes, "Le gâchis," *Jeune Afrique*, October 12–18, 1995; Faes, "Les leçons du 22 octobre," *Jeune Afrique*, October 26–November 1, 1995.

64. *Los Angeles Times*, November 28, 1995, p. 4.

65. Crook, "State, Society, and Political Institutions," p. 225.

Chapter Twelve

Senegal: The Evolution of a Quasi Democracy

RICHARD VENGROFF AND LUCY CREEVEY

Although many African nations are engaged in the process of democratization, Senegal is one of a handful generally considered to be making significant progress in the transition to a fully democratic state.[1] Though it cannot be said that democracy has been fully institutionalized in Senegal, some very important steps have been taken in that direction.[2] The processes associated with political reform in Senegal share some characteristics with other sub-Saharan, particularly francophone, African States. However, there are also very distinct differences in the timing, in the way in which democratic political reform was launched, in the balance of internal and external pressures in stimulating reform, in the incremental nature of the reforms, and in the relative success of those reforms in the long term. For these reasons, Senegal presents an especially interesting and important case for analysis and comparison.

On the positive side, the press is free and unfettered, and it is quite willing to criticize and attack government policy and individual leaders. The broadcast media have been opened up to private organizations, including international cable television, and government radio and television stations must now compete with the private sector for attention. Organizational life is very rich and broad based. The tradition of peaceful participation in local, national, and even international discussions is well established. The opening of the government to democratic coalition building (rather than pure co-optation), even with the most dedicated of opposition leaders, is a sign of political maturity rarely seen in Africa.[3] The military is highly professional and has throughout the history of independent Senegal not intervened directly in the political arena.

On the negative side, the Senegalese polity has not always been committed to democracy, and it occasionally seems to waver in that regard. Some analysts argue that Senegal is at best a "semi-democracy." According to Sheldon Gellar, the Senegalese government "in most instances functions as a patrimonial administrative state which greatly resembles its predecessor, the colonial state, in its approach toward dealing with its citizens."[4] Even today some of the fundamental correlates of democratic rule—a broadly based participant political culture, a sound economic base, a well-educated or at least highly literate population, and strong, institutionalized, opposition parties—are weak or missing. In the rural areas the electorate is still heavily influenced by a well-established system of political relationships linked to the "maraboutic" tradition.[5] Although the Senegalese people have traditionally tried to settle their disputes and disagreements in a relatively peaceful fashion, exceptions are becoming more common. The increasingly violent Casamance secession issue has never been satisfactorily resolved and threatens both the economic and the political stability of the nation. Politically motivated strikes and demonstrations have been regular occurrences.[6] In 1989, the anti-Mauritanian riots produced a type of ugly violence not seen before in the country. The politically motivated assassination of Babacar Sèye, vice president of the Constitutional Commission, in May 1993, was unprecedented in recent Senegalese history.[7] In early 1994, demonstrations against the devaluation of the CFA franc resulted in the deaths of six police and one civilian. Even though this type of mob violence has been relatively infrequent, many fear that a qualitative break with tradition has occurred and a new precedent set which may affect Senegalese politics for many years to come.

The French Colonial Period

The French colonial administration provided little opportunity for the development of serious democratic institutions in Senegal.[8] The relatively autonomous status accorded to the communes of St. Louis and Gorée on August 10, 1872, and later to Dakar and Rufisque, responded to the needs of the French settlers, the Creoles, and the few educated Africans who, early on, were accorded the status and rights of French citizens.[9] The overwhelming majority of the population, the small-scale farmers, remained under the authoritarian rule of a highly centralized, nondevelopmental colonial bureaucracy. The rigidly hierarchical territorial administration was built on an organization based on the *cercle*, the *sous-division* (subdivision), the canton, and finally the village. Only the latter two of these units involved indigenous Africans in any decisionmaking roles. The first election of Senegalese representing the entire country to the French National Assembly in 1946 (Lamine Gueye and Léopold Senghor), although highly symbolic, was based on limited rights of participation and was much more about French politics than local issues.[10]

Political Parties and the Party System

The modern political party system in Senegal was heavily influenced by close links with French political parties, especially after the establishment of the Fourth Republic following World War II.[11] The older, urban-based, elitist Senegalese branch of the International Workers Federation (Fédération Socialiste [SFIO] du Sénégal), founded in 1937 under the direction of Lamine Gueye, gradually gave way to the populist Senegalese Democratic Bloc (Bloc Démocratique Sénégalais, BDS) founded in 1948 and led by Léopold Senghor and Mamadou Dia. The more rural-based BDS was able to absorb several of Senegal's smaller parties while gaining the adherence of the traditional authorities, including the Muslim religious leaders. After the reconciliation between Lamine Gueye and Léopold Senghor in 1958, the BDS and a number of smaller parties transformed themselves into the Senegalese Progressive Union (Union Progressiste Sénégalaise, UPS). With no serious opposition remaining, Senegal was, for all practical purposes, becoming a one-party state.

Unlike many other African nations, the de facto single-party status never became de jure. Having successfully absorbed or co-opted all serious opposition, the UPS during the 1960s was well along the road to capturing permanent control of the state. A crisis was brought on in 1962 by a split in the ruling party between President Senghor and Prime Minister Dia and his supporters in the left (more populist) wing of the party. The success of Senghor and the arrest of Dia following a failed coup led to the suppression of opposition groups, both within and outside of the UPS. The electoral process was changed to create a single, nationwide constituency, with a winner-take-all system based on a party list, thereby ensuring one-party rule.[12] In addition, an effort was undertaken to centralize all political power in the president and the elite, with technocratic cadres serving in the various ministries. This dominance by Senghor and his supporters was confirmed by the results of the 1968 elections, in which only the UPS presented candidates.[13]

The situation of a highly centralized, one-party state lasted until 1974, when the government faced mounting societal pressures, including a most serious threat in the form of rural-based disaffection, the so-called *malaise paysan*.[14] In addition, both desire for international respectability and internal divisions in the ruling UPS forced a liberalization of regulations governing the registration of political parties and a promise to reform the electoral system.[15] As a result of this opening, the most important of the opposition parties, the Senegalese Democratic Party (Parti Démocratique Sénégalais, PDS), was founded by a group under the leadership of Abdoulaye Wade in 1974.

President Senghor thereafter initiated incremental changes designed to expand the democratic option without seriously threatening his ruling party. In 1976, an amendment to Article 3 of the constitution officially transformed Senegal into a de jure three-party system. Each party was required to represent one of the major ideological tendencies identified in the implementing legislation (Marxist-Leninist, democratic-socialist, liberal-democratic).[16] The ruling UPS, which changed its name to the Socialist Party (Parti Socialiste, PS) in 1976, reserved the middle ground (democratic-socialist) among the three options for itself, the PDS reluctantly adopted the liberal democratic label, and the African Independence Party (Parti Africain de l'Indépendance, PAI) took the Marxist-Leninist appellation. A fourth "tendency," conservatism, was legalized in 1978 with the recognition of the Senegalese Republican Movement (Mouvement Républicain Sénégalais, MRS). Other would-be parties such as the National Democratic Assembly (Rassemblement National Démocratique, RND) were accorded the status of associations but not recognized as parties because the "official" legal ideological space for parties was already fully occupied.

Reforms continued to evolve on the basis of both the pragmatic needs of leaders and democratic principles. In 1981, under President Abdou Diouf, the constitution was amended again to remove limits on the number of parties and to allow for a freer form of multipartyism without the restrictions imposed in 1976. Some argue that this strategy was designed to ensure a splintering of the opposition into smaller, less viable and less competitive groupings. In fact, fourteen parties had been recognized in time for the 1983 elections, with eight actually competing for legislative seats and five for the presidency. In this situation the PS won 111 of the 120 legislative seats with 79.9 percent of the vote and Diouf the presidency with 83.5 percent.[17]

Abdou Diouf and the PS won the elections again in 1988, but with a reduced majority and in the face of serious charges of fraud.[18] Supporters of the opposition launched street demonstrations to protest what they viewed as the stealing of the presidential election from the official second-place finisher, the PDS. Official results show Diouf winning the presidency with 73.2 percent of the vote to 25.8 percent for Wade and the PDS. Despite the protests, it is clear that the PS won the election[19] on the basis of superior party organization outside the major cities and the ability to mobilize the rural electorate with the help of the leading marabouts.

Together with four of his PDS colleagues, Abdoulaye Wade was persuaded to join the PS in a government of national unity *("cohabitation")* in 1991. The PDS accepted four ministries (Posts, Literacy, Labor and Professional Training, African Integration), while Wade became the Minister of State without a formal ministry. Although this arrangement temporarily quieted criticism of the government by its strongest competitor, the calm was short-lived. The PDS leaders charged that the PS government did not permit serious discussion of issues, refused to accept criticism, and had given them only weak ministries *("les portefeuilles vides")*. Under pressure from their party, Wade and his colleagues officially withdrew from the government on October 20, 1992. Wade then declared himself a candidate for the presidency in 1993 in opposition to Diouf.

Of greater significance than the existence of a short-lived alliance is the fact that the coalition, during the period of "cohabitation,"[20] produced important political reforms with the involvement of all political parties. These include a new electoral code providing for the representation of all parties at polling stations, a guaranteed secret ballot, a lowered voting age (from twenty-one to eighteen), an easier and expanded system of voter registration, guaranteed access to the state media for all parties, and the acceptance of foreign election monitors.[21] This new system was approved and strongly supported by all political parties. Although several retained some doubts about implementation, the arrangement provided a sound base for free and fair elections.

The hotly contested presidential election of February 21, 1993, again won by the PS on the basis of its ability to mobilize support in the rural areas while sustaining losses in the major urban centers, proved to be yet another major test of Senegal's commitment to democracy. Procedural and administrative difficulties and delays in certifying the vote raised the question of fairness and legitimacy of the entire process to new levels of discourse. President Diouf won the election with a reduced majority (officially 58.4 percent to Wade's 32 percent). The new election system requires that for a first-round victory in the presidential race a candidate must obtain both a majority of the vote cast and the support of at least 25 percent of the registered voters. The officially reported results indicated that Diouf had attained this with the ballots of about 30 percent of the registered voters, a thin but still comfortable margin.

The May 9, 1993, legislative elections, although smoother-running in many respects than the presidential election, were still surrounded by controversy. The PS government had instituted several changes in the electoral code in order to obviate some of the controversy surrounding the presidential vote. The opposition again demonstrated its strength in the major urban centers but failed to match the PS's organizational advantages in the rural areas. The PS obtained nearly 57 percent of the vote and 84 of the 120 National Assembly seats. Five other parties won seats, the most significant being the PDS with twenty-seven. Although only about 40 percent of registered voters took part in the election, this is not surprising given a combination of alienation and fatigue after having just participated in the presidential election several months earlier.[22] Furthermore, the seemingly low turnout may in fact be an indicator that the elections were fairer than usual, with the reported turnout more nearly reflecting the actual turnout.

The demonstrations that followed the 1988 elections were not repeated, to many people's surprise. Instead, immediately after the elections, Diouf and Wade opened secret discussions for establishing a new coalition. The assassination of Babacar Sèye on May 15, 1993, effectively ended those discussions. Sèye, a vice president of the Constitutional Council, the organization that makes final decisions about election results, was shot in Dakar while being chauffeured in his car. Because Wade and the PDS had been strong critics of Sèye's handling of the presidential election returns, they were immediately under suspicion. Wade was interrogated and released. Three individuals directly implicated were arrested and convicted, but those behind the plot were never brought to justice.[23] The two hypotheses most commonly circulated in Senegal are: (1) The PDS assassinated Sèye; and (2) Some elements of the PS staged the assassination to stop the talks of a new Diouf-Wade coalition. Whatever the case, discussions between the PS and the PDS abruptly ended as a result.

Most of the opposition parties, including the PDS, joined together in a new coalition known as Bokk Sopi Senegaal.[24] This new, relatively united opposition included not only most of the political parties, but also the *Moustarchadines*,[25] which represent the forces of an emerging, more fundamentalist Islam in Senegal. Hundreds of *Moustarchadines* were arrested and jailed after the devaluation riots of February 1994. Leaders of the opposition, including Wade, were also imprisoned, and all political rallies, meetings, and marches were banned.

The situation was made more serious because of internal rivalries within the PS government involving Djibo Ka, minister of the interior, on the one hand, and Moustapha Niass, minister of foreign affairs, on the other. Blame for the security breach that left the presidential palace exposed to the antidevaluation demonstrators flew back and forth, but the real issue was the positioning of the ministers for the eventual succession to Diouf, who has indicated that he will probably not run again.[26] International pressure may have helped to alleviate the situation, but Diouf argued that standard legal practices had been followed, and the leading opposition figures were released on that basis in July 1994.

With five opposition parties represented in the National Assembly, the economy in shambles, a tarnished human rights image, continued secessionist violence in the Casamance, and growing religious fundamentalism, the PS again looked to a coalition government to ease the pressure.[27] Both the U.S. and the French embassies facilitated a renewal of discussions between Diouf and Wade. In March 1995 the PDS left the Bokk Sopi Senegaal coalition and joined the government. The PDS received five cabinet posts, including the ministries of National Health and Social Action, Commerce and Industrialization, African Integration, Professional Training, and the title of Minister of State once again for Wade. The new coalition also includes the Party of Independence and Labor (Parti de l'Indépendance et du Travail, PIT) and the Democratic League/Movement for the Party of Labor (Ligue Démocratique/Mouvement pour le Parti du Travail, LD/MPT), each with two ministries, and the Senegalese Democratic Party/Renewal (Parti Démocratique Sénégalais/Rénovation, PDS/R) with one. Of a total of thirty-four ministry level positions, the partners of the PS now hold ten, including some of considerable importance.

The opposition is now limited to the small group of parties led by Iba Der Thiam's Convention of Democrats and Patriots (Convention des Démocrates et Patriotes/Garabi-gi, CDP/G-G), Landing Savané's Unity for Action/African Party for Democracy and Socialism (And Jef/Parti Africain pour la Démocratie et le Socialisme, AJ/PADS), and Madior Diouf's RND. In the National Assembly elections these parties were loosely united as Japoo Ligeeyal Senegaal, a coalition that is now moribund. These remaining fragments of the defunct Bokk Sopi Senegaal[28] group are now attempting to organize at the local level for the coming municipal, regional, and local elections.[29]

The course of political reform and democratization during the 1980s and 1990s has been influenced by other developments. Among the most important have been: the secessionist movement in the Casamance; devaluation; administrative reform; and decentralization. These developments, some of which involve external as well as internal dimensions, have helped to shape the very difficult environment in which efforts to achieve a more democratic state and society have taken place; in turn, democratization has had a variety of influences and impacts upon it. It is to these developments that we must now turn in order to develop a better understanding of the evolution of what we have called a "quasi democracy."[30]

The Secessionist Crisis in the Casamance

Since the 1980s Senegal has been troubled by a secessionist movement in its southernmost region, the Casamance (officially the Ziguinchor Region), which is separated from the main body of Senegal by the Gambia. This area, which boasts some of the highest rainfall and most productive agricultural land in the country, also holds tremendous potential offshore oil reserves, which straddle the border with Guinea-Bissau. The region's dominant group, the culturally and ethnically distinct Jola, remained relatively isolated from earlier historical developments, including the Islamicization that transformed much of the rest of Senegal; the fiercely independent Jola were still battling the French in the 1910s.[31] Feeling both dominated and colonized by northerners, particularly the Wolof, the Jola have become increasingly alienated from their government.[32] Léopold Senghor's failure in the early 1960s to deliver on his pre-independence promises of "land rights and autonomy" resulted in the defection of the Jola from the ruling party to the opposition.[33]

The secessionists in the Casamance belonged to several factions of the Movement of Democratic Forces of the Casamance (Mouvement des Forces Démocratiques de la Casamance, MFDC). The MFDC, which has its roots in the post–World War II independence movement, rose to prominence in Senegalese politics in 1982 when it circulated pro-independence literature and organized antigovernment demonstrations. Numerous arrests were made and an escalating spiral of violence, stimulated by harsh repression by the gendarmes, led to armed attacks in 1983 and again in 1984.

Years of secret negotiations resulted in a cease-fire in 1990 and the release of hundreds of Jola detainees. Again the promised resources and greater autonomy were slow in coming, and so at least one of the armed wings of the MFDC has continued the struggle. Aided by the forest and terrain, easy access to safe havens in Guinea-Bissau and the Gambia, and alleged financial support and equipment from Mauritania, the MFDC revolt has been extremely difficult to suppress. Yet another cease-fire was negotiated in April 1992 in the border town of Cacheu in Guinea-Bissau.[34]

Not satisfied with what they perceived to be empty promises, some factions of the MFDC tried to sabotage the 1993 presidential election.[35] Although the party's agents successfully terrorized many voters, it could not put a halt to the process. At the same time, its weaponry and tactics have become increasingly sophisticated, and the Senegalese army has continued to react in kind, escalating the conflict with a shoot-to-kill policy and increasing troop concentrations. Splits within the MFDC between its northern and southern wings and within the southern group between its political and military arms, make negotiating a long-term peace extremely difficult.[36] The recognized leader of the movement, Father Augustin Diamacoune, called for peace in a radio and television address on June 20, 1995, designed to bring the remaining armed groups of the *Front Sud* to the negotiating table.[37] The Diouf government, for its part, is expected to release more than a hundred MFDC detainees. The intensity of the pressure on the rebels is increasing, with clashes taking place in June with troops from Guinea-Bissau as well as with the Senegalese army.[38]

As noted by Baye Moussé, a journalist for the opposition newspaper *Sud*, the debate continues between those who believe that the Casamance can realize its aspirations only as an independent nation and those who believe that the regional reforms under the new decentralization program can successfully address those ambitions.[39] Pressure on Senegal is also mounting from France, with the new minister of cooperation, Jacques Godfrain, demanding information on four French tourists who disappeared in the Casamance in April 1995.[40] The costs to Senegal in lost revenue from tourism, economic disruptions in agriculture, refugees, political stability, and international respect have been very high. These problems must somehow be resolved. Unable to win militarily, the government is counting very heavily on negotiations and on the success of its proposed reforms concerning regional autonomy.

The Politics of Structural Adjustment

During the presidency of Léopold Senghor the state greatly increased its role in the economy, not merely by regulating the private sector but by establishing a public sector under direct government management. This policy enabled the government to direct a larger share of national income to government employees, labor union members, university students, and urban populations than might otherwise have occurred. Such a policy led to a decline in food production, both for market and for subsistence, as well as in manufacturing, which no longer had to be competitive.[41] This policy also contributed to an increasingly larger percentage of the population's becoming involved in the service sector. The government was able to gain the political support of the groups that benefited from its policy. At the same time, it worked out arrangements with many private businessmen that gave them virtual monopolies as a result of official manipulation of tariffs and controls.[42] State intervention rarely encountered opposition from the country's Muslim leaders as long as the economy appeared to be on sound bases.[43]

It became increasingly evident by the late 1970s, however, that the government's policy was leading to growing stagnation and a high level of external debt.[44] In these circumstances the World Bank and other donor agencies (international financial institutions—IFIs) insisted upon a structural adjustment program (SAP) as the price for continued assistance. Thus a medium-term program for 1980–1984 aimed at raising public savings, increasing investment in productive sectors, liberalizing trade, and reducing the state's role in the economy. The government failed to implement these changes because they risked undermining its support among key groups. As a result of the lack of progress, in 1984 the World Bank canceled a scheduled loan. Subsequently, the government prepared a second plan, for 1985–1992, which led to successive loans from the Bank. During the 1981–1991 period external support for structural adjustment accounted for nearly two-thirds of all development assistance.[45]

Throughout these years, Diouf's government had to undertake a sufficient number of measures to achieve structural adjustment in order to secure the external assistance for its survival. In the process it had to move cautiously and incrementally in order not to destabilize or greatly antagonize the forces that supported its continuation in power. Among the groups that openly criticized the hardships generated by these measures for the population were the fundamentalist Muslims, such as the *Moustarchadines*.

In order to liberalize trade, beginning in 1986 the government reduced import quotas and duties; it also established a moderate but consistent tariff system. Because it did not simultaneously introduce labor reforms and reduce energy costs, and because the exchange rate remained artificially inflated, Senegalese industries found themselves unable to compete with imported products. As a consequence, the government reversed itself. Instead of liberalizing the import trade, it devised a more complex system of protection in 1991 than had previously existed.[46]

The government achieved slightly greater success in the domestic trade sector. By 1988 it allowed prices of food crops to fluctuate according to demand; it also lessened subsidies for cash crops, although the prices of the latter were still not tied to world market prices, which were generally lower. Prices were decontrolled except for sixteen consumer items, including such staples as rice. As a result, the possible political repercussions were contained.

After the 1988 elections, with the assistance of an International Labor Organization study of the Senegalese labor market and a public relations campaign, the government was able to devise the new labor code of 1989.[47] Although the labor unions feared the consequences of diminished job security and benefits, they recognized the impossibility of gaining very much public support against the changes during a prolonged period of recession.

Reforms in banking, a sector in which opposition was more diffuse and less openly threatening, were more substantial.[48] It is in banking, moreover, where serious efforts at privatization since 1985 have shown some success. In other sectors, such as trade, agriculture, and industry, the government still maintains a role.

Taken as a whole, these various reforms move the economy in the direction of liberalization. Nonetheless, the IFIs consider the changes not to have gone far enough and insist that too much state market intervention persists.[49]

Evidence of the malaise produced by several decades of state direction of the economy and by efforts to restore soundness according to norms imposed by the IFIs may be found in the burgeoning informal sector. To supplement shrinking national resources and to pay taxes and other costs of a modernizing society, 60 percent of the population, urban and rural, have become involved in the informal sector.[50] Because activities in this sector were evading taxation on a large scale, the government took more vigorous steps to regulate prices, tariffs, and import quotas as well as prices on domestically produced commodities. Its success has been modest and uneven, in part because of the need to move cautiously for political reasons.

The Political Impact of Devaluation

Senegal's economic problems were further complicated by France's decision in January 1994 to devalue by 50 percent the CFA franc. The devaluation meant that the cost of imports purchased on international markets with the CFA franc doubled and the value of exports from the CFA states was halved.[51] The resulting inflationary spiral, coupled with religious and political unrest, led to street riots in Dakar during the second week in February; the disorders were the most violent political uprising in recent times. The government reacted swiftly, in the wake of the deaths of six policemen and one civilian, plus scores injured, arresting opposition leaders and banning all demonstrations. Although it subsequently released most leaders, several individuals allegedly involved in the violence remained in jail awaiting prosecution.[52]

Rising prices of basic foods, both imported and domestic, had the greatest potential for generating political unrest because they affected everyone. Thus the government acted quickly to restrict and to slow the rises.[53] For example, in April 1995, it allowed the official prices of rice to rise only 25 percent at a time when many traders, due to shortages, were already charging close to 35 percent more.[54] The government also restricted the price increases for medicines and fuels, in the former case by subsidies and in the latter by reducing taxes on gasoline and diesel. Several months later the government removed price controls, carefully timing its action to coincide with the entrance of the PDS into the government. Despite persisting unrest and widespread criticism of the government, the violence of the street riots has not recurred, and an uneasy peace prevails for the time being.

Although decreasing the salaries and benefits of public-sector employees was an important objective of the SAPs, the government was forced to increase them by 10 percent after devaluation. Nonetheless the real income of these employees declined by 15 percent.

These various measures undertaken by the government to mitigate the consequences of devaluation unfortunately decreased its revenues at the very time that they are most needed. As always, short-term political stability has a higher priority than long-term economic recovery. The remarkable ability of the Diouf government to co-opt key elements of the opposition at a critical point has eased the pressure on the regime, at least for the time being. The worst-case scenario is likely to occur if government policy remains reactive, with day-to-day changes producing the kind of uncertainty that makes investment, growth, and increasing exports nearly impossible.[55]

Administrative Reform

By the time Senegal embarked on its first SAP, it was evident that the public sector was much overextended.[56] This situation arose as a result of the government's use of public employment to shore up its political support and stability through a well-articulated patronage system. The government also served as the employer of first resort for secondary school and university graduates in order to relieve socioeconomic pressures on the regime.[57] In these circumstances the government gave priority to creating new positions in preference to providing its employees the operating expenses and equipment necessary for them to do their jobs well. The result was a loss of efficiency and a deterioration of morale. To worsen matters, recruitment was decentralized by ministry and service, which resulted in very little coordination or control over the creation of new positions. Efforts under the first SAP to limit growth of the bureaucracy had only limited success.[58] As a consequence, by the mid-1980s, salaries of functionaries were consuming 60 percent of the budget. By 1991, after new efforts to reduce the numbers through early retirement, voluntary departure, and the privatization of some programs and services, the proportion had declined to 53 percent[59]—but by June 1995 it had risen again, to 56 percent.[60]

During the 1993 elections, many functionaries deserted the PS and transferred their support to the PDS and other opposition parties. Even more of them may be expected to do so in the future because of further losses in real income associated with devaluation and inflation.

Decentralization

During the late 1980s the government, faced with growing economic problems that generated increasing political unrest, turned once more to decentralization, in the forms of deconcentration and devolution, as a promising remedy.[61] Earlier, in the years immediately after independence, Senghor had obtained passage of a revised constitution that involved greater centralization of authority. As a result, local government at the level of the communes saw its powers, already much circumscribed and strictly supervised by the local appointees of the centralized unitary state, greatly reduced. Later, in response to manifestations of growing opposition, Senghor's government recognized the need to provide a mechanism for greater participation by reverting to decentralization. Unfortunately, the reform resulted more from a desire to shore up the regime than from a serious commitment to decentralization.[62] Thus, even though the reform of 1972 establishing rural communities (*communes rurales,* CR) was the most far-reaching administrative change ever undertaken in Senegal, "it did not represent a major departure from French administrative practice in the sense that the state and its agents retained full supervisory control over all aspects of local level actions."[63]

Each of the CRs created starting in 1972 was composed of several villages supposedly linked by a sense of social, economic, and ethnic solidarity. The CRs were expected to undertake development projects on the basis of the perceived needs and priorities of local populations. Administrators appointed by the Ministry of Interior supervised from their headquarters in the regional capitals the activities and finances of the CRs. The reform bypassed the locally elected mayors, who were also agents of the central government. The reform thus involved a contradiction under which greater centralization was instituted as a means of implementing decentralization!

From the start the central government hindered the CRs more than it helped in guiding local development efforts. To worsen the situation, the CRs were never provided with financial resources, technical personnel, or educated or skilled council presidents and members necessary to achieve success. In addition, in many areas traditional authorities continued to oversee the allocation of land in spite of the authority over land use conferred upon the CRs under the reform law. Despite the mediocre and impermanent results from an economic perspective, however, the CR reform created the taste and stimulated the demand for greater autonomy and more local control over community resources and development efforts.[64]

Later, within the context of establishing an SAP in the late 1980s, the IFIs encouraged the government to undertake decentralization under terms that might remedy the previous shortcomings. The PS government agreed to such a direction in the hope that decentralization might generate popular support and maintenance of the democratic initiative.[65] The resulting law of November 25, 1990, sought to empower local units of government, both the CRs and the urban communes, by raising their status to the most complete and autonomous one available under the constitution (*communes de droit commun*). The law gave the elected mayors of urban communes responsibility for developing and managing their budgets.[66]

Two additional reforms transformed some CR headquarters villages into separate communes administratively distinct from their former rural communities and increased the number of elected council members in both the CRs and urban communes. A provision for granting a small salary to council presidents and their assistants may help to professionalize these positions and to attract better qualified, committed, and responsible candidates. In 1995 the National Assembly completely abolished the positions of central government appointees who had previously supervised the budgets of local units, and council presidents of the CRs now have charge of their budgets.

A new electoral code being considered by the national Assembly provides for direct election by universal suffrage of the members of the CR and urban commune councils, ending the system of appointment of one-third of their membership by organizations such as cooperatives. Perhaps the most important innovation in this measure concerns selection of half of the council members on the basis of proportional representation. This change will virtually ensure representation, if not control, of municipal affairs by opposition groups.[67]

In the face of continued economic difficulties and demands for greater autonomy from the Casamance, in particular, on April 4, 1992, Diouf proposed the most far-reaching form of decentralization ever initiated by the government, the creation of strong regional governments.[68] These will involve regional legislative bodies but not executive authorities. The role of the regional governments appointed by Dakar was not spelled out. The reform aimed at better serving the development needs of the country while permitting greater local and popular participation.[69]

In the typical top-down manner in which policy is made in the Senegalese political system, the possible implications of various approaches to regional decentralization are still under study.[70] The basic outline has been developed, and a process of negotiation is still taking place between the government and local and national party elites to work out the details of the arrangement. The final version of the new law awaits action by the National Assembly. The success of these reforms may have an important impact on the future of democratic government in Senegal. Actual implementation of the regional decentralization will probably take place during 1996 at the earliest.[71]

Conclusions

Political reform in Senegal has been an evolutionary process that has moved the nation to the brink of full democracy. Pressures for democratization have been largely internal, although external forces have become more pronounced in the mix in the 1990s. The 1993 elections, though not without problems, were probably among the fairest ever held in Senegal and, indeed, among the fairest in Africa. They have been subjected to intense internal criticism precisely because of their relative transparency. The presence of foreign election monitors, the opposition's increased access to the media, the relatively low reported turnout (51 percent for the presidential election, 41 percent for the legislative elections), and the distribution of the vote between urban and rural areas all suggest that the elections were relatively clean.[72]

Although the peaceful transfer of power from one party to another—the sine qua non of democratization—has not yet occurred, the prospects for such a change in the next presidential and National Assembly elections are good. Some leading elements of the opposition, especially the PDS, are gaining significant experience in governing as part of the latest coalition government, in which they hold several important ministerial posts. Recent reforms in the municipal and rural community electoral codes should ensure some significant success of the opposition parties at this level in the next local elections. Prospects at the regional level are also quite good for the opposition to gain control of the new regional assemblies in one or more regions. This control will provide the local power base and organizational opportunities that have heretofore been the exclusive right of the ruling party. From these bases the opposition will be able to mount a serious national campaign.

In spite of its overwhelming national economic problems, Senegal is brimming over with the results of modernization and change. Virtually no one is untouched by the process, even those in the most remote areas of the country. It even seems that the traditional economic sector—subsistence agriculture and trading—is rapidly disappearing. The society is now largely monetarized; every family must respond by seeking ways to create or increase its revenue. The traditional social roles, never static but slowly changing in the past, defined for all the major ethnic groups how individuals should relate to one another. These roles have been assaulted with the dramatic effects of multiple outside influences and internal changes; as they have been challenged, they alter in response, and some roles are merging into each other and into a variety of new definitions of responsibility and privilege. Even women, traditionally disadvantaged in wage-paying jobs, are moving into new positions, taking on new economic roles. The resultant uncertainties and dislocations have contributed to a growing Senegalese variant of Islamic fundamentalism in the form of several groups of *Moustarchadines*. The role of these groups in the political arena is growing as a counterweight to the more pragmatic Mouride brotherhoods that have kept the PS in power.

Overall economic progress under structural adjustment in Senegal has been somewhat limited, in no small part because political constraints have made it almost impossible for the government to implement seriously the policies to which it has agreed with the donor community. Even in the areas of administrative reform, progress in all but the most cosmetic sense has been quite limited. Though organizational charts were redrawn and functions and personnel policies were given the appearance of transformation, implementation was only halfhearted. In some cases, such as that of the public bureaucracy, retirements resulted in new recruitment in direct contravention of agreed-upon hiring freezes. The ratio of salaries to the national budget has thus risen rather than decreased as planned. Privatization has also proceeded much more cautiously and ineffectively than agreed to.

Decentralization, an important component of overall political and administrative moves toward improved governance, has advanced in fitful steps. The government is looking to regional decentralization to solve the ongoing crisis in the Casamance. Greater autonomy, without the financial resources necessary for policy implementation, without control over local security forces, and under the watchful eye of a governor appointed by the president is not likely to satisfy the independence forces. Having come this far, the MFDC is likely to insist on much greater autonomy than Dakar is willing to grant. Though the new electoral code provides some opportunity for the MFDC to capture local and municipal councils, its members may not be willing to participate or to allow others to do so. In any case, the problem is not likely to be resolved easily or quickly.

Like all governments, the Senegalese variant is attempting at least to survive in a relatively hostile political and economic environment. Until recently it was felt that sufficient wiggle room existed to enable the regime to avoid the most painful aspects of reform, especially those that could result in greater unemployment and cut into the regime's vital patronage network. As the failure of these policies became evident in the slow or absent growth of the economy, the government has finally backed itself into a corner in which the most painful aspects of adjustment and reform must be implemented or new loans required for survival will not be forthcoming.[73] Because it has delayed or circumvented implementation of various aspects of structural adjustment, Senegal is being forced to apply more severe and painful measures today. Senegal has been able in the past to parlay its reputation for democracy into ongoing support from the donor community. With decreasing donor resources available and the cold war over, and with a growing number of democratic competitors in Africa, Senegal may not be able to hold onto its edge. It is ironic that as the state becomes more open and democratic, external pressures in the economic, social, and international political arenas make the growth and survival of democracy and the ability to govern ever more tenuous.

Ultimately, the success of political and economic reforms, including democratization, devaluation, government downsizing, decentralization, and private sector development, will be determined by the fortitude and commitment of Senegal's leaders and the Senegalese electorate. The current round of PS/opposition cohabitation augurs well for this process. Although alienation has increased, the propensities of the people of Senegal appear to be more consistent with a democratic political culture, dialogue, and compromise than with mass demonstrations and violent conflict. The future political stability and survival of democratic rule in the nation depend on the maintenance of these commitments.

Notes

1. African Governance Program, Carter Center of Emory University, *Africa Demos*, no. 3 (1994):27. Even those who label Senegal a "semi-democracy" concede that many of the basic characteristics and support for democracy exist in Senegal. See, for example, Christian Coulon, "Senegal: The Development and Fragility of a Semi-democracy," in Larry Dia-

mond, Juan Linz, and Seymour Martin Lipset, eds., *Politics in Developing Countries: Comparing Experiences with Democracy* (Boulder: Lynne Rienner, 1990), p. 443. For an earlier interpretation of the emergence of Senegalese democracy, see Robert Fatton, *The Making of a Liberal Democracy* (Boulder: Lynne Rienner, 1987), pp. 157–158. For politics during the 1990s, see Sheldon Gellar, *Senegal: An African Nation Between Islam and the West* (Boulder: Westview Press, 1995), pp. 24–51.

2. An ongoing process of constitutional and electoral reform has, in spite of some setbacks, kept the system moving incrementally in the direction of increased democracy. In the conclusion to his insightful analysis of the 1993 elections, Villalon suggests such a balance. See Leonardo Villalon, "Democratizing a (Quasi) Democracy: The Senegalese Elections of 1993," *African Affairs* 93 (1994):192–193.

3. Abdoulaye Wade and the Parti Démocratique Sénégalais (PDS), the main opposition party, have in 1991 and again in 1995, following bitter election campaigns, successfully negotiated participation in the Parti Socialiste (PS) government. Several smaller opposition parties have also joined in these coalitions (for example, the PDS as well as the PIT, LD/MPT, and the PDS/R all hold cabinet posts in the current government).

4. Sheldon Gellar, "State Tutelage vs. Self-Governance: The Rhetoric and Reality of Decentralization in Senegal," in James Wunsch and Dele Olowu, eds., *The Failure of the Centralized State: Institutions and Self-Governance in Africa* (Boulder: Westview Press, 1990), pp. 130–147.

5. See, for example, Leonardo Villalon, *Islamic Society and State Power in Senegal* (Cambridge, England: Cambridge University Press, 1995).

6. For example, this occurred after the 1988 elections. See Crawford Young and Babacar Kanté, "Governance, Democracy, and the 1988 Senegalese Elections," in Goran Hyden and Michael Bratton, eds., *Governance and Politics in Africa* (Boulder: Lynne Rienner, 1992), pp. 57–74.

7. For a detailed discussion of the assassination and its aftermath, see Tidiane Kasse and Abdourahmane Camara, *Affaire Maître Sy* (Dakar: Imprimerie St. Paul, 1995).

8. Sheldon Gellar, *Structural Changes and Colonial Dependency: Senegal, 1885–1945* (Beverly Hills, Calif.: Sage Publications, 1976), p. 23.

9. Makhary Seck, "La gestion des services publics locaux: L'exemple de la Commune de Saint Louis," Thèse de Fin d'Études (Dakar: École Nationale d'Économie Appliquée, 1991).

10. Jacques Mariel Nzouankeu, *Les partis politiques sénégalais* (Dakar: Éditions Clairafrique, 1984), pp. 21–24.

11. Ibid., and Coulon, "Senegal: The Development and Fragility of a Semi-democracy," pp. 411–448.

12. Young and Kanté, "Governance, Democracy, and the 1988 Senegalese Elections."

13. Coulon, "Senegal: The Development and Fragility of a Semi-democracy," p. 443.

14. Edward Schumaker, *Politics, Bureaucracy, and Rural Development in Senegal* (Berkeley: University of California Press, 1975). See also Nim Caswell, "Autopsie de l'ONCAD: La politique arachidière au Sénégal, 1966–1980," *Politique africaine*, no. 14 (1983):39–73.

15. Nzouankeu, *Les partis politiques sénégalais,* pp. 30–31.

16. Ibid., p. 32.

17. Ibid., pp. 128–129.

18. Young and Kanté, "Governance, Democracy, and the 1988 Senegalese Elections."

19. This point is conceded by most analysts of Senegalese politics, including Young and Kanté, "Governance, Democracy, and the 1988 Senegalese Elections," pp. 66–68.

Richard Vengroff and Lucy Creevey

20. The Diouf government preferred the term "majorité présidentielle élargie," rather than coalition.

21. Mamadou Diouf, "Senegal's Uncertain Democracy: The 1993 Elections," *Africa Demos* 3 (1994):11. See also Peter Da Costa, "An End to Cohabitation," *Africa Report* 37, no. 6 (November-December 1992):43; Villalon, "Democratizing a (Quasi) Democracy," pp. 192–193; and Babacar Kanté, "Senegal's Empty Elections," *Journal of Democracy* 5, no. 1 (January 1994):96–108.

22. This election fatigue resulting in decreasing turnout in each round of elections is common in Africa. For a similar phenomenon in a neighboring country, see Richard Vengroff, "Governance and the Transition to Democracy: Political Parties and the Party System in Mali," *Journal of Modern African Studies* 31, no. 4 (1993):541–562. By the standards of a free election in Mali, the turnout in Senegal should be regarded as quite high.

23. Kasse and Camara, *Affaire Maître Sy*.

24. This title combined the Wolof slogan of the PDS, *Sopi* (change), and *Bokk* (together); roughly translated, the new slogan means united for change.

25. "Moustarchadine" is a term applied to several Islamic groups in Senegal that include many Tidianes and members of other brotherhoods. These groups have become quite active politically and favor a move to a less secular, more Islamic-oriented state.

26. Djibo Ka resigned his post in March 1995 and is rumored to being sponsored by Diouf for a post with an international organization.

27. Fundamentalism here refers to Muslims who believe in a complete reform of society to make it conform to Islamic law as it was written down in the first centuries of the religion. See Leonard Caplan, "Introduction," *Studies in Religious Fundamentalism* (Albany: State University of New York Press, 1987), pp. 1–22. In Senegal, the most vocal fundamentalists are often intellectuals who feel that Senegal has been corrupted and exploited by the West and that Abdou Diouf and other government leaders are merely pawns of Western interests. Many such individuals are now associated with the *Moustarchadines*.

28. El Hadj Kasse, "Bokk Sopi Sénégal c'est fini," *Sud*, no. 595 (March 24, 1995):1, 3.

29. Landing Savané, "Notre objectif, les municipales," *Sud*, no. 591 (March 20, 1995):1, 3.

30. Coulon, "Senegal: The Development and Fragility of a Semi-democracy," p. 443.

31. Olga Linares, *Power, Prayer, and Production: The Jola of the Casamance, Senegal* (Cambridge, England: Cambridge University Press, 1992), p. 211.

32. Ibid., p. 222.

33. Peter Da Costa, "The Secessionist South," *Africa Report* 36, no. 1 (January-February 1991):22.

34. Baye Moussé, "Casamance," *Sud*, no. 614 (April 18, 1995):1–2.

35. Peter Da Costa, "The Suffering Southern Province," *Africa Report* 38, no. 3 (May-June 1993):50–51, and Da Costa, "Casamance Quandary," *Africa Report* 38, no. 2 (March-April 1993):60–61.

36. Demba Ndiaye, "Ziguinchor joue la paix," *Sud*, no. 614 (April 18, 1995):1–3.

37. Abdourahmane Camara, "Les à-côté de l'appel de Diamacoune," *L'Aurore*, no. 981 (June 23, 1995):4.

38. "Accrochages entre rebelles et Bissau-Guinéens," *Sud*, no. 663 (June 22, 1995):1–2.

39. Baye Moussé, "Casamance," p. 2.

40. A. Camara, "La France veut des résultats," *L'Aurore*, no. 980 (June 22, 1995):1–5.

41. Moustapha Rouis, "Senegal: Stabilization, Partial Adjustment, and Stagnation," in Ishrat Jusain and Rashid Faruqee, eds., *Adjustment in Africa* (Washington, D.C.: World Bank, 1994), pp. 311–316; World Bank, *World Development Report* (New York: Oxford University Press, 1990), pp. 184, 188.

42. For a discussion of the major power groups within Senegalese politics, see Coulon, "Senegal: The Development and Fragility of a Semi-democracy," pp. 411–448. On the fundamentalist element among Senegalese Muslims, see Barbara Callaway and Lucy Creevey, *The Heritage of Islam: Women, Religion, and Politics in West Africa* (Boulder: Lynne Rienner, 1994), pp. 160–165, 173–176. See also Christian Coulon, *Les musulmans et le pouvoir en Afrique noire* (Paris: Karthala, 1983), pp. 127–141.

43. See the discussion of the changing roles of Islamic leaders as society modernizes and urbanizes in Donal B. Cruise O'Brien, "Land, Cash, and Charisma: Mouride Urbanization, 1945–1986," in Donal B. Cruise O'Brien, *Saints and Politicians: Essays in the Organization of a Senegalese Peasant Society* (Cambridge, England: Cambridge University Press), pp. 59–64; Cruise O'Brien and Christian Coulon, "Charisma Comes to Town: Mouride Urbanization, 1945–1986," in Cruise O'Brien and Coulon, eds., *Charisma and Brotherhood in African Islam* (Oxford: Clarendon Press, 1988), pp. 135–155.

44. One observer has described at length the process of stagnation and decay in the Senegalese economy as "state-sponsored rentierism in the context of an increasingly anarchic political administrative environment." Catherine Boone, *Merchant Capital and the Roots of State Power in Senegal, 1930–1985* (Cambridge, England: Cambridge University Press, 1992), p. 272 (and entire text). See also *The Guardian*, January 13, 1994; Naomi Chazan et al., *Politics and Society in Contemporary Africa*, 2d ed. (Boulder: Lynne Rienner, 1992), pp. 305–316; Timothy Shaw, *Reformism and Revisionism in Africa's Political Economy in the 1990s* (New York: St. Martin's Press, 1993), pp. 103–105; and World Bank, *Adjustment in Africa: Reforms, Results, and the Road Ahead* (New York: Oxford University Press, 1992).

45. Rouis, "Senegal: Stabilization, Partial Adjustment, and Stagnation," pp. 290–292.

46. Ibid., pp. 307–309.

47. The new code differed from the old principally in allowing industry-specific wage scales independent of minimum wage, liberalizing firing practices, and encouraging collective bargaining at the level of the firm. See Rouis, ibid., p. 311.

48. Ibid., pp. 312–316.

49. It is evident from World Bank data that Senegal has continued to maintain its market controls on its two major cash crops (groundnuts and cotton) and to permit preexisting monopolies in the production of all staple items; it has its own persisting monopolies in vegetable oil production and mineral extraction, importation of wheat and rice, and telecommunications. The only changes have come in a relaxing of government control over the import and distribution of fertilizer, the import of cement, the hiring of labor, and urban bus transportation. World Bank, *Adjustment in Africa*, pp. 232–239. The attitudes discouraging the development of local capital in Senegal promulgated by succeeding governments (and captured by Boone in her *Merchant Capital*, especially pp. 252–272) are particularly difficult to eradicate short of a full-scale revolution.

50. Arthur Young Associates, *Informal Financial Markets: Senegal and Zaire. Final Report* (Washington: Bureau for Africa, 1989), p. ii.

51. Amadou M. Dieng, "Partez 13 ans de duperie: Cela suffit," *Sopi*, no. 267 (January 18, 1994):1, 5.

52. Kenneth B. Noble, "French Devaluation of African Currency Brings Wide Unrest," *New York Times*, February 23, 1994.

53. Lucy Creevey and Richard Vengroff, "Devaluation of the CFA Franc in Senegal: The Reaction of Small Businesses," *Journal of Modern African Studies* 33, no. 4 (1995):669–684.

54. *Le Soleil*, April 1995.

55. Creevey and Vengroff, "Devaluation of the CFA Franc in Senegal," pp. 669–684.

56. Amadou Sadio, "The Adaptation of Government to Economic Change: The Case of Senegal," in M. J. Balogun and Gelase Mutahaba, eds., *Economic Restructuring and African Public Administration* (West Hartford, Conn.: Kumarian Press, 1989), pp. 177–185.

57. Richard Vengroff and Alan Johnston, *Decentralization and the Implementation of Rural Development in Senegal* (Lewiston, N.Y.: Edwin Mellen Press, 1987), p. 178.

58. Rouis, "Senegal: Stabilization, Partial Adjustment, and Stagnation," p. 311.

59. World Bank, *Adjustment in Africa*, pp. 122–123.

60. Malick Ba, "Loum écarte toute augmentation des salaires," *Sud*, no. 663 (June 22, 1995):1, 6.

61. Richard Vengroff, "The Transition to Democracy in Senegal: The Role of Decentralization," in Ilpyong Kim and Jane Zacek, eds., *Establishing Democratic Rule* (Washington, D.C.: Indepth Books, 1993), pp. 158–187; Samba Dione, *Évolution des politiques de décentralisation au Sénégal* (Dakar: École Nationale d'Économie Appliquée, 1992).

62. Dione, *Évolution des politiques de décentralisation*.

63. Vengroff and Johnston, *Decentralization and the Implementation of Rural Development*, p. 275.

64. Dione, *Évolution des politiques de décentralisation*.

65. Coulon, "Senegal: The Development and Fragility of a Semi-democracy," pp. 435–437.

66. Papa Mar Sylla, "La nouvelle ère communale," *Le Soleil* (January 1991), pp. 5–6.

67. Vengroff and Johnston, *Decentralization and the Implementation of Rural Development*, p. 48.

68. Abdou Diouf, "Independence Day Address," April 7, 1992 (Dakar: 1992).

69. Modou Mamone Faye, "Regards croisés sur la décentralisation," *Le Soleil*, May 13, 1992, p. 2.

70. Kader Ndoye, Ibrahima Gaye, and Philippe Tersiguel, eds., *La décentralisation au Sénégal: L'étape de la régionalisation* (Dakar: École Nationale d'Économie Appliquée, June 1994).

71. Ibid.

72. Mamadou Diouf, "Senegal's Uncertain Democracy."

73. Per capita gross national product has grown at a rate of only 0.1 percent between 1980 and 1992. World Bank, *World Development Report 1994* (New York: Oxford University Press, 1994), p. 162.

Part Four

Opposition Without Reform

Chapter Thirteen

Togo: The National Conference and Stalled Reform

JOHN R. HEILBRUNN

Economic decline is the Achilles' heel of dictatorship. This fact was clearly demonstrated by the events of 1990 in the Republic of Togo. For General Gnassingbé Éyadéma, a primary strategy to maintain power had been co-optation. When co-optation did not work, he employed repression. Indeed, a judicious combination of both had endowed Togo under his regime with a reasonable degree of political stability for over two decades. In Togo, as across Africa, years of economic depression eventually stripped a petty dictator of his ability to retain power by distributing patrimonial prebends. The Togolese general found that the Cold War's end virtually eliminated the geostrategic rationale for disbursements of foreign aid and military assistance to his anticommunist regime. The Berlin Wall had fallen, people of Eastern European countries rejected further communist rule, and Benin, Togo's eastern neighbor, held a national conference that became the model for similar conventions in francophone Africa.[1]

Political reform in Togo evolved through a convergence of foreign pressures, economic decline, and what may best be characterized as regime fatigue. In short, a decade-long depression had left the single-party state without a means to co-opt the numerous challengers to its rule. Before 1990, a single-party state had survived in Togo by extracting capital from available natural resources and distributing positions to loyal retainers and potential opponents. This strategy of co-optation succeeded as long as there was an expanding economic base to create such positions. Economic depression, however, rendered this form of governance untenable; Éyadéma's slogans ceased to placate a population alarmed by a declining standard of living and an apparent crisis in leadership. Indeed, by 1990, a disgruntled intelligentsia had concluded that it was the leadership of the Togolese Peo-

ple's Rally (Rassemblement du Peuple Togolais, RPT) under Éyadéma that constituted the greatest obstacle to the country's development.

In this chapter it is argued that three variables explain the emergence of the Togolese reform movement and ultimately its success. First, was the severe economic
depression caused by bad economic policies and international shocks that forced
a retreat from a state monopoly over most sectors of the economy. Secondly, this
crisis revealed an inherent weakness in authoritarian rule wherein co-optation
and the use of prebends essentially bought domestic stability. At the same time
that political stability fostered relative economic growth, authoritarian rule excluded significant portions of the population from participating in government.
Finally, reports that dictators in Eastern Europe, Latin America, and elsewhere in
Africa were falling to reform movements had been broadcast on radios and television throughout the world. This final variable had two profound effects. First,
people in Togo were aware of Mathieu Kérékou's fall in neighboring Benin and
desired a similar reform in Togo. Secondly, international development agencies
and Western governments had grown increasingly exasperated with a dictator
who stubbornly refused to liberalize his regime yet continued to request development aid. These three variables, converging in 1990, accounted for the emergence
of the Togolese reform movement.

Structural Adjustment and Economic Crisis

The Togolese economy rests upon exports of phosphate rock, cotton, cocoa, and
coffee, and a vibrant commercial sector. Between 1974 and 1976, a short-lived
boom in the price of phosphate rock provided the government with windfall
profits that it used to nationalize the country's major industries. Togo then joined
a number of African states in establishing state monopolies with restrictive investment codes and regulations on commerce. However, a nationalization of foreign
assets created a massive debt and an inefficient public enterprise sector. Hence,
when prices for phosphate rock, cocoa, and cotton collapsed in 1976, the state
borrowed further to service its existing debts. Subsequently, severe balance of payments deficits forced Éyadéma to turn to the International Monetary Fund (IMF)
and the World Bank. Although these loans carried stiff conditions for fiscal austerity, the government believed the decline in phosphate prices to be cyclical. On
that basis, the state continued to borrow money, until "by the end of 1982 external arrears amounted to CFAF [CFA francs] 58 billion ($177 million) while debt
service payments for 1983 (before any possible debt rescheduling) amounted to
CFAF 53 billion ($161 million) [and] total debt payments formally due corre-
sponded to 135 percent of government revenues."[2]

Togo negotiated its first structural adjustment program (SAP) with the World
Bank in 1983 and received glowing evaluations from Bank analysts for its commitment to fiscal reform. The Togolese program included a familiar combination
of an improved management of public resources, public enterprise reform, and

the promotion of private enterprise. One condition for the SAP was that Togo reform its public enterprise sector. Public enterprise reform meant nothing more than privatization, which was to occur while the state continued to make payments on the loans it had assumed to nationalize the industries. Hence, privatization left the state with fewer holdings, and after each iteration of the SAP, with a greater debt relative to assets. In 1984, the Éyadéma regime sold the Togolese steel company and put ten other public enterprises on the block.[3] Conditionalities that included policies of privatization, subsidy cuts, and strict fiscal austerity were undertaken with little consideration of the hardships suffered by Togo's population.[4] Unfortunately for the government, economic crises left it with little choice but to abide by conditions included in the SAPs.

Before the SAPs, Éyadéma had used money accumulated from phosphate sales to create lucrative public enterprise posts for his supporters. Potential access to the wealth of these companies encouraged income-seeking by individuals who corrupted the management of public enterprises.[5] Hence, a large public enterprise sector enabled a patrimonial regime to prosper, while rampant corruption permeated Togo's society. In 1987, employees reportedly embezzled 2.476 billion CFA francs from the Togolese National Agricultural Savings and Credit Bank (Caisse Nationale de Crédit Agricole, CNCA), causing its collapse and closure.[6] Such episodes highlighted the illegitimacy of Éyadéma's rule and the widening gulf separating the regime from Togo's population.

Although Togo's economy declined over the 1980s (as did the vast majority of African economies), SAPs shielded the state from some of the worst consequences. Indeed, for some residents of the southern Maritime Province and Lomé, the 1980s represented a period of considerable economic prosperity. A growing middle class of merchants and professionals emerged in Lomé, where they dominated commerce and professional activities. A dissonance between promises of economic opportunities and prohibitions on political activity perplexed a generation that had grown to maturity under Éyadéma's rule. The very policies that had contributed to stability also created the conditions under which an influential part of Togo's population demanded political reform. Unfortunately, the government formulated no political response except continued co-optation, banal propaganda, and the increasingly frequent use of repression.

Political Crisis

Each SAP required that Éyadéma further privatize Togo's formidable public enterprise sector. Layoffs resulted in high rates of unemployment, and those bureaucrats who kept their positions came under increasing scrutiny and criticism. As more people lost their jobs, protests increased in number and intensity. Given that urban groups often funneled earnings to rural kinsmen, the rise in unemployment that resulted from compliance with structural adjustment conditionalities had a ripple effect throughout Togolese society. Less advantaged groups resented Éyadéma's favoritism of northern ethnic groups and regions. Although the party included supporters from southern Togo, most high-ranking officials were family members or Kabyè from the president's home region.[7] These individuals occupied the lucrative directorships of public enterprises and preferred posts in the army. Other important positions were reserved for those whom the president wanted to co-opt. But this leadership style was viable only as long as a number of positions in the bureaucracy remained available.

Benign patrimonial rule often thrives in circumstances of relative economic stability in which a leader may rotate positions among loyal retainers. However, patrimonialism becomes more difficult in hard times. Éyadéma had relied upon prebendal politics as well as a charismatic cult and a political mythology to legitimate his regime.[8] For those individuals who refused co-optation, authorities also employed threats and terror. While these strategies had proved effective for most of Éyadéma's rule, they failed to adjust to an increasingly sophisticated populace that demanded a right to participate in Togo's politics. Economic decline compelled the single-party state to relax its political monopoly. When this happened, numerous organizations with cross-cutting memberships demanded freedom of expression, movement, and political participation. These groups spread visions of participatory democracy through their declarations and norms of internal governance. Indeed, the persistence of democratic beliefs and practices despite the prevalence of dictatorship suggests that "fragments of democracy" were present in Togolese society in spite of Éyadéma's ruthless dictatorship.[9]

Yet, it was inconceivable to President Éyadéma that any concessions made to reform movements could result in the overthrow of his regime. Hence, he allowed some reforms while forcefully resisting all efforts to remove him from power and carefully guarding his control of the army. Eventually this close relationship with the military proved critical, and when threatened, the president suggested that any attempts to ban the RPT would result in a vengeful Ewe oligarchy eager to regain power. The president effectively maneuvered the bickering opposition into acts that supported his accusations of tribalism. These strategies accompanied a terror campaign that blocked Togo's political reform.

French Foreign Policy, National Conferences, and Political Reform

A third variable in the Togolese opposition's tragic attempts to overthrow Éyadéma was the role of the international community. Throughout francophone Africa a wave of national conferences took place after 1990. International actors such as the World Bank, the IMF, the U.S. Agency for International Development, and the French government believed that sustainable development was impossible without good governance. Regimes that practice good governance are accountable, transparent, and predictable; in short, a dissatisfied electorate could remove an errant regime from power through action at the polls. To achieve this objective, in 1991, French President François Mitterrand appointed Bruno De-Laye ambassador to democratize the Togolese regime.[10] DeLaye managed to convince the reluctant Éyadéma to allow a national conference. Once organized, Togo's national conference mimicked many others in francophone Africa: A mobilized opposition, composed of trade union leaders, students, teachers, retailers, leading lawyers, and representatives of other social groups, sat as an assembly to judge authoritarian rule. Delegates to the national conference would declare the assembly sovereign, appoint a High Council of the Republic, elect a new prime minister, draft a new constitution, and schedule elections. In short, a national conference would replace an authoritarian regime with a more inclusive government, though it often obscured the reform movement's elitist origins.[11]

By late 1990, Éyadéma had come under direct pressure from French diplomats to permit a national conference. His regime closely resembled that of Mobutu in Zaire, which also relied on a vulgar and ruthless cult of personality. Both regimes were an embarrassment to Paris.[12] During the June 1990 Franco-African conference at La Baule, France, Mitterrand had highlighted democratic changes in Benin as a model for reform in francophone Africa. In his opening speech he explicitly linked continuing French aid to movement toward democratic reform, and he named Togo as one of the worst abusers of human rights in Africa. At the conference's conclusion, Mitterrand warned again that "French aid will be trivial to those countries that continue to rule in an authoritarian fashion with no movement toward democracy."[13] The assumption in French diplomatic circles was that a national conference would succeed in toppling Éyadéma and that elections would bring democracy.

Unfortunately, changing political priorities in France undermined what diplomats had apparently believed would be a successful strategy. At the next conference of heads of francophone states, at Chaillot Palace in Paris in November 1991, Mitterrand declared that France would not interfere in the political affairs of African states and that each country must find its own "rhythm" for reform and political change.[14] Whereas in 1990 Mitterrand had linked bilateral aid to political reform, in November 1991 he effectively untied the hands of those dictators who had managed to keep power during the year following La Baule. For those countries that had succeeded in effecting a transition via a national conference, the future was secure; however, for those that were still reforming, Mitterrand's statement at Chaillot allowed their dictators to repress the reform movements. Within twenty-four hours of Mitterrand's about-face, the Togolese army launched a coup that would eventually return Éyadéma to power.

Negotiations for the Sovereign National Conference

The December 1991 coup derailed Togo's short transition that had only begun six months earlier when the regime and its opposition signed an accord. In these accords, Éyadéma agreed to a national conference after he recognized that he would be unable to establish what Adam Przeworski has coined "a tutelary democracy."[15] Whereas Togo's national conference imitated the Beninese experience structurally in that it established a High Council of the Republic under the leadership of a Catholic prelate, its demands for retribution clearly contrasted with Benin's remarkable achievement of reconciliation.[16] Indeed, this lack of reconciliation was crucial because delegates at the Togolese conference passed resolutions that they had never negotiated with the state. When delegates declared the national conference sovereign, government representatives walked out of the conference and refused to recognize any further resolutions as binding. Thereafter, Togo's conference experience soured, and consensus eluded the Togolese entirely. Although understandable, this proclamation served little benefit for the conference and actually resulted in a reversal of three years of negotiations between the party-state and its local opposition.

Opposition Strategies: Human Rights and Liberalization

The preceding series of crucial developments had forced the government to relax its restrictions on political activity. A reform movement developed rapidly to agitate for political change. These developments resulted from Éyadéma's personal ambitions and his fundamental miscalculations about his opponents' capabilities. In the late 1980s Éyadéma had attempted to portray himself as a man of peace and an advocate of human rights in Africa.[17] Amnesty International's 1987 allegations of torture and arbitrary imprisonment in Togo had, understandably, upset the ambitious Éyadéma. In response, the president established the National Human Rights Commission (Commission Nationale des Droits de l'Homme, CNDH) and appointed as chairman Yao Agboyibor, a delegate to the National Assembly and a loyal member of the RPT.[18] In his keynote address at the CNDH's inaugural meeting in February 1988, Éyadéma suggested that the inauguration of the CNDH proved that a larger process of democratization was occurring in Togo.[19] He condemned all abuses of human rights and, echoing a familiar theme, attributed any that might have occurred in Togo to ethnic conflict. This statement was consistent with Éyadéma's mythology that the RPT alone had enabled Togo to overcome its tribal divisions.

Éyadéma expected that Agboyibor and the CNDH would maintain his position that ethnic conflict was the root cause of any human rights abuses that Amnesty International attributed to his regime. Implicit in his speech was a condemnation of Ewe politicians, whom Éyadéma continued to accuse of encouraging tribal strife. The president, however, had miscalculated the effect of such a commission. Furthermore, he gravely underestimated Agboyibor's ambitions. From all appearances, he intended Agboyibor to discuss human rights abuses in Africa at large and generally to conceal any malfeasance in Togo. What transpired, however, was that Agboyibor used the Commission both to gain national recognition and to transform the theme of human rights into a legitimate reason for autonomous organization.

Subsequent meetings of the Commission publicized politically damaging reports of abuses by gendarmes and police. In essence, the human rights issue served to free organizations from strict government control. Agboyibor used it to become a national political figure. Moreover, this liberalization encouraged others to organize formal groups to "discuss" human rights. In August 1990, Joseph Kokou Koffigoh organized the Togolese League for Human Rights (Ligue Togolaise des Droits de l'Homme, LTDH), wagering that Éyadéma would not risk the international outcry that its suppression would provoke. With a surprising rapidity, the League gained popularity and received support from the international community. By the end of 1990 a plethora of new civic organizations operated in Togo; some had emerged under RPT auspices, and ambitious individuals had established other associations in response to an opening up of political space.

Government Strategies

The emergence of numerous human rights organizations suggested that a controlled liberalization was occurring under RPT tutelage. Both to complement these liberal policies and to satisfy demands from international donors, Éyadéma orchestrated a discussion about the suitability of multiparty pluralism for Togo. Speaking at a convention commemorating the RPT's twentieth anniversary in January 1990, Éyadéma emphasized the unity created by the single party and its ancillary organizations, which helped to prepare the nation for a move to multiparty democracy.[20] However, subsequent events clearly demonstrated that multiparty reform was a hollow promise. In May the RPT held a special congress in Palimé to debate pluralism in Togo. When the convention ended, delegates had rejected the notion of multiparty elections and suggested instead that the party separate from the state.[21] Perhaps Éyadéma actually believed that by generating the appearance of dialogue he could stem a reform movement that was gathering momentum from events in Eastern Europe and Benin.

Continued threats to RPT hegemony prompted Éyadéma to intensify his charismatic cult. At the same time, the government was becoming more defensive; it lashed out at its critics and stepped up its police activities. A pivotal event occurred on October 5, 1990, when a court in Lomé passed sentences on two men accused of distributing seditious tracts. In the closing remarks for the defense, their attorney, Beninese lawyer Robert Dossou, anecdotally related a tale of a pharaoh who so oppressed women and youth that they finally rose up and overthrew his dictatorial regime.[22] The parallels were obvious, and when the two men received sentences of five years, Lomé exploded. At a press conference two days later, General Yao Mawuliklimi Amayi blamed the riots on international plots fomented by dissidents residing in Abidjan.²³ Despite apparent intransigence, Éyadéma pardoned the two men and announced that he would submit a constitutional reform to the people in 1991. This announcement began a pattern of concessions, postponements, and further concessions that characterized the struggle for political reform in Togo over the following three years.

Plays and Counterplays: Bargaining for a National Conference

Éyadéma correctly perceived that repression was ineffective against a growing opposition movement. In July 1990, the government relaxed controls over the press and permitted nonparty newspapers to publish. Three independent newspapers, *La Tribune des Démocrates, Forum-Hebdo,* and *Le Courrier du Golfe,* appeared in late 1990 and presented the opinions of various factions within the opposition.²⁴ Unfortunately, several weeks after the promise of a constitutional referendum, officials accused *Forum-Hebdo*'s editors of inciting tribal violence. Then police closed the *Courrier du Golfe* and arrested its editors for defaming the RPT newspaper, *La Nouvelle Marche.*²⁵ Only Agboyibor's *La Tribune des Démocrates* escaped the harassment of reporters, the seizure of copies, and the destruction of presses that the other papers suffered. Perhaps this freedom was due to his role as chair of the CNDH, or because *La Tribune* had avoided directly criticizing the government.

Despite this renewed repression of the press, liberalization measures emboldened Éyadéma's opposition. The opposition's strategies entailed an attempt to compensate for a lack of military support that left them vulnerable to the state's security apparatus. Through various organizations—first, the Front of Associations for Renewal (Front des Associations pour le Renouveau, FAR), then the Front for Democratic Opposition (Front pour l'Opposition Démocratique, FOD), and finally the Collective for Democratic Opposition (Collectif pour l'Opposition Démocratique, COD)—Éyadéma's opponents would present demands for reform with an ultimatum of general strike, negotiate with the government, call a paralyzing strike, and then return to negotiate again. Exiled opposition leaders began exerting pressure from Paris in coordination with local reformers. Hence, the Democratic Convention of African People, the Pan-African Alliance for Democracy, and the Union of Forces for Change coordinated their action with the Lomé-based LTDH and the Student Movement for Democratic Struggle (Mouvement Étudiant pour la Lutte Démocratique, MELD) to push Éyadéma toward greater reform.²⁶

Éyadéma's strategy was to announce a concession, and then to renegotiate its meaning. In the course of the negotiations, he would reject or so diminish the concession as to render it meaningless. At the same time, a terror campaign kept tensions in the country high. This low-intensity conflict continued through the spring of 1991 until April 11, when soldiers pushed a number of protesters into Lomé's Bé Lagoon, where they drowned.[27] Opposition to the regime coalesced after this incident and successfully coordinated antigovernment demonstrations. International donors balked at the spiraling violence, and when the World Bank threatened to suspend Togo's fourth SAP, Éyadéma recognized that he had to resolve the political crisis. Although Éyadéma agreed to a national conference in principle, he stubbornly continued to obstruct its assembly on points of protocol. On June 4 the opposition leaders called another general strike that completely stopped all movement in every city, except the northern city of Kara, populated primarily by Kabyè. This strike was so successful that the government agreed to resume negotiations. Finally, Kwassi Lanyo Savi de Tovi, representing the opposition, and Yao Komlanvi, the government negotiator, reached an agreement on June 12 to convene a national conference on June 26 and to end the strike immediately.

The June 12 Accord was explicit: The national conference was to debate the political, economic, social, and cultural life of the country and conclude with a general statement; it would organize a transitional period during which a transitional prime minister would lead a legislature; and it would schedule elections. The president was "to guarantee the continuity of the state, its independence and national unity, govern with the dignity of the office in keeping with the attributes the National Conference deems to confer on the prime minister." The government would represent all ethnic interests during the transition period. The chief of state would not postpone any decisions of the national conference or impede general elections, which were to be held at the transition's end. Finally, the government and the Collective for Democratic Opposition made an appeal for civil peace.[28]

For a moment, it appeared as if Togo would follow the path of Benin, where a national conference had successfully overthrown a putatively Marxist dictator. However, Éyadéma was far from relinquishing office. His opponents' narrow objectives, which were to overturn the government and install themselves in political office, gave the president a definite advantage. He possessed an established political organization, whereas his opponents had only rudimentary organizations and were competing with one another. Although Éyadéma had underestimated his opponents' competence at manipulating international perceptions, he continued to control the army, and therefore any reforms were contingent on his consent. Perhaps the president allowed his opposition to hold a national conference precisely because of its internal divisions. More importantly, he knew that they could never enforce their decisions militarily. When the conference finally convened, a tumultuous assembly of previously exiled Togolese dissidents clamored for retribution. All sentiments of reconciliation were drowned in the din of calls for revenge. Yet the Togolese army remained a constant threat that should have reminded reformers of their vulnerability.

Participants' Strategies at the Sovereign
National Conference

The national conference movement had spread from its successful beginnings in Benin throughout francophone Africa. Whereas Benin and Congo experienced relatively rapid transitions, political reform in Togo began slowly, and Éyadéma successfully postponed elections until his victory was certain. Superficially, Togo's national conference resembled the *États Généraux* of the French Revolution, but on a deeper level, the reform movement reflected social cleavages and conflict mediation from Togolese history. For example, the conference hosted close to a thousand participants. For Éyadéma, such an assemblage surely reminded him of the large and similarly vitriolic conventions of the All-Ewe Conference (AEC) after World War II.[29] The AEC was a pillar of support for Togo's first president, Sylvanus Olympio, allegedly assassinated by Éyadéma in 1963. As Ewe politicians had fled into exile, they promised to prosecute all those who had participated in the coup. In a hauntingly similar fashion, delegates at the national conference promised to prosecute all those who had committed atrocities during the previous years. Given that similarity, it is understandable that Éyadéma refused to recognize the conference's claim of sovereignty and fiercely resisted its resolutions.

Before the conference, the government lifted its restrictions on associational activities, which encouraged the formation of numerous groups. These associations became vocal participants at the national conference, which Éyadéma derisively called a "civilian coup d'état." In spite of government intransigence, delegates elected Joseph Kokou Koffigoh prime minister and scheduled elections for June 1992. The fact that Éyadéma negotiated with Koffigoh and the High Council of the Republic suggested a de facto recognition of a shift in political influence. However, without military protection, the transition foundered, and an orchestrated terror campaign forced the bickering leaders of Togo's opposition into exile along with hundreds of thousands of Togolese who had already fled to Benin and Ghana. Presidential elections were twice postponed, and when they were finally held in 1993, Éyadéma won an overwhelming percentage of the vote cast.

Business Associations, Student Associations,
and Trade Unions

Among the leading forces for political reform were members of the business community who sought to end the monopoly of the powerful, semi-autonomous Professional Association of Cloth Merchants (Association Professionnelle des Revendeurs des Tissus, APRT). The leaders of the APRT, known as "Nana Benz," were famous for their near total domination of the cloth trade in West Africa. Younger cloth merchants accused the APRT of enjoying a relationship with Éyadéma that was simply too close. In 1991 the Togolese Women's Association for Democracy and the Association of Women for Democracy in Togo emerged to contest the APRT's domination over business organizations. Not surprisingly, leaders of the APRT were unwilling to relinquish their monopoly. At the sovereign national conference, a number of Nana Benz defended their relationship with the Éyadéma government as unavoidable; they asserted that the dictator had left them without a choice.[30] Quite possibly the leaders of the APRT were making a valid protest; however, there could be no doubt that the relationship had been beneficial for both the APRT and Éyadéma. The Nana Benz supported a political regime that had enabled them to monopolize the West African cloth trade. Despite all the cries of innocence, delegates at the national conference demanded the APRT's dissolution. Of course, such a development would entail an end to the APRT's monopoly and a redistribution of their market share to younger merchants.

Complementing the activities of the business associations were Togo's theretofore passive student groups. Students had fervently opposed the austerity measures that had been conditions of SAPs and desperately wanted a voice in any future negotiations. Each cut in Togo's educational budget deepened discontent over a system of scholarship distribution that favored the less populated northern regions.[31] In addition, students had unhappily endured compulsory membership in the mass organizations affiliated with the RPT. Associations like the National Movement of Togolese Students and Trainees (Mouvement National des Étudiants et Stagiaires du Togo, MONESTO) and the Association of Togolese Students of the University of Benin were all controlled by the Young Togolese People's Rally. In late 1990 at least ten illegal associations emerged, three of which formed an important bloc in February 1991.[32] This coalition sent two letters to the government that outlined students' demands.[33] When neither the president nor the minister of education acknowledged the letters, campus demonstrations erupted. Soldiers allegedly changed out of their uniforms, infiltrated protesting students, and beat and imprisoned demonstrators. There were further reports that students from MONESTO and the party-affiliated Society of Students of Northern Togo had joined with soldiers and savagely attacked protesting students with clubs and knives. These revelations prompted a majority of students to reject the party-run student associations.[34] Southern students then became the opposition's militia, with many participating in an informal group called "Ekpemog" that fought armed soldiers with rocks and Molotov cocktails.

A final defector from the RPT-led state was the labor movement. In January 1973, authorities had formally established the National Labor Federation of Togo (Confédération Nationale des Travailleurs du Togo, CNTT) to consolidate all trade unions under a single, party-dominated organization. Shortly after this decree, the government passed the May 1974 labor codes, imprisoned union leaders, prohibited strikes, and appointed party loyalists to head trade unions.[35] Authorities thereafter brutally suppressed strikes and labor disputes, and trade unions lost all autonomous power. Yet the RPT regime's opening in 1991 allowed a number of trade unions to spin off from the CNTT. The first was the bank employees union, followed shortly afterward by the teachers and dock workers. By June 1991 fifty-four syndicates had registered to send delegates to the national conference.[36] Although the CNTT sought to maintain its position as the representative for all unions, its credibility had suffered much as the APRT's had. A flood of autonomous trade unions emerged to represent Togolese labor and sweep aside the politically bankrupt CNTT.

The Opposition's Miscalculations

In Togo, the principal reformers exchanged no ideas before the national conference and reached no consensus about its desired outcomes. Each leader essentially sought power for himself. Deep splits divided the opposition between those who genuinely wanted to reform the government, and others who sought only to overthrow Éyadéma. Local reformers belonged to a select group of members of the Togolese bar association, university professors, and successful merchants who met regularly at restaurants around Lomé to plan protest strategies. When international donors pressured Éyadéma to liberalize his autocracy, they also encouraged the various iterations of opposition groups to contest single-party rule.

Quite possibly this group of local reformers recognized the need for reconciliation as a precondition of regime change. However, consensus eluded an opposition movement that desperately needed to present a unified front against a military tyrant determined to stay in power. Opposing the local reformers were hard-line voices for retribution. Many of these individuals had returned to Lomé from exile in Paris explicitly for the conference. They advocated a complete dissolution of institutions as constructed by the RPT as well as prison terms for officials of the RPT and the army. This immoderate group quickly took control of the conference, and their rage colored the resolutions of the first weeks.

Unfortunately, local reformers failed to recognize two crucial elements when they convened the national conference. First, they did not sufficiently appreciate that toppling a dictator required removal of the team of people surrounding him. Thus, Éyadéma's clients stood to lose their positions of privilege and power if the conference succeeded in overthrowing the general. Foremost among them were the officers and soldiers in the army, of which approximately 75 percent were Kabyè. These military men were intensely loyal to Éyadéma, and they feared a virtual pogrom if a national conference overturned the RPT state.[37] Rumors of ethnic reprisals were rife in Lomé during early 1991. For example, a series of tracts, signed by "Major Patriot Donzonga," promised revenge for the deaths of Kabyè sharecroppers supposedly killed by Ewe farmers earlier that year. Hence, when delegates to the national conference engaged in diatribes against the president and the army, a quiet resolve formed among the officers to sabotage any attempts at regime change.

The second element was an extraordinarily vindictive group of Togolese exiles and their sympathizers who represented the hard-liners at the sovereign national conference (SNC). Despite Bishop Fanoko Kpodzro's attempts to calm tempers and to seek reconciliation, delegates at the conference repeatedly threatened Éyadéma and members of his state with prosecution. For five days, delegates debated various points without deciding any specific acts. On the sixth day, delegates approved Act No. 1, which declared the national conference sovereign (Article 1), and suspended the January 1980 Constitution with all its ancillary institutions (Article 4).[38] Passage of this act suggested that local reformers had ceded control of their movement to extremists intent only on retribution. The hard-liners, in turn, spared no member of the regime from threats of prosecution and worse. Tragically, after the conference ended, local reformers remained in Togo to bear the wrath of a shunned autocrat while many hard-liners returned to their careers and lives in France.

With the approval of Act No. 1, the government's representatives walked out and accused conference delegates of violating the June 12 Accord by illegally suspending the constitution and the National Assembly.[39] This declaration stipulated that "the Government has noted that the National Conference has allowed a situation to arise for which the June 12 Accord made no provision. In effect, the National Conference has exceeded its recognized position in the June 12 Accord and its competence in declaring itself sovereign. . . . In light of the situation thus created, the Government has decided to suspend its participation in the National Conference."[40] Conference participants riposted that the June 12 Accord was not binding on a *sovereign* national conference. Nevertheless, when government delegates finally returned on July 23, they qualified their return with the statement that because "the Act's [Act No. 1] declaration of sovereignty is contrary to the June 12 Accord, the Government reserves the right to reject any decisions."[41] Hence Éyadéma expressed his intent to reject any or all of the decisions of the national conference, ex post facto, and to retain control.

Despite an awareness of Éyadéma's strategy, participants at the SNC behaved as if a declaration of sovereignty had actually overthrown the government. Condemnations of the RPT regime became increasingly vitriolic, and calls for prosecution animated the discussions. One resolution went so far as to indict Éyadéma's sons for involvement in the Bé Lagoon drownings.[42] This same resolution extended the statute of limitations for anyone implicated in crimes of corruption or violence. This motion also left open the possibility of prosecution for years to come. Indeed, a mass psychosis seemed to grip delegates at the SNC as declaration after declaration threatened members of the government with imprisonment and confiscation of their property. Each resolution appeared to have an intoxicating effect on a people long muzzled by a ruthless dictator, and it would not be until "the morning after" that local reformers would bitterly recall that Éyadéma held all the guns.

Results of the Sovereign National Conference:
A Failed Transition?

Togo's sovereign national conference concluded on August 26, 1991. Koffigoh had been elected prime minister, and the HCR began drafting a new constitution and scheduled municipal, legislative, and presidential elections. Although the HCR sought to establish the political institutions that would enable a transition to democracy, it failed to achieve any of its vaunted goals. One reason for this was Koffigoh's initial actions as prime minister. Initially, Léopold Gnininvi had been the opposition's first choice, but he ceded his place to the better known and popular leader of the LTDH. In spite of his tenuous mandate, Koffigoh committed serious errors almost immediately upon taking office. Perhaps the most damaging was his distribution of the directorships of lucrative public enterprises to loyal followers from his home region. By appointing friends and followers to remunerative positions, Koffigoh exposed himself to accusations of corruption and nepotism. Hence, rather than building coalitions within Togo's fractious opposition, Koffigoh established an independent power base. Consequently, many reform leaders opposed their chosen leader, in spite of the fact that their squabbling played into Éyadéma's hands.

Koffigoh's appointment divided the opposition and further impeded consensus. Internal dissent assured that there would be no pardon for the president, which might have coaxed him to resign. Unfortunately, participants at the SNC indulged in emotional diatribes against the RPT regime and voiced countless demands for prosecution. Éyadéma's reaction was to refuse to recognize any of the conference's resolutions on the grounds that its organizers had violated the June 12 Accord. Meanwhile, Togo's army remained under the president's control, and the HCR had no means to disarm it. This oversight was to prove to be a fundamental miscalculation that would have disastrous results for Togo's reformers.[43]

Dyarchy and Terror

The Togolese sovereign national conference certainly was a missed opportunity to remove an entrenched dictator. A majority of Togo's population, as well as the international community, had formally recognized Koffigoh as prime minister shortly after his election. Obviously, Éyadéma could hardly dismiss such profound changes; yet the president continued to reject categorically the HCR's right to rule. An unstable dyarchy thus emerged in which, essentially, two governments operated at the same time: one that retained a monopoly over violence, and another that claimed popular legitimacy and international recognition. Events would eventually prove military force to be crucial in deciding who would hold power in Togo. In December 1991 the army bombarded Koffigoh's residence, took the prime minister prisoner, and reversed the reforms of the national conference.[44]

Events spiraled out of control after the December "coup." In the summer of 1992, a terror campaign gripped Togo. In July, Éyadéma's partisans attempted to assassinate Gilchrist Olympio, perhaps Éyadéma's most serious rival for the presidency, and succeeded in killing Tavio Amorin, a member of the HCR. Olympio survived his wounds and fled into exile. On September 4, soldiers savagely beat Madeleine Aduayom, a member of the HCR and vice president of the Collective of Women's Associations, after she made a speech on television in which she accused the army of blocking Togo's transition. While a soldier beat her, he punctuated each blow with the chilling statement, "I could kill you, and no one would do anything to me."[45] After this terrifying experience, Aduayom fled to Paris where she joined a growing number of opposition leaders. The terror campaign proved to be highly effective, and by increments Éyadéma reasserted his complete control over Togo. When Koffigoh announced the composition of his cabinet on September 12, high-ranking members of the RPT occupied the essential ministries.[46] Togo had effectively returned to Éyadéma's stewardship.

The Referendum and the Fallacy of Elections

The HCR and Éyadéma's representatives began negotiations on a new constitution in the summer of 1992. In one sense, Éyadéma's concession even to negotiate a constitution reflected how far the SNC's reforms had forced him to modify his behavior. A first constitution contained a controversial article that explicitly excluded Koffigoh and all other members of Éyadéma's previous governments from political office.[47] The president rejected this document and sent it back to the HCR for revision. Then on July 3 the HCR proposed electoral codes that called for a multiple ballot.[48] Éyadéma opposed this provision as well and escalated the debate as a further point of contention between the two governments. Later that month the HCR presented a new constitution that deleted the offending article but added a new article that excluded members of the Togolese Armed Forces from office.[49] Members of the HCR gambled that Éyadéma would either resign his commission as general, and thus allow reform of the army, or he would not run for office. However, General Éyadéma simply rejected the constitution and increased the terror campaign.

On September 21 the government newspaper, the *Togo-Presse*, published a new constitution with the offending Article 62 deleted; and on September 27 it reported that 99.09 percent of voters had approved the referendum.[50] However, on October 22, 1992, troops audaciously entered the parliament building and seized all non-RPT members of the HCR as hostages in exchange for important sums of money that the soldiers asserted belonged to the RPT. This outrageous act ended all hopes of a peaceful transition in Togo. Although the Coordination of the Democratic Opposition–II (Coordination de l'Opposition Démocratique–II, COD-II) called for a general strike, reconciliation between the opposition and Éyadéma remained a distant prospect and violence in the country increased. In January

1993 troops reportedly killed hundreds of people in the Bé district of Lomé, sending thousands fleeing into exile in Benin and Ghana. It was in this environment that a cowed and greatly diminished HCR scheduled presidential elections.

The HCR planned presidential elections for August 25, 1993. In July, an electoral commission disqualified Gilchrist Olympio, and on August 22 Djobo Boukari, Edem Kodjo, and Yao Agboyibor announced that they would boycott the elections. The reason for their withdrawal was a mysterious increase in the electoral register, from 1.6 million who voted for the referendum in September 1992, to 2.2 million who suddenly registered for the presidential vote.[51] After the opposition withdrew, Éyadéma was the sole candidate, and he won an overwhelming percentage of the votes cast. However, in southern Togo, the rate of participation was 17 to 18 percent and as low as 4 percent in some areas.[52] Although the opposition did not similarly boycott the legislative elections, the momentum had shifted back to Éyadéma. His victory in the elections reflected how a determined ruler may corrupt an electoral process to resolidify a weakened hold on power.

In sum, when the transition ended officially on February 20, 1994, the government reported that voters had approved a new constitution, overwhelmingly re-elected Éyadéma with 98 percent of the vote, and elected a National Assembly dominated by past members of the single-party state. Clearly, Éyadéma had successfully resisted the two-year attempt to unseat him. In part, Éyadéma's victory resulted from his refusal to restrain the military. A willingness to employ lethal force against his opponents was evident in the shootings and assassinations of 1991–1993. During all the elections, reports surfaced of soldiers blocking potential voters by their presence near the polls. Little hope remained of a democratic transition except the presence of a legislative opposition that appeared not to be subjected to the kind of terror tactics the army had employed against the transitional government.

The legislature in Togo has always been a weak branch of government. Éyadéma had traditionally used it to reward loyal followers. However, legislative elections in February 1994 gave Yao Agboyibor's Action Committee for Renewal (Comité d'Action pour le Renouveau, CAR) thirty-six seats and thereby became the principal opposition party.[53] In spite of the CAR's mandate, Éyadéma demonstrated once again that he decided political outcomes when he appointed Edem Kodjo prime minister, in spite of Kodjo's paltry showing at the polls.[54] Agboyibor at first refused to participate in this illegitimate government. He soon realized, however, that boycotting the regime only removed any of the constraints that even a weak opposition party might place on the general. In mid-1994, Agboyibor returned to the National Assembly to become the opposition leader. Hence at the elections' conclusion Éyadéma still ruled Togo, but political tides had turned, and he had to acknowledge the power of Agboyibor's CAR. This development represented a major shift from the single-party politics of the years before 1990.

Prognostics for Togo's democratic future are mixed. On a positive note, the 1994 elections ostensibly represented a remarkable evolution in Togo's politics.

Although Éyadéma had successfully resisted being overthrown, he was compelled to govern in a situation of *cohabitation* in which his prime minister was a member of the opposition, and many deputies of the National Assembly are members of opposition parties. Without doubt, Éyadéma still held the reins of power, but now he recognized an opposition and the right of rival parties to contest elected seats in the National Assembly. In short, the reform movement had forced the recalcitrant dictator to share power with other forces in Togolese society. Political reform thus appears to be occurring, but at a far slower rate in Togo than in other francophone African countries.

But there are negative notes as well. Reports from Lomé include talk of a resurgent secret police and the resumption of a culture of silence. Security in the capital, especially for those who oppose the president, is poor. Violent crimes have become commonplace. The mysterious murder of a nonpolitical attorney and the subsequent arrest of Narcisse Djoua, the chief of Éyadéma's presidential guard in January 1995, point to a continuing spiral of violence. It is against this backdrop of violence that the cohabitation of Kodjo and Éyadéma has continued. Reports from Lomé suggest a cessation of violence, yet a tension exits under the calm, and in the autumn of 1995 the streets of Lomé remain deserted after sunset.

Conclusion

Political reform in Togo drew its strength from a convergence of three related variables: economic decline, regime fatigue, and international pressures. Economic decline left the state unable to co-opt opposition through financial reward. The regime tried its oft-used strategies of repression, but the events of October 1990 showed that the Togolese people were unwilling to tolerate the continuing caprices of a petty dictator. Éyadéma was undoubtedly surprised by these events. An even greater surprise was probably that foreign embassies and international donors ceased to support his regime. Opposition groups emerged with the connivance of foreign embassies to maneuver a reluctant Éyadéma into allowing a national conference. However, a national conference was an intermediate process that suggested transition yet promised nothing. Many observers at the time felt that the act of holding a conference and declaring sovereignty would suffice to topple Éyadéma. This notion simply ignored the power accumulated by the president over twenty-five years of rule. Hence the struggle for democracy turned violent and ugly.

Togo then experienced a period of rapid institutional formation as the opposition emerged to contest the continuing single-party rule. Éyadéma resisted reform because he felt that he would be able to do so with minimal costs to himself or his government. In his calculations, the costs of concession to reform were higher than those of resistance. It was therefore incumbent on the opposition to change his calculations. The unfortunate events of December 1991 demonstrated that the president could continue to resist reform indefinitely. Despite Éyadéma's defiance of popular demands for reform, he must still govern in concurrence with Agboyibor and the National Assembly or risk continued alienation from international donors and the diplomatic community.

The failure of Togo's national conference is therefore important as an illustration of the mistakes that prevented a successful transition. Éyadéma had never conceded sovereignty to the conference, and he retained executive power throughout the so-called transition. However, events that culminated in this artificially stable outcome suggest that a transition in Togo remains in motion. How the new government compromises and includes significant portions of the population will determine the future of representative government in Togo.

Notes

1. Sennen Andriamirado, "Conférences nationales: Est-ce vraiment la solution?" *Jeune Afrique,* no. 1591 (June 26–July 2, 1991):16. There is a growing literature on the national conference movement and regime change in francophone Africa. See Gérard Conac, ed., *L'Afrique en transition vers le pluralisme politique* (Paris: Éditions Économica, 1993); F. Eboussi Boulaga, *Les conférences nationales en Afrique noire: Une affaire à suivre* (Paris: Éditions Karthala, 1993); John R. Heilbrunn, "Social Origins of National Conferences in Benin and Togo," *Journal of Modern African Studies* 31, no. 2 (1993):277–299; Pearl T. Robinson, "Democratization: Understanding the Relationship Between Regime Change and the Culture of Politics," *African Studies Review* 37, 1 (1994):39–67; Michael Bratton and Nicolas van de Walle, "Neopatrimonial Regimes and Political Transitions in Africa," *World Politics* 46, no. 4 (1994):453–489.

2. Sven B. Kjellstrom and Ayite-Fily d'Almeida, *Institutional Development and Technical Assistance in Macroeconomic Policy Formulation: A Case Study of Togo,* World Bank Staff Working Papers, No. 786 (Washington: World Bank, 1986), p. 7.

3. *Marchés tropicaux et méditerranéens,* no. 2038 (November 30, 1984):2953.

4. By 1991, two long-term privatization programs had resulted in forty-eight public enterprises' being privatized, liquidated, or rented out by the Togolese government. Among the twenty-six remaining public enterprises are the major hotels, the phosphate mines, and the agricultural marketing board. See Institut National de la Recherche Scientifique, *Économie et société togolaises: Chiffres, tendances, et perspectives: Cahier 1991* (Lomé: ORSTOM, 1991), p. 79.

5. On rent-seeking, see Anne O. Kreuger, "The Political Economy of the Rent-Seeking Society," *American Economic Review* 64 (1974):291–303.

6. *Marchés tropicaux et méditerranéens,* no. 2162 (April 17, 1987):927.

7. Trutz von Trotha, "'C'est la pagaille': Quelques remarques sur l'élection présidentielle et son observation internationale au Togo," trans. Veronique Porra, *Politique africaine,* no. 52 (December 1994):137–143.

8. Prebendal politics is a theme of the influential book by Richard Joseph, *Prebendal Politics in Nigeria: The Rise and Fall of the Second Republic* (New York: Cambridge University Press, 1987).

9. Richard L. Sklar, "Developmental Democracy," *Comparative Studies in Society and History* 29, no. 4 (October 1987):686–714.

10. For a full discussion of DeLaye's mission, see John R. Heilbrunn and Comi M. Toulabor, "Une si petite démocratisation pour le Togo . . . " *Politique africaine,* no. 58 (June 1995):85–100.

11. Gérard Conac, "Les processus de démocratisation en Afrique," in *L'Afrique en transition,* pp. 37–39; Eboussi Boulaga, *Les conférences nationales,* p. 12.

12. For a fine comparison of Éyadéma's regime with Mobutu's, see Michel-Louis Martin, "Réflexions sur la nature et la légitimité du pouvoir martial en Afrique noire contemporaine," in Maurice Duverger, ed., *Dictatures et légitimité* (Paris: Presses Universitaires de France, 1982), pp. 441–466. See also the chapter on Zaire by Thomas Turner in this volume.

13. Jacques De Barrin, "Les dirigeants africains s'engagent à 'associer plus étroitement les populations à la construction de leur avenir,'" *Le Monde,* June 23, 1990, p. 30.

14. Hugo Saga, "Chaillot n'est pas La Baule," *Jeune Afrique,* no. 1613 (November 27–December 3, 1991):4–9.

15. Adam Przeworski, "Democracy as a Contingent Outcome of Conflicts," in John Elster and Rune Slagstad, eds., *Constitutionalism and Democracy* (New York: Cambridge University Press, 1985), p. 61.

16. Again, these similarities are more superficial than deep. Bishop Fanoko Kpodzro belonged to a prominent Ewe family from Palimé. His older brother had been a member of the cabinet of Togo's first president, Sylvanus Olympio.

17. In 1988 *Africa Confidential* (vol. 29, no. 15 [July 29, 1988]:7) related how Éyadéma entertained ambitions for the Nobel Peace Prize as part of his maneuvering to assume Houphouët's influential position as "*le Vieux*" of francophone Africa.

18. République Togolaise, "Loi N° 87–09 du 9 juin 1987 portant la création de la Commission des Droits de l'Homme," *Journal officiel,* June 15, 1987.

19. République Togolaise, "Discours d'ouverture de son Excellence le Général Gnassingbé Éyadéma, Président-Fondateur du Rassemblement du Peuple Togolais, Président de la République," *Seminaire National d'Information et de Sensibilisation organisé les 22 et 23 février 1988 à Lomé* (Lomé: Commission Nationale des Droits de l'Homme, 1988).

20. Cudjoe Kpor, "Festive Moment?" *West Africa,* April 23–29, 1990, p. 665.

21. Atsutsé Kokouvi Agbobli, "Éyadéma réfléchit," *Jeune Afrique,* no. 1536 (June 11, 1990):19.

22. Personal communication with Robert Dossou.

23. Chris Simpson, "Cries for Freedom," *West Africa,* October 22–28, 1990, p. 2701.

24. The use of a newspaper as a political association has had a long history in French West Africa. In many countries, newspapers served as opposition to colonial authorities, often publicizing abuses.

25. Francis Kpatindé, "Status quo à Lomé," *Jeune Afrique,* no. 1569 (January 23–29, 1991):10.

26. Atsutsé Kokouvi Agbobli, "Le Togo gagné par la fièvre démocratique," *Jeune Afrique,* no. 1555 (October 17–23, 1990), p. 22.

27. *Marchés tropicaux et méditerranéens,* April 19, 1991, p. 997.

28. "Accord: Gouvernement/Collectif de l'Opposition," tract distributed in Lomé signed by Yao Komlanvi, minister of the interior and security for the government, and Kwassi Lanyo Savi de Tovi for the COD.

29. For an outstanding analysis of the AEC and Togolese pre-independence politics, see Claude E. Welch, Jr., *Dreams of Unity: Pan-Africanism and Political Unification in West Africa* (Ithaca: Cornell University Press, 1966).

30. Speech by Madame Evelyne Trenou, République Togolaise, Rapport N° 18: Séance du mardi 30 juillet 1991, *Conférence nationale souveraine* (Lomé: 1991), p. 7.

31. Shortly after taking power, Éyadéma decreed that each region would receive an equivalent number of scholarships for study at the university and overseas. Hence the densely populated Maritime Province received the same number of scholarships as the sparsely populated Kara Province, with the effect that of "1,717 Togolese students counted in France between 1970 and 1976, almost two-thirds were originally from the north." Comi Toulabor, *Le Togo sous Éyadéma* (Paris: Éditions Karthala, 1986), p. 242.

32. Students from the Mouvement Étudiant pour la Lutte Démocratique (MELD), the Organisation Universitaire de Lutte pour la Démocratie (OULD), and the Groupe de Réflexion et d'Action des Jeunes pour la Démocratie (GRAD) formed this coalition.

33. "Les mouvements estudiantins adressent une pétition au chef de l'état," *Forum-Hebdo*, no. 27 (February 22, 1991):8.

34. Toyi Hodabalo, "Conflit macabre à l'Université du Bénin," *La Tribune des Démocrates*, no. 6 (March 15, 1991):3.

35. Novisi Agblewonou, "L'indépendance de la CNTT: Bluff ou réalité?" *La Tribune des Démocrates*, no. 11 (May 15, 1991):2.

36. "Conférence nationale: Composition des délégations officielles," *La Nouvelle Marche*, July 6, 1991.

37. Ironically, one of the conditions of the fourth SAP has been that military expenditures be cut. Personnel constitute the mammoth portion of military expenses. This fact has not been lost on any of the military in Lomé.

38. République Togolaise, "Acte N° 1 du 16 juillet 1991," *Conférence nationale souveraine*.

39. Act No. 1 proclaimed that the national conference was sovereign and that its decisions were therefore binding on the government. République Togolaise, "Rapport N° 6 du 15 juillet 1991," *Conférence nationale souveraine*.

40. "Déclaration du Gouvernement," *La Tribune des Démocrates*, no. 18 (July 19, 1991):2.

41. "Deuxième déclaration du Gouvernement," *La Tribune des Démocrates*, no. 19 (July 26, 1991):2.

42. République Togolaise, "Résolution N° 15 relative à la mise sur pied d'une commission d'enquête chargée de faire la lumière sur les massacres de la Lagune de Bé et autres forfaits, sur les déplacements massifs des populations et autres affrontements inter-ethniques, ainsi qu'à la poursuite judiciaire des auteurs reconnus coupables de ces actes," *Conférence nationale souveraine*, August 26, 1991.

43. Francis Kpatindé, "Togo: L'armée contre la démocratie," *Jeune Afrique*, no. 1614 (December 4–10, 1991):4–6.

44. A number of attempted coups occurred in 1991. After a coup attempt in October had failed, Éyadéma publicly requested that the army respect the decisions of the SNC. A week later soldiers attempted a second coup when they entered Koffigoh's residence and tried to take him prisoner. Shortly after his return from the francophone conference at Chaillot, troops seized Koffigoh, and a humiliated prime minister conceded his position on national television. Throughout this period, Éyadéma portrayed himself as seeking to control rebellious troops. However, in an interview in *Paris Match* (November 21, 1991) Éyadéma rejected all the decisions of the national conference as illegal, and he explicitly recognized the demands of his army for his reinstatement in power.

45. Géraldine Faes, "Comment Éyadéma a reconquis le pouvoir," *Jeune Afrique,* no. 1655 (September 24–30, 1992):19.

46. "Togo: La 'gestion consensuelle' selon Éyadéma," *Jeune Afrique,* no. 1654 (September 17–23, 1992):17.

47. For an interview of Koffigoh on this matter, see "Le mandat limité du premier ministre: 'Je voudrais qu'on m'oublie un peu,'" *Jeune Afrique,* no. 1634–1635 (April 30–May 13, 1992):129–133.

48. The electoral laws were published as "Code Électoral," *Togo-Presse,* July 3, 1992.

49. Article 62 of this constitution made military officers ineligible for office. "Projet de constitution de la IVe République," *Togo-Presse,* July 25, 1992.

50. "Le projet de Constitution adopté à 99,09%," *Togo-Presse,* September 29, 1992, p. 1.

51. "Togo: Éyadéma Expects to Win," *Africa Confidential* 34, no. 16 (August 15, 1993):4.

52. von Trotha, "C'est la pagaille," p. 159.

53. Hamza Kaïdi, "Togo: Fin de la transition?" *Jeune Afrique,* no. 1728 (February 17–23, 1994):29.

54. See Ebow Godwin, "Éyadéma Defies All Predictions," *West Africa,* May 2–8, 1994, p. 777.

Chapter Fourteen

Zaire: Flying High Above the Toads: Mobutu and Stalemated Democracy

THOMAS TURNER

I have always considered [Mobutu] to be a human monster . . . without law, morals, principles . . . who is ready to do anything to further his interests. My government will quite simply ignore Mr. Mobutu . . . I do not intend to share power with anyone, whoever it may be.

—Etienne Tshisekedi wa Mulumba, Prime Minister[1]

The chief is the chief. He is the eagle who flies high and cannot be touched by the spit of the toad.

—Mobutu Sese Seko, President[2]

Zaire supposedly entered a twelve-month transition to multiparty rule in April 1990. Eighteen months later, the National Conference forced longtime dictator Mobutu Sese Seko to appoint opposition leader Etienne Tshisekedi as prime minister, producing the stalemate reflected in the contrasting quotations above. Over four years later, Mobutu seems to have ridden out the storm. He remains president and has accepted a premier who is nominally from the opposition but is much more to his liking than Tshisekedi. To understand the survival of the Mobutu regime, we must examine its nature as well as the relationship between that regime and outside forces, particularly the international financial institutions and the governments of Belgium, France, and the United States.

A New Era?

On April 24, 1990, President Mobutu announced that Zaire was entering a new era. Henceforth, that date would rank as a milestone, along with June 30, 1960 (independence from Belgium), and November 24, 1965 (Mobutu's coup d'état, which inaugurated the Second Republic). The new era was to be one of multi-party government, replacing the single-party system that had been in place for twenty-three years.[3]

Mobutu presented this reform, which would usher in the Third Republic, as the product of his own initiative. In an exercise in direct democracy, he had gone to the people and sought their views on the functioning of political institutions. However, responses dealt not only with politics but also with economic hardships and the deterioration of the social infrastructure.

The president claimed that 5,310 of the 6,128 memoranda submitted (to a commission headed by his longtime associate Mokolo wa Mpombo) proposed retaining the single party, the Popular Revolutionary Movement (Mouvement Populaire de la Révolution, MPR), with some administrative and organizational changes, such as reductions in the number and size of party agencies and the recruitment of new staff. Only 13 percent of respondents called for a multiparty system. Apart from the question of keeping or abolishing the single-party system, Zairians offered a number of other political suggestions, among them rehabilitating the legislative, executive, and judicial branches of government; reinforcing legislative control over the executive branch; depoliticizing the civil service and territorial administration; and restructuring the security services so as to guarantee the fundamental rights and liberties of the citizens. In sum, it seemed that the public objected to virtually all the processes, if not the structure, of the party-state Mobutu had constructed.[4]

But Mobutu claimed that after much reflection, he had decided to go beyond the wishes expressed by the majority of the Zairian people. He had opted to experiment with political pluralism, establishing a system of three political parties, including the MPR. Each citizen would be free to adhere to the political formation of his choice. He warned, however, that the new multiparty system would have to avoid the errors of the past: Multipartyism must not become synonymous with "multitribalism."

Mobutu claimed that the Zairian people had demanded that he continue to preside over the destiny of the country. He would continue to serve as chief of state and as such would be above both the political parties and government organs, functioning as a final arbiter. Because he would be above parties, Mobutu was resigning that very day as head of the MPR, permitting the party to choose a new leader to carry out the changes necessary to its new role. (He reassumed leadership of the MPR in April 1991.)

All these changes would take place within twelve months. According to Mobutu, the deliberative bodies, from the National Legislative Council down to the local-level Collectivity Councils, had been judged satisfactory by respondents and would remain in place until the next elections. The National Executive Council (or ministerial council), however, was considered to have resigned. A caretaker premier would be named to assemble a transitional administration, which would be chiefly responsible for carrying out an urgent program "to respond to the expectations of the population in the economic and social domain."[5]

The whole exercise—the three-month "popular consultation" and the speech summarizing the contents of the memoranda received—was vintage Mobutu. He regained the initiative from those opposition groups—the Union for Democracy and Social Progress (Union pour la Démocratie et le Progrès Social, UDPS) at home as well as some of the groups operating from exile—whose demands centered on political reform. He exempted himself and the directly elected deliberative bodies from the condemnation expressed by the public in its memoranda. He declined to accept any responsibility for the country's woes and placed the burden for dealing with them on the back of the new cabinet, which he would not head.

The Kleptocratic Mobutist Regime

Mobutu's Second Republic was a party-state in which the single party absorbed the state. Under the constitution of 1974, "there exists a single institution, the MPR, incarnated by its President." "Mobutism" was declared to be constitutional doctrine. In theory, the gap between state and society was abolished, since the MPR was "the nation politically organized."[6]

In reality, the Mobutu regime was kleptocratic and used the state to extract resources from the civil society and from the international environment.[7] Since the regime lived off of such transactions, attempts by the international financial institutions or foreign governments to curb Zairian financial excesses were bound to fail. At the same time, the gap was growing between the state and the civil society—especially the so-called underground economy—over which the state exercised less and less control.[8] In this sense, then, the stalemated transition to democracy represents a struggle over resources.

In another sense, the stalemate concerns the monopoly of force. Mobutu's regime originated in a military coup d'état and, like other such regimes in Africa, was imperfectly civilianized. Coercion is a major tool of governance in Zaire. Arbitrary arrest and prolonged detention without charges remain common.[9] Major acts of violence, such as the killings that followed the "Kasongo uprising" in Bandundu Region in 1978, the killings of diamond miners in Kasai-Oriental Region in 1979, and, more recently, the massacre of students in Lubumbashi in 1990, intimidate the population.[10]

Through all the reshuffling of ministers, Mobutu was careful to maintain control over the military and the other security forces on which his position ultimately rested. He began with military and police leadership somewhat skewed ethnically toward his Équateur Region and neighboring Orientale, but purges and selective promotion led to further skewing. By the late 1980s the heads of "special" services were all from Mobutu's Ngbandi ethnic community. The intelligence services were coordinated by a Ngbandi civilian, Ngbanda Nzambo ko Atumba. The Israeli-trained Special Presidential Division (Division Spéciale Présidentielle, DSP) reportedly is recruited almost entirely from the Ngbandi—which facilitates use of the DSP against other armed forces such as the mutinous paratroopers in 1992.[11] Through all the political infighting and confusion of the so-called "transitional period," Mobutu retained control over these instruments of coercion, and Tshisekedi's inability to shake that control was a major factor in prolonging the stalemate.

Mobutu and the Western Troika: Belgium, France, the United States

In the colonial era, first as the Congo Free State, Zaire spent twenty-three years as the property of Belgium's King Leopold II, and another fifty-two years as the Belgian Congo, a more orthodox colony of the Belgian state. Since independence, links between Zaire and Belgium have remained close, particularly in the economic and educational spheres. It is thus hardly surprising that Zaire's relations with the former metropole reflect "un mélange d'amour et de haine" unparalleled in its relations with other external forces.[12]

According to Georges Nzongola Ntalaja, "the United States eventually replaced Belgium as the major arbiter of Zaire's destiny, but continues to deal with Zairian affairs within a multilateral strategy of imperialism in which Belgium and France are its key partners."[13] For Crawford Young, in contrast, Mobutu's survival has been due in large measure to his success in multiplying external patrons.[14] These views are complementary, since Zaire has been and remains both dependent and uncontrollable.[15]

Relations with Belgium

Although the young Mobutu apparently was recruited first by the Belgian security police, he was recruited later by the CIA and was known in the early 1960s as a protégé of the Americans rather than the Belgians.[16] The United States and Belgium cooperated in combating the Lumumbist insurrections of 1964, but the coup d'état of November 1965 was widely interpreted as a victory of the American-backed Mobutu over the Belgian-backed Moïse Tshombe.[17]

The rocky relations with the former colonial power since 1965 result mainly from the efforts of Mobutu and the politico-economic elite to pursue their own interests, in the name of nationalism, by expanding the sphere of the state at the expense of the church and the large corporations (formerly the other two elements of the "colonial trinity"). The MPR initially espoused a doctrine of nationalism, borrowed from Patrice Lumumba's Congolese National Movement (Mouvement National Congolais-Lumumbiste, MNC-L) and implying control of the national economy.[18]

Relations with Belgium soured when Mobutu proposed revision of the convention of February 6, 1965, by which Tshombe supposedly had settled the *contentieux belgo-congolais*, that is, the bundle of disputes concerning assets and debts of the former colony. When bilateral negotiations failed to produce substantive results, Zaire broke off relations on July 13, 1966, freezing the assets of certain Belgian organizations and seizing a number of their properties in Kinshasa.[19]

Relations with the Belgian-controlled mining company Upper Katanga Mining Union (Union Minière du Haut Katanga, UMHK) also deteriorated in early 1966. On June 7 the government ruled that all enterprises operating in the country must transfer their headquarters to Zaire and promulgated a law that in effect canceled colonial land concessions.[20] Discussions with Belgium and UMHK continued until December 1966, when Zaire broke them off. When UMHK announced its refusal to transfer its headquarters, Zaire suspended copper exports and blocked the transfer of the mining company's funds. Eventually, a compromise was reached under which a state-owned mining company, the General Quarries and Mines Company (Générale des Carrières et des Mines, GECAMINES) was created. The settlement proved lucrative to UMHK and brought unanticipated costs to Zaire.[21]

In 1973, the government seized some 2,000 foreign-owned businesses and turned them over to Zairians, mainly members of the political elite. Mobutu was the leading beneficiary. Within a few months, the scope of the disaster of "Zairianization" became clear: shortages of goods, tax evasion, abandonment of businesses. Instead of turning back, Mobutu plunged forward into the "radicalization of the revolution," including nationalization of trade and creation of agricultural brigades to relieve food shortages. In its application, however, "radicalization" was transformed from an attack on the Zairianized businesses to an assault on the industrial sector, still primarily Belgian-owned, thus extending the chaos of "Zairianization" to virtually all spheres of the economy.[22]

Starting in 1976, both sides made efforts to improve relations. A new cooperation agreement was signed in March, and Zaire promised to compensate Belgians who had lost assets under Zairianization. Zaire later allowed foreigners whose property had been expropriated to recover 60 percent of their assets, leading to a Belgian renewal of interest in investment. However, Mobutu continued to complain that students and exiles were allowed to carry out antiregime activity from Belgian soil.

When the exile opposition group Front for the National Liberation of the Congo (Front pour la Libération Nationale du Congo, FLNC) invaded Shaba (Katanga) in 1978, Belgium sent paratroopers, as did France, to rescue the stranded Europeans at Kolwezi. Planning to negotiate with the rebels, the Belgians proceeded cautiously, landing their forces at Kamina, more than 200 kilometers away. Their hand was forced when the French landed directly at Kolwezi and counterattacked. Fearing the extension of French influence in their former domain, the Belgians promoted the formation of a joint African defense force to repel future attacks by Zairian dissidents.[23]

Relations with France

Since the 1960s, successive French governments have worked to supplant Belgium as the dominant foreign power in Zaire. During the First Republic in Congo/ Zaire, France backed conservatives and federalists, including secessionist Katanga, against Lumumba and the radical, unitarist forces. Links with Zaire were strengthened after Mobutu's coup of 1965. Despite momentary tension over Mobutu's attempt to form an economic union with Chad and the Central African Republic in 1968, Franco-Zairian relations generally were good. President Valéry Giscard d'Estaing established a personal relationship with Mobutu. Starting in 1973, France became an important military supplier for Zaire, which ordered Mirage jet fighters and Puma helicopters.

Giscard received a triumphal welcome to Kinshasa in 1975, an apparent sign that Mobutu was distancing himself from Belgium and the United States. Giscard called for a meeting of copper producers and consumers, and Zaire reportedly agreed to grant a French company new prospecting rights for copper in exchange for a French moratorium on repayment of debts. The radio and television installations of the Voice of Zaire, the largest in Africa, were built by French companies with French government aid.[24]

When the FLNC invaded Shaba in 1977 and 1978, France was noticeably quicker to respond than Belgium or the United States. Again in 1989, France upstaged Belgium when President François Mitterrand announced at the Francophone Summit in Dakar that his government was writing off debt totaling US$2.6 billion owed by twenty-five of the world's poorest states, including Zaire. The subsequent announcement that Belgium was canceling or rescheduling much of its debt appeared anticlimactic.[25]

Relations with the United States

The heavy U.S. involvement in Zaire since 1960 has been motivated both by geopolitics and by economics.[26] Mobutu has been seen as "our man in Kinshasa," due initially to American involvement in the coups of 1960 and 1965. While Belgian companies and the Belgian government were embroiled in controversy with the Mobutu regime from 1966 onward, relations with the Americans prospered. The promulgation of a generous investment code in 1969 and a moderate political stance lured extensive new investment, including American funds. A substantial aid program was continued.[27]

U.S.-Zaire relations momentarily chilled in 1973 and 1974, when Zaire broke relations with Israel and "Zairianized" foreign property, including facilities owned by international oil companies. However, the Angolan civil war of 1975 apparently convinced the U.S. government that it needed Zaire as an ally in a troubled part of the world. Secretary of State Henry Kissinger's first official trip to Africa included a long stopover in Kinshasa, underscoring the renewed policy of close relations.[28]

The Carter administration, which had declared its number one foreign policy objective to be the promotion of human rights, appeared to pose a threat to Mobutu's abusive regime.[29] However, the FLNC invasions from Angolan soil (especially "Shaba II" in 1978) led to a partial reversal of Carter's skepticism.[30] The United States provided "nonlethal" military assistance, including medical supplies and transportation equipment. In 1980 the House of Representatives, concerned over human rights violations and the misuse of U.S. aid, voted to cut off military assistance to Zaire. Responding to pressure from the White House and from U.S. firms doing business in Zaire, the Senate reinstated the funds.

The election of Ronald Reagan led to the fight against terrorism's becoming the new "number one priority," and hence Zaire's human rights abuses were deemphasized. Zaire was seen as a useful ally in the struggle against Soviet clients such as Libya and Angola.[31] However, the context of U.S. policymaking had changed as a variety of American groups opposed administration support for Zaire.[32] Mobutu responded by hiring two Washington lobbying firms with ties to the Reagan and Bush administrations to promote a positive image of himself and his country.[33] Nonetheless, in November 1990, Congress eliminated military and economic aid (except for some humanitarian aid) to Zaire, crystallizing the longstanding division between Congress and the executive branch and between liberals and conservatives on Zaire policy. The congressional decision was based not only on Mobutu's theft of public funds but also on human rights violations and the May 1990 Lubumbashi massacre in particular.[34]

The end of Cold War competition in Africa, together with the shortcomings of the regime, led the United States to join Belgium and France in promoting peaceful political change in Zaire by pressuring Mobutu to oversee the transition to democratic government and to depart voluntarily. In October 1992 the United States, Belgium, and France all extended official support to the Tshisekedi government.[35]

Zaire, the International Financial Institutions, and the Debt Game

Since 1975 Zaire's massive foreign debt has had a major impact on both its domestic and foreign policy. Some causes of the debt—for example, the rising cost of petroleum imports and the declining proceeds from copper exports—were beyond Zaire's control. Others, including "Zairianization" and "radicalization," the squandering of funds on prestige projects and their diversion into overseas bank accounts, were not.[36]

In 1976 the first of a series of economic stabilization programs was adopted, under the guidance of the International Monetary Fund (IMF) and other external forces. In line with IMF orthodoxy, each successive "Mobutu Plan" was supposed to reduce corruption, rationalize and control expenditures, increase tax revenues, limit imports, boost production, improve the transportation infrastructure, eliminate arrears on interest payments, make principal payments on time, and improve financial management and economic planning.[37]

Zaire's public and publicly insured debt was rescheduled by the "Paris Club" (diplomats of principal creditor nations) at least seven times between 1976 and 1987. Zaire's private creditors rescheduled their part of the debt in 1980, and numerous meetings of World Bank and Western country aid consortia were held to generate further official assistance, starting in 1979.

When the first two standby agreements with the IMF yielded meager results, the IMF and the World Bank decided to send their own experts to run key posts in the Bank of Zaire, the Customs Office, and the Ministries of Finance and Planning. The head of the Bank of Zaire team, Erwin Blumenthal of West Germany, cut off credit and exchange facilities to firms of members of the political elite and imposed very strict foreign exchange quotas, but Mobutu and his colleagues were able to wear down Blumenthal and the other experts.[38]

In 1981, Zaire began to cooperate with the IMF, laying off large numbers of civil servants and teachers. In 1983, it agreed to devalue its currency by 78 percent and to liberalize the economy. In response, the IMF agreed to a fifth standby arrangement and the Paris Club agreed to roll over more than US$1 billion of debt, with a maturity of eleven years, against the eight years normally approved for debtor nations. In 1985 and 1987, the Paris Club rescheduled Zaire's debt for ten years and fifteen years respectively, making it clear that the greater leniency being shown to Zaire was a reward for following IMF guidelines.

The international lenders and Western governments were somewhat successful in controlling the financial abuses of Zaire's rulers during the 1980s, but substituted additional support for the withdrawn financial opportunities.[39] Belgium, France, Israel, and others provided both symbolic and instrumental backing by training new, initially corruption-free military units. Mobutu allowed the United States to ship arms to UNITA rebels in Angola (União Nacional para a Independência Total de Angola, National Union for the Total Independence of Angola) via Zaire and to refurbish the air base at Kamina in exchange for increased aid as well as pressure on the IMF to treat Zaire leniently.[40]

The Opposition, from Shaba I to Multipartyism

Both groups attempting to reform the system and seeking its overthrow played key roles in the struggle for reform at various times. The struggle for political reform was linked to the struggle for economic reform and involved international as well as domestic pressures.

In the aftermath of "Shaba I" (the 1977 FLNC invasion), Zaire's Western backers demanded political reforms. Mobutu responded by allowing multiple MPR candidacies for legislative seats. Earlier that year, the National Legislative Council had rejected the budget submitted to it by the president and denounced excessive presidential spending. Following the elections, the legislature became still more assertive, using questioning of ministers as a mechanism for raising policy issues.

Alone among Zairian opposition groups, the UDPS began as many Western political parties have, as a faction within the legislature. In 1979 a group of deputies defied presidential pressure and affixed their signatures to a report charging the army with responsibility for the massacre of 300 diamond miners at Katekalayi in Kasai-Oriental. In November 1980 these dissident deputies, who became known as "the Thirteen," published a fifty-one-page open letter to Mobutu, providing a comprehensive critique of his autocracy. The Thirteen were careful to include parliamentarians from various regions in their group in order to forestall the charge of tribalism. Invoking the constitution itself as protection for the expression of their views, the authors of the letter dissociated themselves from any advocacy of violence and called for the legalization of a second political party.[41] The thirteen signatories were arrested and stripped of their parliamentary seats.

In July 1982 some of "the Thirteen"—including ex-deputies (Joseph) Ngalula Mpandajila and Tshisekedi—were sentenced to fifteen years in prison for *complot qualifié* (aggravated treason). Their trial was notable for the testimony on behalf of the defense given by (Marcel) Lihau Ebua Libana, former president of the Supreme Court. In 1983 Mobutu lifted the prison sentences of six members of the group but banished them to their home villages.

It was not until 1982 that "the Thirteen" became an opposition party, under the name UDPS. (Frédéric) Kibassa Maliba, a former minister in Mobutu's government, was the group's first president. Whether because it had been founded by former associates of Mobutu, or by strategy, the UDPS stood out among opposition groups as being distinctly moderate. It identified itself as "the Party of Peace and Justice for all . . . committed to achieving democracy in Zaire through nonviolent means by using the following methods: — Free elections — Multiparty system — Freedom of press and associations — Free market economy."[42]

The UDPS did suffer, however, from the perception that it was dominated by Luba-Kasai. In fact, of the original thirteen deputies who signed the open letter in November 1980, only about half were from the Luba or other groups from Kasai-Oriental or Kasai-Occidental, with others representing other southern regions: Shaba, Sud-Kivu, and Bandundu. The most prominent members—Ngalula and Tshisekedi—were Luba-Kasai. As "the Thirteen" transformed their informal grouping into the UDPS, they brought in political figures from other regions, notably Lihau and Bossassi Epole Bolya Kodya, both from Mobutu's home region of Équateur, but the perception of Luba domination remained.

The survival of the UDPS, when so many other opposition groups have vanished, results from its existence within and outside Zaire—that is, the willingness of some leaders, including Tshisekedi, to attempt to function within the country. Also important is the early support of some Americans, notably Democratic Representatives Stephen Solarz of New York and Howard Wolpe of Michigan.[43]

On June 24, 1987, Mobutu announced that the last UDPS leaders had rejoined the MPR, the sole legal party. The seven who rejoined were Kibassa, former minister and one of the earliest MPR officials; Bossassi, president of the Zairian League for Human Rights; (Faustin) Birindwa ci Birhashwrirwa, former president of the Caisse d'Épargne (state-run savings bank); and former deputies Kanana, Makanda, Ngalula, and Tshisekedi. Thus the UDPS apparently came to an end. "Apart from a few dozen noisy supporters, prudently based outside the country— notably in Brussels and Paris—and true militants isolated in Kinshasa—the UDPS had no impact in this too vast country of Zaire," *Jeune Afrique* commented. "In some regions, only a few high bureaucrats and party dignitaries have heard of it."[44]

It was too soon to write off the UDPS, however. Tshisekedi explained that the group had received permission to function as a "tendency" within the MPR. In January 1988, he returned to Kinshasa and attempted to address a public meeting, only to have police beat and arrest him along with hundreds of other participants. In February 1989 thousands of students took to the streets of Kinshasa, protesting IMF-inspired austerity measures that included elimination of student buses and hikes in tuition fees. After suppressing the demonstration, security forces arrested the wife of Tshisekedi, apparently to pressure the UDPS leader into confessing that he had instigated the demonstrations. Other UDPS leaders were arrested on the same occasion, but Mobutu balanced the "stick" with the "carrot," naming former UDPS president Kibassa minister of sports.

In his speech of April 24, 1990, announcing the birth of a multiparty system, Mobutu indicated that three parties would be allowed. In a press conference later that day, he suggested that the three might consist of the long-banned UDPS as well as "moderates" and "hard-liners" of the MPR. Despite Mobutu's attempt to control the process, his speech set off a chain reaction of efforts to publicize existing organizations and to found new ones. The UDPS, the best-structured internal opposition movement, was the first to react. On April 29 a demonstration by supporters of Tshisekedi—released from house arrest on the day of Mobutu's speech—was violently suppressed, with several deaths. Tshisekedi wound up in the hospital early in May, after being attacked at his home by men apparently belonging to a security service.

Political Stalemate and Economic Collapse, 1991–1994

Mobutu was able to cling to power, at least through 1994, for two reasons. First, despite his (temporary) acceptance of Tshisekedi as prime minister, he maintained control of key institutions, including the central bank, the military, and the security police. Mobutu also controlled the network of regional, subregional, and zone administrators, despite the presence of an interior minister drawn from the opposition.

Secondly, Mobutu continued to exhibit formidable political skills, practicing successful divide-and-rule tactics against the domestic opposition as well as his erstwhile backers of the Western Troika. At the elite level, Mobutu stalled and reshuffled the deck, dividing the opposition time and again. In April 1990 he named Professor Lunda Bululu as prime minister of a so-called transitional government. In March 1991, he named another academic (and former minister of planning), Professor Mulumba Lukoji, to replace Lunda. Mulumba has a reputation as a "technocrat" but, like opposition leader Tshisekedi, he is a Luba-Kasai, and the appointment clearly was designed to weaken Luba support for the UDPS.

Early in 1991 the UDPS and other leading opposition parties formed the Sacred Union of the Radical Opposition (Union Sacrée de l'Opposition Radicale, USOR), a group committed to ousting Mobutu. In April Mobutu bowed to domestic and international pressure and agreed to convene a National Conference. Following the model borrowed from Benin, Congo, and other francophone states, this body included representatives of government agencies (including the military), political parties, and so-called "civil society," that is, interest groups of various sorts.[45]

After four postponements, the conference opened in August and elected a Luba-Kasai Protestant pastor and former Senate president, Isaac Kalonji Mutambayi, as provisional chairman. Kalonji had been proposed by the premier, Mulumba Lukoji. A few days later, the conference was suspended once again, as major opposition parties denounced the packing of the meeting by pro-Mobutu delegates.[46]

The conference resumed in September and selected a new president in the person of the Catholic archbishop of Kisangani, Monsignor Laurent Monsengwo Pasinyi. Msgr. Monsengwo was designated after a stormy session during which opposition delegates tore up the official report on the validation of delegates' credentials. The report had proposed validation of the credentials of 2,796 delegates out of 3,450 registered. The previous president, Pastor Kalonji, was forced to leave the room under police protection.[47]

On September 30 Mobutu bowed once again to domestic and international pressure and accepted Tshisekedi as premier, only to replace him a month later with Bernardin Mungul-Diaka, a nationalist of the 1960s from Kwilu (Bandundu Region), who headed a minor party in the Sacred Union (USOR) alliance. The opposition refused to recognize the appointment of Mungul-Diaka.

In November 1991 Mobutu scored a major victory over the Sacred Union by recruiting former foreign minister Jean Nguz a Karl-I-Bond of the Union of Federalists and Independent Republicans (Union des Fédéralistes et des Républicains Indépendants, UFERI) as premier. In September 1992, however, the National

Conference, which had been reopened in response to international pressure, selected Tshisekedi as premier. The country now had two governments.

Mobutu cemented his alliance with Nguz in July 1992 when he transferred nominal control of security forces, specifically the Gendarmerie and the Civil Guard, to the prime minister. But Mobutu retained control of the fighting forces. After ceding the premiership to Tshisekedi, Mobutu countered by forming a sort of countergovernment centering on the presidency. He appointed the previous prime minister, Nguz, as Minister of State to the Presidency, and named other hard-line opponents of change, including the former defense minister, Admiral Mavua Mudima, to key posts.[48] There followed a struggle for control of key state institutions. In September, troops backed by armored cars blockaded the parliament and the national bank.

Mobutu's nomination of former UDPS co-leader Birindwa as premier in March 1993 further divided the opposition. The High Council of the Republic/Transitional Parliament (Haut Conseil de la République/Parlement de la Transition, HCR/PT), created by the National Conference, had named Tshisekedi premier in December 1992, after Mobutu had dismissed him. The HCR refused to recognize Birindwa, as did the United States, Belgium, and France. Nevertheless, he was able to recruit ministers for a government. Co-optation by Mobutu and Birindwa was facilitated by the disastrous economic situation, with some politicians evidently concluding that a job with Mobutu was better than no job at all.[49]

The crudest examples of divide-and-rule tactics involve incitement of ethnic violence. In North Kivu, Hunde, Nyanga, and other "local" people attacked immigrants from Rwanda, with obvious encouragement of Mobutu and his supporters.[50] In mineral-rich Katanga (as Shaba Region was known once more), local people attacked Kasaians as a direct result of Mobutu's policies. Mobutu named Gabriel Kyungu wa Kumwimba, a member of "the Thirteen" and founder of the UDPS, as governor of Katanga (reversing a long-standing policy according to which administrators were named from outside a region). Former premier Nguz declared that his party, UFERI, would not participate in Tshisekedi's government and that his region, Katanga, was "in opposition" to that government. Violence flared in Katanga, directed especially against members of Tshisekedi's ethnic group, the Luba of Kasai. (Nguz is a Lunda, Kyungu a Luba of Katanga.) According to Nguz, the violence was provoked by the "boastful attitude" of Kasaians, who were fueling the "political and ethnic tension," which could lead to "a Yugoslavia situation."[51]

Intertwined with and contributing to the political impasse was the collapse of Zaire's formal economy. The annual inflation rate surpassed 5,000 percent in 1992, in large part because the government abandoned its IMF-drafted economic recovery plan and began spending heavily. Key sectors of the economy were generating greatly reduced foreign exchange earnings. The diamond industry was operating at less than 50 percent of capacity, the copper industry at only 25 percent.[52]

In December 1992, the question of control over currency precipitated a new round in Zaire's political crisis. The Bank of Zaire issued a five million Zaire note, worth about US$3 at the time. Premier Tshisekedi, who contested Mobutu's continuing domination of the central bank, declared the new money "demonetized" and worthless. The consequent refusal of merchants to accept the five million Zaire note led to a military mutiny and other violence. In May 1993, the Bank of Zaire announced that it would issue a new one million Zaire bill.[53]

Throughout the struggle, Mobutu was resisting pressure for reform from his Western allies and from the international financial institutions. In February 1992, when Mobutu and Nguz suspended the National Conference, the United States responded by cutting off all aid, and the European Community suspended all development assistance. Belgium, which had stopped aid following the military's massacre of students at Lubumbashi University, refused dialogue with the Nguz government and said it would provide aid only through the National Conference.

In the first half of 1994, Mobutu's tactics of stalling and of dividing the opposition bore fruit. Mobutu's premier, Birindwa, resigned, and the HCR-PT absorbed members of the pro-Mobutu rival parliament. After five months of political vacuum, the HCR-PT elected a candidate from the "moderate" opposition, Leon Kengo wa Dondo, as prime minister. ("Moderate" and "radical," in Zairian terminology, referred to degrees of hostility to continuance of Mobutu's rule, Tshisekedi being extremely "radical.")

Kengo was a founder of the Union of Independent Democrats (Union des Démocrates Indépendants, UDI), in 1990. Denounced at its founding as "MPR II," it represented a claim to an independent future by politicians and businessmen formerly close to Mobutu.[54] Kengo had been premier twice in the 1980s and allegedly "implemented austerity policies that earned him respect among international financial institutions."[55] His candidacy in 1994 was put forward by the Union for the Republic and Democracy (Union pour la République et la Démocratie, URD), a coalition including the UDI and other "moderate" groups associated with USOR. The radical wing of USOR labeled Kengo's election "illegal and anti-constitutional" and regarded Tshisekedi as the legitimate premier.[56]

Tshisekedi's opposition government continued to meet, but multiple defections and loss of support had rendered it irrelevant. Three Tshisekedi ministers joined Kengo's cabinet, and a fourth was helping to draft Kengo's speeches. Other key elements of the opposition coalition divided. The Democratic and Social Christian Party (Parti Démocrate et Social Chrétien, PDSC) split when one of its leaders, Gustave Malumba Mbangula, accepted the post of deputy prime minister/interior minister. Most deputies from the civil society ended their eleven-week parliamentary boycott, and their former leader, Bahati Lukwebo, accepted the Budget Ministry. Only the trade unions stuck with the radical opposition.[57]

Perhaps the most significant development was that the public had tired of Tshisekedi's repeated calls for resistance. A strike called at the diamond mining company Société Minière de Bakwanga (MIBA) had little effect; the call for a consumer boycott of French interests such as the oil company Elf-Aquitaine and the brewers Brasseries de Kinshasa was largely ignored; and a violent raid on Tshisekedi's house by civil guards, which the opposition press described as a deliberate murder attempt, failed to trigger a single public protest.[58]

Tshisekedi found himself in a no-win situation. Kengo had kept several low-level cabinet posts open for the UDPS and made it clear that he was willing to offer more enticing posts if the UDPS would participate. But Tshisekedi, who has consistently denounced Kengo's government as illegal, risked losing all credibility if he struck a deal. After trying to persuade Tshisekedi to negotiate with the centrists, the Western Troika issued carefully worded statements implicitly recognizing the Kengo government. France, regarded as having backed Kengo from the start, promised aid, and Belgium was ready to help him settle Zaire's differences with the IMF.

The question now is whether Kengo can succeed where Tshisekedi failed in reaching a working arrangement with Mobutu. His promises—ending the irresponsible printing of money, halting public sector corruption, privatizing state companies, ending the security forces' reign of terror—cannot be carried out without cooperation from Mobutu. One key test will be control of the currency. Monetary reform became imperative in 1993, with the highest note in general circulation equivalent to only US$0.0000000014. The new Zaire, which became legal tender on October 31, 1993, was equivalent to 3 million old Zaires, and its convertible value was initially fixed at NZ3.3 to US$1.[59] The new currency enjoyed a period of stability in January and February 1994, when very few notes were being injected into the system because the central bank had trouble paying printers. Rates offered by the Kinshasa banks were little different from those available on the parallel market, and shop prices fell, an almost unheard-of situation in Zaire. By April, however, large quantities of bank notes, still in their plastic wrappings, were being dumped on the black market. By April 9, women currency dealers in Kinshasa's parallel market were buying U.S. dollars at Z235, compared to Z111 a month earlier.[60]

Premier Kengo publicly identified illegal shipments of currency from a printer in Argentina and challenged the presidential intimates (including General Kpama Baramoto of the Civil Guard and businessman Bemba Saolona) running the scheme. He also got Mobutu to approve the dismissal of central bank governor Ndiang Mabul.[61] These measures were not immediately reflected in the inflation rate. Although the annual rate declined from 8,828 percent in 1993, it still totaled 6,030 percent for 1994.[62]

A second test for Kengo concerned the territorial administration. Mobutu was pushing hard for elections to be staged within a year, as laid down in the constitution. Kengo paid lip service to this calendar but clearly considered it ridiculous. With regional governorships in the hands of Mobutu stalwarts, no recent population census, a collapsing transport network, and an interior with little contact with the capital, a free and fair vote was impossible.

The selection of Kengo over Tshisekedi was facilitated by disunity on the part of Zaire's three main external partners. France broke ranks in January 1994, calling for a middle way between Tshisekedi and the Mobutu-designated government.[63] Later, France supported Mobutu and Kengo as essential to its policy of backing the collapsing Hutu regime in neighboring Rwanda. The Clinton administration did little to implement its stated goal of transition to democracy. Before departing, the Bush administration's team seems to have imparted to its successors its deep distrust of Tshisekedi. Msgr. Monsengwo was said to feel that Washington's failure to increase the pressure on Mobutu had become a significant obstacle to effective negotiation. The pressure for meaningful international sanctions against Mobutu, such as a freeze on his multibillion dollar assets abroad, abated after Clinton's team took hold of Zaire policy. When confronted by pressure for sanctions, Assistant Secretary of State for African Affairs George Moose publicly said that they were still being contemplated and privately blamed French and Belgian foot-dragging for the total lack of action. Moose's privately voiced opinion was that both Mobutu and Tshisekedi were part of the problem, and that Zaire's only hope lay in a regime of neutral technocrats (such as Kengo?).[64]

Conclusion

It would be invalid and unjust to overstate the international factor in Zaire's transition to democracy. Certainly the perseverance and courage of individual Zairians—Mme. Thérèse Pakassa of the Unified Lumumbist Party (Parti Lumumbiste Unifié, PALU) and Buana Kabwe of the Zairian League for Human Rights are worthy of mention, along with Tshisekedi—have been crucial in promoting the shift from Mobutu's one-party dictatorship.

At the same time, Zaire's stalled transition to democracy does demonstrate both the heavy impact of international forces upon events in that country and the inability of external actors to impose their will. The Zairian League for Human Rights is based on an imported model and has benefited from support from the United States.

Zaire clearly belongs to a francophone African political subsystem, in that events happening in other French-speaking states are much more likely to be imitated than are those in anglophone Africa. The Voice of Zaire often rebroadcasts international news supplied by France. Taxi drivers in Kinshasa often tune their radios to Radio Brazzaville, located just across the river. *Radio-trottoir*—Kinshasa's rumor mill—spreads this information to other Zairians.

The governments of the Western Troika have exercised considerable influence over events in Zaire over the years. Their support for Mobutu, until recently, represented an important source of strength for his dictatorship. For a time, they supported Tshisekedi, but Mobutu survived that challenge. Part of the problem lies in the fact that the three Western states share an interest in some aspects of reform, particularly that of seeing Zaire follow IMF guidelines on fiscal policy, but they have very divergent interests in other areas. Neither Belgium nor the United States could be expected to sympathize with France's objectives of demonstrating that it is still a great power or of maintaining Rwanda within the francophone bloc.[65] Mobutu's political skills were demonstrated in this context as well, as he exploited every sign of divergent policy on the part of the three Western allies. Will Western support for Kengo prove to be an effective method of clipping the eagle's wings, or will Mobutu continue to soar?[66]

Notes

1. "Mobuto [*sic*] Clings to Power," *Africa Research Bulletin, Political Series*, October 1–31, 1991, p. 10300.

2. Ibid., p. 10301.

3. Mobutu Sese Seko, "Texte intégral du discours prononcé par le Chef de l'État le 24 avril 1990," *Elima*, April 25, 1990 (Kinshasa), pp. 3–5.

4. Ibid.

5. Ibid.

6. Crawford Young and Thomas Turner, *The Rise and Decline of the Zairian State* (Madison: University of Wisconsin Press, 1985), p. 192.

7. Michael G. Schatzberg, *Politics and Class in Zaire: Bureaucracy, Business, and Beer in Lisala* (New York: Africana Publishing Company, 1980.)

8. Janet MacGaffey, M. Vwakyanakazi, et al., *The Real Economy of Zaire: The Contribution of Smuggling and Other Unofficial Activities to National Wealth* (Philadelphia: University of Pennsylvania Press, 1991).

9. Mutua wa M. and P. Rosenblum, *Zaire: Repression as Policy. A Human Rights Report* (New York: Lawyers Committee for Human Rights, 1990).

10. Diocese of Idiofa, "Le soulèvement dit Kasongo," *La vie diocésaine d'Idiofa*, no. 2 (1978):7; "Les massacres de Katekalayi et de Luamela (Kasai Oriental)," *Politique africaine* 2, no. 6 (1982):72–106; V. Digekisa Piluka, *Le massacre de Lubumbashi: Zaïre 11–12 mai 1990: Dossier d'un témoin-accusé* (Paris: L'Harmattan, 1993).

11. "Trial for 'Coup Leaders,'" *Africa Research Bulletin, Political Series*, March 1992, p. 10516.

12. Colette Braeckman, *Le dinosaure: Le Zaïre de Mobutu* (Paris: Fayard, 1992), p. 132. On relations with what became known as the "Western Troika," see pp. 279–315.

13. Georges Nzongola-Ntalaja, "Crisis and Change in Zaire, 1960–1985," in Georges Nzongola-Ntalaja, ed., *The Crisis in Zaire: Myths and Realities* (Trenton, N.J.: Africa World Press, 1986), p. 20.

14. Crawford Young, "Zaire: The Unending Crisis," *Foreign Affairs* 57, no. 1 (1978):177. See also Braeckman, *Le dinosaure*, p. 219, on *"diversification des dépendances."*

15. René Lemarchand, "Zaire: The Unmanageable Client State," in René Lemarchand, ed., *American Policy in Southern Africa: The Stakes and the Stance*, 2d ed. (Washington, D.C.: University Press of America, 1981), pp. 1–16.

16. Sean Kelly, *America's Tyrant: The CIA and Mobutu of Zaire* (Washington: American University Press, 1993); Elise Forbes Pachter, "Our Man in Kinshasa: U.S. Relations with Mobutu, 1970–1983: Patron-Client Relations in the International Sphere" (Ph.D. diss.,

School of Advanced International Studies, Johns Hopkins University, 1987). Braeckman argues that labels such as "homme des belges," "homme des américains," or "agent de la CIA" reflect a simplistic vision of a Mobutu who was out for his own power, in the 1960s as in the 1990s. Braeckman, *Le dinosaure,* p. 145.

17. [Frédéric] Vandewalle, *L'Ommegang: Odyssée et reconquête de Stanleyville, 1964* (Brussels: by the author, 1970); F. E. Wagoner, *Dragon Rouge: The Rescue of Hostages in the Congo* (Washington: National Defense University, 1980).

18. Young and Turner, *Rise and Decline of the Zairian State,* pp. 185–220.

19. Ibid., pp. 276–325; Jean-Claude Willame, "Éléments pour une lecture du contentieux belgo-zaïrois," *Cahiers du CEDAF,* no. 6 (1988):6.

20. J. H. Herbots, "Commentaires de la loi dite Bakajika," *Études congolaises* 10, no. 4 (1967):57–62.

21. Braeckman, *Le dinosaure,* pp. 219–220.

22. Young and Turner, *Rise and Decline of the Zairian State,* pp. 326–362; Michael G. Schatzberg, "The State and the Economy: The 'Radicalization of the Revolution' in Mobutu's Zaire," *Canadian Journal of African Studies* 14, no. 2 (1980):239–257; Braeckman, *Le dinosaure,* p. 198.

23. Romain Yakemtchouk, "Les deux guerres du Shaba: Les relations entre la Belgique, la France, et le Zaïre," *Studia diplomatica* 41, no. 4–6 (1988):375–735; Jean-Claude Willame, "La seconde guerre du Shaba," *Genève-Afrique* 16, no. 1 (1977–1978):10–26; Ghislain C. Kabwit, *The Aftermath of Shaba I and II Crisis: The Illusion of Political Changes and Reforms in Zaire* (paper presented to the annual meeting of the African Studies Association, Baltimore, 1978).

24. Young and Turner, *Rise and Decline of the Zairian State,* pp. 374–375; Théodore Tréfon, "French Policy Toward Zaire During the Giscard-d'Estaing Presidency," *Cahiers du CEDAF,* no. 1 (1989):1; Jean-François Bayart, *La politique africaine de François Mitterrand* (Paris: Karthala, 1984).

25. "Zaire-Belgium: Relations Normalised," *Africa Research Bulletin, Economic Series,* August 15, 1989, pp. 9358–9359.

26. For useful guides to the economic component to American policy, see Immanuel Wallerstein, "Africa, the United States, and the World Economy: The Historical Bases of American Policy," in F. S. Arkhurst, ed., *U.S. Policy Toward Africa* (New York: Praeger Publishers, 1975), pp. 11–37; and Georges Nzongola-Ntalaja, "United States Policy Towards Zaire," in Gerald J. Bender, James S. Coleman, and Richard L. Sklar, eds., *African Crisis Areas and U.S. Foreign Policy* (Berkeley: University of California Press, 1985), pp. 225–238. The view expressed in D. N. Gibbs, *The Political Economy of Third World Intervention: Mines, Money, and U.S. Policy in the Congo Crisis* (Chicago: University of Chicago Press, 1991), according to which the influence of specific American (and Swedish) firms can be detected in U.S. and UN policy, is inaccurate.

27. Braeckman argues that the United States favored the nationalization of the UMHK. Braeckman, *Le dinosaure,* p. 219. On the early years, see Pachter, "Our Man in Kinshasa;" Kelly, *America's Tyrant*; Stephen R. Weissman, *American Foreign Policy in the Congo, 1960–1964* (Ithaca: Cornell University Press, 1974); Madeleine G. Kalb, *The Congo Cables: The Cold War in Africa from Eisenhower to Kennedy* (New York: Macmillan, 1982). For useful overviews of U.S. policy toward Zaire, see Romain Yakemtchouk, "Les relations entre les États-Unis et le Zaïre," *Studia diplomatica* 39, no. 1 (1986):5–115; Michael G. Schatzberg, *Mobutu or Chaos? The United States and Zaire, 1960–1990* (Lanham, Md.: University Press

of America, 1991); Peter J. Schraeder, *United States Foreign Policy Toward Africa: Incrementalism, Crisis, and Change* (Cambridge, England: Cambridge University Press, 1994).

28. Young and Turner, *Rise and Decline of the Zairian State,* pp. 371–373.

29. B. M. Rubin, "Carter, Human Rights, and U.S. Allies," in B. M. Rubin and E. P. Spiro, eds., *Human Rights and U.S. Foreign Policy* (Boulder: Westview Press, 1979), pp. 109–129.

30. B. Gwertzman, "Senators Ask Proof that Cuba Had Role in Invasion of Zaire," *New York Times,* May 27, 1978, pp. 1, 4; Schraeder points to the shift of "world view" within the Carter administration, from Secretary of State Cyrus Vance to National Security Adviser Zbigniew Brzezinski. Schraeder, *United States Foreign Policy Toward Africa,* p. 93.

31. H. Morris, "Warnings from Black Africa," *Today,* April 3, 1981, p. 13.

32. David B. Ottaway, "48 in House Warn Zaire on Rights Abuses," *Washington Post,* February 10, 1988.

33. E. T. Pound, "Congo Drums: With Dictators Falling, Zaire's Mobutu Hires Lobbyists to Make Sure He Retains American Aid," *Wall Street Journal,* March 7, 1990.

34. "Aid Cut," *Africa Research Bulletin, Political Series,* December 16, 1990–January 15, 1991, p. 10211.

35. According to Braeckman, the Americans were the last of the Troika members to abandon their "friend" Mobutu. Braeckman, *Le dinosaure,* p. 294.

36. On diversion of funds, see E. Blumenthal, "Zaïre: Rapport sur sa credibilité financière internationale," *La Revue Nouvelle* 77, no. 11 (1982):360–378; see also the remarks of Congressman J. F. McNulty (Arizona) and appended article, "Mobutu Sucks the Blood from Zaire's Mining Giant," *Africa Now* (London), in *Congressional Record,* reproduced in annexes to Yakemtchouk, "Les relations entre les États-Unis et le Zaïre," pp. 106–109. By far the best source on prestige projects is Jean-Claude Willame, *Zaïre: L'épopée d'Inga* (Paris: Harmattan), 1986; see also Braeckman on "white elephants," *Le dinosaure,* pp. 222–230.

37. Thomas M. Callaghy, "The Ritual Dance of the Debt Game," *Africa Report* 29, no. 5 (September-October, 1984):22–24.

38. Blumenthal, "Zaïre: Rapport sur sa credibilité financière internationale," pp. 360–378.

39. Crawford Young, "Optimism on Zaire: Illusion or Reality?" *CSIS Africa Notes* (Georgetown University), 1985, p. 50; G. Frankel, "18 Months of Harsh Austerity Bring Indications of a Turnaround to Zaire," *Washington Post,* May 22, 1985.

40. J. H. Cushman, Jr., "U.S. Seeking Agreement to Use Air Base in Zaire," *New York Times,* February 22, 1987; B. Harden, "Seeds of Reform Grow Slowly in Zaire," *Washington Post,* November 20, 1987. Kinshasa was the site of the CIA regional training center for Central Africa, according to Braeckman, *Le dinosaure,* p. 73.

41. [Joseph Ngalula Mpandajila], "Lettre ouverte au Citoyen Président-Fondateur du Mouvement Populaire de la Révolution, Président de la République, par un groupe de parlementaires," *Politique africaine* 1, no. 3 (1981):94–140. On Ngalula as the author, see Braeckman, *Le dinosaure,* p. 327.

42. Union pour la Démocratie et le Progrès Social, *Zaire: The New Society* (Oslo: UDPS, Bureau Scandinavie, 1991).

43. According to Braeckman, international support saved the life of Tshisekedi, who otherwise would have been killed by Mobutu's security forces. Braeckman, *Le dinosaure,* pp. 90–91.

44. Sennen Andriamirado, "Kibassa 'sous la houlette' de Mobutu," *Jeune Afrique,* August 19–26, 1987, pp. 56–57.

45. *"Communautés de base,"* organized by Catholics on a Latin American liberation theology model, constituted an important element in the "Civil Society" represented at the National Conference. Braeckman, *Le dinosaure,* p. 178.

46. "Provisional Bureau Head," *Africa Research Bulletin, Political Series,* August 1–31, 1991, p. 10233.

47. "Conference in Uproar," *Africa Research Bulletin, Political Series,* September 1–30, 1991, p. 10266.

48. On the parallel government centering on the presidency, see Braeckman, *Le dinosaure,* pp. 184–186.

49. See Braeckman, *Le dinosaure,* pp. 173–174, on the ongoing process of recruitment and corruption of the "cerveaux désargentés" (literally, "moneyless brains") by the Mobutu regime.

50. "Ethnic Rwandans Massacred," *Africa Research Bulletin, Political Series,* July 1993, p. 11068; "Troops to Kivu," ibid., p. 11097.

51. "[Jean Nguz a] Karl-I-Bond on Ethnic Tension in Shaba Province," *Foreign Broadcast Information Service–Sub-Saharan Africa,* August 28, 1992, p. 2.

52. Diane Hubbard, "Zaire: Economy," *Africa South of the Sahara* (London: Europa, 1996), pp. 1020–1025.

53. The new note would be printed in Kinshasa, an apparent response to the government's unpaid debt to the German firm that printed the earlier currency, including the disputed five million Zaire bill. "Zaire: Mobutu's Monetary Mutiny," *Africa Confidential,* February 5, 1993, pp. 4–5; "Zaire's $2 Bank Note Leads to 300 Deaths," *Africa Report* 38, no. 2 (March-April 1993):5–6.

54. Kengo had been a leader, if not the leader, of one of two "clans" of politicians of Équateur origin orbiting around Mobutu. His group, the so-called *métis* (mulattoes), were hard-liners on the question of compromise with the UDPS. The African "clan," led by Nkema, supposedly advocated reconciliation. Braeckman, *Le dinosaure,* pp. 186–187.

55. U.S. Department of State, *Kengo wa Dondo* [biography], 1994.

56. "Zaire: Deserting a Sinking Tshisekedi," *Africa Confidential,* July 29, 1994, pp. 3–5.

57. Ibid. On the disorder within the UDPS, see "Tshisekedi analyse la crise politique actuelle et rassure," *Tempête des tropiques,* November 10–11, 1994, pp. 4–5.

58. "Zaire: Deserting a Sinking Tshisekedi," pp. 3–5.

59. "Zaire: 1993 Overview," *Keesing's Record of World Events,* vol. 40, Reference Supplement, 1993, p. R29.

60. "Market Flood Undermines Progress," *Africa Research Bulletin, Economic Series,* March 16–April 15, 1994, p. 11645.

61. Interview with an informed source, Washington, December 1994.

62. Hubbard, "Zaire: Economy," p. 1025.

63. "Zaire: Deserting a Sinking Tshisekedi," p. 3.

64. Ibid.

65. Marlise Simons, "France Seeks Partners for Rwandan Venture," *New York Times,* June 17, 1994, p. 51; Marlise Simons, "The French Connection in Rwanda," *New York Times,* July 3, 1994, p. 4; Alex Shoumatoff, "Gallic Mischief: Why Is France in Rwanda?" *New Yorker,* July 18, 1994, pp. 4–5; "Alain Juppé: 'Tenir son rang,'" *Le Monde,* September 2, 1994, p. 9.

66. Steven Greenhouse, "U.S. Tries New Tack with Zaire, Backing Premier to Isolate Mobutu," *New York Times,* November 8, 1994, p. A6.

Part Five

Civil War and Political Change

Chapter Fifteen

Chad: Regime Change, Increased Insecurity, and Blockage of Further Reforms

BERNARD LANNE

During the first half of the 1990s Chad experienced both internal and external pressures for political reform and democratization. These pressures led the regime of Hissène Habré to consider a further softening of its authoritarian character by allowing independent candidates to run against candidates from the official single party in the parliamentary elections of July 1990. At the same time, Habré adamantly resisted the establishment of a multiparty system. Habré's ouster in December 1990 led to the establishment of another authoritarian regime backed by military elements and aided by foreign states.

Under the new regime of Idriss Déby, pressures for reform led to the reestablishment of a multiparty system, the restoration of freedoms of speech and press, the holding of a national conference, and the inclusion of opposition party members in the government and the provisional parliament. Liberalization ceased, however, after mid-1993, mainly for two reasons. Déby and his ruling party sought to delay the holding of a referendum on a new democratic constitution and of parliamentary and presidential elections until after they had further solidified their grip on power. At the same time, the Déby regime proved even less capable than its predecessor in controlling its supporters and eliminating rival armed groups. The resulting failure to establish public order led to chronic inse-

David Gardinier translated this chapter and provided the English-language bibliography.

curity and limited functioning of state institutions, which further blocked efforts by the opposition parties to obtain additional reforms in the direction of democracy.

In this chapter, divided into three sections, the course of political reform and democratization is explored. The first section provides a background from Chad's earlier history, particularly from the period of 1945 to 1987; the second describes the beginning of political reform in Chad from 1988 to late 1990, when President Habré was overthrown; and the third deals with the course of the pressures for change within the evolving context of Chadian life under Déby in the 1990s.[1]

Chad Before 1988

The French conquest of Chad led in 1900 to the creation of a territory two and a half times the size of France. Not only was it landlocked at huge distances from the oceans but also its three major rivers flowed away from them and into Lake Chad. Roughly three-fifths of the estimated million people farmed in the grasslands watered by these streams, while the rest practiced pastoralism over the vast stretches of Sahel and semidesert in the north and east. There were few known natural resources and there was not much economic activity that could be effectively taxed to support the French colonial administration.

The French occupation brought together diverse peoples who had not previously composed a single state. French rule was accepted without much resistance by the animist agriculturalists of the south because it ended centuries of slaveraiding among them by Muslim pastoralists of the north and east. But a legacy of southern hostility toward and distrust of these oppressors persisted throughout the colonial period and, to a certain extent, since then. In the north and east, the French established their control, either through force or the threat of it. Even after most of the country passed under civilian rule in 1920, military administration was maintained over the nomads of the Borkou-Ennedi-Tibesti (BET) Prefecture (far north), Kanem Prefecture (north), and Ouaddai Prefecture (east). Under a system of direct administration the French made Chad's traditional chiefs their agents in carrying out policies to raise revenue to support their administration and its limited services. Many chiefs became extortionate and abusive and, as a result, unpopular with the populations that they administered.

Between the two world wars France created primary schools to train auxiliaries for its administration. Interest in education in French was limited to the animist populations of the south. The Islamicized areas rejected Western education and continued to seek Quranic instruction. In 1928 the administration introduced the cultivation of cotton for export in the southern third of the country as a means of producing tax revenues and raising living standards. In these same regions it also instituted forced labor for public purposes, in part to create a network of roads. Anglophone Protestant missionaries began work in the south in the 1920s, while francophone Catholic missionaries undertook evangelization mainly after 1946.

The activities of the French administration and Protestant missionary efforts helped to create a greater sense of common identity among the Sara cultivators, among whom ten groups had closely related languages and cultural links.[2]

As a result of World War II, France decided to promote the advancement of its Black African territories through their assimilation into the French Republic. Chad became an Overseas Territory of the Fourth Republic and the Chadians French citizens. The territory acquired token representation in the French Parliament. Chadian representatives in the Grand Council of the federation of French Equatorial Africa in Brazzaville and in the Territorial Assembly in Fort-Lamy (the capital, renamed N'Djamena in 1973) acquired a voice in the territory's affairs. The holding of elections led to the formation of parties, often with links to French and interterritorial African parties.

Through the various plans of the Fonds d'Investissement et Développement Économique et Sociale (FIDES) between 1947 and 1959 France provided loans and grants to construct infrastructure and facilities for economic, social, and educational purposes. Cotton production and Western education underwent further expansion. Despite advances, the country's mainly agricultural and pastoral economy generated insufficient income for operating a modern state and even less for development. Western education did not produce enough Chadians capable of assuming positions of responsibility to assure direction of the central government, territorial administration, school system, and economy. Thus the arrival of self-rule in the late 1950s found Chad still dependent upon France for financial and technical aid, including personnel, for maintaining its public institutions.[3]

In November 1958 Chad became an autonomous republic within the French Community. It adopted a parliamentary form of government and democratic institutions. In March 1959 the National Assembly elected François Tombalbaye, a Sara and the leader of the Chadian Progressive Party (Parti Progressiste Tchadien, PPT), as prime minister. The PPT was an anticolonialist party that showed hostility to the colonial administration, French economic interests, and traditional chiefs. The party obtained its strongest support from Western-educated southerners, including many in the civil service. As a result of the rejection of Western education by most Muslims, who comprised at least two-fifths of the population, southern animists and Christians predominated in public employment.[4]

In August 1960 Tombalbaye became president of an independent Chad. The constitution of November 28, 1960, retained a parliamentary system of government. Thereafter he began to Africanize the central government and territorial administration. By the end of 1962 the entire territorial administration lay in Chadian hands. Between 1960 and 1963 the number of French officials in the central government dropped from ninety-five to thirty, though additional Frenchmen served as advisers on development projects. Chadian military officers took over direction of the national army. But only in late 1964 did units of the national army replace French military forces in the BET and Ouaddai Prefectures, a process fully completed by March 30, 1965.

In the meantime, as in the majority of African countries in this era, and with the apparent support of most public opinion, Chad was moving towards a single-party regime in which democracy was no longer any more than a façade. In 1961 Tombalbaye began to eliminate opposition parties, most of which were led by Muslim notables. On January 17, 1962, he dissolved all parties except the PPT. A new constitution, that of April 16, 1962, established a presidential form of government that greatly increased his power.

In January 1963, during a party congress in Fort-Archambault (called Sarh after 1973), the PPT was proclaimed the sole legal party and its executive body, the National Political Bureau (Bureau Politique National, BPN), the republic's supreme political organ. In March 1963, as a result of Tombalbaye's arrest of Muslim cabinet ministers, the BPN came under the control of southerners. Three key Muslim politicians who had exercised influence prior to independence opposed the PPT's political monopoly. The violent protests their supporters staged in the streets of N'Djamena in September 1963 were severely repressed, leading to thirty to forty deaths and the imprisonment of the three leaders. Hence, dominated by Tombalbaye, the regime had evolved towards authoritarianism in spite of the maintenance of representative institutions.

In 1964 reports of widespread discontent as a result of the mismanagement, corruption, and abuses of southern officials in the Islamicized areas reached the capital. These situations, together with the exclusion of Muslims from meaningful roles in the central government, fueled a rebellion in the east in November 1965 and in the BET Prefecture among the Toubou nomads in early 1968. The National Liberation Front of Chad (Front de Libération Nationale du Tchad, FROLINAT), which had been established in Sudan in 1966, later assumed leadership of the revolt. French military intervention in April 1969 at Chad's request under a defense cooperation agreement led to a number of successful offenses against the rebels. After the withdrawal of French troops in August 1972, FROLINAT's northern forces began to receive aid from the regime of Mu'ammar Gadhafi of Libya.[5]

In the meantime, the worsening drought of the early 1970s contributed to a deteriorating political situation. Drought relief efforts by international agencies were hindered by the government's insensitivity to human suffering and by overt profiteering. Erosion of support in the south in the face of continued tyranny and abuses as well as conflict with top military officers led to a coup by army officers originating from the south on April 13, 1975, during which Tombalbaye was killed. Although presidential absolutism ended, the Higher Military Council (Conseil Supérieur Militaire, CSM) headed by General Félix Malloum that resulted from the coup proved to be incapable of dealing effectively with the country's problems and the renewed rebellion of FROLINAT.

Within FROLINAT, which was always a loose coalition of northern and eastern groups opposed to the southern-dominated governments, a major split occurred in 1976 as a result of differences involving personalities and tactics. Hissène Habré (b. 1942), a French university graduate and member of the Anakaza branch of the Toubou people, was replaced as FROLINAT's leader in the north by Goukouni Oueddei. Goukouni was a son of the *derde* or arbiter of a different branch of the Toubou at Bardai. Whereas Habré actively opposed Libya's occupation in 1973 of the Aouzou strip,[6] a desert area believed to contain uranium, Goukouni soft-pedaled the issue in order to obtain arms aid from Gadhafi against the Malloum regime. As Goukouni's forces gained ground, the CSM negotiated an agreement with Habré's Armed Forces of the North giving him the post of prime minister in a new government.[7]

The Fundamental Charter of August 29, 1978, formulated by this coalition specified in its Article 24 the program of action of the new regime: "To elect a Constituent Assembly charged with setting up institutions; to install a democratic political life which guarantees the secular character of the state, [and] the liberty and fundamental rights of the individual."[8] The agreement could not be implemented, however, because of the long civil war that ravaged Chad between 1979 and 1982. During that conflict Libya supported Goukouni, whose gains brought about the collapse of the Malloum-Habré regime in March 1979. But ultimately Habré, aided by France and the United States, defeated Goukouni and came to power in June 1982.[9]

Thereafter, on September 29, 1982, Habré proclaimed the Fundamental Act of the Republic. Article 18 of this provisional constitution declared: "Under the authority of this president of the republic the government has responsibility for . . . the installation of democratic political life that guarantees the fundamental liberties and rights of individuals, associations, and collectivities, [and] the effective participation of all social levels in the management of public affairs."[10] An appointed National Advisory Council functioned as a provisional parliament. Habré proclaimed himself president of the republic, with his party directing the institutions of the state without any limitations on its authority. Anxious to rally the whole country to his side and pressured by France, whose army supported him against Libya, Habré proclaimed on June 22, 1984, the dissolution of the Armed Forces of the North and the creation of a new party, the National Union for Independence and the Revolution (Union Nationale pour l'Indépendance et la Révolution, UNIR), in which "all the sons of Chad" were called to participate.[11]

Thanks to the mediation of President Omar Bongo of Gabon, negotiations resulted in the rallying of the different armed opposition groups. The agreement on national reconciliation signed at Libreville on November 11, 1985, noted "the manifest will of the Chadian people to engage in a real democratic life, enabling them to acquire institutions of their own choice." It also provided for "the adoption by referendum of a constitution that would regulate the political and administrative life of the nation, if circumstances permitted, in a reasonable time frame."[12] A second agreement in Libreville on December 23, 1985, provided for the participation of the signatory political organizations in the management of the state at all levels and the adoption of a new constitution within five years. The primary concern here, however, was the division of power among organizations that had confronted one another with arms rather than the consultation of the people—much less the exercise of individual liberties. There was no free press in the country, and illegal arrests, often accompanied by torture and summary executions, persisted. Membership in the UNIR and payment of party dues were obligatory. Until 1987 the country lived in an atmosphere of war against Libya and the armed opposition groups that Libya supported.[13]

Political Reform Under Habré

In 1988, when peace had been restored, Habré judged it timely to soften the regime. He was encouraged to do this by both France and the United States. Through Decree 333 of July 8, 1988, he created a constitutional committee responsible for the establishment of new institutions within five months. Under the presidency of Jean Bawoyeu Alingué, a former ambassador to Washington and to Paris (1977–1979), the committee included civil servants, jurists, former political figures, and some of Habré's supporters. This committee launched a long inquiry, sent out missions, and distributed questionnaires. Its activities, above all, interested the educated elite. Not surprisingly, after years of conflict and economic distress, the masses of people showed more concern about peace and security than about constitutional arrangements.

In preparation for the UNIR congress that met at N'Djamena starting on November 23, 1988, regional congresses were held in all fourteen prefectures during which people were able to express themselves freely. During these proceedings party members directed virulent criticisms against the abuses of the army, police, and customs officials. At the opening of the congress Habré promised the civil servants full payment of their salaries, which were in arrears, but did not announce any immediate liberalization of his regime. He rapidly reviewed the preliminary projects for a new constitution submitted by the constitutional committee.[14] After a few amendments by the congress, the text was discussed by the National Advisory Committee, the Steering Committee of the UNIR, and finally the Council of Ministers—all bodies that were reluctant to contradict the president.[15]

In the referendum of December 10, 1989, the voters were asked through a single ballot both to adopt the new constitution and to elect Habré as president for seven years. The results contained no surprises. Of the 2,893,275 registered voters, 2,670,825 cast ballots, all but 16,025 of them endorsing both the constitution and Habré. Opponents revealed themselves, mainly in N'Djamena and in the Logone and Middle-Shari. Usually electors arriving at the polling places received only the white "yes" ballot. Nevertheless, a few courageous presidents of polling places let the voters take the red "no" ballot.[16]

The new constitution was promulgated on December 20, 1989, and Habré was inaugurated as president two days later. The constitution discussed at length the liberties and rights of citizens, including respect for physical integrity, freedom of movement and of information, and freedom from arbitrary arrest. Yet this constitution did not provide for the establishment of a truly democratic regime. The institutions were dominated by the president of the republic, who was elected by direct suffrage for a renewable seven-year term. The president nominated and dismissed his ministers, who were responsible only to him. A national assembly elected for five years adopted the laws but lacked the means to censure or remove the government. In fact, the regime was openly authoritarian. The Supreme Court was never nominated. In daily life public liberties were nonexistent as the police and the army continued to extort, arrest, and torture the citizenry.[17]

At the beginning of 1990 the official press announced "a new era of democracy and state of law for our country," which in no way corresponded to reality.[18] Nevertheless, the idea of liberty was taking its course, especially after the collapse of the communist system throughout Eastern Europe in 1989. The Chadian opposition was growing stronger outside the country. France, still the principal financial supporter of Chad, began to preach democratization. On January 5, 1990, Jacques Pelletier, the minister of cooperation, invited Africa not to remain apart from the freedom movement that was shaking Eastern Europe.[19] Then at the conference at La Baule, France, from June 19 to 21, 1990, which brought together the leaders of the countries of francophone Africa, President François Mitterrand joined the campaign for liberal reform.[20] In the Council of Ministers on June 21, Mitterrand declared: "France will aid as many countries as will make efforts to evolve towards democracy."[21] Habré courageously replied: "We are being asked to democratize. This requires an evolution and groundwork. It cannot be a style of the season."[22]

In April 1990 the Chadian government decided that the elections to the National Assembly would be free. Independent candidates would be allowed to compete alongside those of the UNIR, and the latter would have no official endorsement. During the elections of July 8, 1990, 436 candidates competed for the 123 seats to be filled. The balloting took place at the level of the sixty-five subprefectures, which, depending on their population, elected one or more deputies. Numerous indicators show that these elections were as free as they possibly could have been in a country such as Chad, where since May 31, 1959, the voters had been able to endorse only a single list presented by those in power. First of all, 43.9 percent of the registered voters did not cast ballots, which proved that they were not forced to do so and that, more concerned about peace than political debates, they were not interested in the election. Secondly, because the votes were divided among a large number of candidates in a single round of voting, each of the winners received only a small number of ballots and thus represented only a minority of the voters. Finally, some important UNIR personalities were defeated, including Issa Outman at N'Djamena and Colonel Nadjita at Goré in the Eastern Logone, despite secret financial support from those in power.

Those elected included civil servants (54.51 percent) as well as numerous canton chiefs descended from those who had served during the colonial period, which proved the permanence of certain rural elites. Voter turnout was high in the south (73 percent in Tandjilé, 67 percent in Mayo-Kebbi, 65 percent in the Western Logone) but low in the north (30 percent in Batha, 35 percent in Kanem, 39 percent in the Lake Prefecture). These results, with figures resembling those of the 1959 elections, indicated some continuity in political attitudes.[23]

The National Assembly, which met on August 5, elected Jean Alingué as its new president. It began its regular session on October 2, but the subsequent fall of the Habré regime ended its existence prematurely.[24]

In 1988 and 1989 Habré encountered growing dissatisfaction among some of those who had brought him to power concerning the extent of the benefits that they were receiving from his regime. From April 1, 1989, he had to contend with the dissidence of Idriss Déby (b. 1952), a professional soldier and a former commander in chief of the armed forces. Déby, a member of the Bideyat people of Ennedi Sub-Prefecture, had served with Habré's forces against Goukouni. After the failure of a plot by high-ranking Bideyat and Zaghawa officials to overthrow Habré, Déby had fled to Sudan. From a base there, with aid from Libya, he periodically undertook attacks upon sites in eastern Chad. In March 1990 Déby and his supporters, known subsequently as the Patriotic Movement of Salvation (Mouvement Patriotique du Salut, MPS), invaded eastern Chad. France thereupon dispatched military equipment and personnel to Abéché, capital of Ouaddai Prefecture. Although the French contingent did not participate in the military engagements, its presence undoubtedly influenced the rebels' decision to retreat.

But then in November 1990 Déby retook the offensive. Habré's troops, twice defeated, fled or joined the ranks of the victors. On December 2, 1990, Déby's forces entered N'Djamena. Habré fled to Cameroon and from there took refuge in Senegal. The French ambassador failed in his attempt to have National Assembly President Alingué serve as interim president as specified by the constitution. Déby's first deed was the suspension of the constitution and the dissolution of both the National Assembly and the UNIR.[25]

France's motives for not aiding Habré, whom it had been assisting militarily prior to the November offensive, are not entirely clear. Nor is it clear whether France merely stood by and allowed Déby to oust Habré or whether it secretly assisted Déby.[26] What is certain is that France continued its aid to Chad and quite likely encouraged the United States also to do so.[27]

The Course of Political Reform Under Déby

Had Habré been able to remain in power, it is possible that the National Assembly, despite its weakness, could have overshadowed him in the long run and perhaps contributed to the liberalization of his regime. Likewise, if Déby had maintained the Assembly, he could have claimed a certain legitimacy for himself, for it was obvious that Hissène Habré had few supporters among the deputies. Déby's victory, by dislodging a much-feared president, could have preserved Hissène

Habré's finest accomplishment: giving Chad a legislature freely chosen by the people.

But having wiped out the past, Déby was determined to begin the "groundwork" mentioned by Hissène Habré at La Baule. Déby brought with him the new party, the MPS, which he had created in Sudan on March 10, 1990, by merging his original companions of the Movement of April 1[28] with other groups that were unyieldingly opposed to Habré and located outside the country. On December 4, 1990, the National Council of Salvation (Conseil National du Salut, CNS), the MPS's governing body, put together a provisional state council that included a majority drawn from MPS members plus a few who had served in the Habré regime, such as Alingué. Déby's first message to the nation on December 4 promised "the establishment of a democracy . . . a real, complete, and pluralist democracy." Déby claimed that "the patriotic forces were bringing the dearest gift: neither gold nor silver but freedom."[29]

Attempting to keep these promises quickly proved to be difficult, for Déby's power rested on might. For a long time he had belonged to Hissène Habré's group of supporters and had participated in their repressions, notably in September 1984.[30] Following Déby's installation in power, individuals close to the former president began to reappear in public but were not arrested. Those who had fought under the MPS banner wanted government positions and were not about to yield them to others chosen by universal suffrage. Many of them would have preferred that the MPS simply replace the UNIR outright.[31]

On February 28, 1991, in his role as president of the CNS, Déby issued a provisional constitution called the "National Charter."[32] Its preamble proclaimed the regime's commitment to the Declaration of the Rights of Man of 1789 and 1948 and to the principle of pluralist democracy. Inaugurated as president under this charter on March 4, 1991, Déby was to be assisted by a prime minister, whom he would name, and by a provisional advisory council. The charter would become null and void as a soon as a new constitution was adopted, which was supposed to take place at the latest before the end of June 1993. Alingué, who was appointed to the prime ministership, which was a new position in Chad, had very little real power. Déby had thus opted for a temporary quasi dictatorship despite the increasingly intense pressure of the opposition. Nevertheless, freedom of the press was gaining increasing effectiveness,[33] with weekly and bimonthly publications being created in great numbers. Almost all of them showed hostility toward the MPS, the most outspoken being the *N'Djaména-Hebdo*. Public opinion had been awakened, particularly in the cities, and people were no longer afraid to speak out. Moreover, there were no longer any political prisoners.

During the process of consulting representatives from all the prefectures before publishing the National Charter, Déby had received a "Memorandum of the Leaders and Populations of the Southern Zone" dated February 8, 1991, which requested the convening of a national conference.[34] A powerful movement of opinion uniting almost all the elites of the country, both northern and southern, endorsed this request, and the press vigorously backed them up. Though fearful of alienating his entourage, Déby had to deal with these new forces, and in the end he yielded to them. On May 16, 1991, a presidential communiqué announced the convening in May 1992 of a national conference that would draft a constitution for submission in a referendum.[35] This decision marked a complete change in the democratic reform process, since the provisional national charter had given the government alone—essentially Déby—responsibility for creating new political institutions. The press, joyfully orchestrating the retreat of the government, demanded that the national conference be "sovereign,"[36] as had been the case in a number of other francophone African states.

Political reform, however, had actually begun before the convening of the national conference as a result of the legal recognition of opposition parties. A pluralist democracy assumes the existence of more than one political party, and in fact several had been created at various times under legislation dating back to the Tombalbaye era.[37] This legislation, in principle, permitted the creation of new parties, even if earlier opposition parties had been dissolved. In reality, however, such new parties could only function with the approval of the government, and no one since 1990 had dared to request such authorization.[38] Decree No. 15 of October 4, 1991, thus set forth the rules for the creation and organization of political parties. Parties had to have at least thirty founding members originating from ten different prefectures, with at least three from each one. This regulation obviously aimed at avoiding ethnically based parties. Likewise, the decree specified that no party could have a religious or military basis. Furthermore, the request had to be submitted to the Ministry of the Interior, which then would decide within three months whether to grant legal status to the party. A refusal by the ministry could, however, be challenged before an administrative court. Parties could accept donations only from Chadian citizens. The decree exempted the MPS from seeking new authorization. Although the terms of the decree appear restrictive, they were not applied in a repressive manner. Thus the first parties were legalized on March 10, 1992, and by the end of the year there were thirty authorized parties.[39]

The liberalization of political life continued slowly. On November 19, 1991, at the fourth conference of the heads of francophone states at Chaillot Palace in Paris, President Mitterrand recognized the right of African countries to determine their own procedures and pace of democratization.[40] Shortly thereafter, on December 24, Déby created a commission responsible for the national conference, to which a decree granted sovereign powers. This eighty-member commission presented its report in July 1992. Meanwhile, on May 22, the president had nominated a new prime minister, Joseph Yodoyman, who formed a government that included representatives of the opposition parties.[41]

The preparations for the sovereign national conference having been delayed, Déby issued Decree No. 54 of November 1992 creating a tripartite commission composed of representatives from the government, the parties, and civil society (e.g., the unions and the League of the Rights of Man). Chaired by the minister of the interior, Koibla Djimasta, the commission was in fact to prepare for the debates of the conference and deal with the immediate financial problems. The French government had pushed as much as it could in calling for the conference. Both France and the United States promised to subsidize its expenses. Déby traveled to Paris several times and while there was encouraged to accept the existence of a hostile press. In addition, numerous leaders of the new parties enjoyed the support and the assistance of the French Socialist Party, which then held power. The opening of the national conference was rescheduled for January 15, 1993.[42]

Déby's entourage, which included members of his fighting movement, his ethnic group, and the MPS, did not bear sole responsibility for the delay in convening the national conference. Pressing domestic matters in 1991 and 1992 also contributed. Although there had been no freedom under Habré, Chad had at least experienced peace, and most basic services functioned. Beginning in 1991, however, insecurity spread throughout the country, particularly because of the activities of armed former combatants, most of them young people, who had come from Sudan following Déby's victory. They looted, stole, and murdered in both the capital and rural areas. Déby's efforts to reorganize the army and to reduce its numbers achieved little success despite the French financial and technical assistance that was used to reorganize the gendarmerie. Journalists who criticized the army were assassinated and the director of the League of the Rights of Man was killed in the streets of N'Djamena on February 16, 1992. Even within the MPS there was a bloody settling of accounts. Déby's hand was forced by one of his former close fighting companions, Abbas Koti Yacoub, a Zaghawa, who ended up as a dissident in Cameroon in June 1992. In the south an armed opposition movement, the Committee of National Start-Up for Peace and Democracy (Comité du Sursaut National pour la Paix et la Démocratie, CSNPD), surfaced in February 1992. The CSNPD was directed by Lieutenant Moïse Ketté Nodji, who demanded the establishment of a federal republic. The CSNPD gained sympathizers and supporters among southerners who had been victimized by northern officials and herders who pastured on their fields.[43]

The general disorder and the powerful grip of undisciplined soldiers and looters on the customs service led to large-scale fraud that deprived the state of three-fourths of its revenues. Because of the resulting scarcity of funds, civil servants were not paid; strikes began, notably in the educational sector; and the economic situation deteriorated. The few factories that were still functioning closed down one after another, and the state-run cotton purchasing company found itself in very real trouble.

In this unsettling atmosphere much was expected from the national conference. As in other francophone states, the conference did not receive its mandate through elections. Rather, its members were chosen by consensus during the meetings of the tripartite commission. The 830 delegates were drawn from five categories: (1) 116 representatives from among public officials, including cabinet ministers, members of the provisional council, prefects, mayors, judges, army offi-

cers, and ambassadors; (2) 264 representatives designated by the thirty-seven authorized political parties and politico-military organizations, some of the latter of
which were in exile; (3) 130 representatives from civic associations, professional
organizations, and unions (58 members from the latter); (4) 176 representatives
of the population in general, including 112 sultans and canton chiefs, 28 farmers,
28 herders, and 8 from religious bodies (four Muslims, two Catholics, two Protestants) (the chiefs, farmers, and herders had in most cases been selected by the prefects); (5) 144 "resource persons"—a neologism referring to important national
personalities, including political figures and high civil servants who, though no
longer holding office, were considered qualified experts.

Although the national conference thus included 830 voting delegates, its composition was always changing and never more than 780 of them participated in
the most important votes. A majority of the delegates belonged to the middle
class (i.e., civil servants, salaried employees, and party officials whose political
bases were weak because there had been no elections), and individuals largely dependent upon the state (the civil servants and canton chiefs, in particular). All of
the Chadian intelligentsia were there and for the most part were very critical of
the regime.[44]

Opening on January 15, 1993, with a somber speech by President Déby, the
conference lasted nearly three months, until April 7, though it was supposed to
have lasted only one month. Among the body's first decisions was to keep the existing president and government in power during the duration of its sessions. On
January 19, it decided that the sovereignty of the conference would be exercised
only after the completion of its work. The conference wasted much time in personal disputes and unproductive discussions. It failed to focus on its basic mission, which was to formulate proposals for new institutions that could be submitted directly to the people in a referendum. The conference adopted rules of
procedure only on January 28, and not until February 13 was a presidium responsible for directing the debates able to take charge. The presidium was led by Maurice Adoum Helbongo, a former minister under Tombalbaye and one-time official
of the International Labor Organization. He was elected with 409 votes over Kassiré Koumakoye, an administrator who was a former minister under Hissène
Habré and now a leader of an opposition party. Then followed "communications"
in which each delegate depicted an ideal Chad without formulating any concrete
proposals. Pressed for time and short of funds, the conference quickly had to
adopt a provisional constitution called the "Charter of Transition."[45]

Under the same conditions, on April 6, 1993, the conference elected a transitional prime minister. The delegates chose Fidèle Moungar, a southerner who was
formerly a surgeon in France and who now headed an opposition party. Moungar
received 444 votes to Adoum Helbongo's 334. To the new prime minister the conference turned over a rather utopian government program entitled *cahier des
charges* (literally, a compilation of specific things that should be done). The conference elected a Superior Council of the Transition (Conseil Supérieur de la

Transition, CST) composed of fifty-seven members, its majority from opposition parties, to serve as a provisional parliament. To this body it assigned the implementation of a schedule for establishing a new democratic constitution and the holding of elections.

The failure of the national conference deeply disappointed the Chadian people, especially the urban population, which had passionately followed the radio and television broadcasts of the debates. In the end the conference was only able to initiate a slow transitional process that left Déby in power for one year and pushed back the date of the elections, which were the very foundation of democracy. The new parties, which had not obtained legitimacy through popular vote and were as fractious as they were numerous, also showed disappointment.[46]

Moungar's tenure as prime minister was marked by constant conflicts with both President Déby and the CST. Following the massacres perpetrated by the Presidential Guard (PG) in the Eastern Logone in March and April 1993 in the course of suppressing the CSNPD, Moungar sent an inquiry commission to the region. Déby, however, buried its findings, which were critical of the PG. In September Déby forced Moungar to replace the minister of finances, who had taken initiatives that would have reduced the financial resources of the presidency. In a radio broadcast Déby even accused Moungar of amateurism and frivolity.

As for the CST, on June 24, 1993, it forced the prime minister to reduce the size of his government, which its members judged plethoric. Although under the transitional charter the prime minister was responsible to the CST for ensuring the stability of the executive branch, he could only be removed from power by a two-thirds majority. Nevertheless, on October 28 the CST censured Moungar by a vote of forty-five to ten. As a result he was required to yield his office to a new prime minister elected by the CST, Kassiré Koumakoye, who thus obtained his revenge. There is no doubt that President Déby played a role in the fall of Moungar. By this time, through pressures and benefits to CST members, Déby was gaining influence over a majority.[47]

The internal situation remained bad throughout 1993. Often bloody demonstrations took place in Moundou in June, at Ouaddai on August 4, and in the capital on August 8. A high administrator in charge of reorganizing the army was assassinated in the streets on June 26. After having signed a reconciliation agreement, Abbas Koti Yacoub returned to Chad. But he was then accused of conspiracy and was killed at the time of his arrest on October 22. Former and current soldiers continued to close off roads and to extort money from drivers and passengers. In addition, the poor economic situation persisted. The devaluation of the CFA franc on January 11, 1994, substantially increased the cost of living. Civil servants, who had not been paid in months, went on strike on several occasions and, by the end of the year, the paralysis of the state was almost total. School and university examinations could not take place.[48]

On April 5, 1994, in the face of these difficulties and influenced by the president, the CST voted (forty-eight to zero, with three abstentions), under the terms of the charter, to extend the transitional period by one year.[49] Subsequently a constitution of 235 articles was produced by Chad's leading jurists.[50] Unfortunately, the document seems excessively long and complex, and several of its provisions would appear difficult to implement in such a poor country with so little democratic experience. The institutions prescribed by the constitution include a president elected for a five-year term by universal suffrage, a National Assembly, a Senate elected by local collectivities (which do not yet exist), and a government or cabinet responsible to the National Assembly. Moreover, the constitution calls for the establishment of multiple institutions that would be difficult to create and to finance (such as a Constitutional Council, Supreme Court, High Court of Justice, and so on) as well as an administrative decentralization that would be completely new to Chad. This constitution was to take effect only following possible amendments by the government, examination by the CST, and approval by popular referendum at the end of 1994 or in 1995.

Further complicating the picture, part of the elite in the south favors a federal system, which would be difficult to implement, and which would undoubtedly revive tensions between the north and the south. During the national conference these tensions surfaced most sharply during a polemic debate on the language question. Many northerners favored a more extensive use of Arabic, which, along with French, has been an official language since 1978. Southern opposition to such a course led to a lively exchange of hostile words. Nevertheless, few southerners seem disposed to get involved in a struggle over decentralization, which might constitute the first steps towards secession.[51]

In addition, there is the question of economic liberalization. The core of the modern economy rests in the hands of the state and of the public companies that it directs. Although Decree No. 17 of August 29, 1992, provided for a certain number of privatizations, very few have been undertaken so far. The main reason for this situation is the extremely small amount of local capital and the unwillingness of external capital to enter Chad until security has been assured.[52]

During the remainder of 1994 and throughout 1995 adoption of the constitution was stalled, which meant that the holding of parliamentary and presidential elections was delayed. In the meantime, the president, as master of the most solid portion of the armed forces and of the best organized party (the MPS) as well as of the prime minister, who had little autonomy, seemed to dominate the situation.

When Déby announced plans on November 19, 1994, for presidential elections on April 9 the following year,[53] without first securing the agreement of the CST for a constitutional referendum, and launched a grassroots campaign, he collided with the president of the CST, Lol Mahamat Choa.[54] Though Déby succeeded in ousting Lol, whom a compliant CST on October 15 replaced by Mahamat Bachar, a MPS loyalist,[55] he did not get away with having an MPS-dominated commission conduct the required electoral census. The opposition parties successfully challenged his attempts to exclude them in a case before the Supreme Court. At the same time, France, the European Union, and the United States, which had been solicited to finance the census, asked for a consensus among the political parties on the census commission's membership and functioning.[56] Déby had to retreat and name an independent national electoral commission, which was slowly put into place.[57]

Then, when Prime Minister Kassiré Koumakoye indicated that he too wished to become a presidential candidate, the CST granted Déby's request to modify the transitional charter to prevent him from doing so. On April 8, 1995, the CST also replaced Kassiré Koumakoye with Koibla Djimasta.[58] In both of these cases, the CST appeared to be under the control of the president.[59] Earlier, on March 31, the CST had extended the transition and Déby's term as president until April 9, 1996.[60]

Encouraged by these successes, the authoritarian regime once again violated freedom of the press. On June 1, 1995, agents of the National Security Agency (the secret police) sacked the office of *N'Djaména-Hebdo* following its publication of an article claiming that a minority containing many Sudanese continued to dominate the army. This outrage brought forth virulent protests and led to an official apology.[61]

During the same period, the Déby regime experienced both gains and losses in terms of its control of the national territory. At the end of May 1994 Libyan troops left the Aouzou strip in compliance with the decision of the International Court of Justice in early February supporting Chad's ownership of the disputed region.[62] In June the Movement for Democracy and Development (Mouvement pour la Démocratie et le Développement, MDD), composed of partisans of Hissène Habré whom he may be funding from his exile in Senegal, inflicted losses on government troops in the region of Lake Chad.[63] On August 10, 1994, the CSNPD rallied to the regime under terms by which Moïse Ketté and 130 of his followers gained high officer rank in the national army and Ketté later became a cabinet minister.[64] But a dissident faction of the CSNPD, called the Armed Forces for the Federal Republic (Forces Armées pour la République Fédérale, FARF), led by Laokein Bardé, once again took up arms in the Logone, urging among other things the establishment of a federal state that would give southerners a large role in their own affairs. This group wishes to put an end to the continuing abuses by northern officials and troops as well as to control a portion of the revenues from the petroleum around Doba that is scheduled for production starting in 1998.[65] On September 22 the minister of mines and energy, Mahamat Garfa, accompanied by 600 to 1,000 troops, crossed into the Dar Fur Province of Sudan, where they may be joining Zaghawa dissidents still loyal to the late Abbas Koti Yacoub.[66] In July 1995 several different external opposition groups, including that of Goukouni Oueddei, signed an agreement to unite. Such arrangements, however, are only a façade, for practically the only thing they have in common is a desire to overthrow Déby.[67] At the same time, in nearly all of the country, anarchy, banditry, and violence reigned, in large part because of the uncontrolled military elements brought into Chad by Déby's taking of power.[68]

To make matters worse, the administration is dominated by the close relatives of the president, who have multiplied their fraud and diversion of funds.[69] A scandal even broke out in the CST, where embezzlements were committed. As a result, in August 1995 the CST dismissed its executive board, which it judged responsible.[70] Civil servants, whether paid or unpaid, were not working very much. Generally they received their pay only after long delays and because of advances from France to the treasury. Secondary and university students, who often received their scholarships and maintenance grants many months late or in reduced amounts, became more desperate. Violently hostile to the regime, some of them frequently indulged in destructive acts that were becoming increasingly extreme. On top of all of this, Chad became a center for traffic in arms and counterfeit currency.[71]

In July 1995 President Déby blamed the political parties for the delay in the electoral schedule.[72] On August 11 he promised that the transition would end in April 1996 at the latest.[73] In late November, under increased pressure from France, the national election commission set March 31, 1996, as the date for the constitutional referendum, June 2 for the presidential election, and December 22–24 for the legislative elections.[74] Because Déby has the support of the army and the party in power, he is well placed to win, especially since the opposition will doubtlessly divide their votes among many candidates. These elections will be meaningful, however, only if they are fair and if a minimum of security can be reestablished.[75] If the elections take place, they will represent the first time that the people have truly been consulted since the process of democratization began in July 1990.[76]

After thirty years of armed conflict, the masses of ordinary citizens would probably be satisfied with a stable authoritarian regime that would assure them peace, security, and justice. Among them there is no profound movement in favor of democracy. The desire for liberty and participation in public affairs emanates from the elite (civil servants, salaried persons, students, the educated), who are not numerous and who are divided by ethnic and religious differences as well as personal quarrels. At the national conference in 1993 these groups failed to secure meaningful reforms because of such divisions and their lack of realism. The CST, which resulted from the national conference, lacks democratic legitimacy and seems unable or unwilling to challenge the president. Along with the absence of political prisoners, the return of the freedoms of speech and press constitutes the only real progress so far towards the establishment of a democratic polity. Thus, in the face of regime attempts at self-perpetuation, insecurity, rebellion, and only partial functioning of state institutions, the path to further reform and democratization seems blocked.

Notes

1. The most complete bibliographies on Chad before 1990 are found in *Chad: A Country Study* (Washington, D.C.: U.S. Government Printing Office, 1990), and Samuel Decalo, *Historical Dictionary of Chad*, 2d ed. (Metuchen, N.J.: Scarecrow Press, 1987). For works of

the 1990s, see George Joffé and Valérie Day-Viaud, comps., *Chad* (Oxford: Clio, 1995). For works mainly in French, see Bernard Lanne, "Vingt livres sur le Tchad," *Cultures et développement* 14, no. 1 (1982):115–130, and Bernard Lanne, "Quinze ans d'ouvrages politiques sur le Tchad," *Afrique contemporaine*, no. 144 (October-December 1987):37–47. For a brief historical sketch of Chad since 1960, see Bernard Lanne, "Chad: Recent History," *Africa South of the Sahara: 1995* (London: Europa Publications, 1995), pp. 273–280.

2. Jean Chapelle, *Le peuple tchadien: Ses racines et sa vie quotidienne* (Paris: L'Harmattan, 1980), pp. 157–164, 196–234; Virginia Thompson and Richard Adloff, *Conflict in Chad* (Berkeley: Institute of International Studies, University of California, 1981), pp. 2–22.

3. David E. Gardinier, "French Colonial Education in Chad," *Africana Journal* 16 (1994):300–310; Bernard Lanne, "Chad, Chadians, and the Second World War, 1939–1945," *Africana Journal* 16 (1994):311–340.

4. *Chad: A Country Study*, pp. 14–16, 139–140; Bernard Lanne, "Scolarisation, fonction publique, et relations interethniques au Tchad," *Actes du IIIᵉ colloque Méga-Tchad, Paris, ORSTOM 11–12 septembre 1986* (Paris: Éditions de l'ORSTOM "Colloques et Séminaires," 1990), pp. 235–266.

5. Thompson and Adloff, *Conflict in Chad*, pp. 23–61; Bernard Lanne, "Nord et sud dans la vie politique du Tchad," *Le Mois en Afrique*, no. 172–173 (April-May 1980):104–111.

6. Bernard Lanne, *Tchad-Libye: La querelle des frontières* (Paris: Karthala, 1982).

7. Thompson and Adloff, *Conflict in Chad*, pp. 61–86; Michael P. Kelley, *A State in Disarray: Conditions of Chad's Survival* (Boulder: Westview Press, 1986), pp. 2–16.

8. *Afrique contemporaine*, no. 99 (September-October 1978):16–19.

9. *Chad: A Country Study*, pp. 150–151; René Lemarchand, "The Case of Chad," in René Lemarchand, ed., *The Green and the Black: Qadhafi's Policies in Africa* (Bloomington: Indiana University Press, 1988), pp. 106–124.

10. The Fundamental Act was published by decree on October 18, 1982. See *Afrique contemporaine*, no. 125 (January-March 1983), pp. 58–61.

11. *Chad: A Country Study*, pp. 151–153.

12. *Afrique contemporaine*, no. 138 (April-June 1986):62–64.

13. Ibid., pp. 64–65; Lanne, "Chad: Recent History," pp. 275–276.

14. *Infotchad: Bulletin de l'Agence Tchadienne de Presse*, November 15, 1988. For the evolution of the Habré regime, see William J. Foltz, "Reconstructing the State of Chad," in I. William Zartman, ed., *Collapsed States: The Disintegration and Restoration of Legitimate Authority* (Boulder: Westview Press, 1995), pp. 15–31.

15. *Infotchad*, April 1, 1989.

16. The results of the referendum are contained in *Infotchad*, December 15–16, 1989. The figures published in *Marchés tropicaux et méditerranéens*, December 31, 1993, p. 3213, differ slightly.

17. *Economist* Intelligence Unit, *Country Report: Chad* (hereafter cited as EIU, *CR Chad*), no. 1 (1990):31–32.

18. *Infotchad*, January 30, 1990.

19. *Marchés tropicaux et méditerranéens*, January 12, 1990, p. 87. In France the minister of cooperation has charge of aid to African states. For changing French policy in this period, see François Gaulme, "France-Afrique: Une crise de coopération," *Études*, no. 3801 (January 1994):41–52, and Guy Martin, "Francophone Africa in the Context of Franco-African Relations," in John W. Harbeson and Donald Rothchild, eds., *Africa in World Politics: Post–Cold War Challenges*, 2d edition (Boulder: Westview Press, 1995), pp. 163–188.

20. This was the sixteenth Franco-African Summit Conference of Heads of State. See *Marchés tropicaux et méditerranéens*, June 29, 1990, pp. 1833–1838.

21. *Politique étrangère de la France: Textes et documents*, May-June 1990, pp. 125–130.

22. *Le Point,* June 25, 1990.

23. Republic of Chad, Ministry of Interior and Administration of the Territory, National Committee of Legislative Elections, *Summary Table of the Results of the Legislative Elections of July 8, 1990* (N'Djamena, 1990).

24. EIU, *CR Chad*, no. 4 (1990):33; EIU, *CR Chad*, no. 1 (1991):36.

25. Lanne, "Chad: Recent History," pp. 276–277; EIU, *CR Chad*, no. 1 (1991):36–37.

26. French Foreign Minister Roland Dumas observed that "the time is past when France chose rulers for a country, changed governments, and maintained them as she wished. France was present in Chad from February 1986 [on] to stop a foreign invasion. She left in place Opération Épervier (Sparrowhawk) to dissuade any foreign power (in this case Libya) from returning to Chadian territory. But France decided not to interfere in conflicts between Chadians." Also there was in France a legacy of ill-feeling against Habré as a result of the kidnapping of Françoise Claustre and the murder of Major Pierre Galopin, who was sent to negotiate her release, during the 1970s. EIU, *CR Chad*, no. 1 (1991):38. A book published in 1995, *Au coeur du secret*, by Claude Silberzahn, who headed the Direction Générale de la Sécurité Extérieure (DGSE, France's external security service) from 1989 to 1993, "claims that the Chadian president owed his arrival in power in 1990 to the DGSE, which 'could exercise a strong influence on the Chadian system' through him." Cited in EIU, *CR Chad*, no. 2 (1995):33. Further, it was widely believed that France's lack of support reflected Habré's refusal to initiate a transition towards multiparty democracy. Lanne, "Chad: Recent History," p. 277. Ted Killam contends that France allowed Habré to be ousted because he had entrusted the development of Chad's petroleum to a consortium of American companies. Déby acted immediately to replace one of them with the French parastatal, Elf-Aquitaine. Ted Killam, "Chad: A State in Disarray," *Africa Report* 40 (May-June 1995):39–41.

27. EIU, *CR Chad*, no. 1 (1991):38. Chad's national budget during 1994 was $360 million, according to EIU, *CR Chad*, no. 2 (1994):41. During 1992 Chad received $249,400,000 in grants and loans from external sources, including $94.2 million in bilateral aid from France, $24 million from the United States, and $19.4 million from Germany.

28. This is the name that Déby's troops had given themselves.

29. Robert Buijtenhuijs, *La conférence nationale souveraine du Tchad* (Paris: Karthala, 1993), p. 15.

30. In southern Chad there were summary executions of important civil servants, organized massacres, and villages set afire. People in the country called this tragic period Black September. See Lanne, "Chad: Recent History," p. 18.

31. Jean-Pierre Magnant, "Le Tchad," in Gérard Conac, ed., *L'Afrique en transition vers le pluralisme politique* (Paris: Économica, 1993), pp. 387–392.

32. République du Tchad, Mouvement Patriotique du Salut, Conseil National du Salut, *Charte Nationale* (N'Djamena, 1991).

33. No text limited this freedom, but the preceding regimes had not allowed its practice.

34. Personal archives; document signed by sixty-nine individuals representing the Western Logone, Eastern Logone, Middle-Shari, and Tandjilé. The absence of the Mayo-Kebbi was noted.

35. *Le Monde*, May 18, 1991.

36. The adjective "sovereign" was not used in Déby's interview, published in *Jeune Afrique*, June 12–18, 1991, pp. 35–52.

37. Decree No. 27 of July 28, 1962, *Journal officiel de la République du Tchad*, August 15, 1962.

38. The text of Decree No. 15 of October 4, 1991, addressing the creation, functioning, and dissolution of political parties, was published in *N'Djaména-Hebdo*, no. 32, October 17, 1991.

39. EIU, *CR Chad*, no. 2 (1992):32; EIU, *CR Chad*, no. 1 (1993):30.

40. *Marchés tropicaux et méditerranéens*, November 29, 1991, pp. 3085–3089.

41. Buijtenhuijs, *La conférence nationale souveraine*, pp. 41–42.

42. Ibid., pp. 43–44.

43. Robert Buijtenhuijs, "La situation dans le sud du Tchad," *Afrique contemporaine* (July-September 1995):21–30.

44. Buijtenhuijs, *La conférence nationale souveraine*, pp. 45–56.

45. The transition charter (Act 2 of the Sovereign National Conference of April 4, 1993) was published in *N'Djaména-Hebdo*, special edition, no. 81 bis, April 8, 1993, pp. 10–11.

46. Buijtenhuijs, *La conférence nationale souveraine*, pp. 45–56.

47. EIU, *CR Chad*, no. 2 (1993):31–35; EIU, *CR Chad*, no. 3 (1993):27–32; EIU, *CR Chad*, no. 4 (1994):34–38; EIU, *CR Chad*, no. 1 (1994):32–36.

48. EIU, *CR Chad*, no. 3 (1993):33; EIU, *CR Chad*, no. 4 (1993):34–37; EIU, *CR Chad*, no. 1 (1994):37–39.

49. EIU, *CR Chad*, no. 2 (1994):34–46.

50. The constitutional project elaborated by the technical and institutional committee was published in *N'Djaména-Hebdo*, no. 125, March 31, 1994.

51. EIU, *CR Chad*, no. 2 (1993):33.

52. EIU, *CR Chad*, no. 1 (1993):35.

53. *Le Monde*, November 24, 1994, and January 21, 1995.

54. *N'Djaména-Hebdo*, September 15, 1994; October 20, 1994; and November 3, 1994; *Infotchad*, September 14, 1994; October 21, 24, 25, and 26, 1994; and November 29, 1994.

55. *N'Djaména-Hebdo*, October 20, 1994.

56. *N'Djaména-Hebdo*, October 6 and 13, 1994; March 16, 1995; and April 6, 1995; *Jeune Afrique*, February 16, 1995, p. 32, and March 23, 1995, p. 78; *Libération*, October 11, 1994; *Infotchad*, October 8, 1994; *Le Progrès*, February 21 and 28, 1995, and April 11, 1995.

57. *Le Monde*, February 24, 1995; *Jeune Afrique*, May 25, 1995, p. 55; *Infotchad*, June 12, 1995; *Le Progrès*, March 7, 1995; *N'Djaména-Hebdo* contains Law No. 44 of December 14, 1994, and Decree No. 396 of June 6, 1995, creating a national commission of electoral census.

58. *Jeune Afrique*, April 6, 1995, p. 9; *Le Monde*, April 1, 11, and 12, 1995; *N'Djaména-Hebdo*, March 16 and 23, 1995, and April 13 and 20, 1995; *Éléments d'information sur le Tchad*, no. 34, June 1995; *Le Progrès*, March 21, 1995, and April 4, 11, and 18, 1995.

59. *Jeune Afrique*, November 24, 1994; December 1 and 8, 1994; and April 20, 1995, p. 44; *Le Progrès*, May 23, 1995, and July 18, 1995; *N'Djaména-Hebdo*, March 27, 1995.

60. Killam, "Chad: A State in Disarray," pp. 39–41.

61. *Éléments d'information sur le Tchad*, no. 34, June 1995; *Le Journal des journaux indépendants*, June 14, 1995; *Le Progrès*, June 6, 1995; *N'Djaména-Hebdo*, May 18, 1995, and June 8, 1995.

62. EIU, *CR Chad*, no. 2 (1994):36–37.

63. *Marchés tropicaux et méditerranéens*, September 1, 1995, p. 1862; *Jeune Afrique*, November 10, 1994, p. 22–23, December 1, 1994, and July 6, 1995; *N'Djaména-Hebdo*, June 22, 1995; *Le Progrès*, June 20, 1995.

64. *N'Djaména-Hebdo*, September 8 and 22, 1994; *Infotchad*, September 1 and 26, 1994; October 29, 1994; *Jeune Afrique*, September 8, 1994; *Éléments d'information sur le Tchad*, no. 33, October 1994.

65. *Jeune Afrique*, July 6, 1995, p. 47; *Le Monde*, August 18, 1994; *Le Progrès*, March 28, 1995, and April 4 and 25, 1995.

66. EIU, *CR Chad*, no. 4 (1994):35, 38.

67. *Le Progrès*, April 18, 1995; *N'Djaména-Hebdo*, August 10, 1995.

68. *Le Progrès*, January 31, 1995.

69. *Le Monde*, December 21, 1994; *Le Progrès*, May 2 and 9, 1995; *N'Djaména-Hebdo*, August 17, 1995.

70. *Infotchad*, August 24, 1995; *N'Djaména-Hebdo*, July 27, 1995; *Le Progrès*, August 12 and 29, 1995.

71. *Le Monde*, December 21, 1994; *Le Progrès*, May 2 and 9, 1995; *N'Djaména-Hebdo*, August 17, 1995.

72. *Le Progrès*, July 18, 1995.

73. *N'Djaména-Hebdo*, August 10, 1995.

74. *West Africa*, November 27–December 3, 1995, p. 1824. On March 31, 1996, 60 percent of the electorate turned out to approve the constitution, with 63.5 percent voting for it and 36.5 against. The north voted overwhelmingly for the constitution, and the south, except for the Middle Shari (N'Djamena), against it.

75. *Le Progrès*, August 1, 1995; Killam, "Chad: A State in Disarray," pp. 39–41; William F.S. Miles, "Tragic Tradeoffs: Democracy and Security in Chad," *Journal of Modern African Studies* 33, no. 1 (1995):53–65.

76. In April 1993, with assistance from foreign states, Chad undertook a national census that showed a population of 6,287,561, of which 21 percent are urban and only 13.5 percent of those over fifteen years of age are literate. The religious distribution is 54 percent Muslim, 20 percent Catholic, 14 percent Protestant, and 7 percent Animist. *Marchés tropicaux et méditerranéens*, October 27, 1995, pp. 2357–2360. Complete census results are contained in Alain Beauvillain, *Tableau de la population du Tchad des années vingt à 1993* (N'Djamena: Centre National d'Appui à la Recherche, "Travaux et documents scientifiques du Tchad; documents pour la recherche," II, 1993).

Chapter Sixteen

Rwanda: Democratization and Disorder: Political Transformation and Social Deterioration

TIMOTHY LONGMAN

In less than a decade, Rwanda has changed from being a relatively stable country, recognized for its good governance and economic success[1] to being labeled "Africa's hell, pure and simple,"[2] a country torn by ethnic and political violence, civil war, famine, and the movement of millions of refugees. The wave of extreme brutality that swept the country after the death of President Juvénal Habyarimana in a mysterious plane crash on April 6, 1994, appeared to many outside observers to represent a spontaneous reaction to the killing of the president. In fact, as I attempt to demonstrate in this chapter, the cataclysm in which more than 500,000 people were killed in Rwanda in mid-1994 marked the culmination of a program of government-sponsored violence and intimidation intended to frustrate efforts to change the structures of power and democratize the political system. The terrible chaos that a relatively small group of state officials and their allies were able to orchestrate in their ultimately unsuccessful attempt to retain power should stand as a warning of the ease with which authoritarian rulers can obstruct democratic transitions and the difficulty of directing public discontent into constructive political channels.

A Troubled Beginning

Although Rwanda experienced a period of relative peace and prosperity in the 1970s and 1980s, political violence, ethnic conflict, and social turmoil are not new phenomena in the country. In fact, Rwanda embarked on independence with quite bleak prospects. Without access to the sea or substantial natural resources, the country's economic potential appeared dim. Even more troubling, the immediate pre-independence period was marred by violent ethnic conflict that appeared to presage social and political instability. In precolonial Rwanda, a complex and flexible political and social system maintained equilibrium between social groups. The cattle-raising Tutsi, who comprised about 15 percent of the population, dominated the political system, but some chieftaincies were available to Hutu. Furthermore, group membership remained relatively flexible, as wealthy cattle-owning Hutu could be incorporated into the Tutsi group. Twa, who made up only 1 percent of the population, enjoyed less mobility, but they were nevertheless incorporated into the system, pursuing specialized economic activities and providing vital services to the royal court. The three groups shared a common language and lived in close proximity throughout the territory, differing from one another most notably in occupation. Hence, in precolonial Rwanda the categories Tutsi, Hutu, and Twa appear to have been closer to castes than distinct ethnic groups.[3]

German and Belgian colonial policies, however, eliminated the precolonial system's flexibility and complexity and solidified social categories into distinct ethnic identities. Colonial support allowed Tutsi leaders to centralize their rule and gradually to enrich themselves at the expense of the Hutu majority. As a national independence movement began to emerge among the Tutsi elite in the late 1950s, the Hutu, who comprised 85 percent of the population, feared that in an independent country they would continue to be excluded from power and opportunity. Resentment by the Hutu peasants of their exploitation and impoverishment inspired a bloody uprising in 1959 that drove thousands of Tutsi into exile. The Belgian colonial administration suddenly shifted its allegiance to the Hutu, and over a two-year period placed Hutu leaders in nearly all official positions formerly held by Tutsi.[4]

Grégoire Kayibanda, former editor of the Catholic newspaper *Kinyamateka* and leader of the most outspoken Hutu advocacy group, the Party of the Movement for Hutu Emancipation (Parti du Mouvement pour l'Émancipation Hutu, PARMEHUTU), which transformed itself into a political party after the 1959 revolution, became the first president of independent Rwanda after elections in 1962. Although Rwanda under Kayibanda was officially a multiparty democracy, the overwhelming initial electoral victories of PARMEHUTU and the subsequent repression of competing parties made Rwanda a de facto single-party state.

PARMEHUTU's success as an ethnonationalist movement did not, however, translate into the ability to run a government successfully. Throughout the first decade of independence, the government increasingly appeared to suffer from incompetent management and to lack direction, and as a result public support for Kayibanda and PARMEHUTU gradually declined. The economy remained stagnant and ethnic tensions remained high throughout the Kayibanda regime. Sporadic invasions during the 1960s by groups of Tutsi refugees based in Tanzania, Burundi, Uganda, and Zaire led to bloody reprisals against Tutsi living in Rwanda. The perception among Hutu that Tutsi continued to dominate the schools and the economy fueled resentment over the unfulfilled promises of the revolution. The predominance within the government of people from Kayibanda's home region in the central part of Rwanda increased regional tensions, and corruption by public officials undermined the credibility of the government. Discontent with Kayibanda reached a peak in early 1973 when the government failed adequately to control popular protests that drove Tutsi from schools and jobs. In the wake of the resulting instability, Kayibanda moved to consolidate power in the hands of trusted associates from his region. Northern military officers whose positions were threatened staged a coup d'état on July 4–5, 1973, that installed Major General Juvénal Habyarimana as head of state.[5]

The Habyarimana Era and the Genesis of a Democracy Movement

Habyarimana attained power with considerable public support, and for over a decade he was able to maintain an image of competence and fairness both at home and abroad. Under the banner of "peace, unity, and development," Habyarimana directly confronted the conditions that had produced public discontent under Kayibanda. He implemented a system of ethnic quotas in education and employment to ensure that the Tutsi had no unfair advantage. He abolished existing political structures and established a single, populist political party, the National Revolutionary Movement for Development (Mouvement Révolutionnaire National pour le Développement, MRND), whose organization was influenced by the Chinese Communist Party model, to serve as a vehicle for linking people more closely to the government. Under Habyarimana's guidance, the economy improved modestly, with the gross domestic product (GDP) increasing at an annual rate of over 2 percent in the late 1970s and early 1980s. The MRND organized public participation in development in an effort to upgrade the infrastructure throughout the country; the most important program, *umuganda*, brought local communities together to labor in common to build roads and bridges, plant trees, and fight erosion. The image of stability and good governance that Habyarimana promoted attracted extensive international donor aid. This assistance, which grew from US$79 million in 1976 to over $150 million annually in the early 1980s, allowed the government to launch major infrastructural improvements and a variety of other development projects.[6]

Despite these successes, the problems of economic decline, ethnic and regional conflict, and official corruption that led to Kayibanda's demise resurfaced in the late 1980s. These problems served both to undermine Habyarimana's popularity and to inspire a democracy movement. Although the economy grew in the 1970s and 1980s, Rwanda remained among the poorest nations in Africa; in 1982 only eleven African states had lower per capita GDPs than Rwanda. With the second highest population density in the world and an urbanization rate of only 5 percent, overutilization of the land led to serious soil degradation and erosion. Population grew at a rate higher than that of food production beginning in 1977 or earlier, and even during the economic boom, population growth outpaced economic growth. Furthermore, the benefits of the economic growth of the 1970s were concentrated in a small commercial, military, and administrative elite. The standard of living for the majority of Rwandans was actually in decline throughout Habyarimana's tenure. During the 1980s economic decline became more readily apparent as the per capita gross national product fell at an average annual rate of 2.2 percent and a sharp drop in the price for Rwanda's main export, coffee, cut into export earnings. In 1989 alone, real GDP fell by 5.7 percent.[7]

The growing perception of a social and economic gulf between government officials and the majority of the population exacerbated frustrations with the government over the deteriorating economic situation. Even as the poverty of most Rwandans increased, government officials and their allies were able to accumulate substantial wealth. The opportunities for politicians, bureaucrats, and military personnel to gain personal benefits from their offices through both licit and illicit means gradually expanded during Habyarimana's term. With growing frequency, local administrators demanded calabashes of beer or other bribes from their poor constituents to carry out simple government functions. *Umuganda*, originally a means of bringing the population together to address communal needs, became a type of forced labor. For example, in many communities officials required peasants (but not members of the commercial or intellectual classes) to help plant communal forests, ostensibly for the use of the community, but when those who planted the trees needed wood, the officials required them to pay bribes. The wealth gained by the small group of people fortunate enough to be associated with the state was displayed ostentatiously in the construction of new homes and the purchase of cattle, cars, televisions, videocassette machines, and other luxuries, while the majority of the population was struggling simply to pay children's school fees, to buy clothes, and to feed their families. In this context, programs intended to popularize the government—such as *animation* (required public displays of patriotism and loyalty to the regime), *umuganda* (communal labor), and automatic membership in the MRND—were increasingly viewed as onerous and restrictive.[8]

The appearance of regional bias and nepotism in government practices contributed to public disaffection with the state. People in central and southern Rwanda accused Habyarimana of ensuring a disproportionate share of government investment for the north and of providing northerners with an advantage in the distribution of jobs and educational opportunities. A small clique of people from Habyarimana's region and family, known as the presidential *akazu*, increasingly dominated Rwanda's government and economy. The impression that Habyarimana and the *akazu* were running the country for their personal gain while neglecting the needs of the population helped to undermine the populist pretensions of the MRND. The 1987 assassination of Colonel Stanislas Mayuya, a popular public figure considered to be Habyarimana's likely successor as head of state, contributed to an appearance of intrigue in the consolidation of power around the president.[9]

A free press that emerged in Rwanda in the late 1980s confirmed public impressions of official corruption and economic decline. Prior to 1988, the government owned and operated most of the newspapers and periodicals in the country and used persuasion and threats to discourage the country's few independent publications from discussing issues that would reflect badly on the administration. In 1988, however, André Sibomana, the newly installed editor of the Catholic newspaper *Kinyamateka*, historically the most important paper in the country, began to publish candid articles about national economic and political issues. Although the government reacted by arresting several journalists associated with the paper, *Kinyamateka*'s breaking the taboo on honest discussion of public issues inspired other Rwandans to speak out more boldly. Within a two-year period, over twenty new newspapers and journals appeared in Rwanda; many of them, like *Kanguka*, took an overtly antigovernment line. The newspapers juxtaposed reports of official corruption and accounts of the lavish lifestyles of certain government figures against frank discussions of the country's economic troubles, such as a 1989 famine, thus affirming and reinforcing public alienation from the administration and the state.[10]

External political events in the late 1980s provided a model of political action for those Rwandans unhappy with their government. The outbreak of protests in some African countries, such as Sudan, South Africa, and Algeria, and the demise of authoritarian leaders in Burundi, Tunisia, Niger, and Burkina Faso in the late 1980s fueled public discussions of democratization in Rwanda as early as 1988.[11] The example of democracy movements in Eastern Europe and in parts of Africa paved the way for a democracy movement to develop out of the intensifying alienation from the state and general public discontent in Rwanda. By early 1990, intellectuals and others in Rwanda not only had become openly critical of the government but also were demanding specific political reforms to increase government accountability and access to the system.[12]

In 1990 pressure for Habyarimana and the MRND to accept political reforms built very quickly. In February 1990 the Catholic bishops of Rwanda issued a pastoral letter, "Christ, Our Unity," that condemned the growth of ethnic tensions, regionalism, nepotism, and official corruption in the country. Although the bishops specifically exonerated the president and treated the problems as individual rather than systemic, the letter lent credence to public complaints against the government. Following the success of the national conference in Benin in February, some Rwandans began to call for an end to the MRND's monopoly on power, the separation of party and state, the scheduling of a national conference to draft a new constitution, and the observance of free and fair elections. Some Tutsi began to air complaints at the limitations of the quota system and at their near exclusion from military and administrative employment. In May, the Catholic bishops issued a second part to "Christ, Our Unity," more openly critical of the government, in which they defended freedom of the press, supported human rights, and strongly condemned official corruption. In June, when a scuffle broke out at a concert in Butare after someone jumped queue, gendarmes opened fire on the crowd, killing one and injuring five others. In response, university students went on strike in Butare and Ruhengeri, demanding a presidential investigation.[13]

With criticism of the Rwandan government from both inside and outside the country becoming steadily more vocal, demands for reform gaining increasing public support in Rwanda, and authoritarian regimes falling in a number of African states, Habyarimana and his supporters attempted to retake the political initiative and co-opt the process of political reform. Shortly after returning from the Franco-African summit at La Baule, France, where French President François Mitterrand declared that African regimes would have to democratize, President Habyarimana announced in a July 1990 speech that he would initiate a process of political reform in Rwanda. He promised to appoint a commission to chart the country's political future, reform *umuganda* and other unpopular government programs, allow free expression of ideas, and move the country toward multiparty elections. Two months later, the president followed through with one of his promises and appointed the Commission Nationale de Synthèse, charged with proposing constitutional reforms that would be put to a vote sometime during the following year.[14]

Despite the image the president's actions presented, they did not mark a sudden governmental embrace of democratic principles. Rather, they fit into a calculated scheme to retain power by controlling the process of reform. By promoting superficial changes, the ruling group hoped to deflect criticism and exhaust popular enthusiasm for reform without threatening its hold on power. At the same time, the president and his allies sought to discourage and discredit the opposition, making it difficult for opponents to gain support and take power. The Commission de Synthèse fell far short of demands for a national conference, because it was appointed by the president and its proposals were subject to approval by a national legislature, the National Development Council (Conseil National de Développement, CND), composed exclusively of MRND members. By violating the principles of the reforms even as they endorsed them, the ruling group sought to strip reforms of their meaning. For example, while claiming to support freedom of speech, the president and his supporters continued to harass critics of the government. The same month the Commission was appointed, the editor and three journalists from *Kinyamateka* were brought to trial. Even as the president endorsed ethnic harmony, Tutsi who complained about ethnic discrimination found themselves the target of harassment by the gendarmerie.[15]

The efforts of the regime to skirt the reform process appeared initially to have little success. Despite harassment, many intellectual, business, and religious elites continued to increase their demands for reform. In September, thirty-three leading intellectuals issued a strongly worded letter demanding that the government allow serious debate on the country's political future. They called for the government to renounce the use of repression and intimidation, allow free association, separate the party and the state, and eliminate the political monopoly of the MRND.[16]

The War of October

The entire process of political reform was suddenly thrown into doubt when, on October 1, 1990, the northeastern frontier of Rwanda was invaded by an army of mostly Tutsi Rwandan refugees, the Rwandan Patriotic Front (RPF). Small, isolated attacks on Rwandan territory by foreign-based Tutsi refugees had occurred throughout the 1960s, but the 1990 invasion was much larger, and its intent differed substantially from these previous incursions. The primary concern of the leaders of the RPF was neither, as in earlier attacks, to destabilize the country nor to exact revenge against the Hutu who had replaced them in power (the majority of RPF members were born in refugee camps or were too young when they left Rwanda to remember it) nor even to restore the monarchy, despite certain royalist elements in the ranks. Rather, the primary motivation of the RPF was to secure the right of return to Rwanda for refugees living abroad. Since the revolution in 1959, thousands of Tutsi refugees have lived in Zaire, Burundi, Tanzania, Uganda, and elsewhere.

While some refugees have prospered in their host countries, as noncitizens their position has remained tenuous. In Uganda in the early 1980s, for example, the Banyarwanda—both Tutsi refugees and more permanently settled economic migrants, Tutsi and Hutu who had come to Uganda earlier in the century—became targets of repression by President Milton Obote's government. In 1982 some 40,000 Banyarwanda, Bakiga, and Bahima fled into Rwanda, prompting Habyarimana to close the border. Rwanda later repatriated three-quarters of the refugees to Uganda. More recently, Banyarwanda have been the targets of ethnic attacks in eastern Zaire. The Rwandan government claimed during the 1980s that it could not accommodate a return of refugees to the country because of the poor economy and the land pressures created by overpopulation. Thus, despite lengthy negotiations involving the United Nations High Commission on Refugees, the governments of Rwanda and its neighbors, and the refugees themselves, no resolution to the refugee problem seemed imminent in 1990.[17]

Because of their persecution under Obote, many Banyarwanda in Uganda joined Yoweri Museveni's National Resistance Army (NRA), the rebel group that successfully installed Museveni as president of Uganda in 1986. The Rwandan Patriotic Front was formed primarily by ex-NRA soldiers, including several senior officers, who feared that conditions for Banyarwanda in Uganda could again deteriorate despite Museveni's offers of citizenship and other support. Some political opponents of Habyarimana, both Hutu and Tutsi, had fled into Uganda in the 1980s, and they joined with the Tutsi refugees to plan the RPF attack. RPF leaders believed that Habyarimana was vulnerable because of his declining popularity and the momentum of the democracy movement. The RPF hoped to take advantage of this to gain support within the country. They justified the 1990 attack on Rwanda not simply as a means of securing the right of return for refugees but also as the only way to bring down a stubborn authoritarian regime and to allow a democratic government to take power. Hoping to dispel the impression that it was an exclusively ethnic movement, the RPF placed Hutu in some leadership positions.[18]

Impact of the War on Political Transformations

In Rwanda, the "War of October" simultaneously pushed the government to accept substantial political reforms and made a democratic transition more difficult by augmenting the coercive capabilities of the government and increasing the level of insecurity in the country. With assistance from a small number of Zairian troops, and support from the French and Belgians, the Rwandan army was able to repulse the initial RPF offensive, but the presence of rebel troops at the border bolstered critics of the regime and intensified the sense of insecurity in the country. Despite a wave of detentions at the beginning of the war, democratic activism reemerged within only a few weeks. Newspapers continued to proliferate, issuing ever more outspoken criticisms of the regime, and in response to the increased repression in Rwanda several human rights groups emerged to monitor the government and investigate human rights violations.[19]

In an effort to undercut both internal opposition and the democratic claims of the RPF and to take control of the country's political situation, the government instituted a series of reforms over the next several months that changed the face of the regime. Habyarimana announced on November 13, 1990, that the government would soon allow the free formation of political parties and, in response to one of the demands of the RPF, ethnic labels would no longer be placed on national identity cards. The president also announced that because of the turmoil created by the RPF attack, the timetable for the Commission de Synthèse would be shortened. As a result, the Commission released for public discussion initial proposals for political reform in December, and in March 1991 it released a draft constitution. Because of the war, the president did not present the document for a public vote. Instead, in June 1991 the CND adopted a new multiparty constitution, with only a few changes from the Commission proposal. A week later, the CND passed a law on parties eliminating the privileged position of the MRND and allowing the formation of other parties.[20]

After the legalization of multipartyism, a number of political parties emerged and began immediately to push the government to implement more extensive political reforms and to negotiate a settlement to the war. In October 1991 Habyarimana named Sylvestre Nsanzimana, a member of the MRND, to the new post of prime minister, despite demands from opposition parties that the candidate be drawn from an opposition party in order to balance the power of the president and ensure a fair transition to democracy. A coalition of four major opposition parties sponsored a march in Kigali in November that drew 13,000 participants to demand a national conference. When Nsanzimana named a cabinet on December 30 that included only one minister from outside the MRND, the opposition parties organized more protests, and political tensions within the country heightened. At this point, a coalition of Catholic, Protestant, and Adventist church leaders stepped into the political fray to intercede between the MRND, the opposition parties, and representatives of Rwandan refugees and the RPF. After several weeks of negotiation, the political parties reached an agreement to create a "government of transition" with a prime minister drawn from the Republican Democratic Movement (Mouvement Démocratique Républicain, MDR), the successor party to Kayibanda's PARMEHUTU, and ministerial posts evenly divided between supporters and opponents of Habyarimana. The new multiparty government took office in April 1992 under prime minister Dismas Nsengiyaremye.[21]

Beginning in 1990, then, a democracy movement, fed by growing popular dissatisfaction with the government and a war that periodically flared along the country's northern border, was able to force the government to institute a variety of political reforms. In the changing political climate, the press continued to expand and to publish with greater impunity, and the population enjoyed much greater freedom of expression. People were allowed to join the political party of their choice, and private organizations formerly closely supervised by the state, such as cooperatives, were able to act with much greater independence. The political system took on many of the trappings of a democracy, allowing a greater diversity of interests to be represented.

Although these developments increased personal liberty in Rwanda, they did not substantially challenge the location of political, social, and economic power in the country. Habyarimana and the presidential *akazu* retained real control of the state and the primary means of accumulation in the country. Though the War of October may have given impetus to the process of political reform, it also provided the *akazu* with opportunities to strengthen its hold on power. Rumors circulating in 1990 had predicted that Habyarimana would be removed in a coup d'état after Pope John Paul II's visit to Rwanda in September, but the war seemed to improve the president's standing within the military, in the manner wars often have of rallying support for national leaders.[22]

The War of October also provided international support that allowed Habyarimana and his allies to reassert their hold on power. Following the invasion, troops from Belgium and France, sent to Rwanda ostensibly to "protect foreign nationals," as well as troops from Zaire, helped prop up the government. While Belgian and Zairian troops withdrew relatively quickly, French troops remained until 1993, providing Habyarimana with a variety of forms of military assistance, including—according to some reports—direct military backing in several instances. In addition to supplying troops, the French government provided the Rwandan military with arms, training, and technical support, allowing the army to expand from about 5,000 to over 35,000 troops in less than a year. France also provided the Rwandan government with financial assistance and legitimacy in international diplomatic circles. These various forms of support were critical to the ability of the presidential *akazu* to resist reformist pressures and to retain control of power.[23]

Explaining French interest in Rwanda is not simple, since Rwanda, in contrast to other African states where France has played a role, was a Belgian rather than a French colony, but a variety of factors seems to have influenced French policy. During the 1970s and 1980s, as French international prestige was in decline, the French government sought to assert its continuing international significance through increased intervention in Africa. As a francophone country, Rwanda was included in the self-declared French sphere of influence. A close personal relationship developed between the Mitterrand and Habyarimana families, and President Mitterrand's son, Jean-Christophe, who developed a friendship with President Habyarimana, advocated Rwandan government interests in French circles. As a result of these two factors, France greatly expanded its development support to Rwanda in the 1980s, with Rwanda becoming the fifth most common assignment for French volunteers. The French government also began to provide substantial military assistance to the Rwandan army.[24]

The threat to the Habyarimana regime posed by the War of October led to a massive increase in French assistance. France supplied troops and provided the Rwandan military with large arms shipments and training, making possible the huge expansion of the size of the military noted earlier. In addition to the personal rapport between Habyarimana and Mitterrand and the decade of French military and economic involvement in the country, the major factor leading the French to expand their involvement appears to have been the fear that the war threatened Rwanda's standing as a francophone country. Since many of the RPF soldiers were raised in refugee camps in Uganda, Tanzania, and Kenya, English appeared to be a more important language to the RPF than French. France seemed to fear that an RPF victory would remove Rwanda from its sphere of influence. The continuing financial and material support of the French allowed Habyarimana's governing coalition to remain in power despite both the war and internal opposition and gave the government little incentive to implement real reforms.[25]

While the Rwandan government allowed limited political reforms in order to quell popular discontent, and thereby to minimize the degree of force necessary to control the population, it worked simultaneously to diminish the impact of the reforms and to ensure that configurations of power did not change. Although legislation formally legalized independent political parties and a free press, journalists and opponents of the president continued to face substantial harassment. In the days immediately following the October 1 RPF attack, government troops imprisoned 8,000–10,000 people, whom they accused of supporting the RPF—primarily southerners, democracy activists, and Tutsi. Most of those arrested were released within a year, but few were able to return to their jobs after their release; many prisoners were beaten in captivity, and a substantial number died. In subsequent months, the presidential *akazu* employed the expanded army to intimidate political opponents, limiting their ability to challenge effectively the status quo. Beginning in 1992, paramilitary groups—particularly *Interahamwe*, the youth wing of the MRND, and the Coalition for the Defense of the Republic (Coalition pour la Défense de la République, CDR), an extremist Hutu ethnonationalist party—played an important role in intimidating political opponents. In areas where the MRND was dominant, particularly in Habyarimana's base in the north, *Interahamwe* and the CDR made it nearly impossible for opposition parties to organize.[26] In addition, though the government of transition included opposition parties, the most powerful ministries continued to be held by the MRND, and MRND officials hampered the operation of the opposition ministries. In September 1992, after five months in office, Prime Minister Nsengiyaremye sent a letter to Habyarimana bitterly decrying the continuing efforts by the president's allies to obstruct the effective and independent operation of the ministries.[27]

Complementary to the strategy of discouraging opponents through intimidation was the ruling coalition's seeking to discredit both their opponents and the entire process of democratization, thus making it more difficult for the opposition to achieve power. In the years preceding the outbreak of war, a sense of insecurity and disorder had spread across Rwanda, due in part to deteriorating economic conditions and in part to a declining respect for authority, including the authority of law. The War of October accelerated the process of social and economic deterioration. In the north of the country in particular, fighting killed thousands of civilians and drove hundreds of thousands from their homes; a February 1993 RPF offensive alone created 1.1 million internally displaced people. The fighting disrupted supply routes, interrupted the delivery of electricity and water, and destroyed much of the infrastructure, as well as disrupting agricultural production in the north, the country's main food producing region, and in the vast area into which refugees fled.

The government, rather than seeking to reassure the population and to enforce order, contributed to the disorder and sense of insecurity. After the beginning of the war, army and gendarmes became a menacing presence throughout the country, not only harassing political opponents of the government, but also intimidating the population at large, demanding identification papers and maintaining roadblocks ostensibly to find RPF infiltrators. The armed forces and police have been accused of extensive human rights violations and of involvement in robbery and rape of civilians. Beginning in 1992, the *Interahamwe* and CDR militias worked to spread violence and disorder, holding periodic demonstrations, blocking roads, and posing a threat of retaliation against any who opposed them. With the decline in order, crime increased markedly in the country, and authorities made little effort to control it. Creating a climate of terror in the country served not simply to intimidate the population into submission but also to discredit the RPF and the democracy movement.[28] Interviews I conducted in various locations in Rwanda in 1992 and 1993 revealed that many Rwandans believed that multi-partyism had created insecurity in the country, and many expressed nostalgia for the days when Habyarimana ruled the country unchallenged.[29]

One important element in the ruling coalition's program to discredit opponents and create internal insecurity was to reignite ethnic tensions in the country. The Habyarimana government initially had worked effectively to defuse ethnic tensions in Rwanda, but as public resentment of official corruption and profiteering grew in the late 1980s, some officials perceived that rekindling ethnic tensions could serve to deflect public attention and direct popular dissatisfaction and anger toward the Tutsi. With the outbreak of the war, the idea that the Tutsi posed a threat to the Hutu became more tenable. Government-controlled Radio Rwanda disseminated unsubstantiated reports of RPF atrocities against civilians, and government officials claimed that the RPF wanted to reimpose the monarchy. Periodic attacks against Tutsi civilians beginning in 1990 left hundreds dead, forced many others from their homes, and heightened ethnic tensions. The government characterized the attacks as spontaneous expressions of Hutu hatred of Tutsi. In fact, according to convincing reports by both Rwandan and international human rights organizations, these attacks were orchestrated by officials of the government and the MRND. For example, in one commune a massacre occurred when the burgomaster called the Hutu peasants to gather with machetes for *umuganda*, ostensibly to clear brush, then, with gendarmes present, sent them to kill their Tutsi neighbors. In other instances, government officials organized lynch mobs or soldiers themselves carried out the massacres. The human rights reports indicate that many of these massacres were carried out with the direct approval of the president and his close advisers. These attacks helped to raise ethnic tensions throughout the country, with Tutsi facing increasing harassment and living in fear of attack. By raising ethnic tensions, the MRND was able both to appeal to Hutu ethnic loyalty to build support and to frighten most Tutsi from taking an active role in political opposition.[30]

The war and the increase in ethnic tensions allowed the government to take on the mantle of nationalism and characterize their opponents as traitors to the nation. After the multiparty government of transition was installed in 1992, peace talks between the RPF and representatives of the government began in Arusha, Tanzania. Habyarimana and other members of the MRND consistently refused to accept the protocols reached in these negotiations, and they presented themselves as the defenders of the interests of the Hutu majority, characterizing the opposition parties as being allied with the "Tutsi rebels." The massacres of Tutsi in Rwanda inspired the RPF to become more brutal in its own attacks, and as the extent of destruction in the country spread, support for the RPF among Hutu almost entirely disappeared. Portraying the opposition parties as sympathetic to the RPF effectively served to discredit them with a large portion of the population; the interviews I conducted in 1992 and 1993 indicated that many people divided the parties into those "for the RPF" and those against it.

Appealing to nationalist and ethnonationalist sentiments proved a highly successful strategy for the ruling coalition, allowing it to expand its base of support beyond the north. Habyarimana sought to cultivate allies among the opposition, and during 1993 each of the opposition parties in the government split into a faction supporting the Arusha accords and another committed to the interests of the Hutu and opposed to compromise with the RPF. When Nsengiyaremye's term as prime minister expired in July 1993 (he was appointed for one year, then given a three-month extension), Habyarimana appointed Agathe Uwilingiyimana, who had been an outspoken critic of the president but represented a faction of the MDR less sympathetic to the RPF. Her party and the other opposition parties refused to support her appointment, demanding that a new government be established only in the context of a peace treaty with the RPF. She persisted and remained prime minister until her assassination in April 1994.[31]

After over a year of negotiations at Arusha, the growing military success of the RPF and pressure from neighboring governments, international donor agencies, the Organization for African Unity, and other international actors forced Habyarimana and the MRND to accept a negotiated settlement to the war. The comprehensive peace treaty signed in August 1993 called for a new provisional government to prepare the way for elections, with Augustin Twagiramungu of the MDR as prime minister and ministries distributed among the MRND, the opposition parties, and the RPF. The agreement also contained provisions to resettle refugees and to integrate RPF soldiers into the Rwandan army. To work on arrangements for these changes, a group of RPF leaders supported by a contingent of several hundred soldiers arrived in Kigali several months later.

Some of Habyarimana's allies—including, apparently, some of the trusted members of the president's *akazu*—felt that the president had gone too far and compromised too much, and they immediately began to work to ensure that the provisions of the accord would not be implemented. They stepped up harassment of opponents, relying increasingly on the civilian militias, who became a growing threat to individual security in the country. Meanwhile, the divisions in the opposition parties prevented them from being able to decide on appointments to the ministries, which delayed the installation of the provisional government. In early 1994, conditions deteriorated rapidly. The militias received paramilitary training, and opponents of the Arusha agreement provided them with arms. Radio Rwanda began to broadcast personal attacks on opposition figures, human rights activists, and others, and called for certain figures among them to be killed as traitors to the country.[32] In March, the minister of transportation and public works, leader of the Social Democratic Party (Parti Social-Démocrate, PSD) was assassinated, and in retaliation the head of the CDR was lynched the next day. Some reports from Rwanda have indicated that some of Habyarimana's associates developed a plan early in 1994 to kill a large number of opposition figures and democracy activists in order to stop the implementation of the Arusha accords and to crush opposition, but the president considered the plan too drastic.[33]

Although the facts may never be known, the most likely explanation for the downing of Habyarimana's plane on April 6 is that some of the president's own associates plotted the death as an excuse to launch their program of violence in a desperate attempt to hold onto power. Clearly, lists of people to be targeted by the violence were already in existence when the plane went down. Within hours after the accident, the presidential guard began systematically to kill leaders of the opposition parties, Tutsi, human rights activists, journalists, development workers, and others whom they perceived to be capable of challenging them or of inciting the population to resist. Members of the army and the civilian militias then spread the violence throughout the country. According to numerous reports from survivors and refugees, attacks against Tutsi and others were organized by local government officials and militia members, often with support from the military; many of the people who participated in the killings seem to have done so out of fear for their own lives and the lives of their family members. The violence, then, represented a deliberate attempt by a group of people whose power was being threatened—the *akazu* and allied government officials, military personnel, and business interests throughout the country—to take advantage of the chaotic situation in Rwanda to crush opposition and halt the transition to democratic government that would likely deprive them of their power.[34]

Ultimately the massacres created such a degree of chaos in the country that the government's hold on power became untenable. As soon as the massacres began, the RPF renewed its attack and swept rapidly through the north and east of the country, driving millions of Rwandans from their homes as refugees. Within a matter of weeks the RPF controlled most of Rwanda's territory, and the Rwandan army was in shambles. The international community reacted uncertainly to the massacres and the renewed civil war; the United Nations initially withdrew most of the observers it had on the ground as part of the Arusha accords, and then in June authorized the French military to intervene on an ostensibly humanitarian mission. In an action dubbed "Opération Turquoise," French troops entered the southwest region of Rwanda to establish a "safe zone." In fact, by the time the French arrived, the genocidal killing of Tutsi and of Hutu opposition figures was basically complete, and the French presence served primarily to shield the Rwandan military as it fled into exile in Zaire.[35]

Since taking power, the RPF has had difficulty establishing effective control over the country. RPF leaders have attempted to gain popular support and counteract the perception that they are a foreign, Tutsi movement by placing Hutu in the two top positions as president and prime minister, but most people continue to regard RPF leader Paul Kagame, vice president and minister of defense, as the real power behind the throne. The new government has failed to gain popular support and has itself been accused of human rights abuses, particularly in imprisoning without trial thousands of people accused of involvement in the massacres. With hundreds of thousands of refugees afraid to return home for fear of imprisonment and still living outside the country or in camps for displaced people within Rwanda, economic and political life in the country has remained irregular. The ex-Rwandan military has attempted to regroup in Zaire and, according to reliable reports, has received assistance from France and several other countries in its effort to rearm. The threat of an invasion by the people who were responsible for the massacres of 1994 creates a continuing sense of insecurity within Rwanda. The impact of the massacres and the civil war on Rwanda's political system, economy, and society appears likely to endure for a long time, as intense insecurity, authoritarian rule, and severe poverty continue to plague the country.[36]

Implications of the Rwandan Case

The disastrous turn of events in Rwanda provides a number of lessons and warnings for other African countries in the throes of democratic transition. First, the relationship of the general public to the democracy movement in a country may not be as simple and direct as it first appears. In Rwanda, some former political officials and other civic leaders whose political opportunities were limited under Habyarimana, primarily southerners and Tutsi, were able to channel some of the rising public discontent with the political and economic situation into support for political reforms and new political parties. Yet the public's discontent was not associated exclusively with the current government but rather was, for most people, a frustration with politics in general. Most opposition party leaders were familiar faces to the Rwandan public, having served in the past in the Kayibanda or Habyarimana administrations, and to many people they appear to represent nothing new for Rwandan politics.[37] As one of my informants said about the political reforms, "These changes have nothing to do with our poverty. Things are changing for the rich and intellectuals who want to occupy power. But for me power will be the same." Many of my informants agreed that no party really spoke for the common people or defended their interests. Given this gap between the parties and the public, it was easy for the government to discredit the opposition. Recent studies in Kenya, Tanzania, Uganda, and Zimbabwe reveal a similar gap between party politics and public sentiment. The profound social changes taking place in these countries have little connection to the expanding political party system.[38]

Secondly, the same social forces that can empower movements for democratic reform can easily be diverted to other, sometimes destructive, ends. The sense of frustration and growing resentment of authority that appeared in Rwanda in the late 1980s enabled Rwandan dissidents successfully to pressure their government to legalize political party activity and to accept other reforms, but the political changes did not transform public attitudes. Most resistance to authority in Rwanda occurred independently of the formal democracy movement, as in, for example, the spontaneous mass refusal to participate in *umuganda* and *animation* and the burning of public forests by bands of angry peasants that took place in 1992. The establishment of opposition parties did not suddenly encompass and control all of the dissatisfied elements within the country. Conservative forces were able to channel some of the public frustration into ethnic conflict that diverted public anger away from the government and toward the Tutsi minority and the RPF. The line between political protest and simple criminal activity was often murky, and the government was able to use the rise in crime and other elements of social deterioration to serve its own ends. The problems posed by ongoing social unrest to the consolidation of democracy in Congo and Zambia, to name but two cases, demonstrate the difficulties in directing public energies toward constructive ends.

Thirdly, authoritarian rulers demonstrate incredible resilience, even in the face of strong antigovernment sentiments. In Rwanda, Habyarimana and his *akazu* were able to use civilian militias and loyal elements of the army effectively to intimidate their political opponents and frustrate attempts to bring real political change to the country. One of the most disturbing aspects of the violence in Rwanda that began in April 1994 is that it was orchestrated by a fairly small group of individuals who did not have the support of the majority of the population. The use of vitriolic anti-Tutsi, anti-opposition propaganda on Radio Rwanda and threats from military personnel and armed civilian militias were sufficient to induce many Rwandans to cooperate in the massacre, particularly given the low level of support for the opposition. The remarkable ability of Mobutu Sese Seko to hold onto power in the chaotic conditions prevailing in Zaire suggests that the Rwandan government has not been alone in promoting social deterioration to protect existing configurations of power.

Fourthly, international support for democratic reform appears essential. The continued (even expanded) support of the French government for the authoritarian rulers in Rwanda in the 1990s undermined efforts to force reform. Military assistance to Rwanda allowed the Habyarimana regime not only to defend itself against the RPF but also better to control internal dissidents. Without French support, the government might have found it necessary to accept a compromise with both the parties of opposition and the RPF that could have avoided the massacres and ended the civil war. Without international pressure, the government felt little need to implement the Arusha accords and to share power.

Finally, democratization is not an inevitable and one-directional process. In Rwanda, social and political changes simultaneously enabled and hindered the process of democratic reform. Whenever significant reforms seemed imminent in Rwanda, reactionary forces turned to ethnic and political violence to prevent their implementation. The Rwandan case stands as a warning that even when the majority of the population in a country backs some form of democratic change, a limited group of powerful and determined individuals can keep change from occurring. The powerful social forces that stand to lose from democratic change may employ drastic means to protect the status quo. If other countries wish to avoid following Rwanda down the road to chaos as they struggle with their own democratic transitions, then they must find some means of limiting the power of authoritarian regimes and of more effectively channeling public resentments into support for positive change. When political parties and democracy movements lose touch with the population, they become vulnerable to the manipulations of conservative governments seeking to protect their power.

Notes

Much of the data for this chapter was gathered during field research that I conducted in Rwanda in 1992 and 1993. This research was supported in part by grants from the Graduate School of the University of Wisconsin at Madison and the Board of Higher Education of the Christian Church (Disciples of Christ).

1. For example, the World Bank, in its report, *Sub-Saharan Africa: From Crisis to Sustainability* (Washington, D.C.: World Bank, 1989), praised the Rwandan government's economic policies and development program that made possible economic growth even in the face of adverse location and lack of resources.

2. *New York Times*, June 21, 1994, p. A6.

3. Catharine Newbury, *The Cohesion of Oppression: Clientship and Ethnicity in Rwanda, 1860–1960* (New York: Columbia University Press, 1988); Filip Reyntjens, *Pouvoir et droit au Rwanda: Droit public et évolution politique, 1916–1973* (Tervuren, Belgium: MRAC, 1985).

4. René Lemarchand, *Rwanda and Burundi* (New York: Praeger, 1970); Newbury, *The Cohesion of Oppression*; Reyntjens, *Pouvoir et droit*.

5. Reyntjens, *Pouvoir et droit*, pp. 506–509; Christophe Mfizi, *Les lignes de faîte du Rwanda indépendant* (Kigali: Office Rwandais d'Information), p. 293.

6. Mfizi, *Les lignes de faîte*; Catharine Newbury, "Rwanda: Recent Debates over Governance and Rural Development," in Goran Hyden and Michael Bratton, eds., *Governance and Politics in Africa* (Boulder: Lynne Rienner, 1992), pp. 193–219; Filip Reyntjens, "Rwanda: Economy," in *Africa South of the Sahara: 1993* (London: Europa Publications, 1993), pp. 680–682; World Bank, *Toward Sustained Development in Sub-Saharan Africa: A Joint Program of Action* (Washington, D.C.: World Bank, 1984).

7. Reyntjens, "Rwanda: Economy;" Nezehose Jean Bosco, *Agriculture rwandaise: Problématique et perspectives* (INADES-Formation-Rwanda, 1990); Fernand Bézy, *Rwanda 1962–1989: Bilan socio-économique d'un régime* (Louvain-la-Neuve: Institut d'Études du Développement, January 1990); *Economist* Intelligence Unit, *Country Report: Uganda, Rwanda, Burundi*, 2nd quarter 1993; World Bank, *Toward Sustained Development*.

8. Newbury, "Recent Debates," pp. 199–204; Bézy, *Rwanda 1962–1989: Bilan socio-économique*.

9. Christophe Mfizi, "Le Réseau Zéro," Open Letter to the President of the MRND (Kigali: Éditions Uruhimbi, July-August 1992); Sandrine Tolotti, "Le Rwanda retient son souffle," *Croissance*, no. 356 (January 1993):34–39; Marie-Roger Biloa, "Institutions, le prési-

dent et les autres," *Jeune Afrique*, no. 1526 (April 2, 1990):36–38; "Rwanda: Wrapping Democracy in Violence," *Africa Confidential* 33, no. 20 (October 9, 1994):6–7; Newbury, "Recent Debates."

10. Jean-Marie Vianney Higiro, "Kinyamateka sous la 2e République," *Dialogue*, no. 155 (June 1992):29–39; Charles Mutaganzwa, "La liberté de presse, essai d'interprétation conjuncturelle," *Dialogue*, no. 147 (July-August 1991):51–61; Newbury, "Recent Debates."

11. See, for example, Joseph Ntamahungiro, "Sans morale pas de démocratie," *Dialogue*, no. 128 (May-June 1988):26–38.

12. Jean-Damascène Ntakirutimana, "Multipartisme: Leurre ou espoir?" *Dialogue*, no. 144 (January-February 1991):105–119; Ntamahungiro, "Sans morale pas de démocratie;" Joseph Ntamahungiro, "Oui au multipartisme," *Dialogue*, no. 144 (January-February 1991):59–76; Thadée Bagaragaza and Guy Theunis, "L'enjeu du débat," *Dialogue*, no. 144 (January-February 1991):1–10.

13. Newbury, "Recent Debates;" Les Evêques Catholiques du Rwanda, "Le Christ, Notre Unité, Première Parti: L'Unité," (Kigali: Pallotti-Presse, April 1990); Les Evêques Catholiques du Rwanda, "Le Christ, Notre Unité, Deuxième Parti: Justice pour l'homme," reprinted in *Dialogue*, no. 141 (July-August 1990):3–18; François Misser, "Rumpus in Rwanda," *New African*, August 1990, pp. 20. See also Timothy Longman, "Christianity and Democratisation in Rwanda: Assessing Church Responses to Political Crisis in the 1990s," in Paul Gifford, ed., *The Christian Churches and the Democratisation of Africa* (Leiden, Netherlands: Brill, 1995), pp. 188–204.

14. "Pour le multipartisme et la démocratie," *Dialogue*, no. 144 (January-February 1991):144–150; Newbury, "Recent Debates," p. 214; Allison Des Forges, "Recent Political Developments in Rwanda," unpublished paper, March 1992; Stephen Smith, "France-Rwanda: Lévirat colonial et abandon dans la région des Grands Lacs," in André Guichaoua, ed., *Les crises politiques au Burundi et au Rwanda (1993–1994)* (Lille: Université des Sciences et Technologies, 1995), pp. 447–453.

15. Charles Ntazinda, "Les grands problèmes de l'heure au Rwanda," *Dialogue*, no. 144 (January-February 1991):85–98; Misser, "Rumpus in Rwanda."

16. "Pour le multipartisme et la démocratie," reprinted in *Dialogue*, no. 144 (January-February 1991):144–150.

17. [Catharine Watson], "Exile from Rwanda: Background to an Invasion" (Washington, D.C.: The U.S. Committee for Refugees, February 1991); Filip Reyntjens, "Rwanda: Recent History," in *Africa South of the Sahara: 1993* (London: Europa Publications, 1993), pp. 678–680; Gérard Prunier, "L'Uganda et le F.P.R.," *Dialogue*, no. 163 (February 1993):3–18.

18. Watson, "Exile from Rwanda;" La Communauté Rwandaise de France, "Memorandum sur la crise politique actuelle au Rwanda" (Paris, December 1990).

19. Reyntjens, "Recent History;" Monique Mujawamaliya, "The Development of the Rwandan Human Rights Movement and Its Collaboration with International Human Rights Associations" (paper presented at the annual meeting of the African Studies Association, Boston, December 1993).

20. François-Xavier Munyarugerero, "Oui au multipartisme," *Jeune Afrique*, no. 1560 (November 21–27, 1990):7; Reyntjens, "Recent History," pp. 679–680; Danielle Helbig, "Rwanda: De la dictature populaire à la démocratie athénienne," *Politique africaine*, no. 44 (December 1991):97–101.

21. "Carnet," *Dialogue*, nos. 144–151, from January 1991 through February 1992; Des Forges, "Recent Political Developments," pp. 5–7; Michel Twagirayesu [president of the

Église Presbytérienne au Rwanda], "La politique: La réflection de l'Église," speech at the Faculté de Théologie Protestante à Butare, April 2, 1993.

22. Reyntjens, "Recent History," p. 679; "Uganda/Rwanda: Picking up the pieces," *Africa Confidential*, no. 31 (November 23, 1990):5–6; "Rwanda: Death and Democracy," *Africa Confidential*, no. 33 (May 22, 1992):7.

23. [Frank Smyth], "Arming Rwanda: The Arms Trade and Human Rights Abuses in the Rwandan War," *Human Rights Watch Arms Project* 6, no. 1 (January 1994); "Uganda/Rwanda: Picking up the Pieces;" "Rwanda: Death and Democracy;" Smith, "France-Rwanda," pp. 447–451.

24. François-Xavier Verschave, "Connivences françaises au Rwanda," *Le Monde diplomatique* 42, no. 492 (March 1995):10; Smith, "France-Rwanda."

25. Verschave, "Connivences françaises au Rwanda;" Smith, "France-Rwanda; Smyth, "Arming Rwanda."

26. "Rwanda: Civilian Slaughter," *Africa Confidential* 35, no. 9 (May 6, 1994):5–6.

27. Excerpts printed in *Dialogue*, no. 160 (November 1992):57–62.

28. Tolotti, "Le Rwanda retient son souffle"; Nicola Jefferson, "The War Within," *Africa Report* 37, no. 1 (January-February 1992), pp. 62–64; Fédération Internationale des Droits de l'Homme (FIDH) et al., "Rapport de la Commission Internationale d'Enquête sur les Violations des Droits de l'Homme au Rwanda depuis le 1er Octobre 1990 (7–21 janvier 1993)" (Paris: FIDH, March 1993); Association Rwandaise pour la Défense des Droits de la Personne et des Libertés Publiques (ADL), *Rapport sur les droits de l'homme au Rwanda* (Kigali: ADL, December 1992); Africa Watch, "Beyond the Rhetoric: Continuing Human Rights Abuses in Rwanda" (Washington, D.C.: Africa Watch, June 1993); [Josette Thibeau], "Le Rwanda: Ombres et lumières" (Brussels: Commission Justice et Paix, February 1991).

29. With the aid of several research assistants and translators, I conducted interviews with several hundred people, mostly peasant farmers, in Butare, Kibuye, and Ruhengeri Prefectures in 1992 and 1993.

30. Jefferson, "The War Within"; FIDH, "Rapport de la Commission Internationale;" ADL, *Rapport sur les droits de l'homme.*

31. André Guichaoua, "Un lourd passé, un présent dramatique, un avenir des plus sombres," in André Guichaoua, ed., *Les crises politiques au Burundi et au Rwanda*, pp. 19–51; *Economist* Intelligence Unit, *Country Report: Rwanda*, 1993–1995 issues.

32. According to the testimony of a number of individuals, both Rwandan and foreign, who were present in the country at the time.

33. "Rwanda: Civilian Slaughter," *Africa Confidential*, op. cit.; Frank Smyth, "Blood Money and Geopolitics," *The Nation* 258, no. 17 (May 2, 1994):585–587.

34. For information on events surrounding and following the death of Habyarimana, I have relied on a large number of news reports, primarily Associated Press reports, National Public Radio, and the *New York Times*. See also "Rwanda: Civilian Slaughter," *Africa Confidential*, op. cit.; the collection of articles gathered by André Guichaoua in his edited volume, *Les crises politiques au Burundi et au Rwanda*, pp. 675–693; and René Lemarchand, "Rwanda: The Rationality of Genocide," *Issue* 23, no. 2 (1995):8–11.

35. Martin Plaut, "Rwanda: Looking Beyond the Slaughter," *The World Today* 50 (August 1994):149–153; Colette Braeckman, "Autopsie d'un génocide planifié au Rwanda: Condamner les victimes, absoudre les bourreaux," *Le Monde diplomatique* 42, no. 492 (March 1995):8–9; Smith, "France-Rwanda," pp. 452–453.

36. James K. Gasana, "La guerre, la paix, et la démocratie au Rwanda," in André Guichaoua, *Les crises politiques au Burundi et au Rwanda*, pp. 211–237; Kathy L. Austin, "Rwanda/Zaire Rearming with Impunity: International Support for the Perpetrators of the Rwandan Genocide," *Human Rights Watch Arms Project* 7, no. 4 (May 1995).

37. Helbig, "De la dictature populaire," pp. 100–101; Des Forges, "Recent Political Developments," pp. 5–6.

38. See, for example, David Maxwell, "The Church and Democratisation in Africa: The Case of Zimbabwe," in Paul Gifford, ed., *The Christian Churches and the Democratisation of Africa* (Leiden, Netherlands: Brill, 1995), pp. 108–129, and Aili Tripp, "Gender, Political Participation, and the Transformation of Associational Life in Uganda and Tanzania," in the same volume, pp. 205–224.

About the Book

Most African states experienced only a few fleeting years of democratic rule after independence before succumbing to authoritarianism. During the 1970s and 1980s, Africans and Westerners alike came to view dictatorship to be as much a part of the region's social landscape as its grinding poverty. Yet the end of the Cold War and the sharpening of the economic crisis at the end of the 1980s have breathed new life into campaigns for democracy in Africa, shaking the foundations of many long-standing autocracies. In some cases, dramatic transitions took place, though the fate of the new democracies is far from certain.

This volume explores the origins and evolution of political reform movements in several states of francophone Africa. The authors first make the case for the distinctiveness of francophone Africa, based on the influences of colonial history, language, and France's contemporary role in Africa, then survey the challenges of reform, including the problems of transition from authoritarianism and consolidation of democratic regimes. Case studies of thirteen former French and Belgian colonies follow, organized by level of reform achieved: peaceful regime change, incremental reforms, repressed reform efforts, and reform in the midst of war.

About the Editors and Contributors

John F. Clark is assistant professor in the Department of International Relations, Florida International University in Miami. Dr. Clark earned his Ph.D. at the University of Virginia in 1992; he was a Department of State intern in Brazzaville, Congo, in 1990 and conducted field research in Zaire in 1994. He has published articles on ethnic politics and democratization in such journals as *Africa Today*, the *SAIS Review*, the *Journal of African Policy Studies*, and the *Journal of Third World Studies*.

David E. Gardinier is professor of history and former department chairman at Marquette University in Milwaukee. He received his Ph.D. from Yale University, has held two Fulbright Fellowships to Paris, and helped to found the French Colonial Historical Society in 1974. His publications include *Cameroon: U.N. Challenge to French Policy* (Oxford, 1963), *Gabon* (Clio, 1992), and the *Historical Dictionary of Gabon* (Scarecrow, 1981, 1994) as well as numerous articles on the states of Equatorial Africa, including those appearing in the *Revue française d'histoire d'outre-mer*, *Mondes et cultures*, and the *Canadian Journal of African Studies*. In 1994 the French government awarded him the honor of Chevalier dans l'Ordre des Palmes Académiques.

Laura E. Boudon is a doctoral student in international relations at Florida International University in Miami. She holds an M.A. in international studies from the University of Miami and has done research in Senegal. Her dissertation is a comparative study of the effects of the international coffee regime in Côte d'Ivoire and Colombia.

Lucy Creevey is professor of political science and acting dean of international affairs at the University of Connecticut. She is coauthor (with Barbara Callaway) of *The Heritage of Islam: Women, Religion, and Politics in West Africa* (Lynne Rienner, 1994), author of *Muslim Brotherhoods and Politics in Senegal* (Harvard, 1970), and editor of *Working with Women Farmers in Africa* (Syracuse, 1986). Dr. Creevey has also published in such journals as the *Journal of Modern African Studies* and the *Journal of Religion in Africa*.

Samuel Decalo received his Ph.D. from the University of Pennsylvania with specializations in Africa and the Middle East. He has published fifteen books, including *Coups and Army Rule in Africa* (2d ed., Yale, 1990) and the volumes on Benin, Togo, Niger, and Chad in the Scarecrow Press Historical Dictionaries Series, plus some sixty articles. He has taught at universities both in the United States and abroad. He is currently professor of political science at the University of Natal and visiting professor at the University of Florida in Gainesville.

Myriam Gervais is professor of political science at the University of Quebec in Montreal. She has published articles in the *Review of African Political Economy* and the *Canadian Journal of African Studies*. Professor Gervais has done extensive field research in Niger.

John R. Heilbrunn, who received his Ph.D. from the University of California at Los Angeles in 1994, is a specialist on francophone Africa and has published in such journals as the *Journal of Modern African Studies* and *Politique africaine*. He received a Châteaubriand Postdoctoral Fellowship from the French Ministry of Foreign Affairs to spend the 1994–1995 year in residence at the Centre d'Étude d'Afrique Noire at the University of Bordeaux, where he researched democratic transitions in six francophone African states. Dr. Heilbrunn is currently a consultant in Washington, D.C.

Bernard Lanne is a former French overseas administrator who directed the National Administration School in Chad and advised President François Tombalbaye. A graduate of the National School for Overseas France, he earned his doctorate in history from the University of Paris. He is author of *Tchad-Libye: La querelle des frontières* (Karthala, 1982) as well as numerous articles on Chad.

Timothy Longman, having done extensive field work in Rwanda, earned his Ph.D. from the University of Wisconsin in 1995. After teaching at Drake University during the 1994–1995 academic year, he returned to Rwanda with Africa Rights Watch. Dr. Longman has published on Rwanda in *Issue* and contributed to *The Christian Churches and the Democratisation of Africa,* edited by Paul Gifford (Brill, 1995).

Robert J. Mundt earned his Ph.D. at Stanford University in 1972 and is professor of political science at the University of North Carolina in Charlotte. He has studied Côte d'Ivoire since the early 1970s, when he wrote his dissertation on the Ivoirian civil code and served as a lecturer in applied social science at the University of Abidjan. He is also the author of the *Historical Dictionary of Côte d'Ivoire* (1987, 1995) and the chapter on Côte d'Ivoire in the *Handbook of Political Science Research on Sub-Saharan Africa* (Greenwood, 1992).

Thomas O'Toole is professor of interdisciplinary studies at St. Cloud State University in Minnesota. He is author of the *Historical Dictionary of Guinea* (Scarecrow, 1987) and *The Central African Republic: The Continent's Hidden Heart* (Westview, 1986) as well as numerous articles and chapters on the Central African Republic. Dr. O'Toole has taught both in Guinea and at the University of Bangui.

Joseph Takougang obtained the Ph.D. in African history from the University of Illinois-Chicago and is currently associate professor in the Department of African-American Studies at the University of Cincinnati. His articles have appeared in such journals as *Asian and African Studies,* the *Journal of Third World Studies,* the *Western Journal of Black Studies,* and *Revue française d'histoire d'outre-mer.* He is currently coauthoring a book on Cameroon's democratic transition.

Thomas Turner received his doctorate from the University of Wisconsin. He taught for several years at the Universities of Kisangani and Lubumbashi in Zaire as well as at Wheeling Jesuit College in West Virginia. He is the author, with Crawford Young, of *The Rise and Decline of the Zairian State* (University of Wisconsin, 1985).

Richard Vengroff is professor of political science and former dean, Division of International Affairs, University of Connecticut. In the 1995–1996 academic year he was a visiting scholar in the Department of Political Science at McGill University. Dr. Vengroff earned his Ph.D. at Syracuse University and specializes in development administration and management. He has conducted field research in fifteen different African countries; his current research concerns issues of democratic governance, decentralization, and the impact of culture on management. Dr. Vengroff is the author or editor of six books and author of over fifty journal articles and book chapters.

Index

Achu, Simon Achidi, 171, 173–174
Aduayom, Madeleine, 239
Afrique Equatoriale Française, 10, 13, 111–112
Afrique Occidentale Française, 10, 13
Agboyibor, Yao, 230–231, 240
Agip-Recherches, 77, 81(n17)
Agriculture, 45, 87, 121–122, 128, 130, 146, 148, 195, 211,(n49), 226, 268
Agondjo-Okawe, Pierre-Louis, 153–154, 157–158
Ahidjo, Ahmadou, 162–167
Ahomadégbé, Justin, 44, 46, 51
Aikpé, Michel,47
Alingué, Jean Bawoyeu, 272, 274–275
Alphandéry, Edmond, 139
Amadou, Hama, 108(n43)
Amayi, Yao Mawuliklimi, 231
Amondji, Marcel, 188
Amorin, Tavio, 239
Aouzou Strip dispute, 271, 281
Apithy, Sourou-Migan, 44, 47
Armed Forces. *See Individual countries,* armed forces
Arusha Accords, 299–300
Asanga, Siga, 176
Atumba, Ngbanda Nzamobko, 249
Authoritarianism, 26–29, 35, 110, 123(n3), 185–187

Bachar, Mahamat, 280
Bahati, Lukwebo, 258
Bahima, 293
Bakary, Djibo, 87, 90, 105(n2)
Bakiga, 293
Bakongo, 62, 70
Balkanization, 13, 75, 112
Balladur, Edouard, 139, 155–157, 193

Bamba, Moriféré, 191
Bamiléké, 167
Banda, 113
Banking, 53, 213, 227
Banziri, 112–113
Banyarwanda, 293
Bardé, Laokein, 281
Bariba, 44, 57
Barre Mainassara, Ibrahim, 108(n43)
Baule, 193, 198
Bayart, Jean-François, 25, 35(nn6,10), 111
Bédie, Henri Konan, 4, 182, 187
Bemba, Saolona, 259
Bembe, 62
Bendounga, Joseph, 119
Benin, 1, 3, 10, 24, 26, 66, 69, 226, 233, 291
  armed forces, 44–45, 47, 50, 53, 55, 57–58, 60
  civil service, 51, 53, 58
  constitution, 59
  economic problems, 45–53
  elections, 48, 54, 57, 59, 61(nn19,21)
  ethno-regional rivalries, 44–45, 47, 50, 56
  France, 43–44, 47, 54, 56–59
  labor unions, 52, 58
  Marxism-Leninism in, 43–44, 46–48, 51
  National Assembly, 57, 59, 61(n21)
  national conference, 2, 43, 53
  nationalizations, 49
  and Nigeria, 52
  press freedom, 58
  radio and television, 54
  Roman Catholicism, 46
  state companies and parastatals, 48–50
  structural adjustment programs, 50–51, 54, 57